Environmental Politics and Policy

Second Edition

Environmental Politics and Policy

Second Edition

Walter A. Rosenbaum
University of Florida, Gainesville

A Division of Congressional Quarterly Inc.
Washington, D.C.

Copyright © 1991, Congressional Quarterly Inc.
1414 22nd Street, N.W.
Washington, D.C. 20037

Printed in the United States of America

Library of Congress Cataloging-in-Publication Data

Rosenbaum, Walter A.
    Environmental politics and policy / Walter A. Rosenbaum.
—2nd ed.
    p.   cm.
    Includes bibliographical references and index.
    ISBN 0-87187-546-2
    1. Environmental policy—United States. I. Title.
HC110.E5R665   1990
363.7'056'0973—dc20   90-46960
                                                        CIP

Contents

Conclusion   *297*
Suggested Readings   *299*

10. **A New Politics for a New Era: A Political Agenda
     for the 1990s   300**
     The Problem of Regulatory Capability   *301*
     A Hard Look at the "Paradigm Shift"   *304*
     Establishing the Environmental Priority   *309*
     Environmental Forecasting   *311*
     Technology's Institutional Risks   *314*
     Ecology and Social Equity   *318*
     Continuity and Change in the 1990s   *320*
     Suggested Readings   *322*

     List of Abbreviations   *323*
     Index   *325*

Tables, Figures, and Boxes

Boxes

Preface

This book focuses upon *continuity* and *change* in the politics of American environmentalism. Both words matter. The changes have been as important as the continuities in shaping the style and substance of American environmental politics in the 1990s.

In revising this book for the third decade of the nation's environmental era, it seemed especially important to provide some accounting of how far and how well the environmental movement has advanced its policy agenda in the last twenty years, to count failures and successes, to blend explanation with criticism when appropriate, to ask where the movement is headed, and to inquire about the forces shaping its future. And so, while many themes remain from the previous edition to mark the continuities of American environmental politics, the reader will note considerable new material intended to chart and appraise the changes in American environmental politics in its third decade.

A chapter has been added that describes what I call the "quiet crisis of regulatory capacity"—the major deficiencies in institutional and policy design that have become increasingly evident, and deeply disruptive, in environmental regulation over the last twenty years. This chapter (Chapter 4) focuses upon major sources of this crisis: administrative overload, congressional and White House overcontrol, the "single media" approach to pollution regulation, and cost-benefit analysis. The final chapter (Chapter 10) proposes several solutions for these problems, including "integrated" pollution regulation, a new definition of environmental protection as a national security issue, and explicit statutory priority for environmental regulation on the domestic policy agenda.

New material has been added to Chapter 1 to illuminate changes in the political style and policy priorities of the environmental movement over the last twenty years—the transformation from a domestic to a global conception of environmental degradation, to cite one example. The chapter on risk analysis (Chapter 5) includes a discussion, based on an emerging new body of research literature, concerning how social and economic values appear to influence scientific judgment in risk assessment.

This new edition includes assessments of the Reagan administration and its environmental legacy. With Ronald Reagan's departure from the White House, it is now possible to provide a more comprehensive appraisal of his administration's impact on environmental policy and, especially, to appreciate the magnitude of disruption and delay his presidency inflicted upon environmental regulation. This updated appraisal will be found in the chapters dealing with risk assessment, air and water pollution, toxic substances, and the public lands. The general style of the Reagan "administrative presidency" and its objectives are examined in Chapter 3, which focuses on the environmental policy process.

Two issues have been substantially expanded in scope and detail from the earlier edition. In practically every chapter much greater attention has been given to the impact of science and the scientific expert upon environmental policy making and to the problems involved in utilizing science in regulatory decision making. The NIMBY problem—the growing public resistance in the siting of hazardous waste facilities—also gets greater attention in the discussion of hazardous waste management (Chapters 7 and 8) and in the final chapter's prescription for future policy reforms. This enlarged attention is justified, I believe, by the growing importance of these issues in current environmental policy making. Additionally, all the substantive policy chapters have been updated to include the major amendments, passed in the 1980s, to the "Superfund" legislation, the Resource Conservation and Recovery Act, the Safe Drinking Water Act, and the Federal Water Pollution Control Amendments of 1972.

Global climate warming and atmospheric ozone depletion, now major environmental issues but little more than speculation a few years ago, are given appropriately greater attention in the discussion of the environmental policy agenda. In addition, a comprehensive list of readings has been provided at the end of the chapters.

This new edition retains the organizational structure, general themes, and substantive policy chapters of the previous edition and its predecessors. The concepts and characteristics of the "policy cycle" provide the framework in which policy is analyzed. The influence of constitutional design and political culture upon policy is again examined. The policy-making procedures most intimately associated with environmental management are individually characterized, especially the procedures for administrative regulation, risk management, and cost-benefit analysis. Four chapters provide the reader with a brief but informative description of substantive environmental policies, and implementation problems, related to air and water pollution, hazardous and toxic wastes, energy, and the public lands. Numerous illustrations, case studies, and tables or figures are included in an effort to make the material interesting and comprehensible. I hope these features will continue to be as useful and well received as they have been in the past.

For their many diverse contributions to the writing and production of this book I am grateful to my editors, Joanne Daniels and Kerry Kern, and to Michael E. Kraft, James P. Lester, and Geoffrey Wandesforde-Smith for their thoughtful and thorough reviews of the manuscript. Any errors of omission or commission—alas!—will be mine.

When the first version of this book was written twenty years ago, virtually no one—including me—was confident that environmentalism could survive the ferocious competitive pluralism of American public policy. History is a graveyard that memorializes many great and good causes that could not endure. Few issues long command the passionate majorities essential to keep them high on the public policy agenda. Small wonder that environmentalism was frequently dismissed as another trendy and transient public preoccupation. Now, the voices and events from two decades of vigorous environmentalism resonate through every page of this edition. Environmentalism has endured. It is my wish that this book may help environmentalism prevail.

Environmental Politics and Policy

Second Edition

Chapter 1

The Second Environmental Era

*The difficulty of converting scientific findings into political action is
a function of the uncertainty of the science and the pain generated
by the action.*

—William D. Ruckelshaus

Sometime in the late 1980s, deep in the twilight of Ronald
Reagan's final White House years, the United States entered its second
environmental era. Unlike Earth Day in April 1970, the media event
that became the historic signature for the "Environmental Decade,"
Environmental Era II arrived unproclaimed. But there were signs and
portents.

Prelude

One of these events occurred during October 1988, in the small West
Virginia community of Nitro, in the Kanawah River Valley, when the
Environmental Protection Agency (EPA) harmlessly destroyed Elmer
Fike's four-foot cylinder of deadly hydrogen cyanide gas. Thus ended the
EPA's decade-long struggle to compel Fike Chemicals, Inc., a small
custom chemical manufacturer, to control the hazardous substances
contaminating its plant and the nearby surface and ground waters.

Before it played out, the Nitro affair became a $13 million parody
of environmental regulation, "a travesty" in the words of the EPA's
supervising official. It began in 1976, when the EPA obtained a civil
order requiring Fike Chemicals to control its hazardous pollutants. The
company initially complied but failed to maintain the control technology. In 1980, the EPA filed a civil complaint against Fike Chemicals
charging violation of the Resource Conservation and Recovery Act (1976)
because the company's improperly controlled chemicals were endanger-

ing public health. In late 1982 the company signed a consent decree, again promising to clean up its mess and maintain its chemicals properly. But shortly after, in compliance with the newly enacted federal "Superfund" legislation (the Comprehensive Environmental Response, Compensation and Liability Act of 1980), Fike Chemicals was placed on the EPA "priority list" of the nation's most dangerous chemical waste sites and assigned to a category that usually meant the EPA would interfere as little as possible in the facility's operations.

Despite the EPA's intention not to disrupt company operations, Elmer Fike sold his company in 1986 because, he complained, the Superfund listing had driven off his customers. The new owners once again promised to correct the plant's deficiencies, but in June 1986 the EPA discovered that the plant had been closed and abandoned. The site was then upgraded to "an immediate and substantial threat" to public health and the EPA was finally able to act directly to control the on-site contamination. What the EPA found at the site was described as "unbelievable." Among the more than 4,000 abandoned containers were "lethal chemicals that could explode in contact with water, open to the sky; incompatible materials stored in deteriorating drums . . . a bunker full of metallic sodium and a container of methyl mercaptan, both lethal, potentially explosive chemicals,"[1] and Elmer Fike's gas cylinder. A fire or explosion involving these highly volatile chemicals could have been catastrophic for Nitro.

The destruction of the hydrogen cyanide cylinder ended the EPA's ten-year battle to gain access to the Fike Chemical site, but it will take many years to render the site safe for the surrounding community. Critics and defenders of environmental regulation alike regard the Nitro saga as a cheerless metaphor for the entire federal toxic and hazardous waste regulatory program—a warning that something is profoundly wrong with the laws intended to be the foundation of environmental policy during the 1970s.

The Greenhouse Is Coming

In mid-August 1988, the Environmental Protection Agency released a warning to federal and state agencies that marked, as well as any event of the decade, a profound transformation in the nation's environmental politics. All but ignored amid the distractions of the upcoming presidential election, the EPA advised federal and state agencies to begin planning to protect the nation's coastal wetlands from rising sea levels predicted for the next century. "Estimates for sea level rise by the year 2025," the agency commented, "range from 5 to 15 inches above current sea levels and estimates for 2100 from two to seven feet higher."[2] In other words, the nation might lose 30 to 80 percent of its coastal wetlands in little more than a generation. Charleston, South Carolina, didn't need convincing. It was already contemplating a new storm sewer system to accommodate ocean waters raised by melting polar ice caps.

The EPA's barely qualified warning would have been unthinkable a few years earlier. Global warming—the Greenhouse Effect—was then regarded by most atmospheric scientists as speculation. So were acid rain and depletion of the tropospheric ozone layer. Without a potent scientific or political constituency, these issues were fated for "further research." Thus, in the mid-1980s the United States rejected participation in any international agreements limiting worldwide production of pollutants assumed responsible for global warming or the more recently discovered depletion of stratospheric ozone.

In late 1988, Washington reversed itself and signed with twenty-four other nations the Montreal Protocol, which required the United States to cut production and use of chlorofluorocarbons (CFCs) and other halons believed responsible for global ozone depletion. Earlier, Washington agreed with twenty-four other industrial nations to freeze its emission of nitrogen oxides, which are thought to be a major precursor of global acid rain. The sudden ascent of these problems to high priority in the current U.S. public policy debate testifies to the rapidity with which international scientific research is illuminating for Americans the worldwide scale of ecological degradation. The environmental agenda has become global. And issues once thought implausible now abound on the U.S. policy agenda.

Smogbusting in Los Angeles

Even before the EPA released its Greenhouse warning, the board of the South Coast Air Quality Management District, responsible for air pollution control in the sprawling 6,600 square mile Los Angeles basin, had proposed the most radical air pollution management plan in U.S. history. The Los Angeles basin, home to 12 million people, 8 million automobiles, and the nation's worst smog, is the most severe violator of the ozone standards required by the federal Clean Air Act of 1970. In one recent three-year period, the basin violated the standards an estimated 143 days each year. Local authorities must abide with a federal court mandate to produce a plan for complying with EPA air-quality standards for ozone, carbon monoxide, and airborne particulates by the year 2007.

The plan proposed, among other things, within five years to require reformulation of paints and solvents to reduce hydrocarbon emissions, to ban gasoline-powered lawn mowers, to ban the sale of barbecues and fuels requiring a starter fluid, to limit the number of cars each family could have, to raise parking fees for cars carrying a single passenger, and to restrict all new tire purchases to radials that shed less rubber particles into the air. Within an additional five years, the plan proposed to convert 40 percent of the cars, 70 percent of the trucks and other freight vehicles, and all buses to methanol or other "clean" fuels. The plan contained something to offend almost every powerful economic and political interest in the Los Angeles basin, and its prospects seemed bleak. Nevertheless, the plan was a remarkable act of political boldness in its determination to confront Southern Californians with the real social and economic costs of clean air and to challenge the public to accept responsibility for achieving it.

Time will determine how much is substance or symbolism in the environmental rhetoric of the late 1980s. Policies proclaimed are not programs achieved. But the incidents briefly examined above are significant now because they point away from the style and substance of the "Environmental Decade" past. What is evident in the nation's environmental politics in the last decade of the twentieth century is a sharp mood shift, a more expansive sense of scale and causality, a new vocabulary bespeaking an altered agenda, and a pervasive somberness quite unlike the style of the nation's first environmental era.

A New Mood, A Different Agenda

The Reagan years rise like a great divide between America's environmental eras. On the far side lies Environmental Era I, beginning in the 1960s and spanning the 1970s. The Environmental Decade created the legal, political, and institutional foundations of the nation's environmental policies. It promoted an enduring public consciousness of environmental degradation and fashioned a broad public agreement on the need for governmental restoration and protection of environmental quality that has become part of the American public policy consensus. It mobilized, organized, and educated a generation of environmental activists. The environmental movement prospered in a benign political climate assured by a succession of White House occupants tolerant, if not always sympathetic, to its objectives.

The Reagan Legacy

All this changed with the Reagan administration. Ronald Reagan and his advisers believed the president had been elected to bring "regulatory relief" to the American economy, and environmental regulations were an early priority on the "hit list" of laws needing "regulatory reform." The environmental movement regarded the Reagan administration as the most environmentally hostile in a half century and the president's regulatory reform as the cutting edge of a massive administrative assault on the institutional foundations of federal environmental law.[3] The environmental movement, thrown on the defensive, expended most of its energies and resources defending the legislative and administrative achievements of the Environmental Decade from the onslaught of the president's regulatory relief.

The Reagan years severely tested the foundations of the environmental movement. While the foundations held, little was done to advance the implementation of existing policy or to address new and urgent environmental issues. "The contest produced a standoff," concludes historian Samuel P. Hays. "When the political force of public environmental desires became too great, the administration backed down, and when the administration became so zealous that it acted in disregard to established procedures or the intent of legislation, it was forced to change tactics. At the same time . . . the administration could effectively check most innovations in environmental policy that were ripe for action."[4] To environmental leaders, the Reagan years meant, above all, dangerous drift and indecision, almost a decade of lost opportunities and intensifying environmental ills. George Bush's election seemed to promise a far more sympathetic and aggressive White House approach to environmental protection, and promoted a renewed sense of vigor and urgency within the environmental movement. The movement itself was changing in response to the altered political climate and the accumulating experience with environmental management during the prior two decades.

A Global Agenda

When the leaders of thirty national environmental groups met with President-elect George Bush shortly after his victory in November 1988, they presented more than 700 recommendations for his consideration. Among the highest priority issues were global warming, destruction of the planet's ozone layer, loss of tropical rain forests, acid rain, and ocean pollution.[5] Unlike the first environmental era, the politics of Environmental Era II embraces a far more global conception of environmental degradation. It is more aware that ecological ills grow from a complex causality and create an intricate chain of effects that link different ecosystems and natural orders. Thus, it is likely to stress that sulfur oxides polluting Ohio River Valley airsheds create the acid rain that falls into Lake Ontario and deposits the heavy metals that may end up in the body fat of fish consumed by Canadian children. Or the new politics is likely to emphasize that gases and particulates borne in smoke clouds from the deliberate burning of the Brazilian rain forests can be carried by jet streams south to the Antarctic where they can deplete the tropospheric ozone layer.

During the first environmental era the movement leaders spoke most often, and most relevantly, to Americans about the nation's environmental ills. Leaders in the second environmental era speak as naturally of "the Global Commons"—global problems and global solutions. This is an international perspective hardened by a twenty-year accumulation of increasingly sophisticated scientific data suggesting that the gravest ecological problems exist on a scale that defies purely national approaches to their solution. Environmental scientist Barry Commoner once defined ecology as the awareness that in nature "everything is connected to everything else."[6] In this sense, the new rhetoric bespeaks a more truly ecological understanding of the policy problems and solutions involved in environmental management.

Disappointment, Reappraisal, and Reform

The United States enters the second environmental era poised at the intersection of two learning curves: one relates to the body of scientific data, technology, and inference developing about environmental problems; the second relates to experience with the legal and institutional solutions to these problems. One curve seems to climb upward toward a more sophisticated use and understanding of environmental information; the other seems to chart a plummeting confidence in existing institutional and legal capacities to deal with environmental problems.

A conviction is growing among major segments of the environmental movement both inside and outside government that something is fundamentally wrong with many existing approaches to environmental regulation and that action must be taken quickly to change matters. There is ample evidence that many laws considered essential to federal environmental regulation are not working well, and some hardly work at all. Here environmentalists and their opponents often agree, although not about the remedies. Federal laws regulating the manufacture, use, and disposal of hazardous or toxic substances, for instance, are almost a consensus choice as near failures. The specter of Nitro, West Virginia, lingers about the prognosis offered for the current laws by the Conservation Foundation, a respected and moderate environmental organization:

the burgeoning problem of mitigating toxic substances' public health and environmental effects may well exceed the system's regulatory capacity. As the tip of the toxics iceberg gradually enters public view, its perils and complexities may indeed reveal the inadequacy of a segmented approach [to regulation].[7]

Critical reappraisals have affected the environmental movement's policy agenda in several ways. Proposals are now commonly debated to redesign the institutional framework, the incentive structure, and the goals of environmental regulation; some environmental groups, in turn, are changing their viewpoint on such matters. The president's Council on Environmental Quality (CEQ), asserting that "the current environmental program is basically flawed," offered its package of reforms in 1985. CEQ's proposals were rather moderate when judged by the standard of contemporary debates over environmental policy: (1) recognize the "interconnectedness of the environment" by emphasizing multimedia approaches to pollution control instead of the current regulation of air, water, and surface pollution separately; (2) shift the primary objective of environmental regulation to the reduction of risk, not the elimination of all pollutants; (3) improve the communication of information about risk exposure to the public; and (4) redefine the respective role of the state and federal governments in pollution control.[8]

Because the environmental movement has never been a church of one creed, reform proposals exacerbate ideological, programmatic, and tactical disagreements among the faithful. Divisive arguments continue about the validity, the political risks involved, and the extent to which reforms will betray fundamental environmental values. Lee Thomas drew the fire of several major environmental groups, for whom "no pollution" is sacrosanct, when he proposed upon becoming EPA's administrator in 1985 that the agency's primary mission should be to "reduce risk to public health as fast as we can" rather than to attempt what he considered the impossible task of eliminating pollution altogether.[9]

Pervasive dissatisfaction with institutional and legal approaches to environmental management fashioned in the 1970s creates a congenial climate for experimentation and reform. Traditional group alignments and coalitions are more malleable, and new tactical and strategic alliances become plausible in the environmental politics of Environmental Era II. Indeed, major reform seems almost inevitable and, as will be discussed in Chapter 4, the axis about which the new policy dissensions will develop seem relatively clear.

How Much Should Regulation Cost?

During testimony before the Senate Governmental Affairs Committee of which he was chairman, Sen. John Glenn (D-Ohio) was pondering. "The enormity of this thing just sort of overwhelms you," he remarked. Rapping his knuckles on the desk with each word, he continued: "One hundred ten billion, one hundred ten billion, 'B,' billion. . . ."[10] Inspiring this meditation was an estimate by the Department of Energy (DOE) of the cost to clean up radioactive and chemical contamination at twelve sites across the United States where the DOE had negligently supervised the manufacture of nuclear weapons. In fact, the estimate wasn't enormous enough, for it failed to include the additional billions that would be needed to dispose of the radioactive wastes and to decontaminate the reactors themselves.

As rising cost becomes the norm in environmental regulation, economic issues grow increasingly important to all sides. Arguments over the magnitude and acceptability of costs have been customary to environmental regulation from its inception. At the outset of the Environmental Era II, however, the cost of regulation is becoming far more influential in shaping how policy makers evaluate existing programs and define the alternatives for reform. Even more significantly, within the environmental movement a growing sensitivity to cost and a greater willingness to consider proposals for cost reduction are evident among many leaders and organizations.

Environmentalists have approached discussions about the cost of environmental regulation with considerable wariness. They suspect, often correctly, that estimates of regulatory costs produced by business or other regulated interests are deliberately inflated. They also believe that cost-benefit comparisons applied to environmental policies are usually biased because it is much easier to monetize the costs of regulation than the benefits. Moreover, many environmentalists consider it ethically irresponsible to allow economic costs to weigh heavily in making environmental regulations. Protection of human health and safety, and preservation of environmental quality for future generations, are assumed to be preeminent values when compared to any monetary costs that might be attached to their achievement. Thus, almost all approaches to environmental policy evaluation involving some economic calculus are categorically unacceptable to many in the environmental community.

This attitude is changing. Leaving aside predictable and usually unresolvable arguments over the "real" cost of environmental regulations, some adverse economic impacts are now evident, compelling environmental interests to be more sensitive to the importance of regulatory economics for several reasons. First, the costs of almost all major environmental programs have escalated far beyond initial estimates. Massive cost inflation is driving current and projected estimates to a magnitude that forces all sides to reconsider their acceptability. A typical example is the Construction Grants Program, created by Congress in 1972 to provide financial assistance for local governments required to build waste treatment plants to achieve federally mandated water quality standards. Initially, $18 billion was authorized through 1975. Congress authorized an additional $10.5 billion in 1977, then another $4.9 billion in 1981. By 1988, the program—now the second most expensive civilian public works project in U.S. history—had cost the federal government more than twice its original authorization and the EPA estimates that it will require an additional $83.5 billion to meet the total sewage treatment needs of U.S. cities.[11]

Regulatory costs have risen, in good part, because ecological damage has proven to be far more extensive, and its causes more complex, than was imagined when programs were initially designed. The Department of Defense (DOD), for instance, originally assumed it would cost $1.6 billion through 1993 to clean up abandoned hazardous waste sites on its military installations. Eight months later, the estimate soared to at least $5 billion and possibly $10 billion. Cleaning up a "midnight dumper's" single 750-gallon polychlorinated biphenyls (PCB) spill at Ft. Lewis, Washington, cost the DOD $1 million.[12] Moreover, proponents of regulatory programs, particularly the congressional committees and staff writing the laws, are often ignorant (or choose to be) about hidden costs. For example, the Toxic Substances Control Act (1976) was written without discussion of the estimated $130,000 to $240,000 it would cost to gather data necessary for the EPA to defend its procedures for testing each of the twenty-one chemicals or chemical groups it chose to place on a priority list of substances meriting immediate review. In another case, the unanticipated difficulties in controlling the formation of low-level ozone and the emission of nitrogen oxides by trucks and automobiles are a major reason the cost of achieving the Clean Air Act's goals is so steep. The cost is now estimated to be $80 billion more than the $60 billion already spent by federal, state, and local governments.[13]

Regulatory costs also increase as new programs are added. By signing the Montreal Protocols, which limit U.S. manufacture and emission of CFCs in order to protect the global ozone layer, the government and private sector may have to spend an estimated $27 billion in the next century.[14] Depending upon whether one believes its sponsors or its critics, the aforementioned air pollution control plan for the Los Angeles basin will cost either $2.8 billion annually for the first five years or more than twice that much.[15] No small contribution to cost inflation is also made by hundreds of governmental and private sector institutions, such as consulting firms and academic researchers, that depend upon environmental programs for income, staff, or survival. Dependents readily become constituencies, quick to protect and promote the programs. Programs may prove almost impossible to terminate, or may be reformed only after protracted political battles, because the constituencies have a material or ideological stake in the status quo.

Rising program costs affect current policy debates in several ways. First, proposals to shift the primary objective of many current pollution laws, such as the Clean Air Act, from eliminating pollution to reducing exposure to the pollutants have become a major reform issue. Since this issue will be explored in Chapter 6, suffice it to note here that the proponents believe that reducing risk of exposure, rather than attempting to eliminate pollutants, is a far less expensive and more technologically feasible objective. Second, rising regulatory costs have encouraged all sides to give more attention to identifying the trade-offs between regulatory costs and benefits in an effort to identify where the limits of acceptability may lie—in short, to identify the threshold of unacceptably high costs. Third, some environmental leaders and organizations have been more willing to consider substituting economic incentives and other market strategies for traditional administrative procedures to secure compliance with environmental regulations on the assumption that the market approach is more economical. Common proposals have been to permit "emissions trading" among regulated air and water polluters and to use a pollution tax rather than prescribed pollution control technologies to assure compliance with air- and water-quality laws.

Any debate about the importance of economic considerations in environmental regulation arouses an ideological passion among many environmental leaders and groups who profoundly believe that environmental values must never be compromised by marketplace logic. Although the environmental movement will remain internally divided over the economic wisdom of reforming existing laws, reforms will come, albeit slowly and divisively.

The Impact of Evolving Science and Technology

Scientific research and the technological innovation it stimulates have a paradoxical effect on environmental regulation. They vastly improve the capacity to measure the magnitude of environmental degradation, to understand its causes and consequences, and to produce increasingly better techniques for pollution control. But science also creates an unceasing flow of technologies and consumer products freighted with potential ecological risks. Moreover, as environmental science improves, it often diminishes the credibility of existing environmental regulation by discrediting its scientific basis.

The paradox is apparent in the case of disposable diapers, a $3.3 billion annual business in the United States. Americans can buy an array of superabsorbent diapers, colored diapers, and diaper-like bibs and pads to use when changing babies. The adult diaper market has hardly been explored. "In all likelihood," burbled a respected advertising journal, "disposable diapers represent the most dynamic new product category in consumer marketing history."[16] But problems associated with the disposal of this product cast the diapers in a very different light. The 16 billion diapers sold annually in the United States create an estimated 2.8 million tons of urine and excrement that are dumped into landfills. Diapers can contain any of one hundred viruses, including live polio and hepatitis from vaccine residue; this poses a danger to sanitation workers or others brought in contact with the contaminants by flies or ground water. Thus, science and its allied technologies create the diaper problem and define its adverse environmental impacts.

The disruptive effect of new scientific information on existing environmental regulation is more subtle. Scientific research continually grows more sophisticated in its methods of measuring and describing environmental conditions and in understanding the causes and consequences of environmental degradation. This constant infusion of new information, while essential to prudent environmental regulation, unintentionally subverts existing environmental policies when it discredits the scientific premises upon which the policies were originally based. The impact of new information on existing regulation can be illustrated by advances in understanding cross-media pollution, vastly improved techniques for environmental monitoring, and recent research on low-level ozone.

Research on cross-media pollution has revealed that many existing pollution laws are too narrowly focused. After major pollution legislation was written in the 1970s, research revealed that many important pollution problems, such as acid rain and toxic contamination of ground waters, evolve from the movement of pollutants across media—from air to earth to water, for instance. Federal environmental laws were written on a science base that emphasized controlling pollutants in a single media. These laws rarely provide the legal, scientific, or institutional resources for controlling cross-media pollution. Environmental officials have had to define pollution in different ways. Former EPA administrator Douglas Costle observed: "There has been a shift from trying to decrease pollution by gross measures to dealing subtly with more complex issues . . . from dealing with bulk pollutants to such problems as acid rain and ground water contamination. We had to rethink the basic approaches underlying our laws, especially as our knowledge and sophistication increased."[17] In light of this new understanding, the important issue arises of whether the laws should be rewritten to target cross-media pollution.

Increasingly sensitive technologies now reveal that toxic and hazardous substances are far more pervasive than previously assumed. Scientific monitoring has improved from an ability to detect substances in food, air, or water in concentrations of one part per million to one part per quadrillion. As a result of this extraordinary precision, it can no longer be assumed that potentially dangerous substances can be completely removed from air, water, food, or other media. Thus, it appears extremely difficult, perhaps impossible, to eliminate entirely *some* risk, however slight, of human exposure to potentially dangerous substances. However, many environmental laws, such as the famous Delaney Clause in the Food, Drug, and Cosmetic Act (1938) and some portions of the

Safe Drinking Water Act (1974), were written under the assumption that dangerous substances could be eliminated entirely from food, air, or water—in effect, that a "no-risk" level of regulation could be achieved. "You can put a food substance in a process that can measure residues in parts per billion or parts per trillion," commented a spokesman for regulated food manufacturers. "A zero-risk policy makes no sense because you are always chasing zero."[18]

New research continues to yield evidence that some existing air- or water-quality standards may be based on inadequate data. For example, recent tests conducted in EPA laboratories suggest that the existing exposure limits mandated by the EPA for ozone may be inadequate. The results of tests in which healthy people were exposed to currently permissible levels of ozone revealed that serious respiratory problems could arise after exposure for six to eight hours. Many experts now believe that federal ozone standards should be modified to reduce the legally allowable exposure levels.

Research also creates a new order of policy problem through the development of complex forecasting models that enable experts to predict future ecological risks for which the political and economic system may have no existing answers and technology provides no feasible solutions. Both global climate modification and tropospheric ozone depletion are issues first imagined through scientific forecasting. Indeed, a major task for proponents of action to mitigate the impact of ozone depletion and the Greenhouse Effect has been to convince the public and its officials that such forecasting is credible. We can expect environmental issues derived from forecasting to become increasingly common in the future.

The impact of scientific research on environmental policy is magnified by the mass media. The media make environmentalism a populist science. Television, newspapers, and magazines monitor and interpret environmentally relevant science, then translate their findings into terms understandable to laypersons and package the information attractively for mass consumption. One has only to observe how suddenly the Greenhouse Effect became common media fare during the late 1980s to appreciate how rapidly new research enters public consciousness. Equally important, the public opinion climate to which policy makers respond is often created in this manner.

As the scientific basis of environmental regulation evolves, it will remain an institutionalized source of tension, conflict, and change within the environmental policy process by continually forcing a redefinition of environmental problems and solutions. At the same time, an evolving science and technology is essential to effective environmental regulation. And it is to this same science that policy makers must turn for the technology and the theories upon which sound environmental regulation should be grounded.

The Problem of Information Integration

A major issue in Environmental Era II is how the diverse, complex information essential to effective environmental policy making can best be assembled and integrated in the policy process. Experience over more than two decades with different policy-making procedures has made it clear that too many different strategies are required and that many are flawed. Beyond this, disagreement prevails.

Environmental policy making is among the most complex in government because it requires policy makers to arrange an extraordinarily diverse array of information into a coherent decision-making process. Usually, policy makers must be able to obtain and interpret scientific, economic, engineering, legal, and political information and to accord each its appropriate part in reaching policy decisions. For two decades, policy makers have struggled with various schemes for organizing and weighing all this diverse information. The rule seemed to be: Every new law deserves a new strategy. The result has been growing debate about which strategy, or strategies, was most desirable. Much of the current debate over institutional reform is promoted by dissatisfaction with the way information is now used in policy making.

The range of information officials are expected to obtain and integrate in environmental regulation is suggested by a few of the requirements the EPA must fulfill in cleaning up abandoned hazardous waste sites according to the Superfund Amendments and Reauthorization Act of 1986 (SARA), a major revision of the 1980 "Superfund" legislation:

Scientific and Medical Information: EPA officials must determine that the degree of cleanup at the site will, at a minimum, be sufficient to protect human health and the environment.

Economic Information: After choosing how much to clean up a site, EPA officials must decide the most cost-effective approach to the cleanup.

Engineering Information: At the same time EPA officials are wrestling with the scientific and economic issues, they must also assure that the cleanup method they choose will create a *permanent* solution and use alternatives to the dumping of hazardous materials at the site "to the maximum extent practicable."

Legal Information: EPA is expected to come up with a "permanent" solution to site cleanup but the law does not clarify how long "permanent" means. A few decades? A century? Forever? Suppose no proposed solution will last forever. How much less than forever is acceptable?

Political Information: EPA may make financial grants to individuals or groups affected by the cleanup for the purpose of helping them obtain technical help in understanding the problem and weighing the alternative solutions. Who should get these awards? When is it wise to make them?[19]

One major problem, discussed in Chapter 5, is that federal law is notoriously inconsistent in mandating what kinds of information should be considered by regulators when deciding whether a substance should be regulated. The same substance may be regulated by different criteria, depending upon whether it is found in food, water, air, or food crops. Among the thirty-four current federal laws regulating public exposure to hazardous or toxic substances, regulators have many alternative criteria for deciding when a substance should be controlled: seven laws require consideration only of health risks, two require consideration of the available technology, and twenty-five mandate some kind of balancing of risks and costs.

Another problem is how to package information to make it most useful to officials. Quite often, controversy over scientific issues produces such a welter of conflicting and controversial information that policy makers cannot easily decide what information, if any, is valid. In the end, observes scientist and government consultant Allan Mazur, "a dispute itself may become so divisive and widespread that scientific advice becomes more of a cost than a benefit to the policy maker."[20] Cost-benefit analysis provokes one of the great Holy Wars in environmental politics because its many critics within the environmental movement believe it seldom (some would say *never*) provides decision makers with an accurate accounting of all benefits and costs involved in environmental regulations. The packaging problem has long been an issue in the preparation of Environmental Impact Statements (EISs). The National Environmental Policy Act of 1970 requires federal agencies to prepare EISs for any proposed program or decision "significantly affecting the quality of the human environment." Many critics believe the EISs have become too bloated with detail and technical information to clarify for decision makers the important environmental impacts of their decisions.

Arguments continue over when information is best introduced into the policy-making process. This problem provoked some of the most important controversies in environmental politics during the 1980s. One long-running battle concerned how early the public should be given an opportunity for participation and when the public should be excluded.

A second controversy concerns at what point, if any, in environmental regulation is it proper for the president and his staff to attempt to influence agency regulation writing. As will be shown later, both these conflicts have spilled over into the Bush administration.

No issue incites more emotion in environmental decision making than the question of what information should weigh most heavily. Should cost-benefit data be accorded greater importance than health and safety data in deciding how much to control a potentially dangerous substance? How important are the political impacts of a regulation in comparison to its cost or its environmental impact? One reason for this controversy is the congressional habit of writing environmental laws thick with criteria to be considered in making policy decisions but thin with enlightenment on how to weigh them. The Toxic Substances Control Act (TSCA) of 1976 leaves practically nothing unmentioned, and offers no help in deciding what factors are most important, when instructing the EPA on what to consider in deciding whether the risks from exposure to a substance are "unreasonable":

The type of effect (chronic or acute, reversible or irreversible); degree of risk; characteristics and number of humans, plants, and animals, or ecosystems, at risk; amount of knowledge about the effects; available or alternative substances and their expected effects; magnitude of the social and economic costs and benefits of possible control actions; and appropriateness and effectiveness of TSCA as a legal instrument for controlling the risk.[21]

In such situations, administrators must often assume the responsibility for deciding how much weight to accord different factors and how to defend their decisions against political and legal attack.

Even if a law is clear about the relative importance of different criteria in environmental policy making, controversy is likely over whether various participants were biased or prejudiced in the way they created or considered information. In recent years, a growing body of research suggests that scientists and other technical specialists may be influenced by political, economic, or other social values when making apparently professional judgments concerning the extent to which a substance may constitute a hazard to humans or the environment. Almost everyone deplores this bias, but devising a risk assessment process that eliminates it is difficult. The quest for laws and institutional arrangements that reduce or eliminate the influence of undesirable factors in environmental policy making continues with unabated fervor in Environmental Era II—a sign of how difficult it has proven to engineer the legal and institutional arrangements that assure that only the right factors affect decisions at the right time.

The Governmental Setting

The politics of Environmental Era II are shaped not only by current issues but also by an inheritance of laws, governmental institutions, and court decisions evolving over the last thirty years. Governmental institutions become vested interests and actors in the policy process. Laws, administrative regulations, and court decisions create precedents and define limits on existing policy choices. The political, financial, and institutional investments in the current structure of environmental policy making become substantial "sunk costs" that must be taken into account when deciding whether to change existing policy. Many aspects of this governmental setting will be discussed in later chapters. Here it is useful to examine the setting in broad and brief perspective in order to illuminate the range and complexity of the political forces involved in the environmental policy process.

The Administrative Setting

Nearly thirty federal agencies have a mission or authority affecting some aspect of the environment. This bureaucracy is a pastiche of numerous agencies with overlapping and sometimes conflicting authority, of agency rivalries and unceasing "turf" wars, of institutions with differing congressional and interest group clientele. The two agencies bearing the heaviest burden of responsibility for environmental protection and regulation are the Environmental Protection Agency and the Occupational Safety and Health Administration (OSHA).

The EPA, created by an executive order of President Richard Nixon in 1970 and expected to be elevated to Cabinet rank by President Bush in 1991, is Washington's largest regulatory agency in terms of budget and personnel. Its responsibilities embrace an extraordinarily large and technically complex set of programs ranging across the whole domain of environmental management. (The EPA's political and administrative problems will be discussed in Chapter 3.) This staggering range of responsibilities is one major reason why the EPA has been chronically overworked and repeatedly proposed for major organizational reform.

OSHA was created by the Occupational Safety and Health Act (1970) and lodged within the Department of Labor. Its responsibilities include creating and enforcing standards to protect employers and employees in the workplace, creating and maintaining a system to keep records and report job-related injuries and illnesses, encouraging the states to develop and enforce their own workplace health and safety programs, and numerous other duties that routinely plunge the agency into political controversy. OSHA often shares with the EPA a responsibility for risk assessment and enforcement of regulations intended to protect humans and the environment from hazardous or toxic substances.

The Statutory Setting

Current federal environmental legislation is a patchwork of several hundred congressional enactments written over the last half century. Legal scholar Christopher Schroeder's verdict about federal toxic substance laws—that they have "resulted not in a well-designed cabin, but in a pile of logs"[22]—applies as well for the whole of federal environmental legislation. Many controversies prominent in Environmental Era II result from the inconsistencies, contradictions, confusions, and inadequacies of this statutory welter. At the same time, each law memorializes the success of a major environmental coalition in waging a battle for environmental protection that may have lasted decades. Each law acquires a politically vocal and potent constituency from congressional factions, private interests, bureaucratic agencies, and program beneficiaries. A huge volume of judicial opinions girding each law with court-derived interpretations and justifications further institutionalizes the legislation. Collectively, these laws are the legal edifice upon which environmental policy has been erected.

An idea of the variety and range of these congressional enactments can be gleaned from Table 1-1, which summarizes the major legislative enactments currently on the federal statute books relating to just one category of environmental pollutant, toxic substances.[23] Since the vocabulary of policy conflict is fashioned from these laws, many will be discussed further in subsequent chapters. However, cataloging even a few categories of law should be sufficient to emphasize two realities about today's environmental policy controversies: (1) the existing law becomes a conservative force in policy debate because it is difficult to change; and (2) the incompatibilities and omissions in current environmental legislation are a continuing cause of difficulties in policy implementation and enforcement.

Economic Investments

Public and private institutions in the United States are annually spending more than $90 billion for pollution abatement and control. By far the largest portion of this spending is made by the private sector—currently, about four of every five dollars.[24] While this spending represents a relatively small portion of the federal budget or the annual capital outlays of most businesses, the total annual expenditure is only slightly less than the combined U.S. budget for health, veterans' benefits, and education. Between 1980 and 1987, the cumulative U.S. spending on

Table 1-1 *Major Toxic Chemical Laws Administered by the EPA*

Statute	Provisions
Toxic Substances Control Act	Requires that EPA be notified of any new chemical prior to its manufacture and authorizes EPA to regulate production, use, or disposal of a chemical.
Federal Insecticide, Fungicide and Rodenticide Act	Authorizes EPA to register all pesticides and specify the terms and conditions of their use, and remove unreasonably hazardous pesticides from the marketplace.
Federal Food, Drug and Cosmetic Act	Authorizes EPA in cooperation with FDA to establish tolerance levels for pesticide residues on food and food products.
Resource Conservation and Recovery Act	Authorizes EPA to identify hazardous wastes and regulate their generation, transportation, treatment, storage, and disposal.
Comprehensive Environmental Response, Compensation and Liability Act	Requires EPA to designate hazardous substances that can present substantial danger and authorizes the cleanup of sites contaminated with such substances.
Clean Air Act	Authorizes EPA to set emission standards to limit the release of hazardous air pollutants.
Clean Water Act	Requires EPA to establish a list of toxic water pollutants and set standards.
Safe Drinking Water Act	Requires EPA to set drinking water standards to protect public health from hazardous substances.
Marine Protection Research and Sanctuaries Act	Regulates ocean dumping of toxic contaminants.
Asbestos School Hazard Act	Authorizes EPA to provide loans and grants to schools with financial need for abatement of severe asbestos hazards.
Asbestos Hazard Emergency Response Act	Requires EPA to establish a comprehensive regulatory framework for controlling asbestos hazards in schools.
Emergency Planning and Community Right-to-Know Act	Requires states to develop programs for responding to hazardous chemical releases and requires industries to report on the presence and release of certain hazardous substances.

SOURCE: Environmental Protection Agency, *Environmental Progress and Challenges: EPA Update* (Washington, D.C.: Environmental Protection Agency, 1988), 113.

pollution control and abatement exceeded one-half trillion dollars. Most economists predict that this level of spending will prevail, and probably increase, throughout the rest of this century.

The economic burden of environmental regulation varies greatly among U.S. industries. As the data presented in Table 1-2 indicate, the nonfarm sector of the U.S. economy spent an estimated average of 1.7 percent of capital outlays for pollution abatement in 1987, a modest amount. But the chemical, petroleum, and primary metals industries spent an average of 7.2 percent and in the 1970s spent even more on pollution abatement. Most economists do not now consider U.S. expenditures for pollution abatement to be a significant deterrent to U.S. economic growth or capital investment in most U.S. economic sectors. But the magnitude of this spending in the past and its likely continuation well into the next century affect current policy debates in several important ways.

Numerous industries, having invested heavily for many years in required pollution control technologies, strongly resist new regulations compelling them to modify previously installed technologies or to spend more than anticipated on future pollution abatement. Many regulated public and private interests believe this spending can be significantly reduced by new forms of regulation, such as "marketable pollution permits," that will free more pollution abatement dollars for more profitable investment. And many industries believe that their expenditures on pollution abatement are a major damper to future plant expansion and market exploration. Finally, many regulated interests are convinced that their own costs for pollution abatement, and perhaps those of many other economic sectors, are unacceptably high when compared with the benefits.

The Environmental Movement

The many groups marching under the environmental banner have grown in number, sophistication, and aggressiveness throughout the 1980s. They constitute the organizational bedrock of U.S. environmentalism, the political foundation upon which the politics of Era II will be mounted. Many environmental organizations now familiar in the environmental movement first appeared during Era I, but many others were present at its creation.

The environmental movement prospers without a single orthodoxy. Viewed at close range, the movement dissolves into many different organizations with diverse policy agendas, political strategies, and membership credos—a reminder that pluralism, and conflicts born of pluralism, is common within environmentalist ranks. This pluralism is bounded, however, by general values, attitudes, and beliefs—a way of looking at nature,

Table 1-2 *New Capital Business Expenditures for Pollution Abatement, 1975 to 1987*

Selected industry	Pollution abatement expenditures (billions of dollars)							Percent of total capital outlays by business		
	1975	1980	1984	1985	1986	1987[a] (planned)		1975	1980	1987[a]
Nonfarm business, total	6.81	9.19	8.44	8.61	8.45	7.73		4.2	2.9	1.7
Manufacturing[b]	4.66	5.35	4.53	5.13	5.33	5.44		8.7	4.8	3.8
Food, incl. beverage	.30	.26	.26	.25	.27	.25		6.8	3.2	2.3
Paper	.47	.46	.54	.58	.55	.66		16.0	7.1	7.8
Chemicals	.76	.69	.58	.74	.98	1.05		10.7	5.9	6.2
Petroleum	1.21	1.54	1.28	1.25	1.28	1.25		13.3	7.9	7.7
Primary metals	.92	.94	.68	.89	.76	.68		16.9	13.9	7.7
Machinery, except electrical	.09	.12	.19	.15	.10	.10		1.9	1.1	.1
Electrical machinery	.09	.22	.18	.18	.25	.22		2.9	2.3	1.4
Transportation equipment	.15	.48	.36	.55	.60	.53		2.7	3.2	3.1
Public utilities	1.56	3.05	3.25	2.87	2.50	1.76		7.7	8.1	3.8

SOURCE: Department of Commerce, Bureau of the Census, *Statistical Abstract of the United States, 1989* (Washington, D.C.: Government Printing Office, 1989), 205.
[a]Expenditures planned as of January and February 1987.
[b]Includes industries not shown separately.

humanity, and U.S. society—widely shared by environmental leaders and activists. While it lacks the coherence of an ideology, it sets environmentalists apart from mainstream American culture.

The Environmental Ethos

Reduced to essentials, environmentalism springs from an attitude toward nature that assumes that humanity is part of the created order, ethically responsible for the preservation of the world's ecological integrity and ultimately vulnerable, like all earth's other creatures, to the good or ill humans inflict upon nature. In the environmentalist perspective, humans live in a world of limited resources and potential scarcities; like the good stewards of an inheritance, they must use their scientific genius to manage global resources. An enlightened approach to managing nature should stress the interdependency of all natural systems (the ecosystem concept), the importance of ecological stability, resource sustainability, and the enormously long time span across which the impact of ecological change occurs. In its approach to nature, environmentalism emphasizes the sanctity of the created order as a warning against the human assumption that we stand above and apart from the created order by virtue of our intelligence and scientific achievements. All this is summed up for many ecologists in the metaphor of "spaceship earth."

In its cultural stance, environmentalism sharply criticizes marketplace economics generally and capitalism especially, and denigrates the growth ethic, unrestrained technological optimism, and the political structures supporting these. Such an attitude places environmentalists on a collision course with dominant American values. Environmentalism challenges U.S. confidence in market mechanisms to allocate scarce resources for several reasons. It asserts that market economics esteems economic growth and material consumption above concern for ecological balance and integrity. Therefore, the market cannot be relied upon to "signal" resource scarcity efficiently enough to prevent possibly catastrophic resource exhaustion. Many, like William Ophuls, believe marketplace economies are ecologically reckless:

An unregulated market economy inevitably fosters accelerated ecological degradation and resource depletion through ever higher levels of production and consumption. Indeed, given the cornucopian assumptions upon which a market system is based, it could hardly be otherwise; both philosophically and practically, a market economy is incompatible with ecology.[25]

Environmentalism is less hostile to technology itself than to a blind faith in technology's power to cure whatever ecological ills it begets and to a bland confidence in technological expertise to meet humanity's material and spiritual needs. Environmentalists regard the public's confidence in "American know-how" as a secular religion responsible for many of the nation's most difficult environmental problems, such as the management of commercial nuclear technologies.

The environmental movement's political agenda arises from these attitudes toward the natural world and contemporary culture. Many environmentalists believe that the nation's dominant political institutions and processes must be reformed because they are committed to the preservation of ecological, economic, and technological values that are hostile to prudent ecological management. For some, this is summed up as suspicion of the "Establishment" and the traditional institutions and processes associated with it. "If American political ideology and institutions have been successful in encouraging pursuit of happiness through material acquisition," argues Ann Leeson, "they appear incapable of imposing the limits which are required to forestall ecological disaster."[26] Many fear the power of an interlocking economic and political structure committed to controlling technology in environmentally reckless ways. "Many corporations are virtually dependent on governmental contracts," argues Ian Barbour. "The staff members of regulatory agencies, in turn, are mainly recruited from the industries they are supposed to regulate. . . . the particular congressional committees, government agencies, and industries have forced a three-way alliance to promote such technologies as nuclear energy."[27]

Environmentalist politics emphasizes the importance of participatory democracy, decentralized political power, the grass-roots base for political advocacy, and other arrangements that create countervailing power against the Establishment. Environmental groups have increasingly pressed Congress and the White House to provide generous opportunities for public involvement in the implementation of environmental regulations at all governmental levels. They have attempted, whenever possible, to write into laws and administrative regulations various arrangements to frustrate the capture of administrative agencies responsible for environmental management by hostile interests. They have looked to the judiciary as another countervailing institution against legislative and executive agencies dominated by ecologically hostile interests.

Most environmental organizations practice traditional American forms of political advocacy and work within the accepted institutional rules of policy making. But a radical rejection of much considered essential to contemporary U.S. culture is latent within environmentalism. The partisan passion and bitterness of many environmental conflicts are rooted in this fundamental antagonism between the environmental ethic and many traditional American economic and cultural values. In many respects, environmentalism entails not merely reforming existing policies within a framework of traditional American political values and institutions but also recasting the economic and political culture within which policy is made; this leads, ultimately, to a reordering of American cultural values. Nested within environmentalism's familiar political trappings is the hard, sharp edge of a cultural revolution.

Environmental Organizations

The organizational base of the environmental movement has grown almost continuously in number, membership, and political sophistication since the early 1970s. The movement proved its political resilience and skill during the Reagan era, leaving no doubt that it had become a major force in U.S. group politics. Organizations within the movement range across a broad spectrum of political beliefs and styles. Ideologies reach from the "deep ecologists" of the radical left who oppose economic growth, hold all forms of current pollution management inadequate, and advocate small-scale, self-reliant life styles with "appropriate technologies" to the pragmatic, moderate organizations such as the Conservation Foundation who advocate business-environmentalist cooperation and a judicious balancing of economic and ecological values in policy making. Styles vary from the globe-trotting, nonviolent, confrontational aggressiveness of Greenpeace to the more traditional lobbying, public relations, and administrative advocacy of the Audubon Society or National Wildlife Federation.

A major surge in organizational growth within the movement occurred during the 1980s, spurred by adept recruitment through modern direct-mail technology, the environmental crises of the Reagan administration, and growing public support for environmentalist policies. The scale of this recent expansion is suggested in Table 1-3, which compares reported membership figures for five major environmental groups in 1983 and 1989. Altogether, twelve major environmental groups that reported a membership of 2 million in 1983 probably exceed 4 million today. How recently environmentalism acquired its political muscle can be judged by comparing the most recent figures with the total membership of 124,000 reported by the same groups in 1960. Today, national environmental groups probably exceed 7 million members (although there is membership duplication). Many thousands of additional persons belong to more than 3,000 locally organized environmental organizations.

While social support for environmentalism is broadly based in the United States, the membership in most environmental organizations is middle to upper class, white, well educated, and well off. Robert Mitchell found in his 1978 survey of four major environmental organizations that half the members had two years or more of graduate education—an achievement found among only 7 percent of the entire U.S. population.[28]

Table 1-3 *Reported Membership of Five Environmental Interest Groups, 1983 and 1989*

Interest group	1983	1989
Audubon Society	498,000	516,000
Environmental Defense Fund	50,000	125,000
National Wildlife Federation	758,000	5,800,000
Sierra Club	346,000	553,000
Wilderness Society	100,000	330,000
Total	1,752,000	7,324,000

SOURCE: Robert Cameron Mitchell, "From Conservation to Environmental Movement: The Development of Modern Environmental Lobbies," in *Government and Environmental Politics: Essays on Historical Development Since World War II*, ed. Michael J. Lacey (Lanham, Md.: University Presses of America, 1990); "Power of the Earth," *Congressional Quarterly*, January 20, 1990, 146.

Most members are moderately to strongly liberal on political issues and active in other political matters as well. This upscale clientele is often cited by critics to support assertions that environmentalism is elitist and selfish in its social aims, catering to the economic prejudices of the affluent at the expense of the working class and the poor. In the latter 1970s, many environmental groups, aware of their constricted social base, changed (in the words of one leader) by talking less about problems "where we vacation" and more about problems "where we work and live."[29] The new agendas featured issues important to blue-collar workers, farmers, and the underpriviledged: greater workplace safety, better regulation of hazardous and toxic agricultural chemicals, and reduction of inner-city pollution.

The environmental movement has changed in other respects from Era I to Era II. Many organizations today have a scientific and technical staff to provide expert advice and assistance in dealing with the technical issues and controversies common in legislative and administrative policy making. Several organizations, such as the Environmental Defense Fund and the Natural Resources Defense Council, have become highly skilled in litigation by specializing in judicial issues. Over the last two decades national environmental organizations have developed a cadre of seasoned, experienced lobbyists and administrative advocates. The movement has also become much more adept and aggressive in dealing with global issues, to the point of challenging such international economic heavyweights as the World Bank and the International Monetary Fund on the global ecological impacts of their lending policies.

Many observers also detect greater pragmatism and moderation in the strategies of mainline organizations. Environmentalists have become "Washington insiders," claim Richard Harris and Sidney Milkis. "As such they found it necessary to operate incrementally rather than wholistically . . . to moderate their anti-establishment rhetoric, to take seriously economic arguments about market efficiency, and to spend much more time in the corridors of the Capitol than in the streets. . . ."[30] However, many militant organizations and individuals remain for whom "pragmatism" and "moderation" sound like betrayal. It has always been thus. Tension between the impulse to compromise on environmental issues and the determination to reject any compromise in the name of principal permeates the internal politics of the environmental movement and will continue to do so into the next century.

The Public and Environmentalism

Contrary to predictions that environmentalism would be a trendy and transient public enthusiasm, support for the movement and its political agenda has been broad and vigorous among Americans since the inception of the first environmental era in 1970. This support has been politically crucial for the movement, counterbalancing the advantage enjoyed by the opposition in financial resources and governmental access. Environmental organizations have become extremely adept at arousing public concern on environmental matters and turning it to political advantage.

The strength of public support for environmental protection in the late 1980s, measured by public opinion polls, appears robust, widespread, and sometimes unprecedented. In mid-1989, for instance, a *New York Times*/CBS News poll, repeating a question often posed since 1970, asked a representative sample of the American public whether it agreed with the statement: "Protecting the environment is so important that requirements and standards cannot be too high, and continuing environmental improvements must be made regardless of cost." The results of that poll are found in Figure 1-1. Almost 80 percent of the respondents agreed with this assertion while 14 percent disagreed. By comparison, only 45 percent of the respondents had agreed to the same assertion in 1981 and about 65 percent agreed in 1986. Numerous studies suggest that substantial majorities in almost all major socioeconomic groups support the environmental movement and governmental programs to protect the environment—and have done so since the outset of Environmental Era I.[31] The Reagan administration contributed handsomely to its own vexations by failing to appreciate the breadth and tenacity of public support for environmental protection in the face of regulatory reform aimed directly at major environmental programs. Environmental interests effectively mobilized the public against much of the Reagan reform agenda, thereby greatly limiting its scope and effectiveness.

The environmental movement affects public opinion in other signifi-

Question: "Do you agree or disagree with the following statement?
Protecting the environment is so important that requirements and standards cannot
be too high, and continuing environmental improvements must be made regardless
of cost."

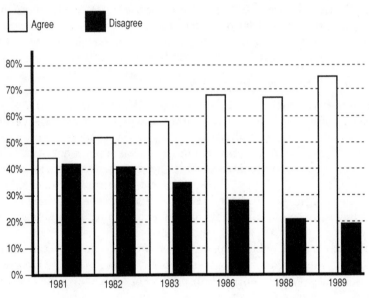

Figure 1-1 Public Willingness to Pay for Environmental Protection

cant ways. Perhaps most important, it has educated the public about the
environmental problems facing the United States and the world. Less
than twenty years ago, ecology and the environment were issues foreign
to almost all Americans. Today many Americans have a rudimentary
understanding of some basic ecological precepts, including the limits
of global resources and the importance of preserving wilderness. The
movement has educated itself and the public to embrace an increasingly
broad conception of "the environment." Before the 1960s, most environmental groups were concerned primarily with land and wildlife management, not air or water pollution or hazardous waste.[32] Their vision was
nearsighted, focused mostly upon domestic issues, and their science was
unsophisticated in its lack of sensitivity to the complex interrelation-
ships among environmental problems. By the early 1980s, viewpoints
were becoming more global, ecologically informed, and expansive in
defining environmental problems. In 1959, for instance, the Defenders

of Wildlife were concerned with individual animals, not survival of species, and with mistreatment of zoo animals. Today the organization stresses, among other issues, worldwide protection of wildlife habitat and protection of endangered species.

Environmental organizations have also encouraged greater public skepticism about the credibility and managerial skills of the scientists, technicians, and other spokesmen for science and technology involved in public affairs. Over the last two decades, environmental organizations have repeatedly challenged the competence of scientific experts and the quality of science supporting opponents in political and administrative battles. These unrelenting technical controversies over the management of commercial nuclear power, the regulation of pesticides, the setting of appropriate air- and water-quality standards, and much else have educated the public on the limits of scientific expertise. Many environmental groups have effectively promoted local citizen involvement in decisions about the siting of real or potential environmental hazards, such as hazardous waste sites. Critics charge that these groups are entirely too successful at grass-roots activism. They blame environmentalists for the rapid spread of NIMBYism (Not in My Back Yard)—the uncompromising public opposition to living next to any potentially hazardous facility. This will be discussed more fully in Chapter 8.

Despite public approval of environmentalism, the political impact may still be restricted in several ways. Environmentalism has become a "consensual value" in American politics, but it is what public opinion analyst Riley Dunlap calls a "passive consensus"—a situation of "widespread but not terribly intense public support for a goal [in which] government has considerable flexibility in pursuing the goal and is not carefully monitored by the public."[33] People may feel much more intensely about other issues, or attribute greater priority to them. In a 1989 Gallup Poll, for example, public responses to a question concerning the funding of federal programs ranked environmental protection eighth among programs deserving more money, well behind such issues as help for the homeless, combating drug problems, health care, and AIDS research. The results of another poll repeated annually throughout the 1980s showed that environmental issues were never among those selected most commonly by the public as "the most important problems."[34]

Moreover, the public may have disliked Ronald Reagan's assault on environmental regulation, but it did not hurt him at the polls. Apparently, environmental values are weakly linked to candidate or party preference for most voters. And Americans frequently resist policies essential to implementing the environmental programs they claim to support, especially when personal cost or inconvenience may be involved (for example, buying smaller, less energy-consuming cars or maintaining pollution control devices on the family automobile). It is not apparent, either, how much the public would support environmental values when confronted by a choice between these and greater energy supply, or more research on cancer, or greater defense spending, or many other possible trade-offs. In short, public sentiments about environmental protection may not always translate into the political or policy impacts most desired by the environmental activist.

Conclusion

In calendar time, 1990 marks the start of the third decade of the "environmental era" proclaimed in 1970. In political time, it is the dawning of Environmental Era II. The momentum of Environmental Era I, begun with the fervor and optimism of Earth Day 1970, gradually dissipated amid the bitter partisan conflicts and policy paralysis of the Reagan administration. Environmental Era II began when the environmental movement regained the political initiative in the closing days of the Reagan administration. Americans were reawakening to the gravity of the nation's ecological condition in the aftermath of numerous highly publicized environmental disasters and increasingly confident predictions by environmental scientists of impending global climate changes with potentially profound significance worldwide. In the United States, the political climate was changing as well. For the first time in nearly a decade, the White House and Congress were prepared to collaborate on a new agenda of major environmental policies.

But the politics of Era II are different from those of Era I. The environmental movement's policy agenda is altered: globalism, radical reform of existing institutions and laws, increased cost consciousness, and greater awareness of limits and problems in achieving environmental goals assume much greater importance in the political agenda of Era II. Tactically, many environmental groups have become more moderate and pragmatic, less confrontational and ideologically rigid in dealing with the opposition. This situation creates greater opportunities for coalition building and policy compromise with the political opposition but also exacerbates existing tensions within the environmental movement between policy moderates and policy militants.

Organizationally, the environmental movement in Era II commands the greatest political resources in its history. At the beginning of the 1990s, most national organizations reported the largest membership and employed the biggest, most skilled staff in their history. The movement has money, direct-mail technology, and politically seasoned organizers. It continues to enjoy broadly based public approval and agreement with its major policy goals. These political resources may still seem inadequate at times in light of the ambitious political tasks the movement has undertaken, but the resources still exceed by far those with which Environmental Era I was begun.

Many questions remain about the intensity and political impact of public support for environmental values, even as polls at the outset of Era II report a broad public consensus on the need for environmental regulation. Yet to be tested is how important ecological values will be in public priority if the public has to choose between environmental policies and other issues claiming limited public resources, such as fighting drug addiction or improving health care. Neither is it clear whether most Americans will vote ecologically when it comes to candidates for public office. What is clear is that Americans are still reluctant to accept the many personal costs and to bear with the many inconveniences that are essential if we are to make environmental protection the reality the public professes to wish.

Notes

1. *New York Times*, October 28, 1988.
2. *New York Times*, August 18, 1988.
3. On the environmentalist viewpoint see Jonathan Lash, Katherine Gillman, and David Sheridan, *A Season of Spoils* (New York: Pergamon, 1984); Norman J. Vig and Michael E. Kraft, eds., *Environmental Policies in the 1980s* (Washington, D.C.: Congressional Quarterly, 1984); and Susan J. Tolchin and Martin Tolchin, *The Rush to Deregulate* (Boston: Houghton Mifflin, 1983).
4. Samuel P. Hays, *Beauty, Health and Permanence: Environmental Politics in the United States, 1955–85* (Cambridge: Cambridge University Press, 1987), 525.
5. *New York Times*, December 1, 1988. See also Kennedy P. Maize, ed., *Blueprint for the Environment: Advice to the President-Elect from America's Environmental Community* (Salt Lake City, Utah: Howe Brothers, 1989).
6. Barry Commoner, *The Closing Circle: Nature, Man and Technology* (New York: Knopf, 1971), chap. 1.
7. Barry G. Rabe, *Fragmentation and Integration in State Environmental Management* (Washington, D.C.: Conservation Foundation, 1986), 147.
8. Executive Office of the President, Council on Environmental Quality (CEQ), *Environmental Quality, 1985: Sixteenth Annual Report* (Washington, D.C.: Government Printing Office, 1987), 18–27.
9. Quoted in Richard A. Harris and Sidney M. Milkis, *The Politics of Regulatory Change* (New York: Oxford University Press, 1989), 266–267.
10. *New York Times*, July 14, 1988.
11. U.S. General Accounting Office, "The Nation's Water: Key Unanswered Questions About the Quality of Rivers and Streams," Report no. GAO/PEMD-86-6 (September 1986), 86–87. See also Margaret E. Kriz, "Effluent, Not Affluent," *National Journal*, March 25, 1989, 740ff; and Paul Portney, *Public Policies for Environmental Protection* (Washington, D.C.: Resources for the Future, 1990), 52–86, 121–145, 176–190.
12. Conservation Foundation, *Newsletter* (September/October 1986): 4.
13. *New York Times*, July 28, 1988.
14. *New York Times*, March 21, 1988.
15. *New York Times*, March 18, 1989.

16. *New York Times*, December 10, 1988.
17. Harris and Milkis, *The Politics of Regulatory Change*, 249. See also Robert V. Bartlett, "Comprehensive Environmental Decisionmaking: Can It Work?" in *Environmental Policy in the 1990s*, ed. Norman J. Vig and Michael E. Kraft (Washington, D.C.: Congressional Quarterly, 1990), 235–256.
18. *New York Times*, October 12, 1988. See also John J. Cohrssen and Vincent T. Covello, *Risk Analysis: A Guide to Principles and Methods for Analyzing Health and Environmental Risks* (Washington, D.C.: CEQ, 1989), chap. 4.
19. Environmental Protection Agency, *Environmental Progress and Challenges: EPA's Update* (Washington, D.C.: Environmental Protection Agency, 1988), 95.
20. Allan Mazur, *The Dynamics of Technical Controversy* (Washington, D.C.: Communications Press, 1981), 29–30.
21. CEQ, *Environmental Quality, 1979*, 218.
22. Christopher Schroeder, "The Evolution of Federal Regulation of Toxic Substances," in *Government and Environmental Politics: Essays on Historical Development Since World War II*, ed. Michael J. Lacey (Lanham, Md.: University Presses of America, 1990).
23. Environmental Protection Agency, *Environmental Progress and Challenges*, 113.
24. U.S. Department of Commerce, Bureau of the Census, *Statistical Abstract of the United States, 1989* (Washington, D.C.: Government Printing Office, 1989), Table 353, p. 204.
25. William Ophuls, *Ecology and the Politics of Scarcity* (San Francisco: W. H. Freeman, 1977), 171. For other significant viewpoints within the environmental movement see David Rothenberg, "A Platform of Deep Ecology," *Environmentalist* 7, no. 3 (August 1987): 185–190; Lester W. Milbrath, *Envisioning a Sustainable Society* (Albany: State University of New York Press, 1989), chap. 7; Fritjof Capra, *Green Politics* (New York: Dutton, 1984); Stephen F. Cotgrove, *Catastrophe or Cornucopia* (New York: Wiley, 1982); Hazel Henderson, *The Politics of the Solar Age* (New York: Anchor Doubleday, 1981); David Orr, "In the Tracks of the Dinosaur," *Polity* 11 (Summer 1979): 562–587; and Donald Scherer and Thomas Attiq, eds., *Ethics and the Environment* (Englewood Cliffs, N.J.: Prentice-Hall, 1983).
26. A. Susan Leeson, "Philosophic Implications of the Ecological Crisis: The Authoritarian Challenge to Liberalism," *Polity* 11, no. 3 (Spring 1979): 305.
27. Ian G. Barbour, *Technology, Environment and Human Values* (New York: Praeger, 1980), 50.
28. Robert Cameron Mitchell, "From Conservation to Environmental Movement: The Development of the Modern Environmental Lobbies," in *Government and Environmental Politics: Essays on Historical Development Since World War II*, ed. Michael J. Lacey (Lanham, Md.: University Presses of America, 1990). See also Robert Cameron Mitchell, "Public Opinion and the Green Lobby," in *Environmental Policy in the 1990s*, 81–102.
29. David Sive of the Environmental Law Institute quoted in Lawrence Mosher, "The Environmental Movement Faces the 80s," *National Journal*, December 13, 1980, 2120.
30. Harris and Milkis, *The Politics of Regulatory Change*, 235.
31. On public support for environmentalism during the 1970s and 1980s see Riley E. Dunlap, "Public Opinion and Environmental Policy," in *Environmental Politics and Policy: Theories and Evidence*, ed. James P. Lester (Durham, N.C.: Duke University Press, 1989), 87–134; Robert Cameron Mitchell, "Public Opinion and Environmental Politics in the 1970s and 1980s," in *Environmental Policy in the 1980s*, 51–74; and John M. Gillroy and Robert Y. Shapiro, "The Polls: Environmental Protection," *Public Opinion Quarterly* 50, no. 2 (Summer 1986): 270–279.
32. The evolution of the conservation movement and its transformation into environmentalism is summarized in Samuel P. Hays, *Conservation and the Gospel of Efficiency* (Cambridge: Harvard University Press, 1959); Joseph M. Petulla, *American Environmentalism: Values, Tactics, Priorities* (College Station: Texas A&M

University Press, 1980); and Henry P. Caufield, "The Conservation and Environmental Movements: An Historical Comparison," in *Environmental Politics and Policy*, 13–56.

33. Dunlap, "Public Opinion and Environmental Policy," 131. See also Everett Carl Ladd, "Clearing the Air: Public Opinion and Public Policy on the Environment," *Public Opinion* 5, no. 1 (February/March 1982): 16–20.

34. *Public Opinion* 10 (July/August 1988): 34–35. See also Gallup Polls published in *Public Opinion* 11, no. 6 (March/April 1989): 25.

Chapter 2

The State of the Environment

In my lifetime, the two biggest advances in raising children have been the clothes dryer and the disposable diaper. . . . If there is a problem with the disposable diapers, they better fix it.
—Kay Willis, founder of Mothers Matter

We have concluded that the Congress does not currently have the information base that it needs to plan appropriately for the management of hazardous waste, either now or in the future.
—U.S. General Accounting Office, February 1987

Between 1988 and 1989 three random events occurred in the United States. First, biologists dredged a small lake located on Isle Royale, a remote island in Lake Superior, the cleanest of the Great Lakes, and discovered significant traces of chemically fresh DDT. There appeared to be no known source for the pesticide, which had been banned for agricultural use in the United States since 1972. Second, fish samples taken from Florida's Everglades were found to contain up to 4.4 parts per million (ppm) of methyl mercury—more than four times the level considered safe by the federal government and one of the highest concentrations ever recorded in the United States. Methyl mercury is rarely found in Florida's rural wetlands. Third, one of the nation's biggest poultry raisers had to destroy 400,000 chickens in Arkansas because they had become contaminated by the carcinogenic pesticide heptachlor, prohibited by the Environmental Protection Agency (EPA) since 1978 for use on food crops.[1]

In each case, explanations were found or suggested. The DDT on Isle Royale had probably traveled on tiny atmospheric particles from Central and South America where DDT is still widely used in agriculture. The mercury contaminating the bass and warmouth of the Everglades might have come from Mexico, or from illegal "midnight dumpers" of toxic wastes, or from the Everglades bottom muck where it had been deposited decades ago, before mercury was banned from pesticides. There was no doubt about what killed the chickens. Poultry raisers had unknowingly fed their chickens sorghum seeds that had been sprayed with heptachlor and sold illegally as feed grain.

These events, apparently different in cause and consequence, have much in common. All were ecological surprises. Each involved a complex web of causality spanning great geographic distances, embracing different environmental media, and posing many alternative modes of explanation. Cause and effect, in each case, spanned years or decades. Each implied related problems not yet discovered, a reminder that ecology is a science rich in surprise and uncertainty. And each incident is one more revelation that the American environment is still dangerously degraded more than twenty years after the nation's "environmental era" began. The politics of Era II grows from this continuing ecological derangement and the sense of urgency it arouses within the environmental movement. Thus, it is important to examine briefly the state of the American environment at the onset of Era II and to start with an obvious question: Why do grave environmental problems persist, or worsen, after more than two decades of governmental effort to arrest environmental degradation?

Why Environmental Problems Persist

No simple and sovereign explanation for the nation's continuing environmental problems will suffice. Most ecological ills are the product of several factors in different, and often interacting, combinations.

While practically every important environmental ill has been targeted by a major federal law, delay and difficulty in program implementation routinely impede enforcement. Implementation is frequently frustrated by decades of deficient agency staffing or budgets. As late as 1988, for instance, the EPA had only forty-five persons available to enforce the Safe Drinking Water Act of 1976 that now applies to more than 200,000 public water systems.[2] Enforcement of most environmental legislation also depends upon voluntary compliance by regulated interests, public and private, who frequently fail to comply. When the U.S. General Accounting Office surveyed 531 major water pollution dischargers in six states in 1983, it found that most had violated their permit conditions several times monthly and almost a third were in "significant noncompliance."[3] Quite often, information essential to effective regulation is missing or fragmentary. The available information is often surprisingly haphazard. Many states, for instance, lack the technical resources to develop numerical standards for many ground water contaminants and depend, instead, upon evidence of environmental damage or public health risks before acting to control these substances.

Economic growth and population expansion often diminish the effectiveness of pollution controls over time. The automobile emission controls and reduced lead levels in gasoline required by the Clean Air Act together lowered the average new car's hydrocarbon and carbon monoxide emissions by 90 percent and nitrogen oxide emissions by 75 percent since 1970.[4] But the number of automobiles in the United States has increased 25 percent, from 147 million to 187 million, and 41 million new trucks have appeared during that time. This vehicle population explosion counteracts the emission reductions achieved for individual vehicles and leads eventually to widespread urban violations of federal air-quality standards. Thus, in the summer of 1988 street-level ozone nearly doubled in many American cities and remained unacceptably high the following summer.

Continuing scientific and technical innovations also contribute to environmental problems by creating new substances or technologies with potentially serious environmental risks. Between 500 and 1,000 new chemical substances are created annually. Advances in biotechnology pose significant questions about the environmental risks associated with the products of recombinant DNA techniques currently being used in academic, commercial, and governmental laboratories. New energy technologies based on fossil fuels or atomic energy always entail potentially adverse environmental consequences that must be weighed in decisions about the course of their development. Scientific and technical innovations, no matter how ultimately beneficial, almost always pose trade-offs between environmental risk and social or economic benefit. Environmental regulation must continually struggle to keep apace of scientific and technical innovation.

Difficulties in environmental protection often arise from limited understanding of the causes and consequences of ecological degradation. Existing data on environmental quality are often scarce; environmental monitoring is often undervalued and underfunded. Data collection has only begun in many environmental domains. Experience with many forms of environmental pollution is too recent to provide carefully tested evidence pointing to firm conclusions about causes, effects, and remedies. Toxic sludge, for example, is a very recent problem resulting from vastly increased municipal waste-water treatment. Since 1972, municipal sludge has doubled in volume to about 7 million dry metric tons annually, and this volume is expected to double again within a decade. Little is known about the composition of these sludges and safe, economical disposal remains a major problem.[5] Time may also change scientific understanding of older environmental problems. When the EPA issued its first National Ambient Air Quality Standards in 1971 for suspended particulates, it made no distinction between small and large particulates. Later research indicated that small articulates (those below ten microns) pose the most serious health risks and, consequently, the EPA had to issue new standards in 1987 specifically for small particulates.[6]

Moreover, as the recent discoveries of acid rain and global ozone depletion demonstrate, nature can surprise science. Natural systems, observes Sandra Postel of the Worldwatch Institute, may absorb stress for long periods without overt evidence of damage. "A point comes, however, when suddenly conditions worsen rapidly," she notes. "Scientists may anticipate such sudden changes . . . but rarely can they predict when they occur. As the scale and pace of human activities intensify, the risk of overstepping such thresholds increases."[7] Widespread scientific concern with environmental quality is so recent that surprise is almost inevitable in ecological policy making. No doubt, such recent environmental discoveries as acid rain, global climate warming, and upper atmospheric ozone depletion will soon become yesterday's news in the face of newer ecological discoveries for which policy makers are equally unprepared.

Finally, it has taken time for environmental scientists to comprehend the global scale of ecological processes and to educate policy makers into perceiving national problems in a world context. Throughout Environmental Era I, U.S. scientists and policy makers emphasized national environmental problems and solutions. The vocabulary of policy discussion in Era II is considerably less parochial, as policy makers are beginning to understand the interdependence of global environments. U.S. climate change is now perceived as one possible consequence of the depletion of Brazil's rain forest. Domestic exposure to pesticide residues on imported fruits and vegetables is now related to U.S. exports worldwide of DDT and other hazardous pesticides. This growing awareness of pollution's global scope sharpens understanding of domestic environmental ills, and at the same time delineates more clearly the limits of purely domestic policy responses to these ills. Dissatisfaction with current environmental programs, in this perspective, reflects scientific progress in defining more accurately the true scope of the problems policy makers must address in Era II.

In short, almost every significant environmental problem is fixed in a matrix of ecological, economic, political, and scientific causes and consequences that usually frustrate quick and simple solutions. This reality was not always apparent to environmental activists in Era I. Undaunted by scientific complexities and beguiled by a faith that "pressing technology" could produce timely solutions to major environmental ills, many ecological activists expected unreasonably quick and thorough environmental restoration.[8] Much of this early optimism has been dissipated by experience with environmental regulation over the last twenty years, and the contemporary environmental movement is generally more realistic and cautious in its expectations about policy accomplishments. Nonetheless, there is ample reason for environmentalists, along with other Americans, to be deeply troubled about the state of the environment in the 1990s and to press for more aggressive, resourceful public efforts at environmental restoration.

In many respects, the American environment is reaching a state of ecological derangement that the nation cannot tolerate much longer. This is apparent if we first examine the traditional indicators used to assess environmental quality over the last twenty years, and then turn to newer indicators pointing to more recently discovered ecological problems.

Traditional Indicators: Air, Water, Toxins, and Consumer Waste

Since the inception of Era I, the federal government has continually monitored a variety of environmental indicators and published current assessments of environmental quality using these indicators. The most important of these relate to the quality of the nation's ambient air, surface and ground waters, hazardous and toxic waste management, and solid waste management. These data provide a useful baseline for observing change in national environmental quality since most major federal environmental programs began in the early 1970s.

Air Quality

The Clean Air Act of 1970 regulated five pollutants (called "criteria pollutants"); lead was added to this list in 1978. These pollutants are emitted by "mobile" sources, mostly cars or trucks, and "stationary" sources such as industry and commercial electric power plants. While the Clean Air Act also currently regulates eight "hazardous air pollutants," the six criteria pollutants are most commonly measured when assessing ambient air quality in the United States. These pollutants and their health effects are summarized in Table 2-1. The EPA has established National Ambient Air Quality Standards for each of the six criteria pollutants.

Generally, ambient air levels of all six criteria pollutants have significantly decreased across the United States since 1970, and many commu-

Table 2-1 *Health Effects of Regulated Pollutants*

Pollutant	Health concerns
Criteria pollutants	
Ozone	Respiratory tract problems, such as difficult breathing and reduced lung function; asthma; eye irritation; nasal congestion; reduced resistance to infection; premature aging of lung tissue
Particulate matter	Eye and throat irritation; bronchitis; lung damage; impaired vision
Carbon monoxide	Impaired ability of blood to carry oxygen; effects on cardiovascular, nervous, and pulmonary systems
Sulfur dioxide	Respiratory tract problems; permanent harm to lung tissue
Lead	Retardation and brain damage, especially in children
Nitrogen dioxide	Respiratory illness and lung damage
Hazardous air pollutants	
Asbestos	A variety of lung diseases, particularly lung cancer
Beryllium	Primary lung disease; effects on liver, spleen, kidneys, and lymph glands
Mercury	Effects on several areas of the brain, as well as the kidneys and bowels
Vinyl chloride	Lung and liver cancer
Arsenic	Cancer
Radionuclides	Cancer
Benzene	Leukemia
Coke oven emissions	Respiratory cancer

SOURCE: Environmental Protection Agency, *Environmental Progress and Challenges: EPA Update* (Washington, D.C.: Environmental Protection Agency, 1988), 13.

nities no longer violate several of these quality standards as they did a decade ago. As long as one concentrates only on national averages and the record on all criteria pollutants, the nation's air quality seems to have improved significantly in the last twenty years. In 1988, for example, the EPA reported that in 1986 (the last year for which estimates are available) carbon monoxide emissions were reduced from 70.9 million tons the previous year to 67.1 tons, sulfur dioxide emissions were reduced from 23.8 million tons to 23.4 million tons, and nitrogen oxides were reduced from 21.7 to 21.3 million tons.[9] The most significant achievement, however, has been a sharp decrease in airborne lead from a national emission of 23,000 tons annually in 1985 to 9,500 tons in 1986—a 59 percent decrease achieved largely by continuing reductions in the lead content of gasoline.

These data fail to reveal that the air in almost all the nation's major cities today is seriously, sometimes dangerously, contaminated much of the year and sometimes virtually every day. The urban pollutants responsible for this pervasive air degradation are ozone and carbon monoxide. Ground-level ozone, in the EPA's opinion "one of the most intractable and widespread environmental problems," is so dangerously concentrated in American urban areas that only one city, Minneapolis, has attained the health-related air-quality standards required by the Clean Air Act.[10] In 1988, a total of ninety-six cities, counties, and other areas associated with a large urban settlement failed to meet federal ozone standards—an increase of 5 percent over the previous record total in 1983 (see "Where Ozone Is Dangerous," page 39).

More than 150 million Americans currently live in geographic areas that exceed the maximum safe levels of ozone exposure a significant portion of the year. Additionally, fifty-nine urban and rural areas in 1988 failed the carbon monoxide standard.

Water Quality

The nation's aquatic inheritance is not just water but different water systems, each essential to modern U.S. society and each currently threatened, or already severely deranged, by different combinations of pollutants.

Surface Waters.   The nation's surface waters—streams, rivers, lakes, and the sea—are the nation's most visible water resource. Almost 99 percent of the population lives within fifty miles of a publicly owned lake. Streams, rivers, and lakes account for a very high proportion of all recreation activities, commercial fishing grounds, and industrial water resources. Because surface waters are so intensively used and so highly visible, their rapidly accelerating degradation became the most immediate cause for congressional action in the 1960s and 1970s to arrest water pollution and restore the nation's once high water quality. Most of the fragmentary data available on national water quality during the last three decades come from monitoring surface-water conditions.

Throughout the late 1970s and early 1980s, the Council on Environmental Quality (CEQ) consistently reported an ambiguous verdict on the nation's surface waters. As late as 1982, the CEQ report was equivocal about progress in cleaning up surface waters: "Despite a growing population and increased gross national product, there has been little or no change in water quality nationally in the last few years."[11] This might seem an impressive accomplishment considering the enormous volume of pollutants that might have been expected with growing population and economic activity over more than a decade. But EPA's conclusion ignored more than 10,000 U.S. lakes considered to have serious pollution problems. And federal agencies such as EPA and CEQ base their surface-

Where Ozone Is Dangerous

The following cities, counties, and other areas are identified by the Environmental Protection Agency as failing to meet federal ozone standards in 1988. Locations are listed by EPA regions.

New England
Boston
Connecticut-Massachusetts
   including Bristol, Hartford,
   Middletown, New Britain,
   New Haven and New
   London, Conn., and
   Springfield, Mass.
Hancock, County, Me.
Kennebec County, Me.
Knox County, Me.
Lincoln County, Me.
Manchester, N.H.
New Bedford, Mass.
Portland, Me.
Portsmouth-Dover,
   N.H.-Maine
Providence, R.I.
Worcester, Mass.
York County, Me.

N.Y./N.J.
Atlantic City
Buffalo
Glens Falls, N.Y., and
   adjacent Essex County
Jefferson County, N.Y.
New York City metropolitan
   area
Poughkeepsie, N.Y.

Mid-Atlantic
Allentown-Bethlehem, Pa.
Altoona, Pa.
Baltimore
Charleston, W. Va.
Erie, Pa.
Greenbriar County, W. Va.
Harrisburg, Pa.
Huntington, W. Va.
Johnstown, Pa.
Kent County, Del.

Lancaster, Pa.
Norfolk, Va.
Parkersburg, W. Va.
Philadelphia
Pittsburgh
Reading, Pa.
Richmond
Scranton, Pa.
Sharon, Pa.
Sussex County
Washington, D.C.

Southeast
Atlanta
Birmingham, Ala.
Charlotte, N.C.
Fayetteville, N.C.
Greensboro, N.C.
Greenville and adjacent
   Cherokee County, S.C.
Jacksonville, Fla.
Knoxville, Tenn.
Lexington, Ky.
Louisville, Ky.
Memphis
Miami-Hialeah, Fla.
Montgomery, Ala.
Nashville
Raleigh-Durham, N.C.
Tampa, Fla.

Midwest
Canton, Ohio
Chicago
Cincinnati
Cleveland
Columbus, Ohio
Dayton, Ohio
Detroit
Grand Rapids, Mich.
Indianapolis

Kewaunee County, Wis.
Lafayette, Ind.
Milwaukee-Sheboygan
Muskegon, Mich.
Toledo, Ohio
Youngstown, Ohio

South Central
Baton Rouge, La.
Beaumont-Port Arthur, Tex.
Dallas-Fort Worth
El Paso
Houston
Iberville Parish, La.
Lake Charles, La.
Tulsa, Okla.

Central
Kansas City, Mo.
St. Louis

Mountain
Denver
Salt Lake City

West
Bakersfield, Calif.
Fresno, Calif.
Kings County, Calif.
Los Angeles
Modesto, Calif.
Phoenix, Ariz.
Sacramento, Calif.
San Diego
San Francisco
Santa Barbara, Calif.
Stockton, Calif.
Visalia, Calif.

Northwest
Portland, Ore.

water quality indices on only six pollutants, excluding such important sources of water degradation as heavy metals, synthetic organic compounds, and dissolved solids.[12]

In the early 1990s, EPA estimates of surface-water quality continued to be ambiguous, vague, and optimistic. Generally, surface-water quality seems at best to have remained in about the same condition as in the early 1980s. The EPA saw progress nonetheless. "State and federal data indicate that our water pollution efforts have made significant headway to restore or protect surface water quality," the agency declared in a major 1988 report.[13] To support its claim, it observed that 99 percent of the nation's streams had been designated by the states for uses equal to, or better than, "fishable or swimmable" and it pointed to "substantially improved" municipal waste-water treatment since 1972. But the same report also noted, with considerable understatement, that "nonpoint sources present continuing problems for achieving national water quality goals in most parts of the country."[14] Nonpoint pollution—any pollution that originates from a diffuse source and not from a single "point" or source—includes runoff from agriculture, urban areas, construction and mining sites, septic tanks, and landfills. The importance of nonpoint pollution in contaminating surface waters can be judged from Figure 2-1, which indicates that nonpoint sources account for almost two-thirds of the volume of pollutants in U.S. streams not currently meeting state quality standards. (Figure 2-1 also ignores nonpoint pollution as an important source of contaminants in other streams as well.) Presently, most forms of nonpoint pollution continue uncontrolled throughout the United States.

The EPA's benign assessment of surface-water quality also neglects growing evidence of confusion and fragmentation in the data used to measure changes in national surface-water quality since 1970. The U.S. General Accounting Office (GAO) evaluated this information, admitted defeat, and left Congress adrift in the data:

GAO was not able to draw definitive, generalizable conclusions ... because evaluating changes in the nation's rivers and streams is inherently difficult, the empirical data produced by the studies sparse, and the methodological problems reduce the usefulness of the findings. Therefore, little conclusive information is available to the Congress to use in policy debates on the nation's water quality.[15]

In the absence of any "definitive, generalizable conclusions," presumably the side mounting the most persuasive figures will win the debate over water quality.

Industrial dischargers remain another serious contributor to surface-water degradation. Many billion gallons of industrial waste, often containing many hazardous and toxic wastes, are still discharged daily into

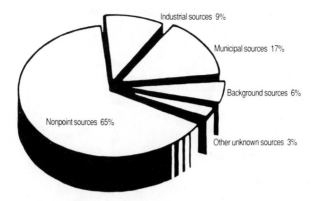

Figure 2-1 *Major Causes of Stream Pollution*

SOURCE: U.S. Environmental Protection Agency, *Environmental Progress and Challenges: EPA's Update* (Washington, D.C.: Environmental Protection Agency, August 1988), 46.

Note: The percentages are based on data from 370,000 stream miles not meeting designated uses.

American surface waters through municipal waste-water systems. The EPA estimates that currently only about 15 percent of the 300,000 industrial dischargers are regulated by federal or state discharge permits.[16]

Ground Water. During the 1980s, the nation's ground water became a major concern. Lying below the earth's upper porous surface and a lower layer of impermeable rock, surface water percolates through the upper layer and collects until it eventually saturates subsurface soil and rock. Much of this water flows slowly to the sea through permeable layers of sand or gravel called aquifers. These aquifers sustain the life and vitality of communities throughout much of the United States. Ground water is as essential as surface water to the nation's existence and far more abundant: the annual flow of ground water is fifty times the volume of surface flows, and most lies within one-half mile of the earth's surface. Almost 50 percent of the U.S. population and 95 percent of its rural residents depend upon ground water for domestic uses.[17] More than 40 percent of all agricultural irrigation originates from ground water. Because ground water filters slowly through many levels of fine soil as it percolates downward and flows onward through the aquifers, it traditionally has been virtually free of harmful pollutants. Today, however, ground water is widely and dangerously degraded.

Almost every state has one or more sources of serious ground-water contamination. Table 2-2 lists the most common sources and the number of states reporting these as a significant problem. Estimates of contamination are crude because reliable data are scarce. Thus, the U.S. Geological Survey first reported the good news that in 1988 the nation's

Table 2-2 *Major Sources of Ground-Water*
Contamination Reported by States

Source	No. of states reporting source[a]	No. of states reporting as primary source[b]
Septic tanks	46	9
Underground storage tanks	43	13
Agricultural activities	41	6
On-site landfills	34	5
Surface impoundments	33	2
Municipal landfills	32	1
Abandoned waste sites	29	3
Oil and gas brine pits	22	2
Saltwater intrusion	19	4
Other landfills	18	0
Road salting	16	1
Land application of sludge	12	0
Regulated waste sites	12	1
Mining activities	11	1
Underground injection wells	9	0
Construction activities	2	0

SOURCE: Environmental Protection Agency, *Environmental Progress and Challenges: EPA's Update* (Washington, D.C.: Environmental Protection Agency, August 1988), 48.
[a]Based on a total of fifty-two states and territories that reported ground-water contamination sources in their 1986 305(b) submittals to the EPA.
[b]Some states did not indicate a primary source.

underground water condition was "generally good" with only 1 to 3 percent contaminated with specific sources; then it delivered the bad news: "available data, especially data about the occurrence of synthetic organic and toxic substances, generally are inadequate to determine the full extent of groundwater contamination in the nation's aquifers or to define trends in ground water quality."[18]

Because of the complexity of ground-water systems and the expense of monitoring, explains the EPA, "we may never have a complete picture of the nature and extent of the problem."[19] But the EPA has identified an enormous number of actual or potential sources of ground-water contamination including:

• about 29,000 hazardous waste sites now potential candidates for the Superfund National Priority List (an inventory of the most dangerous sites);
• millions of septic systems;
• more than 180,000 surface impoundments, such as pits, ponds, and lagoons;

• an estimated 500 hazardous waste land disposal facilities, and about 16,000 municipal and other landfills;
   • millions of underground storage tanks;
   • thousands of underground injection wells;
   • millions of tons of pesticides and fertilizers spread on the ground, mostly in rural areas.[20]

The pervasiveness of ground-water contamination can be illustrated by considering just one of these pollution sources: liquid underground storage tanks (LUSTs). Five to six million LUSTs, most used for retail gasoline or petroleum product storage, are buried throughout the United States. About 400,000 of these are estimated to be leaking now and more will leak in the future. These leaks contaminate the ground water, damage sewer lines and buried cables, poison crops, and ignite fires and explosions. More than 80 percent of the tanks currently in use, constructed of bare steel, are easily corroded and should be replaced with safer containers. Unfortunately, many LUSTs have been long abandoned and forgotten. Located mostly under active or abandoned gasoline stations, airports, large trucking firms, farms, golf courses, and manufacturing plants, these abandoned leaking tanks may never be discovered.[21]

Arguments continue over the magnitude of the threat from many ground-water contaminants. EPA's 1988 interim report, for instance, indicated pesticide contamination in at least thirty-eight states. In twenty-six of these states, pollution was attributed to forty-six different pesticides; in twelve other states an additional twenty-eight chemicals of unknown origin were involved.[22] Generally, contaminants for which the EPA had established standards in drinking water were below levels considered dangerous, but standards did not exist for many of the other chemicals. Most experts agree that the ground water is already seriously contaminated in many places and they expect the problem to worsen in this decade. But evidence about the full scale of this contamination and the actual risks involved to humans and the environment remains elusive. Unfortunately, ground-water contamination is unlikely to receive the governmental money and attention lavished on air pollution or toxic waste until it, too, threatens a national disaster.

Drinking Water.   The nation's drinking water is only beginning to be a major environmental issue. More than 80 percent of the nation's community water systems depend upon ground water, and another 18 percent upon surface waters, for domestic use. The negligent dumping of contaminants into surface and ground waters eventually follows a circle of causality, delivering the contamination back to its source—a reminder that all ecosystems are subtly and intricately interrelated. About half the American population uses a community water system and, altogether, more than three in four Americans daily drink water drawn from surface or underground sources.

In 1976 Congress passed the Safe Drinking Water Act requiring the EPA to establish standards for significant drinking-water contaminants. The agency currently lists standards for twenty-six major pollutants and expects to add more than eighty additional standards by the early 1990s. The EPA has reported that almost 90 percent of the nation's 58,000 public water systems meet the current standards.

Increasing ground-water contamination poses a serious threat to this public water supply. Between 1975 and 1985, 1,500 to 3,000 public water systems exceeded EPA's drinking-water standards for inorganic substances, and at least thirteen organic chemicals known to be carcinogenic to animals or humans have been detected in drinking-water wells.[23] Moreover, private drinking-water systems, a daily source for 36 million Americans, often fail to meet the EPA standards for many regulated pollutants. Most of these private systems draw water from deep wells susceptible to contamination from ground-water pollutants. Toxic organic chemicals have been discovered in wells in every state east of the Mississippi River, with trichloroethylene—a proven carcinogen—being the most frequently discovered toxic organic substance. Many experts believe that drinking-water contamination would appear an even more serious problem if widespread, continual monitoring of well water were conducted by the EPA.

The serious degradation found in most of the nation's water systems testifies that many decades, not just another environmental era or two, will be needed to restore America's water quality. Additionally, the pervasiveness of hazardous and toxic substances in the nation's waters illustrates the difficulty in regulating pollutants traveling readily from one environmental medium to another. Toxic and hazardous chemicals currently contaminate every environmental medium in the United States. For many environmentalists and millions of average Americans, dangerous chemicals are the environmental menace epitomized, the very essence of America's environmental malaise. By any reasonable standard, hazardous and toxic substances must at least be considered a grave and urgent environmental problem throughout the United States.

Hazardous and Toxic Substances

In the environmentalist's hell, the firmament is compacted pesticide awash in toxic sludge. Environmentalists are not alone in attributing to dangerous chemicals a special malevolence. Most Americans apparently believe that the air, water, and earth are suffused with real or potential toxic menaces. The Roper organization polled a sample of Americans in 1989 concerning what environmental risks they considered "very serious" and discovered that dangerous chemicals and other hazardous substances dominated public apprehensions. The public's top three environmental risks, with the percentage of respondents listing each as "very serious," included: (1) active hazardous waste sites (62%), (2) abandoned hazardous waste sites (61%), and (3) workers exposed to toxic chemicals (60%).[24] Nine of the first ten problems ranked in the survey involved hazardous or toxic substances, including radioactive waste, gasoline from leaking storage tanks, and pesticide residues on food.

Many experts note that Americans, often misinformed about the extent of environmental risk in their lives, commonly exaggerate the danger from materials listed high on the Roper poll. But widespread media coverage of hazardous chemical spills, newly discovered abandoned toxic waste sites, and other real or alleged crises involving dangerous substances has forced attention upon hazardous and toxic substances and imparted an air of urgency to resolving the problems. Moreover, mounting evidence about the pervasiveness of potentially dangerous chemicals throughout the United States and uncertainty about the risks they pose to society and the environment increase public apprehension and provoke demands that the government do something to control public exposure to these substances. Thus, hazardous and toxic substances have progressed rapidly from secondary importance in the environmental agenda at the start of Era I to primary importance in Era II.

Chemicals.   Most hazardous and toxic substances are an inheritance of the worldwide chemical revolution that followed World War II. The creation and manufacture of synthetic chemicals have continued at such a prolific pace since 1945 that by the mid-1960s the American Chemical Society had registered more than 4 million chemicals, an increasing proportion of which were synthetics created by American chemists since 1945. Today, more than 70,000 of these chemicals are used daily in U.S. commerce and industry. About 500 to 1,000 new chemicals are created annually. Currently, the EPA has more than 13,000 new chemicals pending its review as required by the Toxic Substances Control Act (TSCA) of 1976.[25]

Despite this profusion of chemicals, about 98 percent of the 55,000 chemical substances used widely in the United States are thought to be harmless to humans and the environment. Perhaps 5 to 10 percent of the new chemicals proposed for review by the EPA will cause concern among the scientific review panels.[26] By the late 1980s, the EPA had prohibited or restricted the manufacture of more than 500 commercial chemicals, including many proven carcinogens such as dioxin, asbestos, polychlorinated biphenyls (PCBs), and the pesticide DDT. This represents a minuscule portion of all the new and existing chemicals that many experts believe merit testing. Even if a substance is restricted or prohibited, the EPA often lacks the resources to implement controls quickly. Although the EPA estimates that more than 500,000 office buildings, apartment houses, stores, and other public or commercial buildings presently contain potentially dangerous loose asbestos, the agency decided in 1988 to take no action because Washington, the states, and the private sector lacked the money and personnel to remove safely the deteriorating asbestos.[27]

Chemical testing itself is time consuming and costly under any circumstances and, when the long-term effects of a chemical are investigated, studies may require decades. Moreover, substances currently suspected of toxic effects often have not been in existence long enough for long-term impacts to be apparent. Today's middle-aged American blue-collar workers may be the first generation of U.S. laborers to reveal the chronic effect of workplace exposure to new chemicals introduced in American industry during World War II. If testing deals with chronic effects of exposure to very small quantities of chemicals—doses as small as parts per billion or trillion—the difficulties in identifying the presence of the substance and the rate of exposure among affected populations may be formidable. For all these reasons, a major problem in regulating dangerous substances has been to obtain, or to create, the essential test data upon which determinations of risk depend.

Although the TSCA authorizes the EPA to control risks from more than 60,000 existing chemicals in the marketplace and to regulate the manufacture, processing, distribution, and use of new chemicals, Chapter 4 illustrates that the agency lacks the resources for such a prodigious undertaking. TSCA is only one of twelve major federal laws the EPA is responsible for implementing in the regulation of hazardous or toxic substances. By the late 1980s, approximately 2,000 to 2,500 of all chemical substances produced in the United States had been tested sufficiently to determine their carcinogenicity, with between 600 and 900 showing substantial evidence of carcinogenicity.

The case of pesticides, which represent only one category of chemicals the EPA is expected to test, illustrates the regulatory burden confronting the agency. Most of the 50,000 pesticide products used in the United States since 1947 were registered before their long-term effects were understood. Amendments in 1972 to the Federal Insecticide, Fungicide, and Rodenticide Act require the EPA to reevaluate all existing pesticides in light of new information about their human and environmental effects. Over 3 billion pounds of pesticide are used annually in the United States. These contain abut 600 active ingredients that must be reviewed by the EPA. The EPA has prohibited, or limited severely, the use of many pesticides, including DDT, aldrin, dieldrin, toxaphene, and ethylene dibromide, and, as a result, levels of persistent pesticides in human fatty tissue have declined from about 8 ppm in 1970 to slightly more than 2 ppm in the mid-1980s.[28] However, the EPA is decades behind in reviewing all the active ingredients and the pesticide compounds made from them.

In the 1990s, airborne toxins will receive major federal attention for the first time, adding an additional large category of substances to EPA's regulatory responsibilities. The Superfund Amendments and Reauthorization Act of 1986, known as SARA, required the EPA to create the first national inventory of toxic releases into the environment from U.S. industry. The latest inventory, released by the EPA in mid-1990, disclosed toxic discharges totaling 4.5 billion pounds in 1988—about 20 pounds per person in the United States.[29] These discharges included:

- 360 million pounds into streams and other surface waters;
- 1.22 billion pounds into underground wells;
- 560 million pounds into landfill;
- 2.4 billion pounds into the air;
- 1.7 billion pounds sent to municipal treatment plants.[30]

The Office of Technology Assessment estimates that this is a small fraction of all releases, however, because firms discharging less than 50,000 pounds of toxics annually are not required to report. Further, in 1988 the EPA also excluded from its inventory any substances released in large volume but with low toxicity. This toxic discharge inventory has become front-page news in many American newspapers and another incitement for public fear about chemical contamination of the environment.

Toxic and Hazardous Wastes.   In the number of individuals affected, the variety of ecosystems at risk, and the persistence of the danger, hazardous and toxic wastes may pose a far greater threat to humans and their environment than those posed by chemicals used in the workplace or home.

More than a decade ago, the discovery of a huge abandoned toxic waste site near Niagara, New York, made Love Canal a national synonym for chemical contamination. The tragedy at Love Canal rapidly escalated into a national media event dramatizing to Americans the growing danger of abandoned toxic wastes throughout the United States. There followed a flood tide of further media revelations about abandoned chemical wastes throughout America, together with intense environmentalist lobbying and growing public pressure for congressional response. In the crisis-driven style characteristic of the 1970s, Congress reacted by passing the Comprehensive Environmental Response, Compensation and Liability Act (1980), popularly called the "Superfund," which included an appropriation of $1.6 billion to clean up the nation's worst abandoned hazardous and toxic waste sites. By the middle of the 1980s, however, it was evident that the magnitude of the abandoned waste problem and the cost to clean up the worst abandoned waste sites far exceeded original expectations. And Superfund's implementation was proceeding at a glacial pace. Between 1980 and 1990, only 34 of the more than 1,100 worst waste sites identified by the EPA had been cleaned up.[31]

Most of the waste annually produced in the United States is not dangerous if properly disposed of. But a ton of hazardous waste for every American is created annually in the United States. Among the more than 14,000 regulated producers of waste, the overwhelming majority are chemical manufacturers or allied industries that produce almost 80 percent of the nation's hazardous waste. Other significant sources include mining and milling, municipal household and commercial waste, and the processing of radioactive materials.[32] America's chemical junkyards are increasing in volume by an estimated 3 to 10 percent annually. At best, no more than 10 percent of this waste has been properly disposed of. As required by Superfund regulations, the EPA has estimated that at least 30,000 dangerous abandoned waste sites currently exist in the United States, but no accurate count is yet available. Many experts believe the actual number of sites may exceed this estimate by at least 10,000.[33] In 1982, the EPA released its first National Priority List of the nation's most dangerous waste dumps, as required by Superfund. By 1988, the list of actual and proposed "priority sites" had grown to 1,177, distributed across the United States as indicated in Figure 2-2.

Contributing to the abandoned waste problem is the deep burial or underground injection, method commonly used to dispose of many hazardous substances. More than 30 percent of all current hazardous waste is stored in landfills or other surface receptacles. About 57 percent of the liquid waste is flushed into deep underground cavities, or water system, where it is presumed to disperse too deeply to contaminate water or soil used by humans.[34] However, such disposal is seldom carefully monitored or regulated. Experts suspect that many hazardous materials thus buried will migrate through subsurface water flows until they contaminate drinking water wells, aquifers used for irrigation, lakes, rivers, or soil. For these reasons, the National Academy of Sciences has recommended that the federal government promote incineration, chemical processing, or other more modern procedures for waste disposal.

Toxic and hazardous waste may haunt the public imagination and agitate legislators, but another serious national waste problem does not. Americans have been loath to confront the implications of their ominously increasing consumer waste—the junk practically everyone

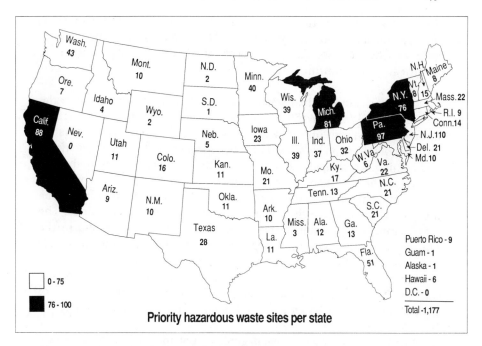

Priority hazardous waste sites per state

Puerto Rico - 9
Guam - 1
Alaska - 1
Hawaii - 6
D.C. - 0

Total -1,177

☐ 0 - 75
■ 76 - 100

Figure 2-2 *Superfund National Priority Sites, 1988*

once loved. Before the end of the 1990s, however, the nation's addiction to individually wrapped cheese slices, throwaway beer cans, plastic razors, styrofoam-swathed hamburgers, and thousands of other consumer conveniences will have contributed substantially to a major national crisis in solid waste disposal. Slowly and reluctantly, all levels of government are recognizing that the volume of municipal garbage, in which consumer items predominate, will overwhelm existing landfill capacity.

Consumer Waste

In 1988, the U.S. municipal solid waste crisis crossed the Atlantic and begot SNAG (Stop North American Garbage). This citizen organization in Great Britain's Cornwall County was agitated at the prospect of receiving imported American garbage. The garbage they intended to stop was 1.25 million tons annually of U.S. solid waste that a private American disposal firm proposed to ship to landfills in Cheshire and Cornwall Counties from unnamed U.S. cities because it was cheaper to ship the garbage abroad than to bury it at home.[35] The American firm argued that Great Britain was already doing a brisk business in imported

European garbage and that the localities would benefit from the substantial revenue and employment generated by disposing of the new waste. Neither Cheshire nor Cornwell accepted the offer. Undaunted, many American cities continue to search the globe for a place to bury their garbage.

The nation's municipal waste has been steadily increasing since the end of World War II. While municipal waste represents only 3 percent of the 6 million tons of solid waste produced yearly in the United States, a small contribution compared to the 90 percent produced by agriculture and mining, municipal waste is very difficult to process and to dispose of safely. Americans are the world's most prolific producers of consumer waste, the major component of municipal garbage, annually tossing away more than twice the average of other industrialized nations. The 1,300 pounds of consumer trash annually produced per capita in the United States includes a rich variety of materials, including 66 pounds of books and magazines, 136 pounds of corrugated cardboard, 4.7 pounds of beer and soft drink cans, 61.7 pounds of soft drink and beer bottles, and 40.2 pounds of food and other glass.[36] The current three pounds of garbage produced daily in each U.S. household is expected to increase by the year 2000.

Most household waste is packaging: cellophane, plastic, paper, styrofoam, and other materials. These materials account for half the volume of American household waste. One dollar in every ten that Americans will spend on food and beverages will pay for packaging that caters to consumer convenience. Paper alone accounts for half the volume of packaging materials. Consumer packaging has, not surprisingly, become a major resource user in the United States. Almost half the paper and glass and a third of the plastics produced in the United States are destined for items whose life span is less than one year.[37] A monument to the economic importance of consumer convenience could be erected with the 1.6 billion pens, 2.6 billion razors, and 16 billion diapers annually tossed into municipal waste dumps.

Disposal of consumer waste and most other components of municipal garbage is increasingly difficult because the land available for garbage dumps is fast disappearing and other methods of disposal are often hazardous and expensive. More than 80 percent of the nation's municipal refuse is still buried in landfills, while 10 percent is recycled and another 10 percent is incinerated. The nation's 6,000 municipalities are so rapidly consuming land for garbage dumps that more than half the nation's cities expect to exhaust their landfill space by 1990.[38] Many cities have resorted to the expensive strategy of shipping their garbage far away, if other places will take it. Philadelphia ships much of its municipal waste to Ohio and southern Virginia, for instance. California's cities will collectively pay $1 billion yearly for disposal of their trash—much of it transported hundreds of miles away for burial.

Waste recycling or incineration, successfully practiced in many nations throughout the world to reduce greatly the volume of their municipal wastes, has not been common practice in the United States. Incineration can reduce the volume of municipal waste and generate energy through the combustion of organic materials in municipal garbage. These organics can also be composted to produce a valuable soil supplement. Proven technologies exist for recycling the most common components of municipal waste: aluminum, paper, and glass. The United States, however, recycles a significantly smaller portion of these materials than almost all other industrialized nations. For example, the United States recycles only one-tenth of its waste glass, while the Netherlands recycles more than one-half and West Germany recycles more than one-third of its waste glass.[39]

There are many reasons for American indifference about recycling or incineration. The nation's tax codes and pricing mechanisms discriminate in many ways against recycled materials when placed in market competition with virgin materials. Most local governments have little experience with recycling or incineration and are seldom pressured by local citizens to explore the possibilities. American culture exalts consumer convenience, not thrifty garbage management. Most Americans regard the household separation of waste into organics and inorganics for collection—a necessary step for municipal recycling or incineration—as a nuisance. Although thirty states encourage residents to separate trash and ten states currently require municipal waste recycling, local governments have felt little real pressure to explore seriously alternatives to landfills for waste disposal. In addition, Washington has been slow to provide the economic incentives or regulatory pressures required to move local governments toward recycling or incineration.

Technical problems must also be overcome. Critics of incineration, including many environmentalists, have argued that the incineration process can liberate dangerous airborne toxins and leave behind hazardous and toxic sludges to be managed. Plastics—an increasingly common component of municipal waste—are difficult to recycle or incinerate safely because they are seldom biodegradable and their combustion creates several toxic gases. Some recycling or incineration technologies especially appropriate to the U.S. market are still experimental. Most experts believe, however, that with the proper governmental regulations, economic incentives, and public support significant recycling and incineration could now be achieved safely in the majority of the nation's larger cities.

If, as predicted, Americans continue to produce municipal waste in the steadily increasing volume of the last three decades, then solutions will be forced upon the nation's governments, industry, and households. The solid waste problem may lack the public appeal and political glamour of other environmental issues like toxic waste management, but its solution will nonetheless become a major issue in the environmental politics of the 1990s.

Three Issues for the 1990s

The important issues emerging in Environmental Era II illustrate how the environmental movement's perspective has become progressively global in the years since Earth Day 1970. This increasingly international conception of environmental problems has been promoted by the growing availability of global environmental indicators and trend data, such as the annual estimates of worldwide environmental quality produced by the United Nations Environment Programme and the World Resources Institute, and by periodic reports on global environmental issues published by the Worldwatch Institute, the Organization for Economic Development and Cooperation, and the World Commission on Environment and Development, among others. Governments in many underdeveloped and developing nations are increasingly aware of the ecological dangers being posed domestically and internationally, and have become more aggressive in seeking international solutions to global degradation. The scientific community has contributed powerfully to this globalization of environmental awareness through increasing worldwide exchanges of environmental information and conferences focused on global issues.

Three of these issues illustrate how rapidly a global ecological awareness has been shaped. Global climate warming, acid precipitation, and atmospheric ozone depletion were little more than scientific speculation at the beginning of the 1970s. By the mid-1980s, evidence had accumulated that these were plausible ecological dangers with potentially catastrophic implications. The Reagan administration refused to concede that these issues merited more than further study and resisted environmentalist pressure to propose new federal programs to combat these dangers. By the late 1980s, however, the Bush administration seemed prepared to accept the reality of these issues and to propose new federal initiatives dealing with each problem.

The political respectability acquired by these global issues has not dissipated the scientific controversy over the existence and magnitude of each problem. In varying degree, the scientific evidence marshaled to persuade policy makers to act upon these problems consists of predictions about future climate trends generated through sophisticated and complex computer models. Critics argue that these computer models are based upon dubious assumptions and unreliable or inappropriate data. Proponents of governmental action admit the uncertainty that always attends climate forecasts based upon computer models, but assert that enough evidence exists to demonstrate that the risks of inaction far outweigh the risks of acting to deal with these prospective climate problems. The debate will not soon be resolved. Policy makers will have to decide when and how to act without the comfort of a scientific consensus on any aspect of the issues.

Global Climate Warming

In mid-1988, James E. Hansen, director of NASA's Goddard Institute for Space Studies, testified to members of the Senate Energy and Natural Resources Committee that it was "99 percent certain" that the unusually hot summer of 1988 was evidence that a global climate warming was underway.[40] That remark instantly caught the attention of Congress and the media. Suddenly, global warming, often called the Greenhouse Effect, was speculation no longer; it bore the imprimatur of NASA science. Thus, Hansen accomplished what the environmental movement could not despite many years' labor. Global warming had acquired political credibility. "The scientific evidence is compelling," concluded Sen. Tim Wirth (D-Colo.). "Now the Congress must begin to consider how we are going to slow or halt that warming trend. . . ."[41]

In fact, the scientific evidence for global warming is less than compelling and, should a warming occur, Congress is unlikely to be able to halt it. But predictions of global climate warming have become persuasive and the Bush administration promises measures to mitigate its impact. Since the United States is the leading producer of the carbon dioxide emissions believed to be the most important cause of climate warming, this U.S. initiative is essential to any worldwide scheme to prevent a climate warming.

Predictions of an impending global warming are based on data demonstrating that the amount of carbon dioxide in the atmosphere has been steadily increasing since the beginning of the Industrial Revolution in the mid-nineteenth century. Until the middle of this century, fossil fuel combustion, mostly from worldwide coal burning and motor vehicles, was the principal source of these emissions. In the last several decades, deforestation (particularly in the tropics) is estimated to have created additional carbon dioxide emissions varying from 12 to 50 percent of that released by fossil fuel combustion.[42] The "Greenhouse" theory asserts that the increasing levels of carbon dioxide will progressively trap more of the earth's heat, gradually warming the global climate as much as three to nine degrees. This warming will greatly accelerate the polar icecap melt and alter world climate zones.

Any effective strategy for mitigating the adverse impacts of a global warming, if such a strategy is feasible, would require global cooperation among all nations burning fossil fuels. But developing nations often blame the industrialized countries for global climate pollution and expect these developed nations to assume the major responsibility, and economic burden, for environmental restoration. Many developing nations like China, India, and Brazil perceive U.S. admonitions to reduce their air or water pollution as an attempt to keep them economically weak by inhibiting their industrialization.

The estimated costs to the United States alone to reduce its carbon dioxide emissions would be enormous. An EPA economist has estimated that the replacement of beaches washed away by rising oceans would cost from $10 to $50 billion.[43] The cost of abating carbon dioxide emissions in the United States would fall heavily upon coal users and producers, particularly electric utilities and industry. The capital cost of installing control technologies for carbon dioxide emissions—and no commercially proven technology yet exists—is estimated to be 70 to 150 percent of the entire cost of a new electric-generating facility. This, in turn, could raise the average American's electric bill by 75 percent.[44] Every American would feel the impact of policies to abate carbon dioxide emissions on life style and pocketbook. The measures EPA has recommended include:

• requiring all new automobiles to achieve an average of at least forty miles per gallon;
• reducing the amount of fuel needed to heat an average American home to half what it took in 1980;
• imposing fees on coal, oil, and natural gas to provide economic incentives to shift away from using fossil fuels as primary energy producers.[45]

This draconian program might be politically acceptable if a global warming were inevitable. But many atmospheric scientists do not find predictions of an imminent climate warming convincing. The computer models used to generate these predictions have been assailed for faulty assumptions and inadequate data about current climate trends. For example, Andrew R. Solow, a statistician at the Woods Hole Oceanographic Institute, argues:

The current warming started before the greenhouse effect could have begun. If the greenhouse effect had begun during the course of the data, then we would see the warming accelerate. No accleration appears in the data. The current warming is consistent with a mild post-glacial period, probably the aftermath of the so-called "little ice age" that ended during the 19th century.[46]

Some experts cite other causes, like solar activity and terrestrial volcanos, as major explanations for climate warming. Still others rely upon different models suggesting that the Greenhouse Effect is not inevitable. Others do not believe sufficient evidence exists to make a responsible judgment about future climate warming. Thus, expert disagreement forces policy makers to become scientific judges and scientists to become salesmen in the struggle to determine whose data will govern policy decisions. Since definitive evidence about when a global warming might begin and how great it might be is unlikely to appear for decades, if at all, proponents of reducing U.S. carbon dioxide emissions have neither a firm public nor a scientific consensus to add political weight to their advocacy. Without a crisis to dramatize the global warming issue, its place on the U.S. federal policy agenda remains precarious.

Acid Precipitation

In late 1988, a public opinion poll commissioned by the National Wildlife Federation revealed that almost 75 percent of the public considered acid rain a "somewhat serious" or "very serious" problem. This is a clear indication of how much the public has been educated into environmental awareness by the media and public policy debates.[47] Unlike global warming, there is now little disagreement among public officials, the public, the scientific community, and the affected economic interests about the existence of acid precipitation. But disagreement persists about practically every other aspect of the matter, including how much industry, utilities, and the automobile each contribute to the acid precipitation problem; how injurious such precipitation is to humans and the environment; and who should bear the costs for abating air emissions causing acid precipitation—if, in fact, abatement is necessary.

The most common chemical precursors of acid precipitation are sulfur and nitrogen oxides emissions from fossil fuel combustion and metal smelting. These gases can be captured by high-altitude winds and transported hundreds of miles from their origin. In the process, these gases become sulfate and nitrate aerosols, then join with other airborne chemical compounds, including ozone and hydrogen peroxide, volatile organic compounds, and water, to become the complex chemicals that return to earth dissolved in water or fixed in ice crystals. Microscopic solids of heavy metals, termed microparticulates, may also become acid deposition. Based on estimates made in several eastern watersheds, between 60 and 70 percent of acid precipitation found in rain or snow is sulfuric acid and the remainder mostly nitric acid.[48]

Some acid precipitation occurs naturally, and scientists have been aware of this for more than a century. During this time, however, acid precipitation has become increasingly widespread and acidic. It now occurs throughout much of the world as well as the United States, and is believed to be ten to thirty times more acidic than it would naturally be in many U.S. industrialized regions.[49] Scientists attribute most of this increase to growing fossil fuel combustion, particularly by electric utilities and industry. The United States, currently discharging about 41 metric tons of nitrogen and sulfur oxides annually, is the global leader, but acid precipitation is a world issue because all industrialized nations and many developing ones discharge significant amounts of the precursors.

The first warning that acid precipitation might be an impending global problem came in the early 1970s when scientists discovered that hundreds of previously normal Swedish lakes had become too acidic to maintain normal biological processes: the usual plant and animal life was absent or dying. Many lakes were deceptively beautiful: "The water is sparkling clear because acid had destroyed everything in it, including the color. It is abnormally peaceful because its natural aquatic life, from fish to crayfish to snails, has ceased."[50] Much of the acid precipitation in Sweden's lakes had originated in Eastern and Western Europe and other parts of Scandinavia. By the middle 1980s, evidence had rapidly accumulated that lake acidification and other ecologically disruptive effects of acid precipitation were increasing at an alarming rate in Scandinavia, Eastern and Western Europe, Great Britain, and North America. By the late 1980s, high levels of acid rain had been discovered for the first time over virgin rain forests in Central Africa. Moreover, wherever acid precipitation was significant, it appeared to be damaging forests, forest soils, agricultural lands, and their related ecosystems.

By the end of the 1980s, evidence mounted that acid rain was economically as well as ecologically costly and increasingly pervasive throughout the United States. The evidence is becoming daily news:

• A massive dying of red spruce and other trees was documented in 1988 along the crest of the Appalachians from Maine to Georgia. Researchers asserted it was "90 percent certain" that the pollution originated in the Ohio and Tennessee River valleys.

• After surveying almost half the 2,700 lakes in New York's Adirondack Mountains, the New York State environmental agency reported in 1989 that one-quarter were so acidic that the vast majority could not support fish and an additional one-fifth were so acidified they were "endangered."

• Scientists employed by the Environmental Defense Fund reported in 1988 that acid precipitation, primarily oxides of nitrogen from automobiles and utilities, accounted for one-quarter of the nitrates entering the Chesapeake Bay. Nitrogen oxides were found to be degrading not only the bay but the waters of Long Island Sound, the New York Bight and North Carolina's Albemarle-Pimlico Sound.[51]

Despite considerable pressure from environmentalists and the states adversely affected by acid precipitation, Washington has been slow to respond to the acid rain problem. The Reagan administration, asserting that insufficient evidence existed about the distribution and dangers of acid precipitation, refused to propose more than further research on the issue. Fashioning a congressional majority in support of new legislation to abate acid precipitation has been difficult for environmentalists and their allies. One reason is that the acid rain controversy has become federalized: the northeastern states most damaged by acid precipitation and the Ohio River states where most of this precipitation originates cannot agree on how the costs for abatement will be distributed. This regional conflict is projected into Congress, making majorities in favor of specific regulatory proposals elusive.

Acid precipitation put Canada and the United States at an impasse throughout the 1980s over how the United States should abate the 20 to 40 percent of Canada's acid precursors that appear to come from the United States. Moreover, there are unresolved technical problems. How can experts determine in an area the amount of acid deposition that is locally produced and the amount that is imported? How much deposition is natural or man-made, new or old? How can one determine how much of the arriving acid deposition eventually affects aquatic or terrestrial life in an area? How can the long-term impact of acid precipitation be identified? Finally, the economic costs and benefits of regulation are continually disputed. Will the costs of abating acid precipitation from the Ohio Valley cause economic depression among the region's "smokestack" industries? How should regulatory costs be apportioned between utilities and industry? And so forth.

The Reagan administration belatedly conceded the seriousness of the acid precipitation problem by signing in late 1988 an international protocol committing the United States in 1994 to limit its nitrogen oxide emissions to 1987 levels. The Bush administration proposed to do more by amending the Clean Air Act to reduce both U.S. sulfur and nitrogen oxide emissions, starting immediately, and to reduce them significantly. The proposal faces an uncertain congressional fate. Environmentalists want faster and deeper cuts in pollution emissions, the affected states cannot readily agree upon how the costs should be apportioned, and the utilities and industries to be regulated are divided on the acceptable regulatory formula. Creating a congressional majority for a regulatory proposal acceptable to the White House, as well, will be difficult under these circumstances.

Atmospheric Ozone Depletion

Scientists first suggested in 1974 that the worldwide use of chloro-fluorocarbons (CFCs) and halons could be destroying the thin but important tropospheric ozone layer encircling the earth at about 43,000 feet. In 1982, British scientists for the first time documented the existence of a large hole in the ozone layer over Antarctica that had been theoretically predicted earlier. Further research has largely confirmed that atmospheric ozone is being chemically depleted at a rate alarming to scientists, and this depletion is occurring across an area far larger than the Antarctic. By the early 1990s, scientists were predicting that a large ozone hole also existed over the Arctic and that rapid depletion might also be found in more temperate regions.

When NASA's Ozone Trends Panel, representing more than one hundred scientists from ten nations, announced in 1988 its estimate that 3 percent of the atmospheric ozone had been depleted between 1969 and 1986, the "findings startled policymakers, industry representatives and researchers around the world. . . . Within a matter of weeks the report's conclusions were widely accepted and public debate on the issue began to build. Suddenly, ozone depletion was real. . . ."[52]

Because tropospheric ozone is a natural shield against the sun's ultraviolet rays, any significant depletion of the ozone layer could mean increased human exposure to ultraviolet light, yielding significantly increased risks of skin cancer and eye damage. A depletion of 1 percent of the atmospheric ozone is estimated to create 3 to 15 million new cases of skin cancer and 555,000 to 2.8 million cataract cases for white persons born before the year 2075.[53] Increased global exposure to ultraviolet rays could produce serious derangements in existing ecological balances, including a major depletion of ocean plankton, which constitutes the foundation of the ocean's food chains.

The culprits in the destruction of the ozone layers are thought to be CFCs and halons, otherwise extraordinarily useful chemicals. CFCs are extensively used worldwide as refrigerants and propellants, for making the bubbles in styrofoam, as solvents for computer circuits, for refrigerator insulation, and for many other purposes. Halons are used primarily in fire extinguishers. The same properties that make these chemicals so commercially and scientifically desirable—they are stable, noncorrosive, nontoxic, and nonflammable—also make them a menace to the ozone layer. Once released into the atmosphere, CFCs and halons slowly migrate upward (they may take five years to reach the ozone layer), chemically interact with ozone, destroy it, and continue to do so for as long as a century.

CFCs, especially, are economic heavyweights among chemicals. An estimated $135 billion in U.S. industrial, commercial, and scientific equipment depends upon CFCs for operation. Replacement chemicals for CFCs may be costlier and less reliable. One available replacement for the widely used CFC-12 is currently three times more expensive and less adaptable.[54] The United States currently manufactures about 30 to 34 percent of the world CFC supply, or about 660 million pounds annually. All industrialized nations, however, are heavy CFC users and producers. The Soviet Union's production of approximately 325 million pounds annually is only slightly less than the production of all the world's less-developed nations. Since developing economies consume increasing amounts of CFCs and halons as they expand, the future availability of CFCs and halons is crucially important to the Third World, as well as to the industrialized countries. Nonetheless, the cost of replacing CFCs and halons still seems modest when compared with the prospective benefits. The EPA has estimated that phasing out U.S. use of CFCs and halons would cost $27 billion by the year 2075, but save $6.5 trillion from cancer deaths averted and other medical benefits, crop damage prevented, and fish populations saved.[55]

Current U.S. policies to protect the ozone layer, while an improvement over the inertia of the 1980s, still seem inadequate to many scientists and environmentalists in light of emerging data about ozone layer depletion. In 1987 the United States and 24 other nations signed the Montreal Protocol, which called for a 50 percent reduction in the production of CFCs by the end of this century and a 1989 freeze in production at 1986 levels. In response to a later agreement by the European Community nations to eliminate all ozone-depleting chemicals by this century's end, the Bush administration made a similar U.S. commitment.

These proposed cutbacks in global production and use of CFCs and halons, even if achieved, will not produce any significant effects for decades. Many atmospheric scientists are now urging a much quicker and larger cutback in their chemical production in light of the ozone depletion discovered at both poles and evidence that ozone depletion is occurring more rapidly than anticipated only a few years ago. The Alliance for a Responsible CFC Policy, the principal industry trade association in the United States, has already called for phasing out CFC use to the maximum extent feasible. E. I. du Pont de Nemours, the major U.S. manufacturer of CFCs, has announced its intention to phase out rapidly all CFC production. Many experts believe that the world's CFC producers and users should be racing against time to eliminate all CFCs and halons and that any delay will be dangerous.

Uncertain Science and Environmental Evaluation

One of the nation's major environmental problems remains the neglect of basic research on environmental quality. Almost all current evaluations of environmental quality are compromised in some way by missing data, constricted time frames, and incompatible measurements. At times, estimates of environmental conditions, or the risks from human or environmental exposure to chemical substances, or predictions about future environmental trends must be made on the basis of data so meager that predictions are little more than the scientists' best guess. Data essential to understanding basic environmental trends, the kind of information "somebody should have," often nobody has. Frequently, the data were never created.

The scope of the missing data problem can be suggested by examining just one important category of environmental problem: chemical hazards. Adequate assessment of the risks from exposure to chemicals used in commerce, science, and industry assumes the existence of a substantial research base. Recent estimates suggest, however, that for almost 75 percent of the ingredients used in cosmetics currently no adequate data exist on toxicity. The comparable figure for food additives is 80 percent, and 64 percent for pesticides or inert ingredients in pesticides.[56] Often, virtually no monitoring of water quality occurred in many major U.S. rivers and lakes before 1970 and much of it today remains the responsibility of state and local governments, research institutions, or corporations whose continuing commitment to research is unpredictable.

The costs, obvious and covert, of missing data are enormous. As later chapters illustrate, this lack of data is one of the most productive causes of controversy and confusion over how environmental policy should be made and implemented. Missing information frustrates needed evaluation of existing programs and hobbles scientists and policy makers alike in anticipating future environmental conditions. It obstructs efforts to evaluate the causes and consequences of existing ecological problems. Inadequacies in the science base of environmental regulation can encourage excessive regulatory costs because policy makers often feel compelled to take the more conservative course and regulate products or activities suspected of creating environmental damage when data demonstrating otherwise are absent or ambiguous. Additional data, no matter how much, will never alone resolve many policy controversies, and an appeal to "further research" can be a tactic to delay decisions, but better data often clarify options and implications of policy choices confronting public officials. Generous research support and well-defined research agendas would seem to be among the first requirements for prudent environmental policy making.

Why, then, are so much essential data still missing, or their acquisition still unplanned, in the third decade of the nation's "environmental era"? One reason is that research and environmental monitoring lack political appeal. They offer few immediate political rewards to elected or appointed officials. They are often difficult to understand or explain to constituents. They seldom produce quick, dramatic solutions to major problems. Lacking political glamour, research funding is an obvious target for budget cutters, a place to find additional money for other, apparently more urgent needs. Further, the EPA and most other federal agencies funding environmental research lack research priorities and agendas matched to current and anticipated policy needs. Rather, research funding and priorities are often reactive to whatever environmental issues or crisis are currently dominating the political agenda—a style guaranteed to produce episodic, unpredictable funding decisions.

The EPA's own Science Advisory Board has for many years urged the agency to formulate long-range research agendas, to match its own research to its policy needs, and to educate Congress and the White House about the need for such an approach.[57] Currently,the EPA does not monitor basic trends for many important ecosystems, such as wetlands and estuarine areas. Almost all monitoring of major ecosystems such as air and water is confined to large metropolitan centers. Much data collection is left to the states. "An awful lot of data collected are not put in a place where they could be used," complained CEQ member Jacqueline E. Schafer. "States collect data about water quality that literally sits in shoe boxes."[58] The scientific community itself often assigns a low priority to data collection on environmental trends in comparison to other research programs.

Environmental data collection also suffers because federal support for any particular research program can be volatile, producing valuable data today and none tomorrow. In 1987, for instance, the EPA was compelled by congressional budget cuts to abandon a key program for measuring human exposure to toxic substances by monitoring chemical accumulations in human body fat.[59] The program would have cost only $2 million a year. It had been a major consideration in EPA's decision to ban U.S. production and use of PCBs after traces of the chemical appeared in the body fat of practically every person studied. Continuation of the program would have provided valuable historical data on the effects of regulation on chemicals considered hazardous to humans.

Conclusion

Twenty years after the United States committed itself to restoring environmental quality and preventing further ecological degradation, achievements have fallen far short of the ambitious goals declared in major pollution control legislation. Progress, at best, has been uneven. The magnitude of the environmental problems now confronting the nation is not wholly the result of regulatory failures, however. Many of the problems have been created, or exacerbated, by continuing techno-logical innovation, by the evolution of techniques to better measure and monitor environmental trends, and by greater scientific understanding of the ecological interdependencies among pollution problems. Still, the nation has failed in many respects to make even limited progress in managing many environmental problems to which an adequate commit-ment of resources and political will could make a difference.

Air quality has improved somewhat outside of the nation's cities, but urban airsheds frequently fail to meet minimum federal air-quality standards for some major air pollutants. Most of the nation's major cities are afflicted with moderate to severe smog problems and two pollutants—carbon monoxide and ozone—have reached dangerous lev-els in many urban areas. The quality of the nation's surface water re-mains ambiguous. While water-quality studies often show significant improvement, they are frequently deficient in the variety of pollutants they monitor and the range of waters surveyed. The evidence of continu-ing, serious ground-water contamination from a variety of chemical and natural pollutants is abundant. As ground-water monitoring becomes more comprehensive and sensitive, evidence of pervasive pollution con-tinues to accumulate.

The United States has yet to regulate adequately the manufacture, distribution, and disposition of chemical and hazardous substances. Reg-ulatory programs intended to accomplish all these goals have been passed, but appropriate resources have been lacking. No area of environ-mental regulation was more adversely affected by the "regulatory re-forms" of the Reagan administration than the control of toxic and haz-ardous substances. Although these programs are likely to receive greater attention and more resources in the 1990s, the variety and distribution of these chemical substances, together with the lack of adequate moni-toring, may exceed the regulatory capacity of existing programs. The nation has yet to mount a serious regulatory program for solid waste and, especially, for consumer waste.

The 1990s also confront the nation's governments with global prob-lems that were little more than scientific speculation a few years ago. Global climate warming, depletion of the tropospheric ozone layer, and acid precipitation have all reached a level of political and scientific importance that requires a governmental response. This response may be delayed and its scope initially limited by continuing dispute within the scientific community concerning the adequacy and implications of the scientific data supporting the existence of these global problems. Moreover, each problem is recognized to be global in its impact, thereby requiring international cooperation among all the nations whose pollutants contribute to the problems. As a major contributor to each of these global problems, the United States bears a major responsibility for contributing to their solution.

Thus, the status of the nation's environment in the third decade of its commitment to environmental protection and preservation is deeply troubling, and sometimes alarming. Measured by its own stated environmental goals more than twenty years ago, the nation has a long, difficult way to go in restoring environmental quality. As scientific evidence increasingly illuminates the global scale of national environmental ills, the challenge of environmental protection becomes even more difficult and an effective response even more imperative.

Notes

1. *New York Times*, July 12, 1988, March 14, 1989, and March 16, 1989.
2. *New York Times*, December 13, 1988. On earlier funding deficiencies, see Conservation Foundation, *State of the Environment: An Assessment at Mid-Decade* (Washington, D.C.: Conservation Foundation, 1984), 425–444; and Richard A. Harris and Sidney M. Milkis, *The Politics of Regulatory Change* (New York: Oxford University Press, 1989), chap. 6.
3. U.S. General Accounting Office, "Wastewater Dischargers Are Not Complying with EPA Pollution Control Permits," Report no. GAO/RCED-84-53 (December 2, 1983), i.
4. *New York Times*, February 21, 1989.
5. Environmental Protection Agency, *Environmental Progress and Challenges: EPA's Update* (Washington, D.C.: Environmental Protection Agency, August 1988), 70.
6. Ibid., 21.
7. Sandra Postel, *Altering the Earth's Chemistry: Assessing the Risks* (Washington, D.C.: Worldwatch Institute, 1986), 7.
8. John E. Bonina, "The Evolution of 'Technology Forcing' in the Clean Air Act," *Environmental Reporter*, Monograph no. 21, July 25, 1975. See also Charles O. Jones, *Clean Air* (Pittsburgh: University of Pittsburgh Press, 1975), chaps. 7, 8.
9. *New York Times*, February 18, 1988. For more comprehensive data see Environmental Protection Agency, *National Air Pollutant Emission Estimates, 1940–1986* (Washington, D.C.: Environmental Protection Agency, January 1988).
10. *New York Times*, March 1, 1989.
11. Executive Office of the President, Council on Environmental Quality (CEQ), *Environmental Quality, 1981* (Washington, D.C.: Government Printing Office, 1982), 52.
12. Ibid., chap. 3.
13. Environmental Protection Agency, *Environmental Progress and Challenges*, 49.
14. Ibid., 70–71. See also Environmental Protection Agency, Office of Water Program

Operations, Water Planning Division, "Report to Congress: Nonpoint Source Pollution in the U.S." (January 1984).

15. U.S. General Accounting Office, "The Nation's Waters: Key Unanswered Questions About the Quality of Rivers and Streams," Report no. GAO/PEMD-86-6 (September 1986), 3.
16. *New York Times*, July 28, 1988.
17. U.S. General Accounting Office, "Ground Water Overdrafting Must be Controlled," Report no. CED-80-96 (September 12, 1980).
18. *New York Times*, October 8, 1988.
19. Environmental Protection Agency, *Environmental Progress and Challenges*, 52.
20. Ibid.
21. Ibid., 102–103. See also CEQ, *Environmental Quality, 1984*, 167–169.
22. Ibid. For an earlier and more comprehensive survey of ground-water pollutants see CEQ, *Environmental Quality, 1981*, 93.
23. Environmental Protection Agency, *Environmental Progress and Challenges*, 52–53. Other drinking water surveys may be found in CEQ, *Environmental Quality, 1986*, C-43; and CEQ, *Environmental Quality, 1984*, 88–89.
24. *New York Times*, May 22, 1989.
25. Environmental Protection Agency, *Environmental Progress and Challenges*, 126. See also U.S. General Accounting Office, "EPA's Data Collection Practices and Procedures on Chemicals," Report no. GAO/RCED-86-63 (February 1986).
26. CEQ, *Environmental Quality, 1984*, 194.
27. *New York Times*, February 29, 1988.
28. CEQ, *Environmental Quality, 1986*, C-133.
29. *New York Times*, April 20, 1990.
30. Ibid.
31. *New York Times*, September 10, 1989.
32. Conservation Foundation, *State of the Environment: A View Toward the Nineties* (Washington, D.C.: Conservation Foundation, 1987), 160.
33. Estimates of potential hazardous waste sites can be found in U.S. General Accounting Office, "Extent of Nation's Potential Hazardous Waste Problem Still Unknown," Report no. GAO/RCED-88-44 (December 1987), 14; and Conservation Foundation, *State of the Environment: A View Toward the Nineties*, 170–179.
34. *New York Times*, August 31, 1983.
35. *New York Times*, June 27, 1988.
36. *New York Times*, July 26, 1989.
37. Cynthia Pollock, *Mining Urban Wastes: The Potential for Recycling* (Washington, D.C.: Worldwatch Institute, 1987), 10.
38. *New York Times*, August 23, 1988.
39. Pollock, *Mining Urban Wastes*, 26.
40. *New York Times*, June 24, 1988.
41. Ibid.
42. Postel, *Altering the Earth's Chemistry*, 8.
43. *New York Times*, June 26, 1988.
44. *New York Times*, August 28, 1988.
45. *New York Times*, March 4, 1989. See also Flavin, *Slowing Global Warming*, 49–74.
46. *New York Times*, December 28, 1988.
47. *New York Times*, September 25, 1988.
48. U.S. General Accounting Office, "The Debate Over Acid Precipitation: Opposing Views, Status of Research," Report no. CMD-81-113 (September 11, 1981). See also Postel, *Altering the Earth's Chemistry*, 25–33; and James L. Regens and Robert W. Rycroft, *The Acid Rain Controversy* (Pittsburgh: University of Pittsburgh Press, 1988), chap. 2.
49. Sandra Postel, *Air Pollution, Acid Rain, and the Future of the Forests* (Washington, D.C.: Worldwatch Institute, 1984), 18.
50. Ross Howard and Michael Perley, *Acid Rain* (New York: McGraw-Hill, 1982), 19.

51. *New York Times,* July 24, 1988, July 7, 1989, and April 25, 1988.
52. Cynthia Pollock Shea, *Protecting Life on Earth: Steps to Save the Ozone Layer* (Washington, D.C.: Worldwatch Institute, 1988), 12–13.
53. Ibid., 14ff.
54. *New York Times,* March 7, 1989.
55. *New York Times,* September 21, 1988.
56. World Resources Institute, *World Resources, 1987* (New York: Basic Books, 1987), 204.
57. Alvin L. Alm, "The Need to Think Ahead," *EPA Journal* 14, no. 7 (November/December 1988): 25–26.
58. *New York Times,* November 8, 1988.
59. *New York Times,* December 12, 1987.

Suggested Readings

Brown, Lester W., ed. *State of the World, 1990.* New York: W. W. Norton, 1990.
Commoner, Barry. *Making Peace with the Planet.* New York: Pantheon, 1990.
Conservation Foundation. *State of the Environment: A View Toward the Nineties.* Washington, D.C.: Conservation Foundation, 1987.
Council on Environmental Quality. *Environmental Trends.* Washington, D.C.: Government Printing Office, 1990.
Schneider, Stephen. *Global Warming.* San Francisco: Sierra Club Books, 1989.
Weiner, Jonathan. *The Next One Hundred Years.* New York: Bantam Books, 1990.
World Resources Institute. *World Resources, 1988–89.* New York: Basic Books, 1989.

Chapter 3

The Politics of Environmental Policy

Mr. Bush told the environmentalists, "I know there is some skepticism about my commitment, but it is real and I am going to surprise you in a good way."
—*New York Times*, December 1, 1988

The White House confirmed today that it had censored Congressional testimony on the effects of global warming by a top Government scientist, but it insisted that the changes reflected policy decisions, not scientific conclusions.
—*New York Times*, May 9, 1989

The Bush administration had been in office less than six months when it blundered into a controversy that seemed to reduce the president's earnest professions of environmental concern to public relations puffery. The occasion was the scheduled testimony of James E. Hansen, director of NASA's Goddard Institute for Space Studies, before the Senate Subcommittee on Science, Technology, and Space on May 8, 1989. Hansen's previous testimony that the Greenhouse Effect was imminent had made him a minor political celebrity. His new testimony on climate warming was again expected to draw considerable congressional and media attention.

But the attention came a day earlier and concerned what Hansen was *not* supposed to say. Newspapers learned that Hansen's testimony had been edited—against his strong objections—by the White House's Office of Management and Budget (OMB), which often reviews proposed congressional testimony by important agency spokesmen. The editing transformed many of Hansen's originally confident predictions about global warming into cautious conjecture. He had intended to tell the subcommittee: "We believe it very unlikely that this overall conclusion . . . [that there will be] drought intensification at most middle- and low-latitude land areas, if greenhouse gases increase rapidly . . . will be modified. . . ."[1] Instead, OMB insisted that he say:

Again, I must stress that the rate and magnitude of drought, storm and temperature change are very sensitive to the many physical processes mentioned above, some of which are poorly represented in . . . models. Thus, these changes should be viewed as estimates from evolving computer models and not as reliable predictions.

He had intended to assure the subcommittee that he and his NASA colleagues who prepared the testimony were "confident that greenhouse gases are primarily of human origin." But OMB insisted he state that the relative contribution of human and natural processes to changing climate patterns "remains scientifically unknown."

This was not the first time Hansen and the White House had crossed swords on this issue. Earlier, he had given congressional testimony as a private citizen rather than agree to the Reagan White House's insistence that he delete from his testimony any recommendation for increased funding for research on climate transformation. This time, however, Hansen chose to go public with his complaints. "It distresses me that they put words in my mouth. They even put it in the first person," he observed. "I should be allowed to say what is my scientific position; there is no rationale by which OMB should be censuring scientific opinion. I can understand changing policy, but not science."[2]

White House representatives quickly asserted that the changes reflected policy decisions, not tampering with science, and argued that Hansen's original conclusions were "not necessarily those of all scientists who have considered this matter" and that "there are many points of view on the global warming issue and many of them conflict with those stated by Dr. Hansen."[3] In fact, there was disagreement within the scientific community over many aspects of the climate warming issue. There was little doubt, however, that OMB's guiding inspiration was a determination that Hansen's testimony square with current White House policy stressing the uncertainty of climate warming.

Conflict between the White House and agency scientists over where science ends and politics begins is hardly peculiar to the Bush administration. Presidents of both parties have usually insisted upon a White House prerogative to review all major policy statements before senior bureaucrats deliver them officially. And many scientists in the bureaucracy have objected. James Hansen, politically skilled and seasoned, knew how to turn his quarrel into a media event. Moreover, Democrats on the Senate subcommittee seized upon the incident to criticize the administration robustly during the committee hearings. Subcommittee Democrats also provided Hansen with ample opportunity in his subsequent testimony to chastise the OMB for its scientific and ethical bungling.

The event embarrassed the White House. It armed George Bush's critics with new ammunition, appeared to contradict the president's professions of concern for an environmental movement whose goodwill he was cultivating, and revealed confusion in the administration's policy management. While environmental policies usually develop less clumsily, this incident featured some characteristics common to environmental policy making. First, policy making is a process that involves a number of related decisions originating from different institutions and actors ranging across the whole domain of the federal government and private institutions. As Hugh Heclo observes, policy is "a course of action or inaction rather than a specific decision or action."[4] Moreover, policy making is continuous; once made, decisions are rarely immutable. Thus, environmental policy is in some respects fluid and impermanent, always in metamorphosis.

Also, policy makers—legislative, White House, or bureaucratic—can seldom act without restraint. Their discretion is bounded and shaped by many constraints: constitutional separations of power, institutional rules and biases, statutory laws, shared understandings about the "rules of the game" for conflict resolution, inherited culture, and more. Collectively, these restraints are givens in the policy setting that mean government resolves almost all issues in a predictable style. Finally, environmental policy making is a volatile mixture of politics and science that readily erupts into controversy among politicians, bureaucrats, and scientists over their appropriate roles in the process, as well as over the proper interpretation and use of scientific data in policy questions.

One useful way to understand public policy, and environmental policy specifically, is to view the process as a cycle of interrelated phases through which policy ordinarily evolves. Each phase involves a different mix of actors, institutions, and constraints. While somewhat simplified, this approach does illuminate particularly well the interrelated flow of decisions and the continual process of creation and modification that characterize governmental policy development. Some of the major constraints and influences on this policy cycle and some of the important institutions involved specifically in environmental policy making will be examined in this chapter.

The Policy Setting

Public policies usually develop with reasonable order and predictability. Governmental response to public issues—the business of converting an issue into a policy—customarily begins when an issue can be placed upon the governmental agenda. Successful promotion of issues to the agenda does not ensure that public policies will result, but this step initiates the policy cycle.

The Cycle of Policy Development

An environmental issue becomes an environmental policy as it passes through several policy phases.

Agenda Setting.   Charles O. Jones aptly called this "the politics of getting problems to government."[5] It is the politics of imparting sufficient importance and urgency to an issue so that the government will feel compelled to place the matter on the "official agenda" of government, the "set of items explicitly up for the serious and active consideration of authoritative decision-makers."[6] This means getting environmental issues on legislative calendars, before legislative committees, on a priority list for bill introduction by a senator or representative, on the schedule of a regulatory agency, or among the president's legislative proposals. In brief, getting on the agenda means placing an issue where institutions and individuals with public authority can make a response and feel a need to do so.

Congressional attention to climate warming, for instance, was largely produced by astute issue positioning and timing. James Hansen's declaration to a congressional committee in mid-1988 that climate warming had already begun immediately vested the issue with prestigious scientific endorsement, instant media exposure, and an air of urgency—a potent political combination. "I've never seen an environmental issue mature so quickly, shifting from science to the policy realm almost overnight," remarked one major environmental group representative. "It took a governmental forum during a drought and a heat wave and one scientist . . . saying loudly and clearly what others were saying privately. That's mighty important in the public policy business."[7]

Formulation and Legitimation.   Governmental agendas can be a graveyard for public problems. Few issues reaching the governmental agenda, environmental or otherwise, reach the stage of policy formulation or legitimation. Policy formulation involves setting goals for policy, creating specific plans and proposals for these goals, and selecting the means to implement such plans. Policy formulation in the federal government is especially associated with the presidency and Congress. The

State of the Union message and the avalanche of bills annually introduced in Congress represent the most obvious examples of formulated policies. Policies once created must also be legitimated—invested with the authority to evoke public acceptance. Customarily, this is done through constitutional, statutory, or administrative procedures, such as voting, public hearings, presidential orders, or judicial decisions upholding the constitutionality of laws—all rituals whose purpose is to signify that policies have now acquired the weight of public authority.

Implementation.   Public policies remain statements of intention until they are translated into operational programs. Indeed, the impact of policies largely depends upon how they are implemented. Thus, what government is "doing" about environmental problems relates in large part to how the programs have been implemented. Eugene Bardach has compared implementation with "an assembly process." It is, he writes, "as if the original mandate . . . that set the policy or program in motion were a blueprint for a large machine that has to turn out rehabilitated psychotics or healthier old people or better educated children. . . . Putting the machine together and making it run is, at one level, what we mean by the 'implementation' process."[8] Policy implementation involves especially the bureaucracy, whose presence and style shape the impact of all public policies.

Assessment and Reformulation.   All the procedures involved in evaluating the social impact of government policies, in judging the desirability of these impacts, and in communicating these judgments to government and the public can be called "policy assessment." Often the federal courts assume an active role in the process, as do the mass media. The White House, Congress, and the bureaucracy continually monitor and assess the impacts of public policy also. Consequently, once a policy has been formulated, it may pass through many phases of "reformulation." All major institutions of government may play a major role in this process of reformulation.

Policy Termination.   The "deliberate conclusion or succession of specific governmental functions, programs, policies or organizations," suggests Peter deLeon, amounts to policy termination.[9] Terminating policies, environmental or otherwise, is such a formidable process that most public programs, in spite of intentions to the contrary, become virtually immortal. More characteristically, policies change through repeated reformulation and reassessment.

Policy Making Is a Combination of Phases.   Because policy making is a process, the various phases almost always affect each other, an important reason why understanding a policy often requires a consideration of the whole development pattern. For instance, many problems encountered by the Environmental Protection Agency (EPA) when enforcing the Federal Water Pollution Control Act arose from congressional failure to define clearly in the law what was meant by a "navigable" waterway to which the legislation applied. This oversight was deliberate, intended to facilitate congressional passage of the extraordinarily complicated legislation. In turn, the EPA sought early opportunities to bring the issue before the federal courts—to force judicial assessment of the law's intent—so that the agency might have reliable guidance for its own implementation of this provision. Additionally, it often happens that aspects of environmental policies, like most other complex federal laws, may appear simultaneously at different phases of the policy cycle. While the EPA was struggling to implement portions of the "Superfund" legislation allocating grants to the states for cleaning up abandoned toxic waste sites, Congress was considering a reformulation of the law to increase funding authorization for more state grants.

Constitutional Constraints

The design of governmental power intended two centuries ago for a nation of farmers still rests heavily upon the flow of policy making in a technological age. Like other public policies, environmental programs have been shaped, and complicated, by this enduring constitutional formula.

Checks and Balances. The Madisonian notion of setting "ambition against ambition," which inspired the constitutional structure, creates a government of countervailing and competitive institutions. The system of checks and balances disperses power and authority within the federal government among legislative, executive, and judicial institutions and thereby sows tenacious institutional rivalries. Yet, as Richard E. Neustadt observes, these are separated institutions sharing power; effective public policy requires that public officials collaborate by discovering strategies to transcend these institutional conflicts.[10]

Federalism disperses governmental power by fragmenting authority between national and state governments. Despite the growth of vast federal powers, federalism remains a sturdy constitutional buttress supporting an edifice of authority—shared, independent, and countervailing—erected from the states within the federal system. "It is difficult," writes one observer, "to find any governmental activity which does not involve all three of the so-called 'levels' of the federal system."[11] And no government monopolizes power. "There has never been a time when it was possible to put neat labels on discrete 'federal,' 'state' and 'local' functions."[12]

Federalism also introduces complexity, jurisdictional rivalries, confusion, and delay into the management of environmental problems. These are partially the result of authority over environmental issues being fragmented among a multitude of different governmental entities and partially the product of Washington's attempts to administer federal environmental regulations through state and local governments. Management of water quality in the Colorado River basin, for instance, is enormously complicated because seven different states have conflicting claims upon the quantity and quality of Colorado River water to which they are entitled. No overall plan exists for the comprehensive management and protection of the river, and none can exist in this structure of divided and competitive jurisdictions. The federal government often attempts to reduce administrative complications in programs administered through the states by the use of common regulations, guidelines, and other devices to impose consistency in implementation. However, the practical problems of reconciling so many geographic interests within the arena of a single regulatory program often trigger major problems in program implementation.

Organized Interests. The Constitution also encourages a robust pluralism of organized interests. Constitutional guarantees for freedom of petition, expression, and assembly promote constant organization and political activism at all governmental levels among thousands of economic, occupational, ethnic, ideological, and geographic interests. To make public policy in the United States requires public officials and institutions to reconcile the conflicting interests of organized groups whose claims not only to influence but to authority in making public policy have resulted in an unwritten constitutional principle. The constitutional architecture of the U.S. government also provides numerous points of access to public power for such groups operating in a fragmented governmental milieu. The political influence broadly distributed across this vast constellation of organized private groups clouds the formal distinction between public and private power.[13] Instead, the course of policy making moves routinely and easily between public institutions and private organizations mobilized for political action.

These constitutional constraints have important implications for environmental policy. Generally, it is easier to defeat legislation and other governmental policies than to enact them, to frustrate incisive governmental action on issues than to create it. Further, most policy decisions result from bargaining and compromise among institutions and actors all sharing some portion of diffused power. Policy formulation usually means coalition building in an effort to engineer consensus by reconciling diverse interests and aggregating sufficient strength among different interests to support effective policies. For instance, administrative agencies have a "thirst for consensus," as James DeLong observes:

Agencies like to achieve consensus on issues and policies. If they cannot bring everyone into the tent, they will try to get enough disparate groups together so as to make the remainder appear unreasonable. If the interested parties are too far apart for even partial consensus, then the agency will try to give everybody something. . . .[14]

Bargaining and compromise often purchase consensus at the cost of disarray and contradiction in the resulting policies. "What happens," remarks Graham Allison, "is not chosen as a solution to a problem but rather results from compromise, conflict and confusion among officials with diverse interests and unequal influence."[15]

Incrementalism

Public officials strongly favor making and changing policy incrementally. "Policy making typically is part of a political process in which the only feasible political change is that which changes social states by relatively small steps," writes Charles A. Lindblom. "Hence, decisionmakers typically consider, among all the alternative policies that might be imagined to consider, only those relatively few alternatives that represent small or incremental changes from existing policies."[16] Generally, incrementalism favors reliance on past experience as a guide for new policies, careful deliberation before policy changes, and a rejection of rapid or comprehensive policy innovation.

Incrementalism is politically seductive. It permits policy makers to draw upon their own experience in the face of unfamiliar problems and encourages the making of small policy adjustments "at the margins" to reduce anticipated, perhaps irreversible, and politically risky consequences. But incrementalism can also become a prison to the imagination by inhibiting policy innovation and stifling new solutions to issues. Especially when officials treat new policy issues as if they were familiar ones and deal with them in the accustomed ways, a futile and possibly dangerous repetition of the past in the face of issues requiring a fresh approach can result.

The Clean Air Act (1970), the National Environmental Policy Act (NEPA) of 1970, and the other innovative legislation of the early 1970s came only after Congress repeatedly failed in dealing with environmental issues incrementally.[17] Beginning with the Water Pollution Control Act of 1956, the first significant federal effort to define a role for Washington in pollution abatement, Congress and the White House continued into the late 1960s to write legislation that treated pollution management as a "uniquely local problem" in which a "partnership" between federal and state governments was considered the appropriate model. This deference to the states was a prescription for inaction; few states voluntarily wrote or enforced effective pollution controls. In the Water Quality Act (1965) and the Air Quality Act (1967) Congress prodded the states a bit more vigorously by setting compliance deadlines for state pollution control plans, yet the legislation was so burdened with ambiguities and constraints on federal action that the legislation was ineffective.

By the early 1970s Congress felt compelled to break with this incrementalism. The environmental movement had grown rapidly in political strength. Although to many observers environmentalism appeared to have been swept to political prominence in a few months, its rise on the national policy agenda had been prompted by years of increasingly skilled, patient, and persistent promotion by a multitude of groups. The Clean Air Act, for instance, had been supported for almost five years by a national environmental alliance, the Clean Air Coalition, before it achieved national attention. Also, the growing severity of environmental degradation was creating a climate of opinion congenial to aggressive, new approaches to pollution abatement. Environmentalists were aided powerfully in their quest for new federal approaches to pollution abatement by the presence of veteran conservationists who assumed crucial congressional positions during this period: Sen. Edmund S. Muskie (D-Maine), Sen. Henry M. Jackson (D-Wash.), Sen. Philip A. Hart (D-Mich.), Rep. Morris Udall (D-Ariz.), Rep. Paul McCloskey (R-Calif.), Rep. Paul Rogers (D-Fla.), and many others. Equally important, environmentalism had become a major media preoccupation.

The time consumed in attempts to attack problems incrementally, the degree of environmental damage necessary to convince Congress that new approaches were needed, and the effort invested by the environmental movement in political action all testify to the tenacity of incrementalism in the policy process. Indeed, one risk in the new environmental programs of the 1970s is that with time they also may settle into an incremental mold resisting necessary changes.

Interest Group Liberalism

It is an implicit principle in American politics, assumed by most public officials as well as those groups seeking access to them, that organized interests affected by public policy should have an important role in shaping those policies. Few interests enjoy such a pervasive and unchallenged access to government as business, for reasons soon to be elaborated, but almost all major organized groups enjoy some measure of influence in public institutions. Many officials, in Theodore Lowi's terms, conduct their offices "as if it were supposed to be the practice of dealing only with organized claims in formulating policy, and of dealing exclusively through organized claims in implementing programs."[18]

Structuring Groups into Government.   Arrangements exist throughout governmental structures for giving groups access to strategic policy arenas. Lobbying is accepted as a normal, if not essential, arrangement for ensuring organized interests a major role in lawmaking. More than

1,000 advisory committees exist within the federal bureaucracy to give interests affected by policies some access and voice in agency deliberations. Hundreds of large, quasi-public associations bring together legislators, administrators, White House staff, and private group representatives to share policy concerns, thereby blurring the distinction between public and private interests. The National Rivers and Harbors Congress, for example, looks after water resource projects, the Highway Users Federation for Safety and Mobility diligently promotes the Interstate Highway System, and the Atomic Industrial Forum pursues the interests of commercial nuclear power corporations. Successful, organized groups so effectively control the exercise of governmental power that, in Grant McConnell's words, significant portions of American government have witnessed "the conquest of segments of formal state power by private groups and associations."[19] In effect, group activity at all governmental levels has been practiced so widely that it has become part of the constitutional order.

An Unusual Kind and Degree of Control.   No interest has exploited this right to take part in the governmental process more pervasively or successfully than has business. In environmental affairs, the sure access of business to government assumes enormous importance, for business is a major regulated interest whose ability to represent itself and secure careful hearing before public agencies and officials often delays or complicates such regulation. But historically and institutionally the influence of business upon government has transcended the agencies and officials concerned with environmental affairs. Business has traditionally enjoyed what Lindblom has called a "special relationship" with government.

Business weighs especially heavy in the deliberations of public officials because its leaders collectively manage much of the economy and perform such essential economic functions that their failure would produce severe economic disorder and widespread suffering. "Government officials know this," observes Lindbolm. "They also know that widespread failure of business . . . will bring down the government. A democratically elected government cannot expect to survive in the face of widespread or prolonged distress. . . . Consequently, government policy makers show constant concern about business performance." So great is this concern that public officials usually give business not all it desires but enough to ensure its profitability. Out of this grows the "privileged position" of business in government, its widely accepted right to require that government officials often "give business needs precedence over demands from citizens through electoral, party, and interest-group channels."[20]

Business also enjoys more practical political advantages in competition with other interests for access and influence within government: far greater financial resources, greater ease in raising money for political purposes, and an already-existing organization available for use in political action. These advantages in strategic resources and salience to public officials do not ensure business uncompromised acceptance of its demands upon government nor do they spare it from defeat or frustration by opponents. But business often, if not usually, is able to exploit its privileged status in American politics to ensure that its views are represented early and forcefully in any policy conflicts, its interests are pursued and protected carefully at all policy stages, and its forces are mobilized effectively for long periods of time. These are formidable advantages, often enough to give a decisive edge in competitive struggles with environmental or other interests that have not the political endurance, skill, or resources to be as resolute in bringing pressure on government when it counts.

Environmental Groups and Governmental Access.   Environmental groups have been no less diligent than others in organizing. Prior to the 1970s environmentalists were at a considerable disadvantage in achieving effective access to government when compared with environmentally regulated interests, particularly business. However, environmental groups—along with public interest groups, consumer organizations, and others advocating broad public programs—were quick to promote a number of new structural and legal arrangements, often created deliberately for their advantage by Congress and administrative agencies. Of these, three were particularly important: (1) liberal provisions for public participation in the implementation and enforcement of environmental regulatory programs as required by statute or administrative regulation; (2) expanded "standing to sue" public agencies, often created within the legislation authorizing environmental programs such as the Clean Air Act, which gave environmental groups far greater access to the courts than in prior years; and (3) the provision by several regulatory agencies for "intervenor funding" to pay the often substantial fees for lawyers and expert witnesses to represent environmental interests in agency proceedings where such groups provided an important, and otherwise unrepresented, interest. Environmental groups continue to defend these arrangements against the administration's effort to limit their scope.

Political Feasibility

"What considerations enter into the selection of priorities and the specific program designed to meet them?" mused veteran Washington observer Ralph Huitt. The answer was political feasibility. That means, notes Huitt, "Will it 'go' on the Hill? Will the public buy it? Does it have political 'sex appeal'?"[21] Policy deliberations involve more than calculations of political feasibility, but there is often a large component in them. Political feasibility involves an intuitive and often highly sub- jective judgment by public officials concerning what policies and pro- grams can be enacted and implemented in some reasonably effective way, given the political realities as they are understood. It is often a judgment quite different from determinations of rationality, economy, or fairness to a policy. The irrationality, vagueness, and apparently sloppy draftsmanship in legislation, environmental or otherwise, are often ex- plicable as an effort to make the law feasible. Calculations of political feasibility affect presidents, judges, and administrators as well as legisla- tors in policy making. In short, political feasibility is another test, and another constraint, on policy.

Examples abound in environmental policy. Political feasibility con- vinced Congress, when it enacted the original $18 billion federal sewage treatment grant program in 1972, that it must also provide a statutory allocation formula ensuring every state, regardless of size or need, a guaranteed and substantial minimum authorization. Political feasibil- ity, in the guise of congressional opinion, dissuaded the Reagan adminis- tration from attempting to abolish the $20 billion synthetic fuels pro- gram authorized under President Carter. Uncounted thousands of executive orders, presidential addresses, congressional bills, and agency regulations have perished unissued because they bore the stigma of political infeasibility.

Policy makers are influenced not only by these general constraints but also by the characteristics of the various governmental institutions that make policy. Each institution has its own characteristic constraints on policy. This is particularly important in understanding environmen- tal policy making in Congress, the bureaucracy, and the courts where different institutional constraints—known as policy "styles"—prevail.

The Political Seasons

The political climate of policy making is seldom constant. Opportuni- ties to make or change policy shift continually. At any given time, there will be differences between what policy makers want and what they can accomplish, between what they are compelled to do and what they would prefer to do, between what is feasible and what is not. This ebb and flow of opportunity is created by different circumstances. The most important include changes in the partisan control of governmental insti- tutions, transient shifts of public mood, and major economic change. These can be called the changing "seasons" of policy making.

Changing Party Majorities. The balance of party strength within Congress and between Congress and the White House powerfully shapes the substance and opportunities for environmental policy making. Generally, opportunities to make or change policy are greatest when the White House and Congress are controlled by the same party. However, since 1970 Republicans have usually occupied the White House and Democratic majorities have controlled both congressional chambers. The floodtide of environmental legislation originating in Washington during the 1970s was, in large part, the result of a broad, bipartisan environmental coalition in both chambers that strongly supported innovative environmental programs proposed or accepted by both Republican and Democratic presidents. The political climate darkened markedly with Ronald Reagan's election, however. The next eight years were largely a record of conflict and impasse between a president and Congress dominated by different parties committed to radically different policy agendas.

During the early Reagan era, Democratic control of the House of Representatives largely prevented the administration from passing in that chamber the manifold changes in existing environmental laws it had pledged to accomplish in the name of "regulatory relief." Even when the Republicans enjoyed a narrow and brief Senate majority from 1980 through 1984, Democrats controlling the major House environmental committees mounted a ferocious campaign of investigations, budget reviews, and other forays against Secretary of the Interior James Watt, EPA administrator Anne Burford, and other important Republicans in environmentally sensitive positions; this threw the Republicans on the defensive and turned much of the media and public opinion against Reagan's most ambitious attempts at regulatory relief. The return of a Democratic Senate majority in 1984 again vested committee control in that chamber to Reagan's opposition. So effective was the congressional Democratic majority in frustrating Reagan's environmental agenda that by the end of Reagan's first term the White House had largely abandoned the legislative strategy for regulatory relief and relied instead on achieving what it could of its reforms through the administrative channels available to the president as the chief executive.

Ronald Reagan's enormous impact upon environmental policy making in the 1980s is evidence, however, that in the hands of a politically skilled president with a clear policy agenda, White House resources can be fashioned into a potent policy-making instrument, with or without congressional cooperation. Reagan's impact on environmental policy was achieved largely by an aggressive, imaginative use of the executive powers inherent in the presidential office.[22] The president's authority to appoint upper- and middle-level administrators of agencies with major environmental responsibilities, such as the EPA and the Department of the Interior, was used to place administrators committed to regulatory reform in policy-sensitive positions where they could affect daily administrative implementation of environmental laws through their discretionary authority. As will be shown in later chapters, these administrators were able in many instances to obstruct, revise, or reinterpret many environmental regulations so effectively that many of the administration's environmental goals were at least partially achieved without any congressional cooperation. Further, the president used the budget and the OMB to reduce personnel and financial resources available for many environmental programs and to change priorities among them through shifting budget allocations.

Not least important, the president used a strategy of selective neglect to delay or prevent the advance of many environmental issues to national importance by denying them a place on his legislative agenda, by discouraging their promotion in legislative priority, and by ignoring them in his public presentations. In this way, for instance, major research funding and regulatory proposals dealing with acid rain, climate warming, and atmospheric ozone depletion were delayed for almost a decade. One barometer of the environmental climate during the Reagan era is the annual report of the Council on Environmental Quality (CEQ), a document closely attuned to White House environmental sensibilities. One could finish the 1986 report unaware that air or water pollution, toxic and hazardous waste, or most other nationally recognized ecological ills might be troubling the nation. From the opening chapter on "Birdlife of the United States" to the concluding chapter on "Take Pride in America"—a paean to voluntary efforts to protect the public lands—scarcely a paragraph addressed a currently important pollution problem.[23]

However, the Reagan administration's resistance to new environmental programs began to falter in the latter half of the president's second term as the public became increasingly concerned about environmental affairs. Even a popular, politically adept president cannot always resist strong tides of public opinion and turn them to his advantage. Often, public opinion, not parties or presidents, will determine policy agendas and the pace of policy implementation.

Shifting Public Moods.   "When President Nixon and his staff walked in the White House on January 20, 1969, we were totally unprepared for the tidal wave of public opinion in favor of cleaning up the nation's environment that was about to engulf us," remembers one of Nixon's close advisers. Congress was quicker to read political prophecy into the polls.[24] By Earth Day, just three months later, recalls the same adviser, "so many politicians were on the stump that Congress was forced to close down."

The Nixon administration's indifference to ecology evaporated when it discovered the political capital to be made by wrapping itself in the environmentalist mantle. The administration's many legislative proposals and executive acts intended to promote environmental protection, such as creating the EPA and issuing executive orders to halt public works projects alleged to be environmentally dangerous, were strongly influenced by surging public interest in environmental protection. And thus it has been ever since. Presidents and Congress alike feel enormous political pressure to respond when confronted by broad public majorities demonstrating a strong interest, or apprehension, about an environmental issue.

The pressure to do something, or look as if something is being done, is strong when sudden spikes of public apprehension rise in the aftermath of a well-publicized environmental crisis or disaster. Many major environmental laws and regulations are a direct response to environmental disasters, real or threatened. Thus, the Three Mile Island reactor accident of 1978 begot new Nuclear Regulatory Commission (NRC) regulations increasing the requirements for emergency planning at commercial nuclear power plants, and the Love Canal toxic waste discoveries inspired the "Superfund" legislation. The tragic 1984 chemical plant disaster at Bhopal, India, almost alone produced the 1986 community "right to know" amendment to the Superfund legislation requiring that industries using dangerous chemicals disclose the type and amount of these chemicals to individuals living within an area likely to be affected by an accident on site. "The Bhopal train was leaving the station," observed one environmental lobbyist about Congress, "and we got the kind of legislation we could put on the train."[25]

This hypersensitivity to public opinion is frequently criticized because it allegedly results too often in hastily written laws difficult to implement. "Congress bears a large share of the responsibility for the problems of environmental regulation," assert economists Robert W. Crandall and Paul R. Portney. "Congress has passed enabling statutes containing unrealistic deadlines and an unnecessary degree of specificity with respect to the standards that [agencies] must issue."[26] The congressional penchant for writing environmental legislation bristling with mandatory deadlines and other "hammer" clauses that appear to demonstrate toughness about pollution has often hobbled governmental efforts to deal with environmental ills. Nonetheless, it is difficult for presidents or legislators to take the longer time and more deliberate approach to ecological problems when issues acquire the guise of a public crisis.

Opinion can also become an obstacle to environmental policy making when the public mood is inhospitable to action. The lack of gasoline and petroleum shortages in the late 1970s, and other evidence that the "energy crisis" was passing, quickly removed energy problems from public concern and thwarted the Carter administration's efforts to pass new energy regulatory programs after mid-1978. By the time the Reagan administration finished its first term, Congress no longer felt pressure to continue mandatory plans for national fuel rationing, to require increased fuel economy standards for automobiles after 1986, or to promote solar technologies and other fuel conservation measures. Thus, advocates of environmental issues must often wait until the public opinion climate is ripe in order to move the White House or Congress to action. And crisis or disaster alone may sometimes be the only force that moves the political will.

Economic Change.   In all environmental policy making, economics is the counterpoint to ecology. The impact of environmental policies on the economy is a continual preoccupation of both environmental regulators and the regulated. And economic conditions, in turn, influence environmental policy making.

The economic impact of environmental regulations is a continual issue in all discussions of environmental policy. Concern most often focuses upon whether environmental regulation will inhibit expansion of the Gross National Product (GNP), how regulations will affect business investments and the market position of firms or industries, and whether regulatory costs are inflationary. Regulated interests frequently assert that specific policies will have most, or all, of these negative effects, while proponents of regulation usually dissent. Data wars erupt: each side summons its economists and econometrics to vindicate itself and discredit the opposition. While the result of these conflicts is often inconclusive, the issues are vitally important. Policies that appear—or can be made to appear—to adversely affect economic growth, market positions, or business investment are likely to command greater and more critical attention from policy makers than those appearing more economically benign. In times of economic recession or depression, the economic impact of policies can become the major determinant of their survival.

Environmental regulations, in any case, do create major public and private costs. Between 1975 and 1986, U.S. public and private expenditures for pollution abatement and control exceeded $564 billion. About 60 percent of this bill was paid by the private sector.[27] Generally, studies suggest that new capital spending for pollution control by public and private sectors has not significantly deterred growth of the GNP or contributed much to inflation or a rise in the consumer price index. For most industries, spending for pollution control has been a diminishing portion of new capital investment over the last decade. In 1987, for instance, business spending on pollution control averaged 1.7 percent of all capital outlays, as compared with 4.2 percent in 1975.[28]

Economic conditions affect environmental policy making in several ways. Most important, the mix of economic activities in the United States largely determines the character and magnitude of the nation's pollution problems and the kinds of stress placed upon its resource base. As the U.S. economy moves away from heavy dependence on manufacturing, the mix of environmental stresses changes. Between 1950 and the late 1980s, employment in U.S. manufacturing declined from 50 percent of the work force to 32 percent, while employment in service and high-technology sectors has climbed to about 51 percent of the labor force. This manufacturing decline reduces the air pollution emissions from U.S. industry, but increases the volume of solid and hazardous waste generated nationally. In the last two decades, the greatest stress on regional resources produced by economic growth has occurred in the South and West.

Perhaps no technology has been more important than the automobile in creating environmental stress. In the United States there is one automobile for every two Americans, the highest density in the world, and that auto will be driven an average of 10,000 miles annually. The U.S. transportation sector currently accounts for approximately 63 percent of the nation's petroleum consumption. It is a major source of air pollution emissions, and contributes significantly to water pollution through ground-water contamination from leaks at refineries and service stations, creates major solid waste problems, and encourages urban blight and growth-management difficulties.

It is widely assumed that a major economic recession, depression, or serious inflation would profoundly affect environmental regulation. The United States, however, has experienced no major depression and only a few short recessions since the 1970s. The serious inflation of the 1978–1983 period, intensified by rising energy prices associated with the "energy crisis" of the mid-1970s, did not appear to create a political climate hostile to environmental regulation. Many experts believe, however, that any prolonged, severe depression, recession, or inflation would make environmental protection much more difficult because regulation would be more vigorously, and probably more convincingly, attacked as a deterrent to economic growth or recovery.

The Institutional Setting

In the United States the tasks of policy formulation, implementation, and assessment are invested largely in the White House, Congress, bureaucracy, and courts. Because the latter three institutions play such a prominent role in environmental policy making, the institutional bias characteristic of each assumes a crucial role in explaining Washington's response to environmental issues.

Congress: Policy Formulation by Fragmentation

The Constitution invests Congress with the principal legislative powers in the federal government. While twentieth-century realities compel the president, bureaucracy, and courts to share these powers, Congress remains preeminent in policy formulation and legitimation. Despite the panoply of party organizations, legislative leaders, and coordinating committees, Congress remains largely an institution of fragmented powers and divided geographic loyalties. Legislative power is dispersed in both chambers among a multitude of committees and subcommittees; local or regional concerns often tenaciously claim legislative loyalties. The electoral cycle intrudes imperiously upon policy deliberations. The public interest and legislative objectivity compete with equally insistent legislative concerns to deliver something, if possible, from Washington to the "folks back home." In environmental affairs, Congress is an assembly of scientific amateurs enacting programs of great technical complexity to ameliorate scientifically complicated environmental ills most legislators but dimly understand.

Committee Decentralization.   Congress has been aptly described as a "kind of confederation of little legislatures."[29] In both chambers the committees and subcommittees—those little legislatures wielding the most consistently effective power in the legislative system—are dispersed and competitive in environmental matters. William Ruckelshaus, the EPA's first administrator, complained in the early 1970s that he had to deal with sixteen different congressional subcommittees.[30] The situation has gotten worse. Today, fourteen of twenty-two standing House committees share some jurisdiction over environmental policy. In the Senate, eleven committees and several dozen subcommittees share jurisdiction over environmentally sensitive energy issues. Water policy is even more decentralized: seventy congressional committees and subcommittees share some jurisdiction. (The array of committees and their environmental jurisdictions are indicated in "Congressional Committees and Their Jurisdictions," pages 84–85.)

Competition among committees, within and between chambers, commonly occurs in formulating environmental programs. The result is protracted bargaining and compromise. With authority over environmental policy fragmented among a multitude of committees in each chamber, competition and jurisdictional rivalry commonly occur as each committee attempts to assert some influence over environmental programs. The result is that, as a rule, environmental legislation evolves

Congressional Committees and Their Jurisdictions

The following are the congressional committees with jurisdiction over environmentally related programs and the programs for which each committee is responsible.

SENATE

Agriculture
Soil conservation, ground water
Forestry, private forest reserves
Pesticides, food safety
Global change

Appropriations
International monetary and financial funds
Forest Service
Army Corps of Engineers
Nuclear Regulatory Commission
Tennessee Valley Authority
Occupational Safety and Health
    Administration (OSHA)
Mine Safety and Health Administration
Soil conservation programs
Food and Drug Administration
Environmental Protection Agency
Council on Environmental Policy
National Oceanic and Atmospheric
    Administration

Armed Services
Military weapons plants
Nuclear energy
Naval petroleum, oil shale reserves
Air Force jet emissions

Commerce, Science, Transportation
Coastal zone management
Inland waterways
Marine fisheries
Oceans, weather, science research
Outer continental shelf
Global change

Energy and Natural Resources
Energy policy, conservation
National parks, wilderness
Nuclear energy, public utilities
Public lands, forests
Global change

Environment and Public Works
Environmental policy, oversight
Air and water pollution
Outer continental shelf
Toxic substances
Fisheries and wildlife
Flood control, deep-water ports
Ocean dumping
Nuclear energy
Bridges, dams, inland waterways
Solid-waste disposal
Superfund, hazardous waste
Global change

Finance
Revenue measures, user fees

Foreign Relations
Nuclear energy, international
International Monetary Fund
International environmental affairs

Government Affairs
Nuclear export policy
Nuclear weapons plant cleanup

Judiciary
Environmental law, penalties

Labor and Human Resources
Occupational health and safety
Pesticides, food safety

HOUSE

Agriculture
Agriculture and industrial chemistry
Soil conservation, ground water
Forestry and private forest reserves
Pesticides, food safety
Global change

Appropriations
International monetary funds
Forest Service
Army Corps of Engineers
Nuclear Regulatory Commission
Tennessee Valley Authority
Occupational Safety and Health
    Administration (OSHA)
Mine Safety and Health Administration
Soil conservation programs
Food and Drug Administration
Environmental Protection Agency
Council on Environmental Policy
National Oceanic and Atmospheric
    Administration

Armed Services
Military weapons plants
Naval petroleum, oil shale reserves
Nuclear energy

Banking, Finance and Urban Affairs
International financial and monetary
    organizations

Education and Labor
Occupational health and safety

Energy and Commerce
Energy policy, oversight
Energy conservation
Health and the environment
Interstate energy compacts
Public health and quarantine
Nuclear facilities
Transportation of hazardous materials
Solid-, hazardous-waste disposal

Foreign Affairs
Foreign loans, IMF
International environmental affairs
Global change

Government Operations
Environment, energy, natural resources
    oversight

Interior and Insular Affairs
Forest reserves (public domain)
Public lands
Irrigation and reclamation
Petroleum conservation (public lands)
Conservation of radium supply
Nuclear energy industry

Judiciary
Environmental law, penalties

Merchant Marine and Fisheries
Coastal zone management
Fisheries and wildlife
Oil-spill liability
Wetlands

Public Works and Transportation
Flood control, rivers and harbors
Pollution of navigable waters
Bridges and dams
Superfund, hazardous waste

Science, Space and Technology
Research and development
National Weather Service
Global change
Nuclear energy, facilities
Agriculture research
National Oceanic and Atmospheric
    Administration

Ways and Means
Revenue measures, user fees
Superfund

SOURCE: Phillip Marwill, *Congressional Quarterly Weekly Report*, January 20, 1990, 151.

only through protracted bargaining and compromising among the many committees. This time-consuming process often results in legislation that is vague or inconsistent. Divided jurisdictions, however, provide different interest groups with some point of committee access during environmental policy formulation, and consequently these groups resist efforts to reduce the number of committees with overlapping jurisdictions and concentrate authority in a few major committees.

Groups hostile to the Clinch River Breeder Reactor, for instance, were aided greatly in their battle to terminate the project by House reforms in 1976 removing jurisdiction over the project from the exclusive control of the Joint Committee on Atomic Energy, the breeder's premier legislative champion, and vesting it in several other less supportive committees. Subsequently, these groups fiercely resisted efforts to reorganize the House committee structure lest they lose their access in the process.

Localism.   During a crucial Senate vote on funding the highly controversial, multimillion-dollar Tennessee-Tombigbee Waterway, a reporter was impressed by what he called "the unabashed display of horse trading among Senators not wanting to endanger their own project." The funding finally passed because many senators of both parties had bartered their support for the project in return for assurances that project proponents would return the favor when other projects were considered. "But that's nothing new," replied Sen. Howell Heflin (D-Ala.) to a critic. "It's happened in the United States Senate since the beginning."[31]

The Senate's unapologetic loyalty to reciprocity in voting for local public works projects, known as political pork, is driven by a powerful tradition of localism in congressional voting. In American political culture, legislators are treated by constituents and regard themselves as ambassadors to Washington from their own geographic areas. They are expected to acquire skills in the practice of pork-barrel politics, capturing federal goods and services for the constituency. They are also expected to be vigilant in promoting and protecting local interests in the national policy arena. Congressional tenure is more likely to depend upon a legislator's ability to serve these local interests than upon other legislative achievements. While not the only influence upon congressional voting, it is deeply rooted and probably the single most compelling force in shaping voting decisions.

This localism affects environmental policy in different ways. By encouraging legislators to view environmental proposals first through the lens of local interests, it often weakens a sensitivity to national needs and interests. At worst it drives legislators to judge the merits of environmental policies almost solely by their impact upon frequently small and atypical constituencies. The Reagan administration learned about the costs of failing to recognize legislators' instinctive localism when, through the Interior Department, it acted to propose in late 1981 the approval of two lease applications for oil exploration in the Los Padres National Forest near Big Sur, one of California's most spectacular coastal vistas. The White House found itself confronting united opposition—regardless of party affiliation—from the entire twenty-two-member California House delegation. Thus did geographic loyalty, awakened by fear of environmental devastation to Big Sur, unite California Republicans against their own party leader and with the opposition Democrats.

Localism also whets the congressional appetite for federal distributive programs freighted with local benefits. Not surprisingly, federal grants to build pollution-control facilities, such as sewage treatment plants, have instant legislative appeal. Even the comparatively tiny federal program for such grants to the states in the mid-1960s appealed. "The program was immensely popular. . . . Congressmen enjoyed the publicity and credit they received every time they announced another grant for another community in their district."[32] The huge $18-billion waste treatment facilities program authorized in 1972, the second largest public works program in U.S. history, was even more popular. By 1982 the $10.5 billion obligated under the program had generated 4.5 million worker-years of employment supporting about 7.3 million Americans. The EPA estimated that for every $1 billion spent, about 50,900 worker-years of employment would be generated in plant and sewer construction.[33]

Elections. The electoral cycle also dominates the legislative mind. The constitutionally mandated electoral cycles of the federal government—two years, four years, six years—partition the time available for legislative deliberation into periods bound by different elections. Within these time frames, policy decisions are continually analyzed for their electoral implications and often valued largely for electoral impacts. This affects congressional policy styles in several ways. First, the short term becomes more important than the long term when evaluating programs; legislators often attribute more importance to a program's impact on the next election than to its longer-term effects upon unborn generations. Second, policies are tested continually against public opinion. While a weak or badly divided public opinion often can be ignored, a coherent majority opinion related to an environmental issue usually wields significant influence on congressional voting, especially when legislators can associate the opinion with their own constituencies.

Bureaucracy: Power Through Implementation

Federal agencies concerned with environmental affairs and closely related matters such as energy, consumer protection, and worker health have grown explosively in the last three decades. More than 150 major new federal laws, most concerned with broad regulation of business and the economy in the interest of public health and safety, have been enacted since 1970. More than twenty new regulatory agencies have been created to implement these programs, including the EPA, Occupational Safety and Health Administration (OSHA), and the Interior Department's Office of Surface Mining Reclamation and Enforcement.

The Power of Discretion. The significance of these agencies rests less upon their size and budget than upon the political realities obscured by a constitutional illusion. The Constitution appears to vest the power to formulate policy primarily in Congress, while leaving to the president and the executive branch the task of seeing that the laws are "faithfully executed." Although implemented and enforced principally in the bureaucracy, public policy develops in both branches of the government.

Delegated authority and administrative discretion provide the wellsprings of the bureaucracy's power. Congress routinely invests administrators with responsibility for making a multitude of decisions it can not or will not make itself about the implementation of policy; often this becomes legislative power delegated to the executive branch. Even when delegation is not clearly intended, administrators assume the power to make public policy when they choose how to implement policies permitting different options—hence the existence of administrative discretion. Consider, for instance, how delegated authority and administrative discretion coalesce as the Forest Service deals with routine responsibilities:

In recommending approval of leases for mining exploration in Los Padres National Forest, the U.S. Forest Service must decide if drilling roads are "potentially erodable," and whether each project lies in "unstable bedrock." The Forest Service landscape architects and area supervisors must also approve the location of drilling and other exploration equipment, the routes of all drilling roads and the types of vehicle used.[34]

Congress and the president, using a variety of constitutional and statutory powers, attempt to discipline the exercise of administrative discretion. Congress usually includes with grants of delegated authority statutory guidelines intended to give administrators various criteria for the exercise of authority. Congress may assert its inherent powers of legislative oversight, budget review and authorization, legislative investigation, as well as others to ensure administrative responsibility in program implementation. The White House, drawing upon the president's powers as chief executive and many congressionally delegated powers, can influence administrative discretion. Still this oversight holds no certain rein on administrative discretion, particularly in light of the vast number and complexity of environmental programs, the elephantine size of the bureaucracy, and competing demands upon presidential and congressional time. The federal bureaucracy, assured of generous discretionary authority well into the future, will continue to be an independent and largely self-regulated influence in environmental policy.

Bureaucratic Competitiveness.   The bureaucracy is no monolith. Its powers in environmental affairs, although collectively vast, also are dispersed and competitive. One source of this fragmentation is the federalizing of environmental administration. Many major environmental laws enacted in Washington are administered partially or wholly through state governments; others give states an option to participate. Under the Federal Water Pollution Control Act, for instance, twenty-seven states currently administer their own water pollution permit systems; all but six states and the District of Columbia administer the Safe Drinking Water Act. The Clean Air Act permits the states to participate in several major aspects of the program, including the control of pollutants and the establishment of emission standards for stationary sources.

Another cause of fragmented administrative authority is the chronic division and overlapping responsibility for environmental programs among federal agencies. For example, twenty-seven separate federal agencies share major regulatory responsibility in environmental and occupational health (see "Federal Agencies with Environmental Regulatory Responsibility," pages 90–91). Regulating even a single pollutant often necessitates a bureaucratic convention. Toxic substances are currently regulated under twenty different federal statutes involving five agencies. To address all the problems in human exposure to vinyl chloride, notes David Doniger, would require the collaboration of all five agencies working with fifteen different laws.[35]

Dispersed authority breeds conflict and competition among agencies and their political allies over program implementation, authority, and resources—the "turf fighting" familiar to students of bureaucracy. While collaboration is common, it is never dependable. State environmental agencies, for instance, often disagree with Washington and among themselves over the proper implementation of the same program. Such a disagreement led to a 1982 suit filed against the EPA by the attorney general of New York charging that the agency was responsible for increasing acid rain in the Northeast by failing to enforce air pollution limits on West Virginia, Michigan, Tennessee, Illinois, Indiana, and Missouri.

Federal agencies are notoriously fitful collaborators in environmental affairs. When the Energy Department, the EPA, and the NRC, all sharing responsibility for the regulation of nuclear power plants, attempted to fashion a procedure for safely closing the plants, the prospect of the NRC becoming the lead agency provoked resistance from the others. "The

Federal Agencies with Environmental Regulatory Responsibility

The following federal agencies share regulatory responsibility in matters concerning environmental and occupational health.

Agricultural Stabilization and Conservation Service. Administers various voluntary land-use programs to protect, expand, and conserve farmlands, wetlands, and forests. (*Agriculture Department*)

Army Corps of Engineers. Regulates all construction projects in the navigable waterways; promulgates regulations governing the transportation and dumping of dredged materials in navigable waters; develops, plans, and builds various structures to protect areas from floods, supply water for municipal and industrial use, create recreational areas, improve water and wildlife quality, and protect the shorelines of oceans and lakes. (*Defense Department*)

Bureau of Land Management. Administers public lands located mainly in the western United States and Alaska. Resources managed include timber, minerals, oil and gas, geothermal energy, wildlife habitats, endangered plant and animal species, rangeland vegetation, recreation areas, wild and scenic rivers, wild horses and burros, designated conservation and wilderness areas, and open-space lands. (*Interior Department*)

Consumer Product Safety Commission. Establishes mandatory safety standards governing the design, construction, contents, performance, and labeling of consumer products; develops rules and regulations to enforce standards. Hazard-related programs include acute chemical and environmental hazards.

Federal Aviation Administration. Establishes and enforces rules and regulations for civil aviation safety standards, including noise and exhaust emissions from aircraft (in cooperation with the EPA). (*Transportation Department*)

Federal Energy Regulatory Commission. Issues licenses for hydroelectric power; provides for recreational opportunities, flood control, and the efficient and safe operation of project dams. (*Energy Department*)

Federal Highway Administration. Sets functional safety standards for the design, construction, and maintenance of highways; establishes safety standards for commercial motor carriers in interstate or foreign commerce; regulates the movement of dangerous cargoes on highways and administers programs to reduce motor carrier noise. (*Transportation Department*)

Federal Maritime Commission. Certifies the financial responsibility of vessels that carry oil or other hazardous material to cover costs of cleaning up spills in navigable waters.

Federal Trade Commission. Protects the public from false and deceptive advertising, particularly involving food, drugs, cosmetics, and therapeutic devices. Issues report on "tar" and nicotine contents of cigarettes.

Food and Drug Administration. Administers laws to ensure the purity and safety of foods, drugs, and cosmetics. Develops programs to reduce human exposure to radiation; conducts research on the effects of radiation exposure and toxic chemical substances found in the environment. (*Health and Human Services Department*)

Materials Transportation Bureau. Develops and enforces operating safety regulations for the transportation of all materials by pipeline; carries out inspection, compliance, and enforcement actions for transport of all hazardous materials (including radioactive materials) by air, water, highway, and rail. (*Transportation Department*)

Mine Safety and Health Administration. Develops, promulgates, and ensures compliance with mandatory mine safety and health standards. (*Labor Department*)

National Bureau of Standards. Researches and provides technical information on the protection of public health and safety, environmental quality, industrial productivity, and the promotion of better materials use. (*Commerce Department*)

National Institute for Occupational Safety and Health. Researches and develops occupational safety and health standards. (*Department of Health and Human Services*)

National Oceanic and Atmospheric Administration. Describes, monitors, and predicts conditions in the atmosphere, ocean, sun, and space environment; disseminates environmental data through meteorological, oceanographic, geophysical, and solar-terrestrial data centers; manages and conserves living marine resources and their habitats, including certain endangered species and marine mammals. (*Commerce Department*)

National Park Service. Administers programs to conserve the scenery, natural and historic objects, and wildlife in the nation's parks. (*Interior Department*)

National Transportation Safety Board. Investigates and reports on the transportation of hazardous materials. (*Transportation Department*)

Nuclear Regulatory Commission. Licenses the construction and operation of nuclear reactors and other facilities; licenses the possession, use, transportation, handling, and disposal of nuclear materials.

Office of Conservation and Renewable Energy. Directs energy conservation programs; expands use of biomass, alcohol fuels, and urban waste; studies effects of acid rain and carbon dioxide associated with coal burning. (*Energy Department*)

Office of Surface Mining Reclamation and Enforcement. Protects against the adverse effects of coal mining operations; establishes minimum standards for regulating surface effects of coal mining; promotes reclamation of previously mined lands. (*Interior Department*)

Office of Water Research and Technology. Supervises the nation's water quality and quantity; researches controls for the quality and quantity of ground and surface water, conservation techniques and technologies, protection of fragile water ecosystems, and water management planning. (*Interior Department*)

Soil Conservation Service. Administers program to develop and conserve soil and water resources; offers technical assistance on agricultural pollution control and environmental improvement projects. (*Agriculture Department*)

U.S. Coast Guard. Works with Materials Transportation Bureau to ensure that ship-owners clean up oil or hazardous materials discharged into navigable waters. (*Transportation Department*)

U.S. Fish and Wildlife Service. Regulates the development, protection, rearing, and stocking of wildlife resources and their habitats; protects migratory and game birds, fish and wildlife, endangered and threatened species; enforces regulations for hunters of migratory waterfowl; preserves wetlands as natural habitats. (*Interior Department*)

U.S. Forest Service. Manages the national forests and grasslands; regulates the use of forest resources and the activities of commercial foresters working in national forests. (*Interior Department*)

U.S. Geological Survey. Classifies and manages mineral and water resources on federal lands, including the outer continental shelf. Maintains the Earth Resources Observation System Data Center that conducts and sponsors research to apply data findings in mapping, geography, mineral and land resources, water resources, rangeland, and wildlife and environmental monitoring. (*Interior Department*)

Water and Power Resources Service. Develops and manages water and power resources in the western states. Projects include flood control, river regulation, outdoor recreation, fish and wildlife enhancement, and water-quality improvement. (*Interior Department*)

SOURCE: *Environment and Health* (Washington, D.C.: Congressional Quarterly, 1981), 130–131.

underlying reason for their disagreement," explained the U.S. Comptroller General's Office, "was that such an action would give NRC additional regulatory authority over their programs."[36]

Dispersed authority also explains much of the contradiction and confusion in federal environmental regulation. In the mid-1980s, for instance, ground-water users were regulated, and often confounded, by forty-four different federal programs scattered among more than a half dozen agencies.[37] The agencies responsible for pesticide regulation often send contradictory messages. One such instance occurred in late 1983 when the EPA announced an emergency suspension of the use of EDB as a soil fumigant and its intention to phase out all remaining agriculture uses in a year. At the same time, the Animal and Plant Health Inspection Service in the Department of Agriculture was requiring the use of EDB on commodities imported from the Caribbean and the U.S. Agency for International Development was promoting EDB's use in developing countries.[38]

In this milieu of dispersed and competitive agency authority, policy implementation often resolves into a continual process of collaboration and conflict between coalitions of agencies and their allies shaping and reshaping policy as the relative strengths of the conflicting alignments change. Moreover, administrative conflict crosses the institutional divisions of the federal government, spreads downward through the federal system to state and local governments and outward from government to organized private groups. Indeed, agencies failing to enlist diverse and active allies in their policy struggles may frustrate their own mission and leave their future hostage to more politically skilled opponents.

The Courts: The Role of Appraisal

Judges actively participate in the environmental policy process in several ways. They continually interpret environmental law, an inevitable task in light of the ambiguities and silences common to environmental legislation. This statutory interpretation often amounts to policy making by the judicial branch. Judges also attempt to ensure that agencies discharge their mandated responsibilities under environmental legislation and otherwise comply with administrative obligations. Additionally, the federal courts enforce the Administrative Procedures Act (1946), the code of administrative procedure applicable to all federal agencies. Finally, the courts ensure that environmental laws and their administrative implementation comply with constitutional standards.

The Courts and Environmental Policy.   The federal courts, particularly the Supreme Court, have made several significant contributions to environmental policy. During the 1970s the courts greatly expanded opportunities for environmental groups to bring issues before the bench by a broadened definition of "standing to sue." Prior to the 1970s environmental interests were greatly inhibited in using the courts by the traditional requirement that standing—the right to have one's suit heard by the court—could be obtained in environmental issues only when states were a party or when the private party initiating the action had suffered a clear injury or property loss. This precluded judicial consideration in cases where plaintiffs charged another party with environmental harm (this was not a personal injury) or attempted to sue governmental agencies for failure to discharge environmental responsibilities (personal injury or loss was difficult to document). Beginning with the Scenic Hudson case (1971) the Supreme Court gradually expanded standing over the next few years until a generous variety of individuals and environmental groups were able to initiate litigation to protect various public interests.[39] In more recent years the courts have not always been consistent or generous in their definition of standing. Nonetheless, the earlier decisions enabled environmental interests to use litigation effectively to bring pressure on Congress, administrative agencies, and regulated interests for more effective environmental policies during a crucial decade when major environmental laws were being written.

The federal courts' substantive interpretations of environmental laws during the 1970s also had a major impact in strengthening the scope and impact of many programs. The federal district court's 1972 *Sierra Club v. Ruckelshaus* decision, for instance, interpreted the goals of the Clean Air Act to require that all states prevent the degradation of any airsheds with ambient air quality higher than national standards. This decision in effect forced the EPA and Congress to create the Prevention of Significant Deterioration (PSD) policy to protect all high-quality airsheds throughout the United States. According to R. Shep Melnick, "PSD was born in the courtroom and has resided there almost constantly for the past decade."[40] Indeed, as his meticulous study of the federal courts and the Clean Air Act indicates, the courts have been a major factor in the evolution of extremely stringent air pollution control standards by Congress and the EPA.[41]

Environmentalists, impatient with the faltering pace of the EPA's development of a priority list of hazardous pollutants for examination as required under the Toxic Substances Control Act, used the federal courts—particularly the District Court for the District of Columbia, an especially sympathetic forum for environmentalists—to force the EPA to speed up its priority setting. While environmentalists also suffered defeats in federal litigation during the 1970s, generally it was a period when judicial interpretation of environmental law worked to the environmentalists' advantage.

The federal courts also have been extremely instrumental in enforcing strict procedural compliance and reasonable adherence to the intent of the law in enforcing the requirement of the National Environmental Policy Act for Environmental Impact Statements (EISs) in the federal bureaucracy. Perhaps in no other area of environmental law have the federal courts been more consistent. "Judicial enforcement of NEPA has resulted in increased administrative disclosures by federal agencies, more detailed analysis of environmental considerations by these agencies and more thoughtful future planning in this area on their part."[42] The EIS process has been particularly useful to environmentalists by disclosing the implications of administrative issues that otherwise might not have been apparent, by serving as an early warning system to alert environmental groups to impending new issues, and by compelling federal agencies to give environmentalists an opportunity to influence decisions with environmental consequences.

The Growth of Business Litigation.   In the latter 1970s business and other regulated interests began to use the federal courts to their advantage far more adeptly than they had earlier. During the 1970s environmentalists had been the primary beneficiaries of federal litigation; in the 1980s this advantage seems to have been substantially diminished.

One major reason for the increased effectiveness of business interests in federal litigation was the great growth in number and activity of specialized not-for-profit legal foundations representing regulated industries in environmental litigation. Reasoning that the devil should not have all the good tunes, business patterned these associations after the public interest legal foundations created in the 1970s to represent environmental interests. The most effective of these regionally organized business foundations have been the Pacific States Legal Foundation and the Mountain States Legal Foundation. The Midwest Legal Foundation and the Northeast Legal Foundation are two others. Like environmental public interest groups, these business associations maintain they are suing the government in the public interest and enjoy tax-exempt status. However, business public interest groups are financed principally by organizations, such as the Adolph Coors Company and the Scaife Foundation, who have fought vigorously against most of the major environmental regulatory programs that have been passed during the last three decades.

While business legal foundations have been highly aggressive in initiating cases against federal and state environmental regulations, the growing strength of business in environmental litigation also has been the result of greater skills and more attention by individual corporations and trade associations. Initially many corporations had little experience with environmental litigation, but they learned quickly.

"Starting in 1970," observes Lettie Wenner, "environmentalists were the most active groups at both the trial and appellate levels [of the federal courts]. . . . However, as the decade progressed and business corporations and trade associations added attorneys conversant with environmental law to their staffs, the numbers of economic interest groups' demands on the courts increased dramatically."[43] Suits initiated by business organizations were more often directed against emission standards established by the EPA under air and water pollution control legislation. In the early 1980s both the number and success of these business challenges to EPA emission standards appeared to be increasing.

The benefit to business interests from this growing strength in environmental litigation does not solely rest upon an ability to win cases. Exhaustive and relentless challenges to federal regulation can delay enforcement of environmental laws for many years and throw environmental groups on the defensive, compelling them to invest scarce resources in protracted legal battles. Often the battles are won ultimately not by the side with the best case but by the side with the best endurance. With its much greater legal and financial resources and capacity to sustain litigation, business has gradually eliminated many of the organizational and legal advantages once enjoyed by environmental interests in the federal courts.

Litigation as a Political Tactic. The impact of the courts upon policy, as the previous discussion suggests, arises not only from the substance of court rulings but also from the use of litigation as a tactical weapon in policy conflict. The courts become another political arena where losers in prior policy battles fought in Congress, the bureaucracy, or the White House seek yet another opportunity to prevail. For instance, when the major U.S. automakers failed to persuade the EPA to delay for a year the enforcement of the 1975 auto emission standards required by the Clean Air Act, they appealed successfully to the federal courts for a judicially imposed delay. The federal court asked the EPA to conduct further hearings and to assemble more evidence justifying its decision. Faced with this prospect and the likelihood of further litigation, the agency granted a delay in the compliance deadline rather than invest further resources in a struggle of very uncertain outcome. Not surprisingly, environmental groups specializing in litigation, such as the Environmental Defense Fund, increased their activity during the Reagan administration in an effort to counteract through the courts what they alleged to be massive regulatory resistance to their interests within the administration.

Litigation is also a stall in the policy process, a frustration to the opposition. Litigation creates a bargaining chip to be bartered for concessions from the opposition. Both environmentalists and their opposition have used the obstructive capacities of litigation to good advantage. When the Interior Department attempted in late 1981 to sell for energy exploration 111 tracts of offshore land in California's coastal zone, the state of California and numerous environmental groups joined in litigation blocking the sale of 32 tracts, among the most desirable, thereby freezing sale of the others also. This persuaded the department to reconsider the leases rather than risk a prolonged freeze on the sale of all valuable tracts. Litigation initiated in the mid-1970s by environmental opponents of the Seabrook, New Hampshire, nuclear power plant cost the facility owners almost $15 million monthly in delay and almost succeeded in shutting the facility permanently.

Many critics have pegged NEPA's requirement for EISs as an especially productive source of lawsuits working to the advantage of environmentalists, but the data suggest otherwise. The number of lawsuits challenging federal agency actions under NEPA has been decreasing generally since 1970 and remains relatively low. Between 1970 and 1980 more than 10,000 impact statements were filed by federal agencies, yet only 1,911 lawsuits challenging the adequacy of the statements were initiated—many by business, state and local governmental entities, and other nonenvironmental organizations. This litigation seems particularly modest in light of the large number of impact statements actually written in the past two decades and the much greater number of agency decisions that might have been challenged on grounds that EISs should have been written for them. In 1975 alone, federal agencies assessed more than 30,000 decisions to which NEPA might apply. In short, environmentalists did not appear to have gained an especially strategic legal advantage from NEPA.[44]

Though the institutional styles of Congress, the bureaucracy, and the courts all contribute to shaping environmental policy, the Reagan administration's especially crucial role in policy implementation during the 1980s imparted a special importance to the agencies most active in this implementation. These agencies became perhaps the decade's most visible institutions in environmental policy making. Their attributes, consequently, deserve more detailed consideration.

The Administrative Setting

A great diversity of administrative agencies share responsibility for environmental administration. By far the most important, most visible, and largest of the environmental regulators is the Environmental Protection Agency.

The EPA

Asked if his job had been rewarding, a former EPA administrator replied that it was "like beating a train across a grade crossing—if you make it, it's a great rush. If you don't, you're dead."[45] An insider's guide to Washington ranks the EPA administrator job among the one hundred toughest positions in Washington. Created by an executive order of President Richard Nixon in 1970 and scheduled for elevation to Cabinet status in 1991, the EPA is Washington's largest regulatory agency in budget and personnel. Its responsibilities embrace extraordinarily complicated and technical programs running across the whole domain of environmental management and touching almost all major sectors of the U.S. economy. Under these conditions, political controversy is the daily bread of EPA's leadership. "The Administrator rarely goes to the President with good news and is more often the bearer of bad news," observed Lee Thomas, EPA's administrator from 1985 to 1988. "You almost never have a decision where many people applaud it."[46]

The size of EPA's regulatory burden is suggested in "Major Responsibilities of the EPA," pages 98–99, which summarizes the EPA's current statutory responsibilities. These regulatory programs represent the major environmental legislation of the last two decades, including the Clean Air Act; the Clean Water Act; the Noise Control Act; the Safe Drinking Water Act; the Resource Conservation and Recovery Act; the Toxic Substances Control Act; the Marine Protection, Research and Sanctuaries Act; the Federal Insecticide, Fungicide, and Rodenticide Act; the Superfund Act; and the Superfund Amendments and Reauthorization Act. Beginning with a staff of approximately 8,000 and a budget of $455 million in 1972, the EPA steadily grew to almost 13,000 employees and a budget of $1.35 billion until 1981 when the Reagan administration severely reduced its budget and personnel. The agency recovered somewhat in the late 1980s and presently has about 15,000 employees and an annual budget of approximately $4.9 billion, most of which is committed to waste treatment grants for local governments and Superfund grants to clean up abandoned toxic waste sites.[47] The agency, whose administrator is appointed by the president, consists of a Washington headquarters and ten regional offices, each headed by a regional administrator. Unlike most regulatory agencies, the EPA administers both regulatory and distributive programs such as the huge federal waste treatment grants, the Superfund program, and various research activities.

During the early Reagan administration, bitter controversy thrust the agency into the national limelight. The president's first administrator, Anne Burford, was a former Colorado legislator and corporate attorney whose clients included many industries hostile to federal environmental

Major Responsibilities of the EPA

The following are the major regulatory tasks assigned to EPA in each important pollution control program.

In the area of air quality, the EPA:
• Establishes national air quality standards.
• Sets limits on the level of air pollutants emitted from stationary sources such as power plants, municipal incinerators, factories, and chemical plants.
• Establishes emission standards for new motor vehicles.
• Sets allowable levels for toxics like lead, benzene, and toluene in gasoline.
• Establishes emission standards for hazardous air pollutants such as beryllium, mercury, and asbestos.
• Supervises states in their development of clean air plans.

In the area of water quality and protection, the EPA:
• Issues permits for the discharge of any pollutant into navigable waters.
• Develops "effluent guidelines" to control discharge of specific water pollutants, including radiation.
• Develops criteria that enable states to set water quality standards.
• Administers grants program to states to subsidize the cost of building sewage treatment plants.
• Regulates disposal of waste material, including sludge and low-level radioactive discards, into the oceans.
• Cooperates with the Army Corps of Engineers to issue permits for the dredging and filling of wetlands.
• Sets national drinking water standards to ensure that drinking water is safe.
• Regulates underground injection of wastes to protect purity of ground water.

• With the Coast Guard, coordinates cleanup of oil and chemical spills into U.S. waterways.

To control the disposal of hazardous waste, the EPA:
• Maintains inventory of existing hazardous waste dump sites.
• Tracks more than 500 hazardous compounds from point of origin to final disposal site.
• Sets standards for generators and transporters of hazardous wastes.
• Issues permits for treatment, storage, and disposal facilities for hazardous wastes.
• Assists states in developing hazardous waste control programs.
• Maintains a multibillion-dollar fund ("Superfund") from industry fees and general tax revenues to provide for emergency cleanup of hazardous dumps when no responsible party can immediately be found.
• Pursues identification of parties responsible for waste sites and eventual reimbursement of the federal government for Superfund money spent cleaning up these sites.

To regulate chemicals, including pesticides and radioactive waste, the EPA:
• Maintains inventory of chemical substances now in commercial use.
• Regulates existing chemicals considered serious hazards to people and the environment, including fluorocarbons, PCBs, and asbestos.
• Issues procedures for the proper

safety testing of chemicals and orders them tested when necessary.

• Requires the registration of insecticides, herbicides, or fungicides intended for sale in the United States.

• Requires pesticide manufacturers to provide scientific evidence that their products will not injure humans, livestock, crops, or wildlife when used as directed.

• Classifies pesticides for either general public use or restricted use by certified applicators.

• Sets standards for certification of applicators of restricted-use pesticides. (Individual states may certify applicators through their own programs based on the federal standards.)

• Cancels or suspends the registration of a product on the basis of actual or potential unreasonable risk to man, animals, or the environment.

• Issues a "stop sale, use, and removal" order when a pesticide already in circulation is found to be in violation of the law.

• Requires registration of pesticide producing establishments.

• Issues regulations concerning the labeling, storage and disposal of pesticide containers.

• Issues permits for pesticide research.

• Monitors pesticide levels in the environment.

• Monitors and regulates the levels of radiation in drinking water, oceans, rainfall, and air.

• Conducts research on toxic substances, pesticides, air and water quality, hazardous wastes, radiation, and the causes and effects of acid rain.

• Provides overall guidance to other federal agencies on radiation protection matters that affect public health.

In addition, the EPA:

• Sets noise levels that are acceptable for construction equipment, transportation equipment (except aircraft), all motors and engines, and electronic equipment.

---

regulations. Environmentalists interpreted her appointment as a signal that the White House intended to move the agency's sympathies toward business and other regulated interests and away from the environmental groups that considered themselves the agency's natural constituency. Between 1981 and 1983, the administration sharply reduced the EPA's budget and personnel across nearly all programs. Critics charged that the changes had reduced the agency's budget by 30 percent and its employees by 23 percent during this period.[48] Environmentalists and their congressional allies in both parties, by now a durable coalition, also asserted that Burford and other administration appointees to EPA were attempting to obstruct implementation of environmental regulations in other ways.

By 1983, EPA's internal changes had badly disrupted its programs and demoralized its personnel. The agency's credibility appeared to be damaged and its leadership increasingly preoccupied with congressional investigations and running battles with environmental groups. The situation threatened to degenerate from a White House embarrassment to an electoral liability in 1984. Burford finally resigned after strong White House prompting and soon thereafter most of the other Reagan appointees within the agency followed.

In a more enlightened effort to manage the agency, the president next appointed William D. Ruckelshaus as its administrator. Ruckelshaus, the agency's first administrator, was widely regarded among environmentalists as an able and concerned environmental administrator. His considerable bipartisan support in Congress and strong following among EPA staff brought greater stability, an end to most partisan bickering with Congress, and a modest increase in funding and personnel to the agency. Environmentalists generally approved, as well, when Lee Thomas, an experienced, highly competent career EPA employee, replaced Ruckelshaus in 1985. Under Ruckelshaus and Thomas, the EPA restored a measure of credibility to its regulatory enforcement. The budget and staff resources also improved and the agency's political woes were no longer major media fare. At the same time, environmentalists complained that the agency's resources had not kept pace with its growing regulatory responsibilities and mounting environmental problems. And many were convinced that the agency was still tardy and half-hearted in implementing its programs and would stay so until the Reagan administration left office.

President Bush's appointment of William K. Reilly, a veteran, highly respected environmental leader, as EPA's new administrator and the president's generally conciliatory attitude toward environmental groups seemed a portent of better times for the EPA. The Bush administration seemed to assign environmental issues, including especially acid rain, climate warming, and tropospheric ozone depletion, a high priority in its legislative agenda. Yet many environmentalists remained skeptical that the Bush administration would advocate the politically tough policies that seemed essential to deal with environmental ills in the 1990s. Nonetheless, EPA's leadership seemed to most environmentalists to be in far better shape than it had been at the start of the Reagan administration.

The Occupational Safety and Health Administration

Created in 1970 to write and enforce regulations to implement the Occupational Safety and Health Act, OSHA is located within the Department of Labor and headed by an assistant secretary nominated by the president. The agency's responsibilities guarantee that it will be embroiled in political controversy. These responsibilities include improving safety standards in the workplace, creating rights for employees and employers to improve workplace health and safety, maintaining records of job-related injuries and illness, developing and enforcing mandatory job safety and health standards, monitoring federal agency safety programs, and much more.[49]

During the first six years of its operation, OSHA adopted thousands of rules for workplace safety that provoked continual criticism from both business and labor. Business complained that the standards were too often complex, trivial, or incomprehensible. And, so the complaint went, OSHA was heedless about the costs of its regulations. Labor unions asserted that the agency was too slow and indecisive in enforcing its regulations. What seemed clear was that the agency had to set safety standards for many workplace hazards with inadequate data about safe levels of exposure. In these many instances, OSHA often decided to limit exposure to the lowest levels technologically possible—the most conservative approach. Critics charged that these standards were prohibitively expensive and scientifically indefensible. In fact, OSHA was grappling with a problem inherent in its mission. Among the different factions concerned with OSHA's work, there is no commonly accepted calculus for deciding how regulatory costs are to be weighed against worker health or safety when determining appropriate policies. Rather, Congress, the courts, and the White House have imposed differing standards, often at the same time.[50]

Between 1976 and 1980, the Carter administration encouraged major changes in OSHA's operations. Rules and regulations were simplified, hundreds of workplace standards were revoked or relaxed, and unannounced workplace inspections—an infuriating practice to small business, especially—were reduced. OSHA's authority was further limited when Congress exempted more than 1.5 million small businesses with an estimated 5 million workers from OSHA's regulations and the Supreme Court ruled that employers had a right to refuse access to OSHA inspectors. Also, the agency discovered in the latter 1970s that it would get much more political support by concentrating on health hazards widely publicized in the media or a special concern to specific unions. By the early 1980s, writes John M. Mendeloff, "most of OSHA's choices about which hazards to address reflected the sustained interests of particular unions: asbestos (a broad coalition of unions), coke oven emissions (Steelworkers Union), arsenic (Steelworkers Union), benzene (Oil, Chemical and Atomic Workers Union), cotton dust (Textile Workers Union, backed by the AFL-CIO), and lead (Steelworkers Union)."[51]

OSHA's fate in the Bush administration remains problematic. The Reagan administration brought a strong shift of emphasis to OSHA. Cutbacks in personnel and budget greatly reduced OSHA's inspection and enforcement actions and slowed its pace of standard setting. Labor unions and environmentalists charged that OSHA's leadership was deliberately obstructing program implementation and gutting its resources in response to business pressures. Although environmentalists and unions were able to compel OSHA to take some major enforcement actions by appealing to the courts, environmentalists and many congressional critics in both parties believed that "regulatory relief" had left OSHA hobbled and half-hearted in implementing its responsibilities. Most of these critics believed OSHA's vigor would improve with the Bush administration. Early statements by administration spokesmen suggested that it viewed OSHA's work more sympathetically than had the Reagan administration. Whether OSHA would receive increased funding, personnel, and freedom from White House antiregulatory pressures—the tangible stuff that turns promises into realities—was not apparent.

The Council on Environmental Quality

The National Environmental Policy Act included a provision for the establishment of a commission to advise the president on environmental matters. To be headed by three members appointed by the president, the Council on Environmental Quality was to be part of the president's staff. Among the major responsibilities prescribed for the council in section 203 of NEPA were (1) to gather for the president's consideration "timely and authoritative information concerning the conditions and trends in the quality of the environment both current and prospective"; (2) "to develop and recommend to the President national policies to foster and promote the improvement of environmental quality"; and (3) "to review and appraise the various programs and activities of the Federal Government" to determine the extent to which they comply, among other things, with the requirement for writing EISs. Thus the CEQ was created, like other major presidential advisory commissions, to provide policy advice and evaluation from within the White House directly to the president.

Ever since its first year of operation in 1971, the CEQ has published a widely distributed and densely documented annual report, a periodic appraisal of major environmental trends, issues, and new developments. The council also administers the process for writing and reviewing EISs within the federal government. Although the CEQ is a small agency with no regulatory responsibilities or major environmental programs beyond modest research activities, it assumes enormous symbolic importance and political value to environmental interests. Its presence within the White House implies a high national priority to environmental programs, and the council's opportunities to influence the president directly mean that it can act, in the words of environmental leader Russell Peterson, as "the environmental conscience of the executive branch." Nonetheless, like all other presidential advisory bodies, it can exercise no more influence in White House decisions than the president cares to give it; it may carry on its NEPA-mandated activities, but the president is free to ignore any of its recommendations or other initiatives.

The CEQ's rapid decline in status between the Carter and Reagan administrations illustrates how much its effectiveness depends upon presidential favor. The council enjoyed considerable influence under President Carter, a strong environmentalist, but its influence plummeted rapidly during the Reagan administration. One of Reagan's earliest acts after his inauguration was to reduce the CEQ's staff from forty-nine to fifteen and its budget by 50 percent; the symbolism was obvious to environmentalists.[52] CEQ's publications and other research activities immediately declined in number and quality. The president waited almost three years to appoint the council's third member. Throughout the remainder of the Reagan administration, the CEQ seemed to inhabit a White House nether region where it was seldom seen or heard. Environmentalists hoped that President Bush's pledges of environmental concern prophesied better days for the CEQ in the 1990s.

The Department of the Interior

Established as a Cabinet-level department in 1845, the Department of the Interior has acquired responsibilities over more than a century that leave few national environmental issues untouched. The department's important environmental responsibilities include (1) protection and management of more than 549 million acres of public land—roughly 28 percent of the total U.S. land area—set aside by Congress for national parks, wilderness areas, forests, and other restricted use; (2) administration of Indian lands and federal Indian programs, including authority over western tribal lands containing a very large proportion of the coal, petroleum, uranium, and other largely unexploited energy resources in the western United States; (3) enforcement of federal surface mining regulations through its Office of Surface Mining; (4) conservation and management of wetlands and estuarine areas; and (5) protection and preservation of wildlife, including endangered species. Headed by a cabinet secretary appointed by the president, the department's programs historically have been a primary concern to environmentalists; the interior secretary, although not always identified with the environmental or conservationist movements, in recent decades has been compatible with their interests.

At the beginning of the Reagan administration, the Department of the Interior—and particularly Reagan's first choice as the department's secretary, James Watt—became the source of continual controversy as a result of its efforts to make sweeping changes in personnel and programs. Critics charged that the department's programs to protect the environment had been placed on the agenda for an administration "hit list" applied by Secretary Watt. The secretary, more than any other official, epitomized to environmentalists all that seemed wrong with the Reagan administration's environmental record; he became the movement's archvillain. Watt, who seemed to relish bare-knuckle political brawls, insisted he had a public mandate to accomplish long-overdue reforms thwarted—until the Reagan administration—by a small clique of selfish and narrow-minded environmental interests.

These controversies were rooted in environmental groups' strong convictions about the nature of the department that shaped their response to any departmental leadership. Environmentalists maintain that the Interior Department's leadership, like the EPA's, should be acceptable to the environmental movement and reasonably supportive of the department's programs. Watt's political associations prior to his appointment, including especially his leadership of a conservative public interest law firm representing many corporations and state governments opposing federal regulation, seemed enough to disqualify him for office in the environmentalist view. Watt's subsequent actions seemed to vindicate the environmentalists' worst premonitions. He proposed to accelerate oil and gas exploration on the outer continental shelf, open more federal lands to fossil fuel development, give concessionaires in the national parks wider influence in making park policies, and give the states greater control over federal lands within their boundaries. The enforcement staff for surface-mine regulation was gutted. Numerous persons previously critical of programs to protect resources were appointed to administer those programs.

The department has always been a battleground between interests seeking to conserve the resources in the public domain and those seeking generous access to them. The department's mandate to ensure "balanced use" of resources between conservation and development—a mandate that continually thrusts the department and its secretary into a storm of controversy concerning which use shall dominate—is a certain source of trouble for every secretary. Moreover, the department's programs serve a clientele including not only environmentalists, but also the timber and cattle industries, mining companies, sportsmen, a multitude of private corporations, and many other interests who expect the department to be solicitous of their viewpoints. Finally, the western states historically have maintained that they have not been given sufficient voice in the administration of the federal lands that often constitute the vast majority of land within their boundaries. The desire of these states to assume greater control over the public domain within their jurisdictions and the resulting tensions with Washington will outlive any administration.

But Watt's strident conflicts were unusually nasty, even for the occupant of an office rich in controversy. In October 1983, James Watt, having accumulated too many enemies for White House tolerance, resigned his position, the victim of his own ideological and rhetorical intemperance. Republicans and environmentalists both lost their best fund raiser. In an effort to diminish controversy, Reagan replaced Watt with Judge William P. Clark; he was followed by Donald P. Hodel, a former secretary of energy. Hodel successfully removed the department from the headlines and took a more conciliatory approach to its environmental critics. Environmentalists, convinced that only the leadership style had changed, continued to assert that the department was hostile to conservation values and the regulatory programs intended to promote them. Environmental spokesmen were convinced that the department's political leadership had worked until the Reagan administration's end to implement policies that would accomplish Jim Watt's objectives.

The Nuclear Regulatory Commission

The NRC was created by Congress in 1976 to assume the regulatory responsibilities originally vested in the Atomic Energy Commission (AEC). An independent agency with five commissioners appointed by the president, the NRC regulates most nonmilitary uses of nuclear facilities and materials. The commission's major activities related to the environment include the (1) regulation of the site choice, construction, operation, and security of all civilian nuclear reactors; (2) designation and supervision of all nuclear waste repositories; (3) regulation of uranium mining and milling facilities; and (4) closing of civilian nuclear facilities after their use (called decommissioning). In 1989 the NRC employed about 3,500 individuals with a budget of approximately $420 million.

Environmental groups have been most concerned with the NRC's supervision of nuclear power plants and repositories for radioactive wastes. Although 124 nuclear plants were operating or approved for construction by 1990, the majority of these have been criticized by environmental groups for alleged deficiencies in structural safety, control of radioactive emissions, and waste storage.[53] Additionally, environmental groups have often been very aggressive in seeking NRC safety reviews of operating plants and personnel training procedures. The NRC will assume a major responsibility for the review of site selection and the supervision of waste disposal at the nation's first permanent nuclear waste repository at Yucca Flats, Nevada. Environmental groups regard the process of site construction and waste disposal as a major issue of the 1990s.

The NRC and environmental groups have been adversaries and allies. The environmental movement generally has supported the NRC's stricter enforcement and review of regulations for operating nuclear facilities and its increasingly rigorous standards for new facility licensing. Yet environmentalists also have criticized the NRC for allegedly siding too often with the nuclear power industry against its critics, for bureaucratic inertia and conservatism, and for ignoring technical criticism and data from sources not associated with the nuclear power industry or the commission. Like other regulatory agencies, the NRC is bound to its own clientele—the nuclear power industry—by professional associations, common technical and economic concerns, and historic sympathies; it is also committed to regulating the industry in the public interest while maintaining sufficient objectivity and disengagement from the nuclear power movement to do that job. These often conflicting responsibilities lead the NRC into controversies with environmental interests. Nonetheless, the NRC and its mission remain among the most environmentally significant elements in the executive branch.

The Department of Energy

Despite its size and importance the Department of Energy (DOE) has been the stepchild of the executive branch. Widely criticized and burdened with difficult and often unpopular programs, the department continues to exist largely because Congress cannot agree upon how to replace it. The department was created in 1976 when Congress combined a number of independent agencies with programs already operating in other departments in order to bring the federal government's sprawling energy activities within a single bureaucratic structure. Under the DOE's jurisdiction are a number of regulatory activities and energy programs affecting the environment. Among these, the more important include the (1) promotion of civilian nuclear power activities; (2) regulation of military nuclear facilities and radioactive wastes; (3) administration of the federal government's research and development programs in energy production and conservation; (4) regulation of price controls for domestic petroleum and natural gas; and (5) administration of federal research and development grants for commercial synthetic fuels production in the United States. With approximately 18,700 employees and a budget of $10.5 billion in 1988, the DOE is the principal executive agency involved in the regulation and production of many different energy technologies with significant environmental impacts.

From its inception, the DOE lacked strong leadership and internal stability.[54] Its important research and development programs were plagued by delays, maladroit administration, and controversy. Constant internal reorganizations left the agency's staff demoralized and confused about its mission and viability. Nonetheless, the DOE's authority embraces a multitude of programs with potentially significant impacts for the 1990s, including research and development of energy conservation, technology, the siting of nuclear waste facilities, and supervision of the military reactors and other installations involved in manufacturing atomic weapons.

In the waning days of the Reagan administration, the military nuclear weapons program, inherited from the Atomic Energy Commission, suddenly erupted into controversy and hurled the DOE into a crisis that will impact environmental politics throughout the 1990s. Beginning in late 1987, the DOE reluctantly revealed evidence of gross mismanagement, deliberate deception, and suppression of information continuing for decades at almost all its fourteen military nuclear facilities. Dangerous technology problems forced the DOE to shut down major military reactors at the Savannah River (Georgia), Hanford (Washington), and Aiken (South Carolina) facilities. Large amounts of dangerous radioactive waste were discovered to have been leaking for many years from failing containment structures at the nuclear fuel processing plants at Rocky Flats, Colorado, and Fernald, Ohio. In mid-1988, documents revealed that the AEC had concealed evidence of major accidents and failures at nuclear facilities during the 1950s and 1960s.[55] In late 1988, Secretary of Energy John S. Herrington conceded that severe problems existed in the management of the DOE's military reactor program and cited the severe cuts in the budget and staff of the nuclear safety programs within DOE in the early 1980s as the primary cause. When the military reactors might be reactivated was problematic. The damage to public health from uncontrolled releases of radioactive materials at the installation sites had to be assessed and remedied.

This legacy of mismanagement burdened the new Bush administration with huge political and economic problems. The nation's military weapons programs would be dangerously crippled if the military reactors could not be reactivated and replaced. The reckless release of radioactive wastes and suppression of information about site management were likely to involve criminal negligence. Estimates of cleanup costs at the military facilities—highly speculative at best—exceeded $150 billion. Residents at high risk of exposure to uncontrolled radioactive wastes from the sites were outraged; as were the affected state and local governments. This was more high-visibility bad news for an agency with a talent for collecting misfortune.

Conclusion

In an important sense, environmental degradation is a twentieth-century problem resolved according to eighteenth-century rules: fundamental government arrangements such as institutional checks and balances, interest group liberalism, congressional localism, and much else reviewed in this chapter are explicitly created by the Constitution or implicit in its philosophy. In contrast, bureaucracy has imparted to environmental policy making, as to other federal policies, a distinctly twentieth-century character; administrative politics are now as fundamental in shaping environmental policy as any other, older element in the Constitution.

The explosive growth within the last few decades of federal environmental legislation, together with a specialized environmental bureaucracy, has added distinctly new elements to the federal policy cycle and indicates that environmental management has become a permanent new policy domain within federal and state governments with its own set of institutional and political biases. In short, environmental policy making today occurs within a context of many political givens whose collective impact upon the substance of environmental policy has been the focus of this chapter.

Notes

1. *New York Times*, May 8, 1989.
2. Ibid.
3. *New York Times*, May 9, 1989.
4. Hugh Heclo, "Issue Networks and the Executive Establishment," in *The New American Political System*, ed. Anthony King (Washington, D.C.: American Enterprise Institute, 1979), 89.
5. Charles O. Jones, *An Introduction to Public Policy* (North Scituate, Mass.: Duxbury Press, 1978), chap. 2.
6. Roger W. Cobb and Charles D. Elder, *Participation in American Politics* (Baltimore: Johns Hopkins University Press, 1972), 86.
7. *New York Times*, July 23, 1988.
8. Eugene Bardach, *The Implementation Game* (Cambridge, Mass.: MIT Press, 1971), 36.
9. Peter deLeon, "A Theory of Termination in the Policy Process: Rules, Rhymes and Reasons" (Paper delivered at the annual meeting of the American Political Science Association, Washington, D.C., September 1–4, 1977), 2.
10. Richard E. Neustadt, *Presidential Power* (New York: Wiley, 1960).
11. Morton Grodzins, "The Federal System," in *American Federalism in Perspective*, ed. Aaron Wildavsky (Boston: Little, Brown, 1967), 257.
12. Ibid. See also Charles E. Davis and James P. Lester, "Federalism and Environmental Policy," in *Environmental Politics and Policy: Theories and Evidence*, ed. James P. Lester (Durham, N.C.: Duke University Press, 1989), 57–86; and James P. Lester, "A New Federalism? Environmental Policy in the States," in *Environmental Policy in the 1990s*, ed. Norman J. Vig and Michael Kraft (Washington, D.C.: Congressional Quarterly, 1990), 59–80.

13. This mingling of private and public power is well explored in Grant McConnell, *Private Power and American Democracy* (New York: Vintage Books, 1967). See also Helen M. Ingram and Dean E. Mann, "Interest Groups and Environmental Policy," in *Environmental Politics and Policy*, 135–157.
14. James V. DeLong, "How to Convince an Agency," *Regulation* (September/October 1982):31.
15. Graham Allison, *The Essence of Decision* (Boston: Little, Brown, 1971), 163.
16. Charles A. Lindblom, "The Science of 'Muddling Through,' " *Public Administration Review* (Spring 1959): 86.
17. The reasons for this departure are examined carefully in J. Clarence Davies III and Charles F. Lettow, "The Impact of Federal Institutional Arrangements," in *Federal Environmental Law*, ed. Erica L. Dolgin and Thomas G. P. Guilbert (St. Paul, Minn.: West Publishing, 1974), 26–191.
18. Theodore Lowi, "The Public Philosophy: Interest Group Liberalism," *American Political Science Review* (March 1967): 18.
19. McConnell, *Private Power*, 162.
20. Charles A. Lindblom, *The Policy Making Process*, 2d ed. (Englewood Cliffs, N.J.: Prentice-Hall, 1980), 73.
21. Ralph Huitt, "Political Feasibility," in *Policy Analysis in Political Science*, ed. Ira Sharkansky (Chicago: Markham Publishing, 1970), 410.
22. Richard P. Nathan, *The Administrative Presidency* (New York: Wiley, 1983), chaps. 1, 5, 6. See also Edward Paul Fuchs, *Presidents, Management and Regulation* (Englewood Cliffs, N.J.: Prentice-Hall, 1988), chaps. 4, 5; Peter M. Benda and Charles H. Levine, "Reagan and the Bureaucracy: The Bequest, the Promise, and the Legacy," in *The Reagan Legacy*, ed. Charles O. Jones (Chatham, N.J.: Chatham House, 1988), 102–142; Jerry W. Calvert, "Party Politics and Environmental Policy," in *Environmental Politics and Policy*, 158–178; and Norman J. Vig, "Presidential Leadership: From the Reagan to the Bush Administration," in *Environmental Policy in the 1990s*, 33–58.
23. Executive Office of the President, Council on Environmental Quality (CEQ), *Environmental Quality, 1986* (Washington, D.C.: Government Printing Office, 1988).
24. John C. Whittaker, "Earth Day Recollections: What It Was Like When the Movement Took Off," *EPA Journal* 14, no. 6 (July/August 1988): 14.
25. Margaret Kriz, "Fuming over Fumes," *National Journal*, November 26, 1988, 3008.
26. Robert W. Crandall and Paul R. Portney, "Environmental Policy," in *Natural Resources and the Environment: The Reagan Approach*, ed. Paul Portney (Washington, D.C.: Urban Institute Press, 1984), 56.
27. U.S. Department of Commerce, Bureau of the Census, *Statistical Abstract of the United States, 1989* (Washington, D.C.: Government Printing Office, 1989), 204–205.
28. Ibid.
29. Ralph Huitt, "Political Feasibility," in *Policy Analysis in Political Science*, ed. Ira Sharkansky (Chicago: Markham Publishing, 1970), 414.
30. Barry G. Rabe, *Fragmentation and Integration in State Environmental Management* (Washington, D.C.: Conservation Foundation, 1986), 16–17; see also Michael E. Kraft, "Congress and Environmental Policy," in *Environmental Politics and Policy*, 179–211.
31. *New York Times*, November 5, 1981.
32. R. Douglas Arnold, *Congress and the Bureaucracy* (New Haven: Yale University Press, 1979), 133.
33. Lawrence Mosher, "Clean Water Requirements Will Remain Even if the Federal Spigot Is Closed," *National Journal*, May 16, 1981, 874–878.
34. *National Journal*, November 21, 1981, 2078.
35. David D. Doniger, *The Law and Policy of Toxic Substances Control* (Baltimore: Johns Hopkins University Press, 1978), 3.
36. U. S. General Accounting Office, "Cleaning Up Nuclear Facilities—An Aggressive and United Federal Program Is Needed," Report no. GAO/EMD-82-40 (May 25,

1982), v. See also Walter A. Rosenbaum, "The Bureaucracy and Environmental Policy," in *Environmental Politics and Policy,* 212–237.

37. U. S. General Accounting Office, "Groundwater Quality: State Activities to Guard Against Contaminants," Report no. GAO/PEMD-88-5 (February 1988), 13.

38. CEQ, *Environmental Quality, 1985,* 230.

39. Werner J. Grunbaum, *Judicial Policymaking: The Supreme Court and Environmental Quality* (Morristown, N.J.: General Learning Press, 1976), 31. See also Lettie McSpadden Wenner, "The Courts and Environmental Policy," in *Environmental Politics and Policy,* 261–288.

40. R. Shep Melnick, *Regulation and the Courts: The Case of the Clean Air Act* (Washington, D.C.: Brookings Institution, 1983), 73.

41. Ibid., especially chap. 4.

42. Grunbaum, *Judicial Policymaking.*

43. Lettie McSpadden Wenner, "Interest Group Litigation and Environmental Policy," *Policy Studies Journal* (June 1983): 674.

44. See summaries of NEPA litigation in the 1980 and 1981 CEQ annual reports; see also Richard A. Liroff, "NEPA Litigation in the 1970s: A Deluge or a Dribble?" *Natural Resources Journal* (April 1981): 315–330.

45. John H. Trattner, *The Prune Book: The 100 Toughest Management and Policy-Making Jobs in Washington* (Lanham, Md.: Madison Books, 1988), 250.

46. Ibid., 249.

47. U.S. Department of Commerce, Bureau of the Census, *Statistical Abstract, 1989,* 318, 321.

48. Conservation Foundation, *State of the Environment, 1982* (Washington, D.C.: Conservation Foundation, 1982), chap. 9.

49. Congressional Quarterly, *Congressional Quarterly's Washington Information Directory, 1988–1989* (Washington, D.C.: Congressional Quarterly, 1988), 410.

50. Congressional Quarterly, *Environment and Health* (Washington, D.C.: Congressional Quarterly, 1981), 94–100.

51. John M. Mendeloff, *The Dilemma of Toxic Substance Regulation: How Overregulation Causes Underregulation* (Cambridge, Mass.: MIT Press, 1988), 147.

52. Lawrence Mosher, "Environmental Quality Council Trims Its Sails in Stormy Budget Weather," *National Journal,* July 24, 1982, 1306–1307.

53. The environmentalist viewpoint may be found in Ralph Nader and John Abbots, *The Menace of Atomic Energy* (New York: W. W. Norton, 1979); and Stephen Hilgartner, Richard C. Bell, and Rory O'Conner, *Nukespeak: The Selling of Nuclear Technology* (San Francisco: Sierra Club Books, 1982).

54. Christopher Madison, "The Energy Department at Three—Still Trying to Establish Itself," *National Journal,* October 4, 1980.

55. *New York Times,* October 27, 1988, November 13, 1989, and December 14, 1989.

Suggested Readings

Harris, Richard A., and Sidney M. Milkis. *The Politics of Regulatory Change.* New York: Oxford University Press, 1989.

Jones, Charles O. *An Introduction to Public Policy,* 2d ed. North Scituate, Mass.: Wadsworth Publishers, 1984.

Lester, James P., ed. *Environmental Politics and Policy: Theories and Evidence.* Durham, N.C.: Duke University Press, 1989.

Melnick, R. Shep, *Regulation and the Courts: The Case of the Clean Air Act.* Washington, D.C.: Brookings Institution, 1983.

Nathan, Richard P. *The Administrative Presidency.* New York: Wiley, 1983.

Chapter 4

To Govern Is to Choose
Institutions, Economics, and Policy Reform

> It was the real world. It was a clarification to me that getting this
> stuff out was going to be a real bitch.
> —William Reilly, EPA administrator, on early opposition
> to his programs in the Bush administration

The echoes of Earth Day had barely faded when the writers of
the Council on Environmental Quality's first annual report, unbruised
by experience, looked ahead from 1970 and saw the future of environmental policy. "We already know what problems are most pressing,"
they concluded. "Clearly, we need stronger institutions and financing.
We need to examine alternative approaches to pollution control . . .
better monitoring and research . . . to establish priorities and comprehensive policies."[1] That first CEQ report made no mention of acid rain,
atmospheric ozone depletion, the Greenhouse Effect, biotechnology,
preservation of biological diversity, estuarine pollution, ground-water
contamination, or growth management, among many other currently
important environmental issues. History seldom respects prophecy. Environmental degradation now looks quite different—more comprehensive, more intractable, more subtle—than it appeared at the beginning
of Environmental Era I. Time also chastens and changes assumptions.
Today what seems most urgently needed is not stronger institutions but
different ones, not alternative policies but *newer* ones, not only better
monitoring and research but also *better ways to use* the resulting data.
    Problems in environmental policy making have become the quiet
crisis of the contemporary environmental movement, as serious as any
global ecological derangement apparent at the beginning of Era II. In
the years since 1970, environmental regulation has become thoroughly
institutionalized through numerous laws, regulatory agencies old and
new, and the development of political structures linking governing insti-

tutions, regulatory agencies, states, environmental groups, regulated interests, and others in a continuing policy-making network. The policy-making process thus institutionalized appears as much a problem as an accomplishment.

When the Conservation Foundation asserted in 1989 that the foremost domestic problem in environmental policy making was "an overarching need to rethink the whole structure of the apparatus that we have in place for solving the problem of pollution and waste," it captured a pervasive sentiment within the environmental movement.[2] In this chapter, two interrelated problems in the structure of contemporary environmental policy making will be examined: institutional design and the economic logic of regulation. In the following chapter we will look closely at the complex procedures and problems created by risk assessment, a decision-making process fundamental to environmental management. These matters have become priority items on any reform agenda for contemporary environmental policy.

Institutional Problems

The institutional problems in environmental policy making appear to be less a failure of institutions to perform as designed than a failure in design, which may be inappropriate to the requirements of environmental policy making. In effect, the government often seems to be mounting a war on modern high-tech ecological degradation armed with policy muskets and bureaucratic cavalry. This disparity between means and ends is apparent in the style of congressional policy making on environmental issues, in EPA's current organizational structure, in the impact of federalism on policy implementation, and in the continuing bureaucratic pluralism and competition in environmental policy implementation.

Congress: Too Much Check, Too Little Balance

In a Madisonian government of separated institutions sharing powers, environmental administrators have good reason to look warily toward Congress. The Constitution invests the Congress with enormous authority over the daily conduct of the president and the executive branch. Congress may enact, rescind, or amend an environmental law. It can use its appropriations authority to alter levels of funding or manpower in a regulatory program; it can reward or punish environmental agencies at annual budget reviews, at congressional committee hearings and investigations. It may use its inherent "oversight" powers to delay or speed a program's implementation. Congress further enlarges its influence through numerous understandings, informal arrangements sanctified by tradition, and assertions of prerogative that administrators ignore at their peril. Members of Congress, for instance, assume that they have a right to look after their constituencies' interests in federal programs like pollution regulation. Thus, Congress collectively and legislators individually become involved continually in the implementation of almost all environmental programs affecting "the folks at home."

Congress has become, as the constitutional framers anticipated, the most potent institution in the intricate structure of "checks and balances" erected about the president and the executive branch. Congress has also become a rich source of delay, confusion, and waste in both making and implementing environmental policy. Most of these problems arise from excesses and exaggeration in the authority the Constitutional framers prudently invested in Congress—a case of checks and balances gone awry. Many of these difficulties could be eliminated or mitigated by a self-imposed discipline of which Congress may be incapable.

A Crisis Mentality.   The congressional response to environmental problems is highly volatile, waxing and waning according to changing public moods, emerging environmental crises, economic circumstances, or today's front-page ecological disaster. Congress easily falls into a "pollutant of the year" mentality, mandating new programs or sudden changes in existing ones according to what pollution problems currently seem most urgent. Thus, the 1978 Love Canal disaster hastened enactment of the Comprehensive Environmental Response, Compensation and Liability Act of 1980 ("Superfund"), and the 1984 chemical plant explosion in Bhopal, India, assured passage of the "community right-to-know" provision in the 1985 Superfund Amendments and Reauthorization Act (SARA).

One result of this crisis mentality has been administrative overload. The EPA and other environmental agencies have often had to implement quickly a multitude of new programs, hastily enacted without sufficient time or resources provided for the tasks. In one six-year period, for instance, Congress required the Environmental Protection Agency (EPA) to implement the Clean Air Act (CWA) of 1970, the Federal Water Pollution Control Act Amendments (FWPCAA) of 1972, the Safe Drinking Water Act (SWDA) of 1974, the Toxic Substances Control Act (TSCA) of 1976, and the Resource Conservation and Recovery Act (RCRA) of 1976. Congress felt no urgency, however, about providing the EPA with the resources commensurate with this avalanche of new responsibilities. As a result, the agency has struggled continually and unsuccessfully to find the means to carry out all the program mandates. This crisis mentality also begets constantly mandated changes in regulatory priorities or program deadlines. One example was the sudden congressional decision in 1977, dignified as a "midcourse correction," to switch emphasis in the FWPCAA away from controlling industrial pollutants (such as suspended solids or oxygen-demanding materials) and toward control of toxic pollutants whose dangers were then becoming obvious. Such changes, however imperative they seem at the moment, are highly disruptive to the orderly implementation of existing laws.

Guidance: Too Much and Too Little.   Behind every major environmental law's impressive facade of high purpose and ambitious action there is likely to stretch a terrain mined with muddled language, troublesome silences, and inconsistent programs. Some of this is inevitable. Mistakes in statutory design will occur because federal environmental regulations address problems of great scientific and administrative complexity with which legislators have had no prior experience. Moreover, members of Congress are typically lawyers, business executives or other nonscientific professionals who depend upon the expertise of administrators to clarify and interpret the law appropriately in regard to specialized environmental programs. The constant pressure of legislative affairs discourages most members of Congress from giving considerable attention to environmental issues, or developing an adequate understanding of them. "It's tough to get Congress to focus on bills with sufficient time to develop an adequate depth of understanding," observed John A. Moore, EPA's former acting deputy director. "You've got 1 or 2 Congressmen who truly know it; there are 400 others that are going to vote on it."[3]

Environmental legislation is often vague and contradictory because Congress cannot or will not resolve major political conflicts entailed in the law. Instead, Congress often papers over the conflict with silence, confusion, or deliberate obscurity in the statutory language. This results in a steady flow of political "hot potatoes" to the bureaucracy, which must untangle and clarify this legal language—often to the accompaniment of political conflict and legislative criticism—or leave the job to the courts. The EPA thus becomes enmeshed in protracted litigation and political bargaining, and program regulations essential to implementing the law often are held hostage to these procedures. Moreover, many regulations can be competently formulated only after research that might require years or decades.

Congressional frustration with the Reagan administration's continual delay in implementing environmental laws lead to the extravagant use of a contrasting legal style equally freighted with administrative difficulty.[4] In the past, congressional suspicion of the bureaucracy occasionally resulted in laws, such as the Wilderness Act (1964), that bristled with mandated deadlines and precise directions about how the law was to be implemented. Since the early 1980s, Congress has habitually in-

cluded extraordinarily detailed and inflexible language in new environmental laws, mandating precise deadlines for the completion of various
programs and describing in exquisite detail how administrators were to
carry out various program activities. The Superfund Amendments and
Reauthorization Act of 1986 is a monument to overcontrol. In SARA's
five sections, Congress mandated 150 deadlines, not only for the EPA.
The boxscore:

EPA is solely responsible for 59 deadlines . . . and jointly responsible . . . for 5
others. The law imposes 14 deadlines on [other] nonspecified federal entities . . .
9 other federal entities are tasked with 48 specific deadlines. The law also imposes
5 deadlines on states, 8 deadlines on local community government groups, and 11
deadlines on private sector business facilities that handle hazardous substances.[5]

One section of SARA contains a provision concerning how local communities are to implement required emergency planning for local facilities
using highly dangerous chemicals. This requires the EPA to set a threshold quantity for the release of these toxic chemicals that will automati-
cally trigger community emergency procedures. If the EPA fails to set
this threshold, however, the law mandates that the threshold will auto-
matically be two pounds—no matter what the chemical. A threshold
this low would almost assure a local emergency response to every toxic
chemical release in a community.

Congressional overcontrol does not leave enough flexibility in the
law when justifiable delays may be essential. Overcontrol practically
assures frequent agency failures to meet some deadlines, thereby eroding
the credibility of programs and agencies. Additionally, overcontrol often
drives agencies to set up their own informal, unannounced timetables
for completing assigned programs and to set their own program priorities
in an effort to deal with the law more realistically.[6] Finally, agency
failures to conform to congressional overcontrol are a provocation to
litigation and further congressional oversight of the programs involved,
thus delaying and complicating rather than hastening implementation.

The Legislative Bluff.   Congress has written into the nation's major
environmental laws a multitude of sanctions, many ostensibly severe,
intended to encourage compliance with environmental regulation and
to arm regulators with the power to compel it. The Clean Air Act, for
instance, authorizes the EPA to impose a moratorium on the construction and operation of any new stationary source of air pollution in any
urban area that fails to attain federally required air-quality standards by
the mandated deadlines; this, in effect, gives the agency the authority
to stop major urban economic development. The CAA also empowers
the EPA to issue documents halting all federal highway construction

funds and other major federal grants to any state with urban areas failing to meet deadlines for compliance with federally required air-quality standards. The Superfund legislation authorized federal and state regulators to sue the creators of abandoned hazardous waste sites to recover all the costs of removal and remedy involved in making abandoned sites safe. The RCRA empowers the EPA to secure a court injunction stopping any activity by any person or firm that endangers public health or safety by failing to comply with the act's requirements for the handling of dangerous substances.[7] And so forth.

Such tough penalties cannot be used routinely. Effective regulation requires that the sustaining sanctions be varied and selectively used. Regulators often need both authority and opportunity to bargain about when and how penalties will be applied to regulated interests failing to comply with the law. Nonetheless, powerful sanctions unused, or merely threatened, eventually become a rusty regulatory blunderbuss, their power more apparent than real.

Congress itself has diminished the credibility of many tough sanctions written into environmental legislation by repeatedly extending compliance deadlines for regulations, thereby sidestepping the sanction problem. Consider, for example, the Clean Air Act's deadline for the nation's metropolitan areas to meet national air-quality standards for ozone or face a moratorium on new factory construction and loss of federal highway funds. Congress first set the deadline for 1976, then extended it to 1982, then to 1987, then to late 1988, then to 1990 to save more than sixty metropolitan areas from sanctions. Once Congress authorized the EPA to extend the CAA deadlines, writes legal scholar R. Shep Melnick, the message was clear: "Congress and the EPA once again showed that they would not stand behind the standards and deadlines previously announced with great seriousness. Every major participant now knows that loopholes will always appear in the nick of time, thus obviating the need to impose sanctions in areas that fail to meet air quality standards."[8] Continuing congressional setbacks in compliance deadlines have also been made for automobile emission requirements in the CAA, in water-quality standards for municipal waste treatment systems regulated under the FWPCAA, and many programs in other environmental laws.

Among the many plausible reasons customarily given for this congressional habit are the legislators' concern about the adverse economic impact of sanctions on the local and national economy, the alleged difficulties in developing the technologies needed to meet compliance deadlines, and the administrative or judicial delays that impede program implementation. Equally important, however, is a lack of political will to face the consequences of the commitments the Congress has made to enforce the law. In effect, the toughest sanctions often amount to little more than impotent fictions in much environmental legislation.

Subgovernments. One of Washington's most venerable institutions is the subgovernment, sometimes described as a "policy whirlpool" or "iron triangle." The classic subgovernment is a trinity comprised of a congressional committee, agency personnel, and an interest group, all united by a common commitment to a narrow policy objective, most often the implementation of some portion of major federal law and the promotion of the interests it serves.[9] Subgovernments vary in durability and membership, but many tenaciously preserve a large measure of influence, if not control, over routine policy making in their own domain. Subgovernments often facilitate communication, negotiation, and consensus building among the different institutional interests involved in routine policy making. They bridge the gap between separated governmental institutions and private interests, often promoting policy implementation and appraisal. Thus, subgovernments often become helpful, even essential, political infrastructures in Congress's daily struggle to carry out its constitutional responsibilities.

Among the most important subgovernments involved with environmental policy making are those joining congressional committees with the agencies over which they have jurisdiction and with the interest group constituencies for those agencies. A number of congressional committees, for instance, possess significant oversight or budgetary authority over the EPA: the House Energy and Commerce Committee; the House Government Operations Committee; the House Science, Space, and Technology Committee; the Senate Environment and Public Works Committee; and the Appropriations Committee in each chamber.[10] Like all congressional committees, those concerned with environmental agencies like the EPA, Department of the Interior, NRC, and OSHA have acquired a strong political stake in maintaining their jurisdiction and their working relationships and understandings with the agencies involved in their oversight. Indeed, the chairmen of many congressional environmental committees and subcommittees—men like Rep. John D. Dingell (D-Mich.), Rep. Henry A. Waxman (D-Calif.), and Sen. John H. Chafee (R-R.I.), and Sen. George J. Mitchell (D-Maine)—have become national figures through their environmental activities.

The congressional committees anchoring environmental subgovernments also have a strong vested interest in perpetuating their jurisdiction over specific agencies and programs. They are likely to resist vigorously any effort to reorganize environmental agencies, or the congressional committee structure, or the environmental laws over which they exercise oversight when such change threatens to diminish committee influence over the agencies involved. This perpetuates the multitude of committees and fragmented authority over environmental affairs in Congress and erects almost insurmountable obstacles to major reorganization of agencies and programs when fundamental change may be essential to better regulation. A case in point is the "integrated environmental management" concept now advocated by many environmental policy reformers and discussed later in this chapter. The environmental subgovernments were "responsible for undermining various consolidation proposals in environmental and conservation management during the early and middle 1970s . . . [and] effectively blocked enactment in 1979 of the proposed Integrated Environmental Assistance Act, which had offered some promise as a source of environmental integration."[11]

These problems are not peculiar to environmental policy. Rather, they reveal historic political values and institutional processes nurtured by the constitutional design of Congress and two centuries of American political culture. The tyranny of the immediate—the congressional tendency to respond to the most compelling problem of the moment and to be preoccupied with the short-term consequences—is inevitable in a legislature whose entire lower chamber and a third of its upper one is elected every two years. Preoccupation with the next election easily constricts the congressional time horizons of most importance to a period of a few years and compels attention to the problems most likely to be on the public's mind at the moment. A desire to sidestep possibly intractable legislative conflicts by shifting them to administrators, or to avoid the threatening political and economic consequences of enforcing the law, is instinctive to all politicians. So is the impulse to hold fast to whatever legislative arrangements give one power and influence. Behaviors so strongly inspired by the fundamental political order become all but immutable.

Some improvement may be possible through relatively moderate reforms, such as reorganization of the congressional committee structure and better legislative draftsmanship in the law. Perhaps, as will be elaborated later, fundamental institutional redesign may be the only solution. But at least two reforms merit brief mention because they deal not with changes in congressional design or habit but with how legislators have been taught to think about the natural order. First, many congressional obstacles to better environmental regulation might be greatly reduced if Congress were convinced that the nation's present environmental ills constituted a crisis of such extraordinary order as to threaten national security and community survival. Second, many legislators might be more willing to forgo their customary approach to environmental policy making if they were individually better educated about the character of environmental problems and how public institutions are helping to solve the problems or to exacerbate them.

EPA's Organizational Structure

"The simple fact is that the Environmental Protection Agency cannot possibly do all the things its various mandates tell it to do," declared the CEQ in 1985.[12] Critics and defenders of current environmental regulation disagree about the solution to EPA's malaise, but almost all agree that the agency is implementing most of its mandated programs inadequately and failing entirely to implement many others. A vocal but small clan of critics favor abolishing the agency altogether. A larger, more influential group advocates abandoning exclusive reliance on the "command-and-control" philosophy presently guiding the agency programs and placing greater reliance on marketplace incentives—of which much will be said in later chapters. Most reform proposals, however, range from relatively conservative alterations in the agency's existing resources and mandate to a radical restructuring of the agency's organization and mission.

Administrative Overload. "By requiring the EPA to accomplish so much, Congress has virtually ensured that the agency's rule-making and enforcement efforts will be inadequate," writes economist David Vogel. "The price the EPA has paid for its successful effort at strict enforcement in selected policy areas—such as control of automobile emissions . . . has been the virtual neglect of its regulatory responsibilities in a whole host of other areas. . . ."[13] The evidence of EPA's current administrative overload is written in the statistics of missed deadlines, lagging research, and impossibly distant completion dates for existing program responsibilities. The doleful litany includes the following:

The Federal Insecticide, Fungicide, and Rodenticide Act (1947) has been amended to require the EPA to evaluate more than 50,000 individual pesticide products containing over 600 active ingredients and 900 inert ingredients. "If EPA has to prepare interim registration standards for all 600 active ingredients," concludes the General Accounting Office (GAO), "then the Agency may finish the first round reviews in about 2004."[14]

The EPA's air program has issued emission standards on less than ten substances of approximately 1,500 thought to be hazardous air pollutants.[15]

The EPA's Office of Solid Waste and Emergency Response estimates that the nation produces 247 million metric tons of hazardous waste and 200 million metric tons of municipal solid waste annually. There are also estimated to be 22,000 inactive or abandoned waste sites, of which approximately 2,000 will eventually be designated as national priorities for cleanup. Cleanups are in progress in about 500 of these cases. Over a million underground storage tanks exist in the United

States, of which an indeterminate number may be leaking. The EPA's underground tank program is just underway.[16]

Confronted with a daunting multitude of program responsibilities, data requirements, testing needs, and program deadlines, the EPA frequently resorts to improvised strategies for deciding which programs and pollutants will get priority. Sometimes it depends upon litigation initiated by private interests—most often environmental groups—to force its attention to specific programs. The agency was able to give priority to a TSCA requirement that it act within one year on recommendations from its experts concerning whether a substance merited testing for carcinogenicity only because the Natural Resources Defense Council sued the EPA and obtained a judicial order for the EPA to speed up the review process. Sometimes the agency ignores portions of the law (perhaps deliberately) to make its workload manageable. In order to cope with the otherwise impossible task of screening 60,000 chemicals presently in commercial use, as the TSCA seems to require, Ned Woodhouse observes that the EPA "simply misinterpreted the law: the agency placed its focus exclusively on new uses of new chemicals. . . . EPA apparently decided (probably implicitly) that its staff and funds were inadequate to cover tens of thousands of existing chemicals."[17] Sometimes agency managers explicitly establish their own priorities among programs.

The Program Integration Problem. The EPA has come to resemble a regulatory holding company, a conglomerate of offices, each focused narrowly on problems in a single environmental medium (such as air, land, or water) or on one kind of pollutant (such as toxic waste). Further, each office is responsible for numerous regulatory laws written with little attention to their mutual consistency or compatibility. "Each program has staked out an environmental problem that it is required to 'fix,' according to the peculiar rules embodied in its statutory mandate," observes the CEQ.[18] The EPA was originally conceived very differently. The advisory council recommending the EPA's creation to President Nixon had argued that environmental policy had a unique character because there were "interactions and trade-offs inherent in controlling different types of pollution." The EPA was expected to be the means to "rationalize the organization of environmental efforts" and "give focus and coordination to them."[19] In short, the EPA was intended to synthesize approaches to specific environmental problems into an "integrated and holistic approach"—which is precisely what the EPA has not done.

Circumstances conspired against this integrated approach from the EPA's inception. Its most grievous fault was its lack of political allure. Congress and the White House, under intense public pressure to do something quickly about specific pollution problems, needed to promote what seemed the quickest solution to the most apparently urgent problem of the moment. Integrated management, in contrast, seemed strange and complicated, too difficult to explain and too unpredictable in results to appeal to Congress or the public.[20]

Also, the media offices concerned with air, water, and land quickly dominated the EPA and defeated most efforts to create more integrated programs; these offices had powerful constituencies while the multimedia programs did not. "Each environmental medium and the separate programs within each medium have attracted politically potent constituencies that are likely antagonists toward any attempt to transform— or integrate—the existing system," notes Barry Rabe. "They include environmental professionals and agencies, representatives of business and industry, and various policy-making committees and subcommittees that operate in Congress and state legislatures."[21] Environmental groups were usually unsympathetic, perhaps because they feared that integrated management would subvert existing programs. Moreover, environmental law usually regulates the impact of specific pollutants, such as threats to public health or ground-water quality, and legislative pressure to produce results gives regulators little incentive to take the longer time necessary to develop more holistic approaches to pollution management.

The segmented approach to pollution management embodied in EPA's organization and programs is often unsatisfactory because it does not effectively deal with cross-media pollution and interactive pollutants. Consider, as an example of the cross-media problem, the task of regulating the hazardous wastes from the nation's more than 3,500 electroplating firms. If such firms are permitted to flush their wastes into municipal waste treatment systems, these wastes (including heavy metals like cadmium, copper, and nickel) can kill the bacteria essential for municipal water treatment. If the heavy metals are removed from the wastes before they are flushed into the municipal system, a toxic sludge is left to manage. In 1984, the EPA decided to phase out the use of landfills for the disposal of these sludges. If electroplating firms then decide to stabilize the waste sludge by mixing it with other agents like cement kiln dust, the poisons may be secured and acceptable for landfill but the metals then cannot be recycled and the wastes create much greater bulk in landfills rapidly filling to capacity. Under present law, these toxic metals will be managed differently according to which medium they affect. Thus, regulating these wastes by one approach creates a new form of pollution and transfers costs from one program to another. Presently, no federal law empowers the EPA to manage these toxic sludges by calculating the costs and risks involved in their migration from one environmental medium to another and by selecting a strategy that creates the least total cost, or risk, when all the different media are considered.

The problem of interactive pollutants is illustrated by the increased health risks that may be associated with metals exposed to acid precipitation. Studies of regions with heavy acid precipitation indicate that metals in soil and lake sediment (such as aluminum, cadmium, mercury, and lead) become more soluble as the acidity increases in the water. Acidified water can "leach metals from soils and lake sediments into underground aquifers, streams, and reservoirs, potentially contaminating edible fish and water supplies. It can also dissolve toxic metals from the pipes and conduits of municipal or home water systems, contaminating drinking water."[22] No current federal program or EPA office exists with the authority to manage acid precipitation through comprehensive study of its multimedia effects and interactive consequences. Instead, acid precipitation is regulated by different methods, according to different criteria, depending on whether it is airborne or deposited in soil, and whether its chemical products affect surface waters.

Developing an integrated approach to pollution management would take considerable time. One obstacle is the lack of reliable, accurate scientific models explaining cross-media pollution processes and identifying the costs and risks involved. Additionally, few scientific professionals are trained in integrated management, and few resources are currently invested in developing such training programs. But the approach has much to recommend it. It would produce regulatory methods that create significant cost reductions, greater overall risk reduction, and perhaps quicker results than the segmented approaches currently applied to pollution problems. It could also encourage greater compatibility and consistency between regulatory programs than now exist, and it might appreciably improve coordination and reduce inefficiencies in the operation of the EPA's present program offices.

Needed: More Money, More Staff. The EPA has been badly underfunded and understaffed throughout the 1980s. Many of the agency's current problems with missed deadlines and laggard enforcement are an inheritance from the Reagan administration's severe budget reductions in the early 1980s. Between 1980 and 1983, the agency lost almost one-third of its budget and more than one-fifth of its personnel.[23] Congress subsequently rejected many additional budget and personnel cuts, but the agency's budget failed to keep pace with the EPA's growing regulatory responsibilities throughout the 1980s. Excluding grants for waste treatment plants and Superfund cleanup, which do not fund agency personnel or program activities, the agency's budget, adjusted for inflation, fell from $1.49 billion in 1980 to about $1.43 billion in Ronald

Reagan's proposed 1990 budget. Agency staff had increased by a modest 3 percent between 1980 and 1988, hardly enough to provide the additional personnel required by new program responsibilities in the 1980s and by unmet staffing needs lingering from the 1970s.[24]

The EPA's research and development (R&D) programs have been a continuing casualty of the budget squeeze. When adjusted for inflation, the agency's R&D budget fell from $395.8 million in the last Carter budget to $319.3 million in the last Reagan budget. With little money to invest in its own research, the agency has been unable to initiate the development of databases essential for anticipated new regulatory problems involving integrated pollution management, or global warming, or a multitude of new chemical substances and biotechnology products. Program enforcement, essential for the credibility of any regulatory program, has waxed and waned throughout the 1980s as funding and personnel were first drastically reduced during the early 1980s and then moderately increased in the latter years of the Reagan administration. (During the Reagan years, the EPA's proposed budget ceased to specify funding levels for enforcement, thus making it more difficult to identify cutbacks.) The lack of adequate funding for agency R&D or enforcement illuminates the continual disparity between congressional or White House professionals of commitment to environmental protection and the actual strength of that commitment when a crisis is not compelling the president or Congress to "do something."

Missing Priorities.   Like the man who mounted his horse and galloped off in all directions, the EPA has no constant course. With responsibility for administering nine separate statutes and parts of four others, the EPA has no clearly mandated priorities, no way of allocating scarce resources between different statutes or between programs within a single law. Nor does the EPA have a congressional charter, common to most federal departments and agencies, defining its broad organizational mission and priorities. While the agency has had to make informal, ad hoc decisions about program priorities to survive, these are much less satisfactory legally and politically than a clear, congressionally mandated agenda.

Congress has little inclination to provide the EPA with a charter or mandated priorities, in good part because the debate sure to arise on the relative merit and urgency of different environmental problems is an invitation to a political bloodletting most legislators will gladly avoid. Intense controversy would arise among states, partisans of different ecological issues within the environmental movement, and regulated interests over which problems to emphasize; the result would be a political brawl sure to upset the existing policy coalitions, which themselves were fashioned with great difficulty. Moreover, setting priorities would invite a prolonged, bitter debate over an intensely emotional issue: Should the primary objective of environmental protection be to reduce public risks associated with environmental degradation as much as seems practical or—as many environmentalists feverently believe—to eliminate all significant forms of pollution altogether? However, many experts within and outside the EPA have argued that unless Congress sets priorities enabling the agency to concentrate its resources on a relatively few feasible, measurable objectives, the nation will be dissipating its environmental resources among a multitude of different programs and objectives with few significant results.

The Impact of Federalism

The Constitution creates more than a government of countervailing and competitive institutions. The tenacious institutional rivalries inherent in the U.S. constitutional system are moderated because, as Richard E. Neustadt observes, the institutions share power.[25] Effective policy requires that public officials collaborate by discovering strategies to transcend these institutional conflicts. So it is with the federalism through which environmental regulations are usually implemented.

Federalism disperses governmental power by fragmenting authority between national and state governments. Despite the historic enlargement of federal powers, federalism remains a sturdy constitutional buttress supporting the edifice of authority—shared, independent, and countervailing—erected for the states within the federal system. "It is difficult," writes one observer, "to find any government activity which does not involve all three of the so-called 'levels' of the federal system." And no government monopolizes power. "There has never been a time when it was possible to put neat labels on discrete 'federal,' 'state,' and 'local' functions."[26]

Environmental programs are usually federalized, and sometimes regionalized, in their implementation, thereby introducing another political dimension to the policy process. Federal air and water pollution legislation is administered, for instance, through the EPA's Washington headquarters, its ten regional offices, and the majority of state governments, which assume the responsibility for issuing to pollution dischargers a permit specifying the acceptable control technologies and emission levels. This two- and three-tiered design ensures that state and regional interests take part in the regulatory process and that, consequently, state and local governments, together with their associated interests, actively pursue their individual, often competitive objectives during program implementation. Even if the states are not formally included in the administration of federal environmental regulations, they are likely to insist upon some voice in decisions affecting them. Thus, states with Department of Defense (DOD) nuclear weapons processing facilities insisted they be consulted when the DOD determined the priority list for site cleanup after widespread mismanagement of nuclear materials was discovered at more than twenty sites in the late 1980s.[27]

Federalism in environmental regulation guarantees voice and influence to the multitude of different states involved, providing an essential representation for various geographic interests affected politically and economically by federal environmental law. Federalism also encourages diversity and experimentation in program administration, at times producing valuable innovation in program implementation. But federalism also multiplies the number of local government environmental agencies issuing permits. In Washington state, for example, there are six state permitting agencies, a regional air pollution authority, five county permitting agencies, and three municipal ones.[28] Regulated interests often complain about the time and difficulty required in getting all their required permits and plea for the creation of a "one-stop shopping" system that would enable them to obtain the necessary permits through one coordinating agency.

Federalism also involves bargaining between federal, regional, and state agencies when writing and enforcing regulations. State governments, in particular, have a habit of using their own congressional representatives to influence federal environmental regulation to their own advantage. Much of the delay, conflict, and confusion in program implementation also arises because state governments have been so adept in persuading their congressional delegations to intervene in the regulatory process on behalf of a state interest.

Few issues arising from federalism in environmental programs arouse state concern as much as federal aid and administrative discretion for the states in program management. Federal aid comes in many forms: grants for program administration, staff training, salary supplements, program enforcement, and pollution-control facilities; technical assistance in program development or enforcement; research cost sharing; and much more. In 1988, the EPA alone provided more than $2.9 billion in aid to the states, mostly in grants for the construction of waste treatment facilities. The states understandably favor generous federal cost sharing in the administration of federally mandated environmental programs. This aid represents a large proportion of the spending on environmental programs for many states and the pressure on Washington to maintain or increase it is unceasing. Many proponents of environmental regulation believe that the amount of federal aid directly affects the quality of environmental protection, particularly in many states where the state governments lack staff and technical resources to implement programs unaided.

The amount of discretion permitted the states when interpreting and enforcing federal regulations within their own borders is a matter of ceaseless controversy in American environmental administration. Generally, the states prefer Washington to leave state administrators with enough discretion to adapt federal environmental regulations to unique local conditions and to be responsive toward local economic and political interests. States frequently complain that federal regulations force them to conform to Washington-inspired rules that are inappropriate, economically wasteful, or politically unfair to local interests.

Assailing Washington for imposing regulations upon the states without respect for local interests is political ritual among state officials. Major state industries and other locally important economic interests affected by environmental regulation usually join the crusade for generous administrative discretion to the states where their political clout may be much greater than in Washington. The "Sagebrush Rebellion" of the early 1980s exemplified the western states' perennial grievance against administration of the public lands within their boundaries by a distant Department of the Interior (DOI). More than half of Alaska, Nevada, Idaho, Oregon, Utah, and Wyoming is federally owned, as is more than a third of Arizona, California, Colorado, and New Mexico. The western governors and their allies launched a determined campaign to persuade Congress and the White House to grant the states much greater voice in deciding how these lands, and particularly their economic resources, should be developed. Both President Reagan and his first secretary of the interior, James Watt, enthusiastically embraced the Sagebrush Rebellion and promised to use their administrative powers to give the states more voice in the DOI's management of western lands. The rebellion proved little more than a skirmish, however, when Congress and the federal courts blocked early Reagan administration efforts to make most of the promised changes and the western states grew apprehensive about the environmental destruction that might accompany massive economic development on the public lands.

The Sagebrush Rebellion was but an episode in the Reagan administration's sweeping campaign to change fundamentally the relationship between Washington and the states in the administration of federal environmental regulations. Bundled together as "decentralization," the key strategies were "devolution" and "defunding"—giving the states more responsibility for deciding how to implement federal regulations while diminishing federal aid for environmental regulation. During Reagan's first four years, federal aid, which accounted for at least half the regulatory budgets in two-thirds of the states, was significantly reduced.[29] Subsequent studies suggest that a majority of states did not replace these lost federal dollars and, consequently, implementation and enforcement of environmental regulations were apparently adversely affected. The states were defunded at the same time Washington enlarged their administrative responsibilities, in effect leaving them with less money to do more work. By the end of Reagan's first term, state disenchantment and congressional opposition virtually ended the reform effort. In one perspective, as David Beam observes, little was accomplished. "No large-scale devolution of federal . . . regulatory functions has been accomplished. Indeed, once the heat of battle dissipates, it is possible that the changes that have actually emerged . . . will be regarded as relatively moderate."[30] But implementation and enforcement of environmental laws had been delayed, or prevented, for more than three years.

The larger issues of federalism raised by devolution and defunding will reemerge again, in some new incarnation. Conflicts over the respective roles of federal and state governments in writing and funding environmental regulations are inherent in the federalized administration of environmental laws.

Bureaucratic Pluralism and Competition

Regulatory politics involves not only frequent bargaining and conflict between federal, regional, and state regulatory agencies, but also recurrent competition between different regulatory agencies. Few environmental problems lie within the jurisdiction of a single agency. Several agencies—sometimes as many as nine or ten—will share responsibility for some aspect of environmental management. Organized interests with a stake in an environmental issue will promote, if possible, a major role for whatever relevant agency is most sympathetic to their viewpoint. Conversely, various interests will fight tenaciously to keep sympathetic agencies from losing their regulatory influence on crucial issues. American farmers fought long but largely in vain to prevent Congress from investing the newly created EPA with the Agriculture Department's former authority for pesticide regulation. The farmers reasoned correctly that the Agriculture Department would be considerably more sympathetic to the viewpoint of pesticide users and hence less inclined to restrict agricultural chemicals than would the EPA. More successful was the Pentagon's campaign to prevent the Nuclear Regulatory Commission (NRC) from inheriting authority to regulate military reactors and nuclear fuel facilities when the Atomic Energy Commission was abolished in 1976. Instead, authority went first to the Energy Research and Development Administration and later to the new Department of Energy—both of which the Pentagon assumed to be more responsive to military interests than the NRC.

Often, regulating environmental pollutants becomes primarily a struggle between federal bureaucracies—perhaps state agencies as well, each with a different viewpoint and constituency. Twenty-five different federal laws concern some aspect of hazardous and toxic wastes, dispersing major authority for their implementation between the EPA, Food and Drug Administration, Department of Transportation, and the Consumer Product Safety Commission. "Federal control of all exposures from the manufacture, use, and disposal of vinyl chloride would have required the participation of five federal agencies and involvement of 15 separate laws," notes Barry Rabe.[31] Just how complicated the bureaucratic infighting over a regulatory issue can become is illustrated by the following story.

In mid-1981 farmers sprayed more than 200,000 acres of eastern Montana wheat land with the acutely toxic pesticide endrin.[32] High levels of endrin subsequently were found in a variety of migratory and native fowl. Residents in sixteen states along the central and Pacific migratory flyways eventually might have been affected by the contaminated birds; several Canadian provinces were also involved. The Montana Department of Agriculture asserted that local residents would be seriously endangered if they were exposed to contaminated soil or ate the tainted birds. The U.S. Fish and Wildlife Service in the Department of the Interior agreed. But the EPA found the pesticide levels in the contaminated birds well below the human danger level, and with an adequate margin for safety. Other Interior Department officials decided that the affected states would have to decide for themselves whether to curtail hunting seasons because of the pesticide. The Canadian Wildlife Service, not waiting, immediately ordered hunters in Alberta and Saskatchewan provinces to stop eating ducks and geese. This multitude of squabbling bureaucracies is testimony to the overlapping authority and competitive clientele that routinely politicize the administration of most environmental programs.

Economic Issues

Controversy over the economic rationality of environmental regulation has been unceasing from the inception of Environmental Era I. Critics—most often the regulated interests—assert that both the process and objectives of environmental regulation are flawed by economic inefficiency, irrationality, and contradiction. Spokesmen for the business sector, state and local governments, and other regulated interests often join many economists in advocating fundamental changes in the criteria used in formulating environmental regulations and in the methods used to secure compliance with them. As regulatory costs and dissatisfaction over regulatory achievements mount, even the environmental movement, traditionally hostile to proposals for economic reform, has felt compelled to examine critically the economic basis of current environmental laws. Controversy over economic reform focuses primarily on two issues: the value of cost-benefit analysis as a major criterion in writing environmental regulations and the effectiveness of marketplace incentives rather than "command-and-control" methods for securing compliance with environmental standards.

The Cost-Benefit Debate

A common complaint about almost all environmental regulations written since 1970 is that the congressionally mandated procedures for setting environmental standards are insensitive to costs. "Cost-oblivious" laws, such as the Clean Air Act or the Occupational Health and Safety Act where cost-benefit considerations are forbidden as regulatory criteria, are cited as examples of legislatively ordained disregard for the economic consequences of regulation. Other laws, such as RCRA, have been criticized for failing to require specifically that regulatory agencies consider costs among other factors in setting environmental standards. In the view of critics, this mandated rejection or indifference toward cost-benefit analysis breeds a cost carelessness among regulators that inflicts economic penalties upon regulated interests.[33]

The Case for Cost-Benefit Analysis. Proponents of cost-benefit analysis argue that it can, at the very least, point decision makers to the most economically desirable, or cost-effective, policies for achieving a regulatory goal. "Even if one objects . . . to basing environmental policy on benefit-cost analysis," argues Resources for the Future's economist A. Myrick Freeman, "it still makes good sense to be in favor of cost-effective environmental policies. Cost-effectiveness means controlling pollution to achieve the stated environmental quality standards at the lowest possible total cost." Moreover, the proponents add, critics of cost-benefit analysis are really objecting to *incompetent* analysis, sometimes deliberately created to produce a desired outcome. Competent cost-benefit analysis can sometimes identify policies that are both economically and environmentally wiser than those currently implemented. A case in point, argues Freeman, are the federally financed water resource developments such as dams, stream channelization, and flood control projects that were originally justified by questionable cost-benefit analyses. He notes that "these analyses used techniques that systematically overstated the benefits and water resource development, understated the economic costs, and ignored environmental costs. The result was construction of a number of projects that were economically wasteful and environmentally damaging and serious consideration of such misguided proposals as the one to build a dam in the Grand Canyon."[34]

When all the regulated sectors of the U.S. economy are considered, so the critics reason, a huge inflationary diversion of capital from more economically desirable uses results. Eugene Bardach and Robert A. Kagan, for instance, cite Labor Department figures suggesting that the standards proposed by the EPA for coke oven emissions might result in a 29 percent drop in worker production in that industry. They also refer to data from the Commerce Department indicating that compliance with federal environmental, health, and safety regulations would cost the U.S. copper producers $3.5 billion between 1978 and 1987, "resulting in slightly lower production, fewer jobs, increased copper imports, and a substantial increase in price."[35] Critics frequently allege that excessive regulatory costs will drive some firms out of business or out of the country. Spokesmen for major national business associations, such as the Business Roundtable and the U.S. Chamber of Commerce, have alleged that excessive regulatory costs have significantly depressed the growth rate of the Gross National Product (GNP).

A commonly proposed solution for these alleged extravagances is the mandatory use of cost-benefit analysis by agencies writing environmental regulations. The intent is to provide regulatory officials and regulated interests with an estimate of the net costs and benefits associated with a particular environmental standard. Few proponents of cost-benefit analysis would argue that it should be the sole criterion for regulatory strategies. Most believe that the routine use of this procedure would make regulators more sensitive to the cost of their regulatory decisions and more likely to select regulatory procedures with net benefits, or with the least cost among alternatives. Many also believe that cost-benefit analysis leads to a better quality of decision making. As Paul Johnson observes, "The value is that it injects rational calculation into a highly emotional subject. . . . It offers you a range of alternatives. Without stringent analysis, nobody knows whether costs imposed by regulatory programs are money well spent."[36] And, though seldom admitted, many advocates hope the publicity given regulatory costs, especially when net benefits are lacking, will deter agencies from choosing such regulations.

The Case Against Cost-Benefit Analysis.   Environmentalists have traditionally opposed the routine use of cost-benefit analysis in setting environmental standards. Some still regard cost-benefit analysis as a categoric evil, wholly inappropriate to the selection of environmental regulations. Others recognize that economic considerations may sometimes merit attention in writing environmental laws, but believe cost-benefit calculations are easily distorted to the advantage of regulated interests. Most environmentalists regard cost-benefit analysis as nothing less than a covert assault on environmental regulation whenever it is used.

Environmentalists assert that cost-benefit analysis often distorts economic reality by exaggerating regulatory costs and underestimating benefits. Regulated interests, the argument continues, often deliberately magnify their compliance costs; it is difficult, in any case, to obtain accurate economic data from them. Further, regulated interests give little attention to the economic "learning curve," which often yields a substantial saving over the full period of regulation as they gain experience and expertise in controlling their pollutants. Benefits from regulation, in contrast, are often underestimated because they are not easily calculated. For instance, how are the health benefits from significantly cleaner air over the next several decades to be calculated? What value is to be placed upon rivers, streams, and lakes made fishable and swimmable again? What is the dollars-and-cents value of an irreplaceable virgin forest conserved for another generation?

Some benefits almost defy monetizing when, for instance, regulations involve the possible saving of lives. An agency may consider regulatory alternatives involving different levels of risk to populations from exposure to hazardous or toxic substances. What is the appropriate value to be placed upon a life saved? A variation of cost-benefit analysis sometimes advocated in such a situation is to compare the costs of regulation with estimates of the lives saved from the different strategies. Such a comparison implicitly requires regulators to decide how much an individual human life is worth. As a practical example, an EPA study of acid rain prevention suggested that stricter controls on air emissions from electric power plants in the Ohio River Valley would cost several hundred million dollars. It also would avert an estimated 54,000 additional pollution-related deaths by the year 2000. Comparing lives saved with dollars spent on pollution controls in this instance makes economic sense only if one assigns a dollar value to each life—a politically perilous act sure to seem arbitrary, if not morally repugnant, no matter what value is assigned.

But perhaps the most persuasive reason for resisting cost-benefit analysis, in the environmentalists' view, is that reducing an environmental value such as clean air or water to a monetary figure makes it appear to be just another commodity that can be priced, bought, and sold. "Many environmentalists," explains Steven Kelman, "fear that subjecting decisions about clean air or water to the cost-benefit tests that determine the general run of decisions removes those matters from the realm of specially valued things. . . . The very statement that something is not for sale enhances and protects the thing's value in a number of ways. . . . [It] is a way of showing that a thing is valued for its own sake, whereas selling a thing for money demonstrates that it was valued only instrumentally."[37] Indeed, environmentalists often believe they stand apart from regulated business through a profound ethical disagreement over the intrinsic worth of wild places, uncontaminated air and water, and other environmental amenities that the movement defends. This conviction of moral purpose imparts to the movement much of its passion and persistence. It also elevates arguments over cost-benefit analysis to the level of ethical principles that makes it so difficult for environmentalists to compromise on the issues.

Cost-Benefit Analysis and the Reagan Administration. The Reagan administration mounted the most determined campaign in White House history to impose cost-benefit analysis upon federal regulatory agencies by means of executive order (EO). Presidents Ford and Carter, concerned about the inflationary impact of federal regulations, had encouraged cost-benefit analysis among regulatory agencies, but did not mandate it.[38] The Reagan administration demonstrated how fundamental cost-benefit analysis was to its gospel of regulatory relief when one of the president's earliest official acts was Executive Order 12291 in February 1981, requiring environmental agencies and all other federal regulatory authorities to produce Regulatory Impact Analyses (RIAs) for all "major" regulatory proposals—new regulations, or revisions of existing ones, with an estimated impact exceeding $100 million. The most important provision of this order was its requirement that "regulatory action shall not be undertaken unless the potential benefits to society from the regulation outweigh the potential costs." Enforcement of this new requirement was left to the Office of Management and Budget (OMB).

Environmentalists were convinced that EO 12291's real purpose was to stifle environmental regulation. Reagan's order affected both the quantity and quality of environmental regulations written during his two terms. Yet EO 12291 never achieved the epic impact its proponents wished because its implementation was flawed from the outset. Several major environmental laws, like the Clean Air Act and the Occupational Safety and Health Act, prohibited cost-benefit analysis or severely limited its application in regulations implementing them (although the EPA spent $2 million preparing an unused cost-benefit analysis for an air-quality standard anyway).[39] Many other regulatory proposals escaped EO 12291 because their impact did not exceed $100 million. Agencies often prepared cost-benefit analyses but, lacking confidence in the results, turned to other criteria for guidance in regulation writing.[40] And agencies showed little consistency in how they prepared their analyses, notwithstanding OMB guidelines.

Experience demonstrated that cost-benefit analyses were severely limited and inherently biased in dealing with environmental regulations because of data deficiencies. A GAO evaluation of EPA's experience summarized the problems:

EPA's benefit-cost analyses cannot provide exact answers to regulating complex environmental problems largely because of gaps in underlying scientific data. . . . This data gap is troublesome in estimating physical measures of the benefits of environmental regulation, such as improvements in water quality or better visibility. Problems also arise in calculating dollar values for these improvements . . . in estimating the costs of complying with environmental regulations. These data weaknesses . . . affect other federal agencies dealing with health and environmental regulations.[41]

None of this troubled the Reagan OMB. It processed more than 2,000 RIAs annually, accepting most RIAs accompanying regulatory proposals and, when possible, using them in arguments for revision or rejection of environmental regulations. It was here that EO 12291 had its major impact on environmental laws. The OMB, together with Reagan-appointed officials in the environmental regulatory agencies, exercised administrative discretion to apply these cost-benefit analyses selectively to some proposals but not to others. Cost-benefit analysis was seldom used when proposals were made to *deregulate* some aspect of the environment or some relevant private firm. The OMB and its agency collaborators often allowed costs and benefits to be evaluated improperly, or their distribution to be ignored, in ways that favored reduction or elimination of regulation. The Reagan administration's use of cost-benefit analysis created a pervasive bias. "Policy evaluation during the Reagan administration proved to be a blatant exercise in the pursuit of actions that helped promote business interests," concludes one recent study of EO 12291. "Benefit-cost analysis. . . became nothing more than the simple addition of business compliance costs. The erosion of the benefit side of the benefit-cost evaluation equation . . . had been finalized during the Reagan Administration. The pretense of weighing benefits with costs to determine net societal costs, as prescribed in Executive Order 12291, was no longer tenable."[42]

Realities and Rhetoric.　　Much has been learned about cost-benefit analysis. The blizzard of econometric data normally accompanying arguments over the cost of regulation is often unreliable. Willfully or not, regulated business often overestimates the costs of regulation and proponents of regulation often underestimate it. Also, as the Reagan experience illustrates, cost-benefit analysis is so vulnerable to partisan manipulation that it is often discounted by officials even when they can consider the economics of regulation. "In executive branch meetings," recalls a former adviser to President Nixon, "the EPA staff repeatedly seemed to minimize pollution costs, while other agencies weighed in with high costs to meet the identical pollution standard. Often, we halved the difference. . . ."[43] Many regulatory decisions are ultimately made on the basis of political, administrative, or other considerations and later sanctified with economics for credibility.

But individual regulations or regulatory programs can impose what appear to be excessive costs. Jimmy Carter, an outspoken environmentalist, nonetheless established in the White House the Regulatory Analysis Review Group in an effort to make environmental programs more economical. Studies of the Occupational Safety and Health Administration under both presidents Carter and Reagan have identified some regulations seemingly too costly for their benefits. Sometimes, costs are grossly inflated not so much by individual regulations as by the multiplicity and unpredictability of regulatory procedures.

All this should clarify at least a few aspects of the cost-benefit controversy. First, there is no substantial evidence that regulatory costs have become so excessive that cost-benefit analysis must be routinely imposed on all environmental regulation programs. Second, there are doubtless instances, perhaps a substantial number, where cost-benefit analysis might suggest better solutions to environmental regulation that would be otherwise selected. For this reason, such analysis should not be categorically excluded from consideration unless Congress specifically mandates an exclusion. Third, it matters a great deal who does the calculating. All cost-benefit analyses should be open to review and challenge during administrative deliberations. Fourth, Congress should explicitly indicate in environmental legislation or in the accompanying legislative history how it expects regulatory agencies to weight economic criteria alongside other statutory guidelines to be observed in writing regulations to implement such legislation. Finally, regulatory costs might be significantly diminished not by using cost-benefit analysis but by using economic incentives in securing compliance of regulated interests with environmental programs.

In the aggregate, regulatory costs have had a very modest impact on the American economy. Few firms have been driven from the marketplace by these costs. Major industries seldom flee states with tough regulatory standards. Although American business spends an estimated $90 billion annually to comply with environmental regulations, most studies suggest that these expenditures have only a slightly inflationary or depressive impact on the U.S. economy. Altogether, the United States has been spending about 1.5 percent of its GNP on pollution control in recent years—a figure most economists would not consider burdensome.[44]

Using the Marketplace Incentives

In 1979 the EPA moved sharply away from the traditional standards-and-enforcement approach to air pollution by introducing its "bubble policy" for controlling emissions from existing air pollution sources. This policy substituted economic incentives for legal prescriptions in an effort to secure compliance with environmental regulation. Properly used, marketplace incentives can be a practical means to reduce the costs of regulation.

What's Wrong with Standards and Enforcement?   The traditional standards-and-enforcement approach to environmental regulation described in Chapter 6 has much to recommend it, but it also has at least two economic flaws.[45] First, it offers regulated interests few economic incentives to comply rapidly and efficiently with mandated pollution standards. In the economist's perspective, standards and enforcement lack an appeal to the economic self-interest of the regulated. Even severe penalties for noncompliance with the law often fail to motivate polluters to meet required pollution-control deadlines. Penalties are often unassessed or severely weakened by negotiation with regulatory agencies. Some firms find it more profitable to pay penalties and to continue polluting in violation of law than to assume the far steeper costs of compliance.

A second problem is that traditional regulatory approaches require the federal government to specify the appropriate technologies and methods for their utilization in practically every instance where pollutants are technologically controlled. Highly complicated, exquisitely detailed specifications that make poor scientific or economic sense for particular industries or firms can result. One reason is that neither Congress nor administrators may have sufficient scientific training or experience to make correct judgments about the appropriate technologies for pollution abatement in a specific firm or industry. Also, regulators sometimes lack sufficient information about the economics of firms or industries to know what technologies are economically efficient—that is, which achieve the desired control standards the least expensively. In general, write economists Allen V. Kneese and Charles L. Schultze:

Problems such as environmental control . . . involve extremely complicated economic and social relationships. Policies that may appear straightforward—for example, requiring everyone to reduce pollution by the technologically feasible limit—will often have ramifications or side affects that are quite different from those intended. Second, given the complexity of these relationships, relying on a central regulatory bureaucracy to carry out social policy simply will not work: there are too many actors, too much technical knowledge, too many different circumstances to be grasped by a regulatory agency.[46]

Examples of costly mistakes in specifying technological controls are not hard to find. Instances occurred in the writing of regulations to implement the Surface Mining Control and Reclamation Act of 1977.

Utah International Inc., a General Electric subsidiary, complained that the EPA and the Office of Surface Mining in the Interior Department required that all runoff from areas disturbed by surface mining must pass through a sedimentation pond although other management practices, such as the use of straw dikes and vegetative cover, would achieve substantially the same results. The company had to build at its Trapper Mine near Craig, Colorado, a $335,000 sedimentation pond when alternative methods could have achieved the same results at 10 percent of the cost.[47]

The Conoco Company complained that Consolidation Coal, a subsidiary, unnecessarily spent $160 million annually to meet engineering standards imposed on surface mines by Washington. The National Academy of Sciences, speaking through its National Research Council, had recommended a different approach.[48]

Bubbles, Nets, and Offsets: Emissions Trading at the EPA. During the last two decades the EPA has approved various schemes, collectively called emissions trading, that created marketplace incentives for interests regulated by the Clean Air Act to control their pollutants.[49] In 1974, the EPA allowed firms creating a new emissions source within a plant to reduce emissions from another source in the same plant so that net emissions did not significantly increase (a procedure called netting). In 1976, the agency approved emissions trading through "offsets." A new pollution source—a coal-fired electric utility, for instance—could locate in a "nonattainment area" (a region not meeting national air-quality standards) only if it could offset its new pollution emissions by reducing emissions from other sources already in the area, such as those from another power plant. It could also buy pollution reductions by other firms in the area to offset its own net pollution.

In 1980, the EPA introduced bubbling, its most ambitious form of emissions trading. This policy assumed "that an imaginary enclosure, or bubble, is placed over an industrial plant. From this enclosure, or bubble, a maximum allowable level of emissions is permitted. A firm in this bubble would be free to use more cost-effective pollution controls than are usually allowed."[50] For example, a firm with three stacks emitting pollution might find it least costly to cut back severely on the emissions from one stack while leaving the others only slightly controlled. If the total emissions leaving the imaginary bubble over the plant did not violate air-quality standards, the firm would be free to decide how best to comply with the law. Advocates of the approach assumed that the result would be a substantial cost saving for the firm and quicker compliance with pollution standards because the firm would be free to choose the solution best suiting its economic self-interest. With bubbling the EPA also allowed "emissions banking," which permitted a regulated firm to earn "credits" for keeping pollutants below the required level. Firms could apply these credits against their own future emission-control requirements, sell them to other firms, or save them.

The results have been inconclusive since air pollutants have been netted, offset, bubbled, and banked. Estimates suggest that the aggregate cost savings for firms have been modest. By the mid-1980s, the 132 federal and state sanctioned "bubbles" had saved firms an estimated $435 million, netting about $4 billion, both relatively small sums when compared to the total compliance costs for firms regulated by the Clean Air Act.[51] Some experts believe that the savings from emissions trading have been exaggerated to the private sector. Others argue that the rules have not been vigorously enforced. In any case, few firms have seized the opportunity to start emissions trading. One reason is that emissions trading requires precise, reliable information about a firm's pollution emissions that is usually unavailable to either the firm or its regulators. Also, many firms avoid emissions trading because of uncertainty about the ultimate legal status of emission credits. The EPA itself is divided and irresolute about the future of emissions trading. Environmental organizations remain almost unanimously hostile to any regulatory scheme, like emissions trading, that appears to create a right to pollute.

The future of emissions trading is clouded. Marketplace strategies in the Bush administration have lost the political chic they enjoyed during the Reagan years, and the economic advantages have never been clear and persuasive to most regulated firms. The implacable opposition of environmentalists leaves the legal status of emission trading problematic. Yet the potential savings suggest that emissions trading is worth a longer trial. Federal and state governments will have to make a major investment of money and personnel to acquire the emissions data essential to increase the scope and appeal of emissions trading to private firms. The states, especially, will have to take greater initiative in encouraging emissions trading. None of this seems predictable in the early 1990s.

Conclusion

To most Americans, the nation's environmental troubles are epitomized by polluted air, fouled water, dangerously unregulated hazardous and toxic wastes, and a multitude of other ecological derangements. This chapter illuminates a less obvious dimension of the environmental crisis that is equally dangerous in its ecological implications: the institutional and economic obstacles to implementing environmental policy effectively. In many critical respects, the institutions and policies the nation now depends upon to reverse its ecological degradation are failing, sometimes badly. Equally as imperative as new technological solutions to ecological ills are new economic and institutional solutions. Finding these solutions will require critical, difficult debate within the environmental movement and among public policy makers at all government levels concerned with ecological restoration.

These problems are especially refractory because they often originate in the fundamental constitutional design of the political system, or in deeply rooted political traditions. Among these problems are congressional overcontrol of the agencies implementing environmental policy, legislative reluctance to create clear mandates and priorities within regulatory programs, the excessive fragmentation of committee control over environmental policy, and the resistance of subgovernments to structural and policy reform. While federalism is essential to the political architecture of any environmental regulatory program in the United States, it also complicates policy implementation by introducing competitive, pluralistic interests.

Other problems arise from the excessive dependence upon traditional policy approaches to environmental problems, particularly the standards-and-enforcement method of regulation and the single-media approach to controlling specific pollutants. While other approaches often seem more appropriate, and in some cases have been tried experimentally, they are strongly resisted by a multitude of institutional, professional, and economic interests with a stake in the status quo. Often, the environmental movement itself has been excessively conservative in resisting policy innovation.

Among the significant economic problems arising from environmental regulation, none is more often debated than the high cost of environmental regulation. As costs continually rise well above expectations, the need to find cost-effective, cost-saving approaches to policy making grows more apparent. While cost-benefit analysis is sometimes a useful strategy for reducing regulatory costs, its serious political and economic deficiencies suggest that other approaches, involving more economic incentives for pollution abatement in the private sector, are likely to be more broadly effective. None of the problems now associated with regulatory incapacity are likely to be solved easily or quickly. But it seems that reform is essential.

Notes

1. Executive Office of the President, Council on Environmental Quality (CEQ), *Environmental Quality, 1970* (Washington, D.C.: Government Printing Office, 1970), 232.
2. Conservation Foundation, *Newsletter* no. 1 (1989): 1.
3. Margaret E. Kriz, "Pesticidal Pressures," *National Journal*, December 12, 1988, 3125–3126.
4. Walter A. Rosenbaum, "The Bureaucracy and Environmental Policy," in *Environmental Politics and Policy: Theories and Evidence*, ed. James P. Lester (Durham, N.C.: Duke University Press, 1989), 214–216.
5. U.S. General Accounting Office, "Superfund: Missed Statutory Deadlines Slow Progress in Environmental Programs," Report no. GAO/RCED-89-27 (November 1988), 3.
6. Richard N. L. Andrews, "Environment and Energy: Implications of Overloaded Agendas," *Natural Resources Journal* 19, no. 3 (July 1979): 487–504.
7. R. Shep Melnick, "Pollution Deadlines and the Coalition of Failure," *Public Interest* no. 75 (Spring 1984): 125.
8. R. Shep Melnick, *Regulation and the Courts* (Washington, D.C.: Brookings Institution, 1983), 378.
9. Louis Fisher, *The Politics of Shared Power* (Washington, D.C.: Congressional Quarterly, 1987), 222–223.
10. Congressional Quarterly, *Congressional Quarterly's Washington Information Directory* (Washington, D.C.: Congressional Quarterly, 1989), 141–142.
11. Barry G. Rabe, *Fragmentation and Integration in State Environmental Management* (Washington, D.C.: Conservation Foundation, 1986), 128–129.
12. CEQ, *Environmental Quality, 1985*, 14.
13. David Vogel, *National Styles of Regulation* (Ithaca, N.Y.: Cornell University Press, 1986), 167.
14. U.S. General Accounting Office, "Pesticides: EPA's Formidable Task to Assess and Regulate Their Risks," Report no. GAO/RCED-86-125 (April 1986), 35.
15. CEQ, *Environmental Quality, 1985*, 14.
16. Ibid.
17. Edward J. Woodhouse, "External Influences on Productivity: EPA's Implementation of TSCA," *Policy Studies Review* 4, no. 3 (February 1985): 500.
18. CEQ, *Environmental Quality, 1985*, 12–13.
19. Richard A. Harris and Sidney M. Milkis, *The Politics of Regulatory Change* (New York: Oxford University Press, 1989), 228.
20. Peter W. House and Roger D. Shull, *Regulatory Reform: Politics and the Environment* (Lanham, Md.: University Presses of America, 1985), 106ff.
21. Rabe, *Fragmentation and Integration*, 126.
22. Sandra Postel, *Altering the Earth's Chemistry: Assessing the Risks* (Washington, D.C.: Worldwatch Institute, 1986), 36.
23. Conservation Foundation, *State of the Environment: An Assessment at Mid-Decade* (Washington, D.C.: Conservation Foundation, 1984), chap. 9.
24. Michael Gruber, "Are Today's Institutional Tools Up to the Task?" *EPA Journal* 14, no. 7 (November/December 1988): 2–6.
25. Richard E. Neustadt, *Presidential Power* (New York: Wiley, 1960), 33.
26. Morton Grodzins, "The Federal System," in *American Federalism in Perspective*, ed. Aaron Wildavsky (Boston: Little, Brown), 257.
27. Conservation Foundation, *Newsletter* (September 1986): 6.
28. Rabe, *Fragmentation and Integration*, 26–27.
29. Charles E. Davis and James P. Lester, "Decentralizing Federal Environmental Policy: Correlates of Federal Aid Replacement by the American States" (Paper presented at the annual meeting of the Southwestern Political Science Association, San Antonio, Texas, March 19–22, 1986). See also Charles E. Davis and James P. Lester, "Federalism and Environmental Policy," in *Environmental Politics and*

Policy, 57–86; and Michael E. Kraft, Bruce B. Clary, and Richard J. Tobin, "The Impact of New Federalism on State Environmental Policy: The Great Lakes States," in *The Midwest Response to the New Federalism,* ed. Peter K. Eisenger and William Gormley (Madison: University of Wisconsin Press, 1988), 204–233.

30. David R. Beam, "New Federalism, Old Realities: The Reagan Administration and Intergovernmental Reform," in *The Reagan Presidency and the Governing of America,* ed. Lester M. Salamon and Michael S. Lund (Washington, D.C.: Urban Institute Press, 1984), 440.

31. Rabe, *Fragmentation and Integration, 14.*

32. *New York Times,* September 13, 1981; September 16, 1981; September 18, 1981.

33. The arguments are usefully summarized in Allen V. Kneese and Charles L. Schultze, *Pollution, Prices, and Public Policy* (Washington, D.C.: Brookings Institution, 1975).

34. A. Myrick Freeman III, "Economics, Incentives, and Environmental Regulation," in *Environmental Policy in the 1990s,* ed. Norman J. Vig and Michael E. Kraft (Washington, D.C.: Congressional Quarterly, 1990), 150, 153.

35. Eugene Bardach and Robert A. Kagan, *Going by the Book: The Problem of Regulatory Unreasonableness* (Philadelphia: Temple University Press, 1982), 28.

36. Paul Johnson, "The Perils of Risk Avoidance," *Regulation* (May/June 1980): 17.

37. Stephen Kelman, "Cost-Benefit Analysis: An Ethical Critique," *Regulation* (January/February 1981): 39.

38. On the history of cost-benefit analysis see Richard A. Liroff, "Cost-Benefit Analysis in Federal Environmental Programs," in *Cost-Benefit Analysis and Environmental Regulations: Politics, Ethics, and Methods,* ed. Daniel Swartzman, Richard A. Liroff, and Kevin G. Croke (Washington, D.C.: Conservation Foundation, 1982), 35–52; and Richard N. L. Andrews, "Cost-Benefit Analysis as Regulatory Reform," in ibid., 107–136.

39. U.S. General Accounting Office, "Cost-Benefit Analysis Can Be Useful in Assessing Environmental Regulations, Despite Limitations," Report no. GAO/RCED-84-62 (April 1984), iii.

40. W. Norton Grubb, Dale Whittington, and Michael Humphries, "The Ambiguities of Benefit-Cost Analysis: An Evaluation of Regulatory Impact Analyses Under Executive Order 12291," in *Environmental Policy Under Reagan's Executive Order,* ed. V. Kerry Smith (Chapel Hill: University of North Carolina Press, 1984). 121–166.

41. U.S. General Accounting Office, "Cost-Benefit Analysis," 7.

42. Edward Paul Fuchs, *Presidents, Managers and Regulation* (Englewood Cliffs, N.J.: Prentice-Hall, 1988), 124. See also Joseph Cooper and William F. West, "Presidential Power and Republican Government: The Theory and Practice of OMB Review of Agency Rules," *Journal of Politics* 50, no. 4 (November 1988): 864–895; and National Academy of Public Administration, *Presidential Management of Rulemaking in Regulatory Agencies* (Washington, D.C.: National Academy of Public Administration, 1987).

43. John C. Whitaker, "Earth Day Recollections: What It Was Like When the Movement Took Off," *EPA Journal* 14, no. 6 (July/August 1988): 11.

44. Paul R. Portney, "EPA and the Evolution of Federal Regulation," in *Public Policies for Environmental Protection,* ed. Paul R. Portney (Washington, D.C.: Resources for the Future, 1990), 11.

45. Thomas G. Ingersoll and Bradley R. Brockbank, "The Role of Economic Incentives in Environmental Policy," in *Controversies in Environmental Policy,* ed. Sheldon Kamieniecki, Robert O'Brien, and Michael Clarke (Albany: State University of New York Press, 1986), 210–222.

46. Kneese and Schultze, *Pollution, Prices and Public Policy,* 116.

47. *National Journal,* May 30, 1981, 971–973.

48. Ibid.

49. Robert W. Hahn and Gordon L. Hester, "EPA's Market for Bads" *Regulation* 11, no. 3/4 (1987): 48–53.

50. Ibid.
51. Ibid.

Suggested Readings

National Academy of Public Administration, *Presidential Management of Rulemaking in Regulatory Agencies.* Washington, D.C.: National Academy of Public Administration Press, 1987.
Portney, Paul R., ed. *Public Policies for Environmental Protection.* Washington, D.C.: Resources for the Future, 1990.
———. *Natural Resources and the Environment: The Reagan Record.* Washington, D.C.: Urban Institute Press, 1984.
Rabe, Barry G. *Fragmentation and Integration in State Environmental Management.* Washington, D.C.: Conservation Foundation, 1986.
Vogel, David. *National Styles of Regulation: Environmental Policies in Great Britain and the United States.* Ithaca, N.Y.: Cornell University Press, 1986.

Chapter 5

More Choice
Risk Assessment

I just had an eight-hour briefing on fine particulate standards. . . .
Our scientists told me we can defend any standard between 150 and
250 parts per million. So pick a number.
—William Ruckelshaus, former administrator of the EPA

In February 1989 the Environmental Protection Agency (EPA) alarmed Americans, including most of the nation's commercial apple growers, with the ominous announcement that daminozide, a chemical ripening agent used on red apples, posed "a significant risk of cancer to humans."[1] The EPA estimated that the chemical could cause cancer in 5 of 100,000 persons exposed to it over a seventy-year period—a risk unacceptable under current law—and pose higher risks to children. Then came confusion. EPA announced that it would not suspend the chemical's use for an additional eighteen months because test results "did not show conclusively that [daminozide] posed an imminent hazard to human health." The agency explained that it was making the announcement in advance of the actual suspension date to speed the process of removing daminozide, known by the trade name Alar, from the market.

Although Alar was used on only 5 percent of red apples, getting it off the market would not be easy. Food processors and retail food chains might promise to accept no more apples treated with Alar, but the chemical was impossible to detect on apple skins because it penetrated the surface. In addition, Alar could not be removed, or readily detected, in apple juice or other processed foods made with treated apples.

The EPA's announcement provoked a battle over the scientific and administrative wisdom of the decision. Like most controversies over pesticide regulation, the scenario was highly predictable. The chemical's producers, the Uniroyal Corporation, challenged the scientific basis for the EPA decision and announced that it "completely disagreed" with the pronouncement because independent laboratories used to evaluate Alar had found it posed "no significant risk to public health."[2] Representatives for environmental groups denounced the EPA for not banning Alar immediately and charged that the announced policy "would not be protective of children's or the public's health." The president of a grower's trade group, the International Apple Association, protested that "available data have not confirmed any health threat" from Alar. Finally, the experts were heard. Bruce Ames, a University of California biochemist and expert on the genetic effect of chemicals, dismissed the EPA estimates as "worst case piled on worst case and none of it true."[3] Nonetheless, many schools and other institutions feeding children were hastily removing red apples from their menus and consumers were avoiding them.

Several weeks after the EPA announcement, the Natural Resources Defense Council, a public interest law firm, inflamed the Alar controversy by issuing a report alleging that 5,500 to 6,200 children, roughly 5 in every 20,000 children among the current preschool population, "may eventually get cancer solely as a result of exposure before 6 years of age" to chemical residues on fruits and vegetables.[4] Scientific contradiction was almost instantaneous. "Voodoo statistics," concluded the executive director for the American Council on Science and Health. "No evidence [has been found] of even one case of human cancer in children and adults linked to exposure to the minute pesticide residue in food."[5] No matter: sales in the apple industry, usually a $1.1 billion annual business, were down.

The apple was further embattled when the Consumers Union reported in late March that 75 percent of the apple juice samples it examined from store shelves contained Alar.[6] The Processed Apple Institute, the trade association representing a majority of apple juice producers, retorted that its own testing of 4,623 samples from a cross-section of brands produced only eight with detectable levels of Alar. The Consumers Union asserted that its tests were more sensitive to Alar. The Processed Apple Institute responded that Consumer Union's tests were inaccurate and unapproved by the federal government. The thrust and parry continued for months; one side's risk assessments countered the other's. The one certain loser was the apple industry, whose sales did not recover for almost six months.

In the end, which side was correct? The true extent of public risk from exposure to Alar, or to many other agricultural chemicals, remains uncertain; the wisdom of the EPA's solution remains arguable. The EPA's decision was complicated by many circumstances. The agency first received studies in the mid-1970s suggesting that daminozide might cause human cancers, and by 1985 was considering a proposal for daminozide's cancellation. But the EPA's own science advisory board, arguing that data were still insufficient, urged more testing.[7] Further tests on laboratory animals produced both cancerous and noncancerous tumors in mice—but daminozide did not produce tumors in rats. This posed an interpretation problem because both animals were used to assess risks of human exposure to carcinogens. Further, the carcinogenic risk was not Alar itself but a chemical by-product left on food when Alar was heated. And Alar was only one of more than one hundred chemicals used on apple trees in the United States. An average grower might use between six and twenty chemicals in a single growing season. Thus, Alar might not be the most dangerous among these chemicals.

Ironically, the EPA would have had an easier decision if Alar had been a new chemical. The Toxic Substances Control Act (TSCA) would have placed the burden of proving Alar's safety upon its manufacturer and the EPA could have suspended its use with the evidence it already had available. Since Alar was a chemical already in use, the burden of proving its toxicity to humans rested with the EPA.

The final decision was a fabric of suppositions. The EPA had to assume that its animal data were accurate and applicable to human beings with the probabilities it had calculated. The agency had to assume it had enough data to create a strong presumption that daminozide was carcinogenic to humans, even when the data were inconsistent. It had to assume it had sufficient information to prove it was better to accept the risks and costs in suspending daminozide than to tolerate the risks associated with continuing public exposure to the chemical—even though those risks were estimates, at best. These problems were not unique to Alar. They appear in various guise in most decisions to regulate toxic or hazardous substances. The Alar controversy is one episode in a continuing conflict over the proper means for measuring the risks and costs from exposure to a wide range of substances suspected to be environmentally hazardous. This chapter explores the reasons why these conflicts arise and persist.

The Limits of Science in Environmental Policy

Environmental issues draw public officials and scientists into a treacherous zone between science and politics, where collaboration is essential and difficult. Public officials seek from scientists information accurate enough to indicate precisely where to establish environmental standards and credible enough to defend in the inevitable conflicts to follow. Scientists want government to act quickly and forcefully on ecological issues they believe to be critical. Yet science often cannot produce technical information in the form and within the time desired by public officials—indeed, it often cannot provide the information at all—leaving officials to make crucial decisions from fragmentary and disputable information. Scientists often discover that public officials and agencies are unwilling, or unable, to await the slow testing and validation of data before reaching decisions about scientific issues; data are needed now, or tomorrow. And policies often are made, and unmade, without resort to the scientific materials supposed to govern such decisions.

In short, environmental issues often raise difficult scientific and political questions. They compel public officials to make scientific judgments and scientists to resolve policy issues for which neither may be initially trained. The almost inevitable need to resolve scientific questions through the political process and the problems that arise in making scientific and political judgments compatible are two of the most troublesome characteristics of environmental politics.

Science Issues in Political Settings

The growth of environmental legislation in the last two decades is evidence of the federal government's increasing concern with science and technology since World War II.

Legislation concerning atomic power, air and water pollution, workplace and consumer safety, and hazardous wastes all have put before public officials and agencies the need to make determinations of public policy depending heavily upon scientific evidence and scientific judgments. Environmental issues, indeed, routinely require administrative agencies, Congress, judges, the White House staff, and even the president to make these determinations.

The range of scientific judgments required of administrative agencies in implementing environmental programs seems to embrace the whole domain of ecological research.

The Coast Guard is authorized "in order to secure effective provisions . . . for protection of the marine environment . . . to establish regulations for ships with respect to the design and construction of such vessels . . . and with respect to equipment and appliances for . . . the prevention and mitigation of damage to the marine environment." (Ports and Waterways Act of 1972)

The EPA is to set effluent standards for new sources of water pollution so that each standard reflects "the greatest degree of effluent reduction . . . achievable through application of the best available demonstrated control technology, process, operating methods, or other alternatives, including, where practicable, a standard permitting no discharge of pollutants." (Federal Water Pollution Control Act of 1972)

The EPA is required to establish "standards of performance" for classes and categories of new air pollution sources "which contribute significantly to air pollution or contribute to endangerment of public health or welfare." (Clean Air Act of 1970)

Congress, and particularly the congressional committees writing legislation, also may have to resolve a multitude of technical issues. When regulating hazardous substances, for instance, what is a reasonable period to specify for chemical manufacturers to produce reliable data on the human effects of potentially dangerous substances? Is it necessary to regulate air emissions from diesel trucks in order to reduce harmful air pollutants? Is it appropriate to include heavy metals in the list of water pollutants for which standards must be created by the EPA? Eventually judges will be compelled to weigh scientific evidence and render judgment upon environmental issues. Did the Interior Department have sufficient information to file a valid environmental impact assessment on a proposed coal mining lease on federal lands? Do federal standards for nuclear reactors adequately protect public safety as required by law? The fabric of environmental policy is so interwoven with scientific issues that it is impossible to exclude them at any stage of the policy process.

Policy Pressures and Scientific Method

Few public officials are scientists. Faced with the technical questions inherent in environmental policy, officials customarily turn to scientists and technicians for answers or, at least, for a definition of alternative solutions to clarify choices. As a matter of practical politics, solving issues by resort to credible scientific evidence can also deflect from officials the criticism they might otherwise endure—sometimes science alone legitimates policy. But the politician and the scientist live in fundamentally different decision-making environments.

There are significant differences in the time frames for problem solving. "In his search for truth," observes Roger Revelle, "the scientist is oriented toward the future; the politician's orientation is usually here and now. He desires quick visible pay-offs for which he often seems willing to mortgage the future. For the politician in a democratic society, infinity is the election after the next one."[8] Often, public officials are compelled to act swiftly. The Clean Air Act, for example, required the EPA administrator to set standards for sulfur oxides and nitrogen oxides within two years. The Superfund Amendments and Reauthorization Act (SARA), passed in 1986, included among its 150 deadlines a requirement that the EPA issue a plan to implement SARA's radon research program, produce an annual report on radon mitigation demonstration programs, and provide a report on its national assessment of the radon problem in less than two years after the legislation was passed.[9] If a crisis erupts—a newly discovered leaking hazardous waste dump or a potentially catastrophic oil spill—information is needed immediately.

Public officials, moreover, must often craft environmental policies amid continuing disagreement between experts and the public over the degree of risk associated with various environmental problems. Table 5-1, for instance, compares how the EPA's risk experts and the public evaluated various environmental risks. While the public rated chemical waste disposal as the highest environmental risk, the experts ranked it considerably lower. In contrast, the experts assigned much greater risk to stratospheric ozone depletion and indoor radon than did the public. Chemical plant accidents were rated a major risk by the public, but not by the experts. Other major differences are apparent. In effect, these differences amount to two different agendas of priority for environmental regulation. Critics of current environmental regulation, pointing to these disparate views of ecological risk, often argue that public opinion has intimidated policy makers into following the wrong environmental priorities. Many argue that the public needs a much better education in the nature of environmental risks. For elective officials, however, the reality is that what the public believes to be a significant environmental risk can be ignored only at great political risk. In fact, it is difficult for most policy makers to weigh expert and public assessments of risk equally and even more difficult to yield to the experts when they disagree with an aroused public.

Further, the scientist tends to measure the correctness of a policy, when possible, by the standards of experimentation and empiricism. For example, the appropriate standard for an air pollutant would be determined by careful dose-response studies involving animals and perhaps human beings. The public official, in contrast, has to calculate a standard's correctness using several additional criteria: Will it satisfy enough public and private interests to be enforceable? Can it be enforced with existing governmental personnel and budget? Does the standard appear credible? (It must not be so controversial as to shake public confidence.) The public official may be content to set environmental standards within a range of acceptable figures, according to what best will balance political, economic, and administrative considerations. But the scientist may measure acceptability by the single standard of precision; accuracy, not acceptability, matters. Under these circumstances, it is understandable that policy makers and their scientific consultants often disagree about what data should be used, and in what manner,

Table 5-1 *How Experts and the Public Estimate Environmental Risks*

Experts	Public
High to medium risk	
Criteria air pollutants from mobile and stationary sources (includes acid precipitation)	Chemical waste disposal
	Water pollution
	Chemical plant accidents
Stratospheric ozone depletion	Outdoor air pollution
Pesticide residues in or on foods	Oil tanker spills
Hazardous/toxic air pollutants	Exposure to pollutants on the job
Indoor radon	Eating pesticide-treated food
Indoor air pollution other than radon	Other pesticide risks
Tap water used for drinking	Contaminated drinking water
Exposure to consumer products	
Worker exposure to chemicals	
Low risk	
Hazardous waste sites—active	Indoor air pollution
Hazardous waste sites—inactive	Exposure to chemicals in consumer products
Other municipal and industrial waste sites	Biotechnology (genetic engineering)
Underground storage tanks	Strip-mine wastes
Contaminated sludge	Nonnuclear radiation
Accidental releases of toxic chemicals	Greenhouse Effect
Accidental oil spills	
Biotechnology	

SOURCE: Adapted from the *EPA Journal* 13, no. 9 (November 1987): 11.

in policy decisions. Such situations are replete with opportunities for conflict over how accurately and appropriately information was used in arriving at policy prescriptions.[10]

Derelict Data and Embattled Expertise

Controversy among experts commonly arises in environmental policy making. Contending battalions of experts—all garlanded with degrees and publications, and primed to dispute one another's judgments—predictably appear at congressional and administrative hearings. Substantial expert consensus upon environmental issues is rare; policy makers more often are left to judge not only the wisdom of the policies but also the quality of the science supporting the policies.

Missing Data. Why is controversy so predictable? Frequently there is a void of useful data about the distribution and severity of environmental problems or possible pollutants. Many problems are so recent that public and private agencies have only begun to study them. Many pollutants—hazardous chemicals, for instance—have existed only a few decades; their ecological impacts cannot yet be reliably measured. Quite often the result is that nobody has basic information, the kind "somebody ought to have":

No information is available on the toxic effects of an estimated 79 percent of chemicals used in commerce. Less than one-fifth have been tested for acute effects, less than one-tenth for chronic (for example, cancer-causing), reproductive, or mutagenic effects. In mid-1985 the EPA's assistant administrator for pesticides and toxic substances stated that the data bases for many previously registered pesticides were "woefully inadequate and the existing data have not been evaluated by current standards."[11]

Very little information is available to provide accurate estimates of the volume of hazardous waste generated by location. State estimates are so disparate, concluded the General Accounting Office, that they "preclude any conclusive statements about how much waste is being generated within a state."[12]

It is difficult to determine whether the federal Construction Grants Program has significantly reduced discharges from waste-water treatment plants because "little methodologically defensible work has been done to determine the program's effects on in-stream characteristics and other aspects of water quality."[13]

A federal government study of coal waste concluded: "Much of the information presented on coal wastes was speculative and not universally agreed upon. . . . Although coal has been around longer than nuclear [power], its environmental and health effects are not as fully understood. In fact, coal wastes were not even recognized as potentially hazardous until recent years."[14]

Lacking high-quality data, experts often extrapolate answers from fragmentary information; plausible disputes over the reliability of such procedures are inevitable. The scarcity of fundamental information on ecological trends and pollutant characteristics is a major reason why environmental monitoring is essential to prudent policies. However, monitoring is customarily underfunded and undervalued by government because it lacks the political "sex appeal" attracting public interest and official enthusiasm.

Late and Latent Effects. Disagreement over the severity of environmental problems also arises because the effects of many substances thought to be hazardous to humans or the environment may not become evident for decades or generations. The latency and diffusion of these impacts also may make it difficult to establish causality between the suspected substances, or events, and the consequences.

Asbestos, a hazardous chemical whose malignancy has been documented recently, illustrates these problems.[15] Since World War II approximately 8 million to 11 million U.S. workers have been exposed to asbestos, a mineral fiber with more than 2,000 uses; its heat resistance, electrical properties, immunity to chemical deterioration, and other characteristics made it appear ideal to a multitude of major industries. It has been used widely to manufacture break and clutch linings, plastics, plumbing, roofing tile, wall insulation, paint, paper, and much else. Asbestos is also highly carcinogenic. Among those highly exposed to asbestos, 20 percent to 25 percent died of lung cancer, 7 percent to 10 percent perished from mesothelioma (cancer of the chest lining or stomach), and another 8 percent to 9 percent died from gastrointestinal cancer.[16]

This toxicity has become apparent only recently because cancers associated with asbestos do not become clinically evident until fifteen years to forty years after exposure; illness may appear from two years to fifty years later. Added to the incalculable cost of human suffering is the immense economic impact of these delayed effects. By 1984 more than 12,500 liability suits had been filed by 35,000 plaintiffs against almost 300 companies involved in the past use or manufacture of asbestos. One major manufacturer, the Johns Manville Company, has been involved in more than 100,000 lawsuits, with claims in excess of $8 billion.

Many other substances used in American commerce, science, and domestic life are suspected of producing adverse impacts upon humans or the environment.[17] These impacts may be diffuse and latent; conclusive evidence might appear in decades. Yet government must decide whether to regulate these substances now. In effect, experts are estimating the risks from continued use of a substance when the actual effects on man or the environment are largely unknown. Difficult as such calculations are, a failure to act, as in the case of asbestos, may eventually prove so costly in human suffering and economic loss that scientists may be reluctant to wait for conclusive data. Experts also must weigh in their risk calculus the possible irreversibility of anticipated future impacts. These complex and often tenuous determinations lead to honest disagreements over the validity of most risk assessments associated with hazardous substances.

The Risks in Risk Assessment.   The current controversy within the scientific community over the Greenhouse Effect illustrates the difficulties inherent in determining the magnitude of risk from exposure to potentially hazardous substances. The Greenhouse Effect theory holds that an increase in the atmospheric content of carbon dioxide will result in heat becoming trapped in the earth's atmosphere, producing a dramatic warming of the earth. This theory has spawned predictions of polar ice caps melting, Miami Beach being awash in a foot of the Atlantic Ocean, and the gradual changing of the Midwest into a vast desert.

Critics dismiss this scenario as wild speculation, yet responsible scientists can find reputable scientific studies suggesting such apocalyptic visions.

Disagreement arises over how latent and irreversible these effects of rising concentrations of carbon dioxide in the earth's atmosphere might be. The Council on Environmental Quality (CEQ) has estimated, for instance, that a doubling of the preindustrial levels of carbon dioxide in the world's atmosphere would be a significant threshold at which major atmospheric changes are likely. But when will such a doubling occur? If global fossil fuel use were held at existing levels, it probably would not occur until the year 2175. But a rise of 2 percent annually in fossil fuel burning probably would advance the same doubling to the year 2050. And a 4 percent annual growth of world fossil fuel combustion, about the actual growth rate for the period 1940 to 1973, would produce the important threshold in the year 2025, within the lifetime of millions living today.[18]

Which figure is acceptable? The most conservative estimate leaves a considerable period for further study since the problem would not become critical for several generations. But if future world fossil fuel use holds to the pattern of the last quarter century, the problem may become acute within the lifetime of this generation and immediate abatement of world fossil fuel use may seem imperative. Should governments delay, in any case, taking action on the carbon dioxide issue in light of the disruptive and probably irreversible climatic changes to be expected whenever such a doubling happens? "When the 'signal' announcing the gradual global warming due to carbon dioxide has been clearly identified, the change will already be well established, if the climate models are correct," notes the CEQ.[19] By this time, governmental action would seem futile:

It would then probably be too late to avoid continued climate change, should the countries of the world decide to do so. As a consequence of the ocean's extremely slow takeup of CO_2, it is estimated that centuries might then be required to restore present atmospheric temperatures, even if all CO_2 emissions were somehow to stop in the next century.[20]

Inevitably, differing estimates of the latency and diffuseness of the carbon dioxide problem, based on differing technical data, will yield conclusions so varied that one will often seem highly implausible compared with another. Perhaps most distressing to those seeking "objective" and "reliable" data, no such data may be available within decades of the time decisions about the Greenhouse Effect must be made.[21]

Animal and Epidemiological Experiments. Estimates of a substance's danger to human beings, particularly the cancer risks, based on animal or epidemiological studies are a rich source of controversy and confusion. Having rejected most controlled human studies as ethically repugnant, scientists are left with few alternatives in arriving at risk estimates. They may attempt to characterize a substance's danger based on existing knowledge of how chemical carcinogens affect human cells. Little knowledge exists about the precise way in which these chemicals alter the structure and chemistry of cells. One common alternative is controlled animal experiments in which test animals are exposed to substances, the effects monitored, and the risks to human beings extrapolated from the findings.

Animal studies are particularly controversial when estimating the human effects from low levels of chemical exposure—for instance, a dose of a few parts per million or billion of a pesticide or heavy metal in drinking water over thirty years. The human risks of cancer or other serious illnesses will be small, but how small? And how reliable is the estimate? Animal studies do not and can not use enough animals to eliminate possibilities of error in estimating the human effects of low-level exposure. To demonstrate conclusively with 95 percent confidence that a certain low-level dose of one substance causes less than one case of cancer per million subjects would require a "mega-mouse" experiment involving 6 million animals.[22] Instead, researchers use high doses of a substance with relatively few animals and then extrapolate through statistical models the effect on humans from low-level exposure to the tested substance. But these models can differ by a factor of as much as 100,000 in estimating the size of the dose that could produce one cancer per million subjects. A whole litany of other problems attend small animals studies. Failure to observe any response to a substance among a small group of animals does not imply a substance is safe. Animals, moreover, differ greatly in their sensitivity to substances; dioxin is 5,000 times more toxic to guinea pigs than to hamsters.[23] And so forth.

Epidemiological studies depend upon surveys recording the relationship between known human exposure to suspected hazardous substances and the known effects; the investigator does not deliberately expose humans to possibly dangerous substances but does attempt to capitalize upon exposure when it occurs. Such after-the-fact studies have been used to establish the cancer risks of exposure to cigarette smoke and asbestos, for example. Epidemiological studies can establish statistical relationships between exposure to suspected hazardous substances and adverse effects, but they cannot prove causality; consequently they are open to dispute. Challenges often are raised because such studies cannot be scientifically controlled to eliminate other possible factors affecting the results. Some connections between exposure to substances and effects often can be drawn for the general population, observes David

Doniger, but "humans are exposed to too many different substances at unknown doses for unknown periods to permit statistically reliable conclusions to be drawn. Moreover, there are synergistic and antagonistic interactions between chemicals that drastically complicate drawing conclusions about the effects of each chemical."[24]

The Limited Neutrality of Scientific Judgment

Perhaps fifty opportunities exist in normal risk assessment procedures for scientists to make discretionary judgments. Although scientists are presumed to bring to this task an expertise untainted by social values to bias their judgment, they are not immune to social prejudice, especially when their expertise is embroiled in a public controversy. "The more an issue is in the public eye," observes physicist Harvey Brooks, a veteran of many such public controversies, "the more expert judgments are likely to be influenced unconsciously by pre-existing policy preferences or by supposedly unrelated factors such as media presentations, the opinions of colleagues or friends, or even the emotional overtones of certain words used in the debate."[25]

Scientific judgment on environmental issues can be influenced by one's beliefs about how government should regulate the economy, by one's institutional affiliation, or by other social and political attributes. For example, a recent study of 136 occupational physicians and industrial hygienists working in government, industry, and academia, examined the link between their political and social background and their opinion about a proposed Occupational Safety and Health Administration (OSHA) standard for carcinogens. Scientists employed in industry were more politically and socially conservative than those employed by universities or government. The industry scientists were more likely to favor scientific assumptions about identifying carcinogens that would decrease the probability that a substance would be deemed a risk to human health—in effect, they favored scientific premises that made regulation of a substance less likely.[26]

In another study, political scientists Thomas M. Dietz and Robert W. Rycroft interviewed 228 Washington risk professionals—experts on risk assessment involved in environmental policy making—to determine if a relationship existed between their professional judgments in risk assessment and their social, political, and institutional background. Among the many linkages discovered, they found that "place of employment is significantly linked to differences in . . . the use of both risk and cost-benefit analysis," and that once risk professionals became involved in policy making there was "a weakening of disciplinary perspectives and a strengthening of viewpoints based on politics and ideology."[27] In general, concluded Dietz and Rycroft, risk professionals working for corporations or trade associations differed from those working for government or academic institutions in their technical judgments about how risk should be determined and when substances should be regulated, as well as in broader attitudes about governmental regulation.

Social or political bias can be particularly influential, and often pernicious, when unrecognized or unadmitted by the experts. Yet the impact of such bias upon scientific judgment is often subtle and elusive. No barrier can be contrived to insulate science entirely from the contagion of social or economic bias. Knowledge that such bias exists, however, has important implications for risk assessment and its related controversies. The existence of this bias is a strong argument for keeping scientific and technical determinations open to examination and challenge by other experts and laypersons. There should be no domains of science quarantined from public inquiry. Scientists working in the public sector have a professional and personal responsibility to encourage rigorous self-examination of their own technical judgments in light of their vulnerability to social bias. The myth of a socially neutral science should not be unchallenged within the scientific professions. Moreover, it is now evident that many technical controversies in policy making may not be resolvable by resort to scientific evidence and argument because "scientific" solutions will be permeated with social, political, or economic bias. Indeed, political controversy often subverts scientific integrity. Experts can be readily, even unintentionally, caught up in the emotionally and politically polarizing atmosphere of such disputes, their judgment so badly compromised that, as Dorothy Nelkin remarks, their expertise "is reduced to one more weapon in a political arsenal."[28]

The Value of Science in Environmental Policy Making.   Despite the scientific disputes attending environmental policy making, it remains important to recognize how often science provides useful and highly reliable guidance to policy makers. Often the scientific data relevant to an issue clearly point to the adverse impacts of substances and define the magnitude of their risk; this was certainly evident in the data leading to the federal government's decision to ban most domestic agriculture uses of the pesticides DDT, aldrin, and dieldrin, for instance. Furthermore, even when one set of data does not alone provide definitive evidence of human risks from exposure to chemicals, numerous studies pointing to the same conclusion together can provide almost irrefutable evidence; such was the case in the epidemiological evidence indicting asbestos as a human carcinogen. Often the reliability of data will be routinely challenged by those opposed to the regulation of some substance regardless of the ultimate merit to their case. Finally, public officials must make decisions on the basis of the best evidence available. For all their limitations, scientific data often enable officials to define more carefully and clearly the range of options, risks, and benefits involved in regulating a substance even when the data cannot answer all risk questions conclusively.

Even if indisputable data were available on the risks of human exposure to all levels of a substance, controversy would continue over the acceptable level. It is asserted sometimes that science should be responsible for determining the magnitudes of risk from exposure to chemicals and that government should define the acceptability—that is, defining acceptable risk is largely a political matter. Such a division of labor is rarely possible. Scientists usually are drawn together with public officials into the nettlesome problem of determining what levels of exposure to substances ultimately will be acceptable.

What Risks Are Acceptable?

It was not surprising that William Ruckelshaus began his second season as EPA's administrator with a plea that Congress or some other authoritative institution establish guidelines for deciding what risks are acceptable in regulating hazardous substances. The EPA, like several other federal agencies, wrestles daily and inconclusively with the problem. Discretionary judgment also permeates the process of determining acceptable risks, which invites pressures and counterpressures for contending sides struggling to influence official decisions to their advantage. The language of the law may conceal it, but determining acceptable risk is ultimately an intensely political affair.

Expert Uncertainty

Defining acceptable risk in environmental regulations would be far less contentious if science could reliably provide evidence clearly indicating when levels of exposure to hazardous or toxic substances become dangerous to humans or the environment. Often, as we have seen, the appropriate tests have never been conducted for thousands of chemical substances currently used throughout the United States. Even when tests have been made, competent experts may disagree over interpretation of the data. Sometimes technology frustrates the search for acceptable risk.

Consider the problem of determining safe blood levels for lead. Many experts consider 20 to 25 micrograms per deciliter of blood a toxic level. But recent research implies that 10 to 15 micrograms per deciliter in children or fetuses might be slightly harmful.[29] But 25 micrograms remains the most accepted figure for two very practical reasons: (1) the most commonly used screening tests cannot detect blood levels of lead much below 25 micrograms, and (2) the drugs used to remove lead from the body do not work very well on levels below 20 micrograms. Often, scientific standard setters have had to develop their own criteria for defining safe levels of exposure in the absence of other guidance. In testing the effects of pollutants on animals, for example, scientists try to cope with the uncertainties inherent in using animals as test subjects by adopting a rule-of-thumb measure when extrapolating their findings to humans. Test animals should show no adverse health effects from a pollutant when exposed to doses at least one hundred times greater than likely human exposure.

Thus, "acceptable risk" can seldom be defined precisely by scientific criteria alone, even though scientists often make discretionary judgments that define it. Rather, acceptable risk is increasingly a political judgment, something settled through governmental institutions. Acceptable risk is usually defined in environmental regulation by statutory criteria—that is, standards written into law to guide regulators in determining when to regulate a substance.[30]

A Multitude of Risk Criteria

A multitude of different congressional standards guide regulatory agencies in making determinations of acceptable risk. Different substances are often regulated according to different standards. The same agency may have to use as many as six or seven standards depending upon which substances, or which laws, are involved. The same substance may be subject to one regulatory standard when dumped into a river and another when mixed into processed food. Statutory risk standards are commonly vague and sometimes confusing; congressional intent may be muddled, often deliberately. Agencies must, nonetheless, render from this confusion defensible judgments.

Generally, regulatory agencies encounter one or more of the statutory formulas listed below in determining the permissible exposure levels to various substances. The examples are drawn from existing legislation:

1. No-Risk Criteria. Regulatory agencies are to set standards ensuring no risks to human health from the use of a substance. These standards are also "cost oblivious" because they do not permit agencies to use the cost of regulation as a consideration in standard setting. "No additive shall be deemed to be safe if it is found to induce cancer when ingested in man or animal, or if it is found, after tests which are appropriate for the evaluation of the safety of food additives, to induce cancer in man or animal. . . ." [Food, Drug and Cosmetic Act (1938), 21 U.S.C.A. section 348 (3) (A)]

2. Margin-of-Safety Criteria. Congress orders regulatory agencies to set standards that protect human health with an additional margin for safety, which allows agencies to introduce an extra degree of control in case their original standards prove too lenient. "National primary ambient air quality standards . . . shall be . . . in the judgment of the [EPA] Administrator, based on [air quality] criteria and allowing an adequate margin of safety . . . requisite to protect human health." [Clean Air Act (1970), U.S.C.A. section 7409 (b)(1)]

3. Cost-Regarding Criteria. Congress mandates that an agency consider, in varying extent, the costs of regulation alongside the benefits in setting a standard for human or environmental exposure; or Congress may permit cost considerations to be among other criteria an agency may consider. Statutes define how costs are to be weighed with other criteria differently:

A. *Cost-Sensitive Criteria:* Agencies are permitted but not necessarily required to balance the benefits for a given regulatory standard against the costs of its enforcement. Different formulas may be provided in assigning priorities to cost and benefit. "The Secretary [of Labor], in promulgating standards dealing with toxic materials or harmful physical agents under this subsection, shall set the standard which most adequately assures, to the extent feasible, on the basis of the best available evidence, that no employee will suffer material impairment of health or functional capacity . . . other considerations shall be . . . the feasibility of the standards, and experience gained under this and other health and safety laws." [Occupational Safety and Health Act (1970), 33 U.S.C.A. section 655(b)(5)]

B. *Cost-Benefit Criteria:* Agencies are ordered to balance the benefits against the economic costs in setting standards for exposure to a substance. "The Commission shall not promulgate a consumer product safety rule unless it finds . . . that the benefits expected from the rule bear a reasonable relationship to its costs; and . . . that the rule imposes the least burdensome requirement which prevents or adequately reduces the risk or injury for which the rule is being promulgated." [Consumer Product Safety Act (1972), 15 U.S.C.A. section (f)(3)(E)-(F)]

A close reading of these guidelines will reveal the enormous discretion customarily left to regulatory agencies in determining how to balance the various statutory criteria.[31] It is often difficult to separate scientific from nonscientific issues; scientists usually become activists in standard setting as well as in determining the magnitude of risks upon which the standards should be based. For instance, the Food and Drug Act's requirement that no food additive may be permitted in the United States if it is "found to induce cancer when ingested by man or animal" raises scientific issues even as it attempts to serve as a criterion for regulators in setting policy: Over what period of time must the risk of cancer exist?

Must substances be banned even if they are used in quantities so small that only extremely small risks may exist to man? Are the cancers produced by a substance in animals the result of exposure to that substance alone? In the end, determining acceptable risks becomes both a political and a scientific question.[32]

Limited by its lack of scientific expertise yet reluctant to leave agencies with too much discretion in determining acceptable risk, Congress often packs regulatory laws with so many criteria for risk determination—lest any important consideration be ignored—that regulatory decisions become enormously cumbersome and technical. Consider, for instance, the criteria the EPA is ordered to use in the Toxic Substances Control Act (1976) when deciding whether the risks from exposure to a substance are "unreasonable":

The type of effect (chronic or acute, reversible or irreversible); degree of risk; characteristics and number of humans, plants and animals, or ecosystems, at risk; amount of knowledge about the effects; available or alternative substances and their expected effects; magnitude of the social and economic costs and benefits of possible control actions; and appropriateness and effectiveness of TSCA as the legal instrument for controlling the risk.[33]

Agencies often spend considerable time working out detailed internal regulations to translate these complexities into workable procedures. They may attempt to reach understandings concerning how criteria will be balanced with interest groups active in the regulatory process. But agencies often are faced with limited time for making regulatory decisions, with fragmentary information relevant to many criteria for standard setting, with disputes between interest groups concerning the validity of information and the priorities for criteria in policy making. In the first years of a new regulatory program, moreover, an agency can expect virtually all its major decisions to be challenged through litigation, usually by an interest alleging the agency has failed to interpret properly its statutory responsibilities. Agencies frequently encourage either openly or tacitly such litigation because it can work to their advantage. By interpreting the manner in which risk determinations should be made by agencies, judges often dissipate the fog of uncertainty about congressional intent and provide agencies with firm guidelines for future determinations.

Political Bias

Agency formulas for determining acceptable risks also have proven to be highly sensitive to political pressures and to ideological biases. Given the great discretion left with agencies in determining acceptable risks, it is possible for the process to be biased toward differing philosophies of regulation. During the Carter years the White House directed the

Occupational Safety and Health Administration to treat any suspected carcinogen as a proven hazard until tests proved otherwise—a stance well within OSHA's authority.[34] Moreover, a substance was deemed "suspect" if it induced either benign or malignant tumors in at least one laboratory study on animals. This approach, strongly biased toward regulation of workplace hazards, environmental protection, and strict control of suspected hazardous substances, fit comfortably into the activist regulatory bias of a liberal Democratic administration.

The Reagan administration, however, rapidly changed these guidelines. In the future much more convincing proof would be required before a substance was considered even "suspect." OSHA abolished its list of suspected workplace carcinogens regularly published during the Carter years. And the levels of acceptable risk from substances were raised by factors of ten to one hundred over the earlier Carter criteria. Not surprisingly, these new guidelines were far more compatible with the Reagan administration's determination to place fewer substances under regulatory control and to decrease the compliance costs for business and other regulated interests. These changes, too, generally could be reconciled with OSHA's discretionary authority in determining acceptable risks from workplace exposure to hazardous substances.

The Disappearing Threshold

One of the most politically controversial aspects of determining acceptable risk remains the *threshold problem*, a largely unanticipated result of three tendencies among Congress and agencies concerned with environmental regulation. First, in writing and enforcing most environmental legislation during the 1970s, officials remained *risk averse* in dealing with potential hazards; risk reduction was preferred to risk tolerance. Second, Congress generally assumed that with many, or most, regulated substances there would be some threshold of exposure below which the risks to humans or the ecosystem were negligible. Congress certainly did not anticipate removing *all* traces of human or ecological hazards. And third, legislators, who were largely indifferent to regulatory costs compared with health criteria in setting regulatory standards, discouraged agencies from using cost-benefit analyses when determining acceptable risks.

Economics and technology now present regulation writers with some very difficult decisions growing from these circumstances. Extremely sophisticated technologies enable scientists to detect hazardous substances in increasingly small concentrations, currently as small as parts per billion or trillion. It is usually impossible to assert scientifically that such low concentrations are wholly innocent of averse risk, however slight, to humans or the environment. Further, the cost of controlling hazardous substances often rises steeply as progressively higher standards are enforced; after reducing, for instance, 85 percent of a substance in a waterway, it may cost half as much or more to remove an additional 5 to 10 percent. In effect, the risk threshold once presumed by policy makers vanished; all measurable concentrations of a substance apparently held some possible harm to humans or their environment. To eliminate conclusively *any* probable risks from such substances, regulators would have to require the total elimination of the substance—an extraordinarily expensive undertaking. The threshold problem thus was created: Should a trade-off be made between the costs and benefits of risk prevention, and, if so, what criteria should govern the choice?

Critics assert that regulators err in this trade-off by insisting upon extremely high standards for controlling risks out of all proportion to the benefits to society or the environment and without sensitivity to the economic burden imposed upon regulated interests.[35] This is, in critic Paul Johnson's terms, the "Custer Syndrome." Regulators "take action at any cost, do it as quickly as possible, and leave the thinking to afterwards." This leaves the public with "unrealistic expectations" about the benefits, which will in most cases be extremely small if not undiscoverable when regulators insist upon eliminating even minuscule risks from hazardous substances.[36] Advocates of strict risk management, however, usually will respond that the full extent of risk is unknown or may be greater than currently estimated; they may dispute the accuracy of opposing data. Often, they are especially indignant at the suggestion that human lives may be endangered if the cost of protection is deemed excessive—an assertion that, skillfully delivered, implies that officials are venal or inhumane for imperiling lives to save money for a regulated interest.

Elected officials are understandably wary in dealing with these publicly sensitive issues, especially when they may be cast as the villains by advocates of strict regulation. It is easy to make tolerance for even small risks appear to be a cruel gambling with the destinies of innocent people. When the Nuclear Regulatory Commission (NRC) proposed to set standards for reactor safety at a level that would make the risk of immediate death or lethal cancer from an accident 1,000 times smaller than the actual fatalities from all other causes, that may have seemed a negligible risk indeed. But when critics argued that this meant the NRC was tacitly accepting the possibility of 13,000 American deaths from reactor accidents in the next thirty years, the NRC found itself embroiled in a conflict.[37] In fact, risk assessment deals in *probabilities*, not certainties, of accident, or death, or disease. Still, it is often politically difficult to defend some risk threshold, no matter what the economic advantages and despite the relatively few additional benefits that might occur from removing the threshold.

Recently, the EPA has attempted to deal with the threshold problem by creating its own threshold criteria when the law permitted. The EPA revised several of its regulations to allow public exposure to extremely low levels of several known or suspected carcinogens, in effect establishing a threshold for these substances. In 1987, the agency allowed continued agricultural use of the herbicide alachlor because the EPA deemed that the chemical did not pose an "unreasonable" cancer risk to humans.[38] The agency asserted that the risk of cancer to humans was generally one in a million over a seventy-year period from current levels of alachlor in food and water. In 1988, the EPA promulgated a broad new regulation affecting pesticides known to be carcinogenic in processed or raw food. Henceforth, the agency would permit residues posing no more than a "negligible" risk to humans—the same one in a million risk previously assigned to alachlor. Environmental and consumer groups, vehemently opposed to the EPA's new thresholds, have initiated legal and administrative action to overturn these regulations. Thus, the future of the reappearing thresholds at the EPA is problematic.

The Politicizing of Science

Environmental issues place scientists in a highly charged political atmosphere where impartiality and objectivity, among the most highly esteemed scientific virtues, are severely tested and sometimes fail. Scientists are often consulted by public officials in good part because the scientists' presumed objectivity, as well as technical expertise, makes them trustworthy advisers. But impartiality may be an early casualty in the highly partisan and polarizing atmosphere of policy conflict. Even if scientists can maintain impartiality, they cannot prevent partisans of one or another policy from distorting technical information to gain an advantage. Scientists often correctly suspect that their work will be misrepresented when used in political arguments and their credibility consequently diminished. In any case it is characteristic of environmental policy that scientific evidence and opinion are frequently divided for political reasons and that consequently expert disagreements tend to reinforce political conflicts; often these expert cleavages yield no conclusive answers to difficult issues.

Scientific disagreement in complex environmental issues is, in fact, almost predictable because so many opportunities exist for political issues to create, or exacerbate, technical disputes. Scientists, bringing to their work the full human measure of political bias and preconception, cannot always purge scientific opinions of such influence. Especially when political conflict tends to polarize views and force division over issues, an expert can intentionally, or unwittingly, shade opinions to fit a favored position or manipulate materials until they fit a simplistic policy position. "Experts tend to behave like other people when they engage in a controversy," observes Allan Mazur, himself a sociologist and a physicist. "Coalitions solidify and disagreements become polarized as conflict becomes more acrimonious."[39]

Particularly when a technical issue involves ambiguous data or several plausible alternative explanations, experts often will select the viewpoint congenial to their political, social, or economic convictions. Mazur observes that experts favoring nuclear power tend to support the notion that there exists a threshold of radiation exposure below which human risks are negligible; opponents of nuclear power plants, in contrast, favor a linear conception of risk that permits no such threshold.[40] Apparently, there are Republican and Democratic theories of genetic chemistry. In the mid-1980s many Reagan administration officials and some experts sympathetic to the president's program to reduce environmental regulations were supporting the *epigenetic theory* of cell chemistry.[41] This theory asserts that many carcinogenic substances affect cell mechanisms other than the DNA strands with their genetically coded materials; such a theory could be interpreted to permit greater human exposure to known cancer-causing substances—and also less regulation of such substances—than previously had been federal policy. Under Administrator Anne Burford, the EPA did approve tolerance limits for several carcinogenic pesticides, including the potent pesticide permethrin, on the basis of this epigenetic theory. Under the Carter administration, however, the *genotoxic theory* had prevailed; it asserted that all carcinogens cause changes in genetic cell materials and hence must be considered dangerous. Although the genotoxic theory has been more generally accepted by experts, reputable scientists have supported the conflicting interpretation. One need not accuse either side of willful deceit in order to suggest that political and economic bias could, and probably does, play some part in convincing experts of the truth of a position.

Even when experts qualify their opinions appropriately, policy partisans often distort technical information for their own purposes. In policy conflict one's data become a weapon, and science a bastion against one's critics. Policy advocates and public officials, constantly pressured to take positions and defend them convincingly, often attempt to force upon scientific data a clarity and a simplicity that do not exist. Indeed, torturing technical data to fit some partisan position can be considered an art form in policy debates.

Regulatory agencies, no less than individuals, are guilty of using scientific data selectively, sometimes with gross negligence. One of the worst examples became evident in the 1980s when it was revealed that the Atomic Energy Commission had suppressed deliberately and consistently for more than twenty years scientific evidence suggesting that radioactive fallout from nuclear weapons tests in Nevada may have endangered ranchers and others in its path during the 1950s. All agencies at some time practice some type of data manipulation. One of the virtues in wide public exposure of regulatory proceedings is that opportunities exist for experts to expose and challenge such manipulation.

The great potential in policy conflict for disrupting sound scientific inquiry and distorting data emphasizes the importance of permitting an open, prolonged, and comprehensive scientific review of major environmental policy decisions. Such a process does not ensure that any scientific consensus will emerge upon strategic issues. But it does permit the widest latitude for scientific debate—for the uncovering and publicizing of information as well as for challenging and refining interpretations of data. It encourages among policy makers greater clarity about the full range and limits of the technical information confronting them. It invites a public airing of issues that experts otherwise might keep to themselves or confine to a small cadre of governmental and scientific insiders who become by virtue of their privileged information a powerful technocratic elite. It helps to discriminate between plausible and unrealistic policy options. If the politicizing of science in environmental issues is inevitable, it should at least be exploited to advantage when possible.

Gambling with the Future

The complex new problems of risk assessment in environmental regulation confirm that we live in a historically unique era of technocratic power. American science and industry, in common with those of other advanced industrial nations, now possess the capacity to alter in profound but often unpredictable ways the biochemical basis of future human life and thus to change future ecosystems radically. In its extreme form, represented by nuclear weapons, modern technology has the power to eradicate human society, if not humanity itself, as we know it. But modern technologies also can alter the future ecosphere in a multitude of less dramatic but significant ways: through the deliberate redesign of genetic materials in human reproduction, through the depletion of irreplaceable energy resources such as petroleum or natural gas, through the multiplication of long-lived hazardous substances whose biological impacts upon humans and the ecosystem may magnify through hundreds of years, and much more. We are practically the first generation in the world's history with the certain technical capacity to alter and even to destroy the fundamental biochemical and geophysical conditions for societies living centuries after ours. It is, as one social prophet noted, a power that men of the Middle Ages did not even credit to devils.

With this new technocratic power comes the ability to develop technologies, to manufacture new substances, and to deplete finite resources so that the benefits are largely distributed in the present and the risks for the most part displaced to the future. Future societies may inherit most of the burden to create the social, economic, and political institutions necessary for managing the risks inherent in this generational cost transfer. Such technical capacity can become an exercise of power undisciplined by responsibility for the consequences.

The status of nuclear wastes in many ways provides a paradigm for this problem. Because the wastes from civilian nuclear reactors currently cannot be recycled, as was assumed when the nuclear power industry began in the United States during the 1950s, the federal government now must find a safe and reliable way to dispose of the growing amount of nuclear wastes from these facilities.

Among the most dangerous of these substances are "high-level" wastes—those highly toxic to humans for long periods—found in the spent fuel rods from civilian reactors. Strontium-90 and cesium-137, for instance, must be isolated from human exposure for at least 600 years; other high-level wastes must be isolated for perhaps a thousand years. Equally dangerous and much more persistent are the "transuranic" wastes forming over long periods from the decay of the original materials in the spent fuel rods after they are removed from the reactors. Plutonium 239 remains dangerous to humans for at least 24,000 years, perhaps for as much as 500,000 years. This plutonium, notes one commentator generally sympathetic to the nuclear power industry, "will remain a source of radioactive emissions as far in the future as one can meaningfully contemplate."[42] Other transuranics include americium-241 (dangerous for more than 400 years) and iodine-129 (dangerous for perhaps 210,000 years).

Practically speaking, such figures mean that hazardous wastes must be prevented from invading the ecosystem for periods ranging from centuries to hundreds of millennia. Not only must they be securely isolated physically, but human institutions also must survive with sufficient continuity to ensure their responsible administration throughout these eons. Many other chemicals created in the last few decades, including widely used pesticides such as DDT, 2-3-5-T, and dieldrin are not biodegradable and may persist throughout the world ecosystem indefinitely. Though less dangerous than nuclear wastes, these and other substances also represent a displacement of risks to human health and to the ecosystem well into the future.

This transfer of risk raises fundamental ethical and social questions for government. Should public institutions be compelled in some formal and explicit way to exercise regard—and how much?—for the future impacts of decisions concerning environmental management today? Should they be forced, if necessary, to consider not only the future ecological implications in developing dangerous technologies but also the ability of future societies to create institutions capable of controlling these technologies when deciding whether to develop them?

This issue is significant because governmental and economic institutions have a tendency to discount the future impacts of new technologies or newly developed chemicals when compared with the immediate impacts. In economic terms this is done in formal cost-benefit analysis by discounting future benefits and costs rather substantially. In political terms it amounts to adopting a strategy that favors taking environmental actions on the basis of short-term political advantage rather than long-term consequences. (Elected officials, especially, often treat as gospel the legendary advice of a former House Speaker to a new colleague: "Remember that when it comes time to vote, most folks want to know 'what have you done for me lately?' ") It is particularly difficult for public officials to develop a sensitive regard for the distant future when there are no apparent political rewards for doing so. At some time whispers the political cynic in practically all public officials: "What has posterity recently done for you?"

Conclusion

Scientific issues so permeate environmental problems that the scientist's substantial involvement in making environmental policy is essential. Science, however, has not proven to be an oracle in the environmental policy process. As we have seen, there are limits to the capacity of technical experts to resolve environmental problems and, sometimes, even to clarify them. These limitations arise from the frequent absence of essential technical data, or the ambiguity of available data, or disagreements among experts over the proper evaluation of scientific evidence relevant to environmental problems. Thus, expert opinions on environmental issues may run on a continuum from consensus to dissension; quite often differing opinions tend to leave public officials without any clear and immediate policy options to adopt. Further, many environmental issues involve policy choices that are, as one commentator has remarked, "transcientific." These are issues in which matters such as the acceptability of risks from alternative policies are involved—questions for which the scientist can claim no special competence or superior understanding.

It is also apparent that policy partisans, public agencies, and others attempting to advance one policy or another often will attempt to use scientific evidence, or the scientist's own opinions, to legitimate their policy bias. This tactic often can amount to willful, or unwitting, misrepresentation of technical materials; it is also an almost irresistible temptation to someone in the policy process. Thus, major concerns in evaluating environmental policy should always be an alertness to the limits of scientific evidence in resolving policy issues and a sensitivity to the potential abuses of technical excerpts and evidence.

Often environmental policy must be formulated not only in the absence of definitive data concerning key issues but also with a likelihood that such data will not be available before a final decision must be made. In many cases, technical data that indisputably resolve scientific conflicts in environmental policy may never become available. Those who appeal for "more time to study the problem" or advise "waiting until more evidence is available" may only be attempting to prevent action as long as possible. It is among the most difficult, yet common, problems facing environmental policy makers that they must make prudent judgments concerning when "further study" will truly yield constructive new evidence and when it is only a pretext for prolonged inaction.

In the end science cannot relieve public officials and institutions from making many difficult and controversial environmental decisions. Nor are scientists and their work invulnerable to the pressures and prejudices of political life. Science can make essential and constructive contributions to environmental policy making by clarifying the impacts of policies, by identifying policy alternatives and suggesting their feasibility, and by suggesting new environmental issues for public consideration. There will always remain, however, a domain of choice for public officials that lies beyond the proper capacity of science to resolve, just a there are vast domains of scientific inquiry that ought to remain beyond the ability of politics to manipulate.

Notes

1. *New York Times*, February 2, 1989.
2. *New York Times*, March 30, 1989.
3. *New York Times*, February 2, 1989.
4. *New York Times*, February 5, 1989.
5. *New York Times*, February 25, 1989.
6. "Apple Juice: A Long Way from the Tree," *Consumer Reports* 54, no. 5 (May 1989): 293–296.
7. *New York Times*, February 2, 1989.
8. Roger Revelle, "The Scientist and the Politician," in *Science, Technology and*

National Policy, ed. Thomas J. Kuehn and Alan L. Porter (Ithaca, N.Y.: Cornell University Press, 1981), 134.

9. U.S. General Accounting Office, "Superfund: Missed Statutory Deadlines Slow Progress in Environmental Programs," Report no. GAO/RCED-89-27 (November 1988), chap. 2.

10. See, for example, Thomas R. Dunlap, *DDT: Scientists, Citizens and Public Policy* (Princeton, N.J.: Princeton University Press, 1981), esp. chap. 8.

11. U.S. General Accounting Office, "Pesticides: EPA's Formidable Task to Assess and Regulate Their Risks," Report no. GAO/RCED-86-125 (April 1986), 21–22.

12. U.S. General Accounting Office, "Hazardous Waste: Uncertainties of Existing Data," Report no. GAO/PMED-87-11BR (February 1987), 15–16.

13. U.S. General Accounting Office, "The Nation's Water: Key Unanswered Questions About the Quality of Rivers and Streams," Report no. GAO/PEMD-86-6 (September 1986), 4.

14. U.S. General Accounting Office, "Coal and Nuclear Wastes—Both Potential Contributors to Environmental and Health Problems," Report no. EMD-81-132 (September 21, 1981), 2.

15. See Executive Office of the President, Council on Environmental Quality (CEQ), *Environmental Quality, 1979* (Washington, D.C.: Government Printing Office, 1980), 194ff.

16. Ibid.

17. A useful compendium of such substances may be found in Samuel S. Epstein, Lester Brown, and Carl Pope, *Hazardous Waste in America* (San Francisco: Sierra Club Books, 1982), appendix I; and CEQ, *Environmental Quality, 1979,* chap. 3.

18. CEQ, *Global Energy Futures and the Carbon Dioxide Problem* (Washington, D.C.: Government Printing Office, 1981), 5.

19. Ibid., 54.

20. Ibid.

21. A general review of the issues may be found in Sam H. Schurr et al., *Energy in America's Future* (Baltimore: Johns Hopkins University Press, 1979), chap. 14.

22. On the general problems of animal experiments, see David D. Doniger, *The Law and Policy of Toxic Substances Control* (Baltimore: Johns Hopkins University Press, 1978), part I.

23. Animal data are cited in the *New York Times,* June 25, 1983.

24. Doniger, *The Law and Policy of Toxic Substances Control,* 12.

25. Harvey Brooks, "The Resolution of Technically Intensive Public Policy Disputes," *Science, Technology and Human Values* 9, no. 1 (Winter 1984): 40. For estimates of discretionary judgments in risk assessment see National Research Council, Commission on Life Sciences, Committee on the Institutional Means for Assessment of Risks to Public Health, *Risk Assessment in the Federal Government: Managing the Process* (Washington, D.C.: National Academy Press, 1983), chap. 1.

26. Frances M. Lynn, "The Interplay of Science and Values in Assessing and Regulating Environmental Risks," *Science, Technology and Human Values* 11, no. 2 (Spring 1986): 40–50.

27. Thomas M. Dietz and Robert W. Rycroft, *The Risk Professionals* (New York: Russell Sage Foundation, 1987), 111.

28. Dorothy Nelkin, ed., *Controversy: The Politics of Technical Decisions* (Beverly Hills, Calif.: Sage Publications, 1984), 17.

29. *New York Times,* September 1, 1988.

30. A comprehensive review of the various statutory standards for risk in federal law is found in John J. Cohrssen and Vincent T. Covello, *Risk Analysis: A Guide to Principles and Methods for Analyzing Health and Environmental Risks* (Washington, D.C.: Council on Environmental Quality, 1989), 14–15.

31. I am indebted to my colleague Albert Matheny for these illustrations.

32. See William W. Lowrence, *Of Acceptable Risks* (Los Altos, Calif.: William Kaufmann, 1976).

33. CEQ, *Environmental Quality, 1979,* 218.
34. *National Journal,* June 18, 1983.
35. A sampling of this literature may be found in the collection of articles by Peter Lewin, Gerald L. Sauer, Bernard L. Cohen, Richard N. Langlois, and Aaron Wildavsky in the *Cato Journal,* "Symposium on Pollution" (Spring 1982): 205ff.
36. Paul Johnson, "The Perils of Risk Avoidance," *Regulation* (May/June 1980): 17.
37. *New York Times,* February 12, 1982.
38. *New York Times,* December 15, 1987.
39. Allan Mazur, *The Dynamics of Technical Controversy* (Washington, D.C.: Communications Press, 1981), 29.
40. Ibid., 27.
41. *National Journal,* June 18, 1983.
42. *New York Times,* May 12, 1983.

Suggested Readings

Bosso, Christopher J. *Pesticides and Politics: The Life Cycle of a Public Issue.* Pittsburgh: University of Pittsburgh Press, 1987.
Cohrrsen, John J., and Vincent T. Covello. *Risk Analysis: A Guide to Principles and Methods for Analyzing Health and Environmental Risks.* Washington, D.C.: Council on Environmental Quality, 1989.
Committee on Risk Perception and Communication, Commission on Behavioral and Social Sciences and Education, Commission on Physical Sciences, Mathematics and Resources, National Research Council. *Improving Risk Communication.* Washington, D.C.: National Academy Press, 1989.
Jasanoff, Sheila. *Risk Management and Political Culture.* New York: Russell Sage Foundation, 1987.
Krimsky, Sheldon, and Alonzo Plough. *Communicating Risks as a Social Process.* Dover, Mass.: Auburn House, 1988.

Chapter 6

The Unfinished Agenda
Air and Water

> *The air accompanying this planet is not replaceable. . . . It may be cleaned in part if excessively spoiled. The passengers' lungs will help. . . . However, they will discover that anything they throw, spew or dump into the air will return to them in due time. Since passengers will need to use the air, on average, every five seconds, they should treat it accordingly.*
> —David Brower, "Third Planet Operating Instructions"[1]

Clean air and clean water are powerful public images. The environmental movement regards the Clean Air Act (CAA) of 1970 and the Federal Water Pollution Control Act Amendments (FWPCAA) of 1972 as foundations of the first environmental era. Public opinion polls show that Americans universally recognize the nation's gravely degraded air and waters as major ecological problems. And so clean air and water have acquired political chic. Politicians so routinely assure constituents of their unceasing regard for clean air and clean water that both have become clichés instead of realities.

After twenty years of sustained effort by federal, state, and local governments to eliminate air and water pollution and an estimated public expenditure exceeding $700 billion, the nation's air and water remain dangerously degraded.[2] A few dramatic achievements, many lesser but impressive gains, and a multitude of marginal improvements comprise the cosmetic veneer of success that brightens reports about implementation of the CAA and FWPCAA. But air and water quality have deteriorated so gravely in many places throughout the United States that governmental efforts to restore them sometimes seem more desperate than prudent.

So it was in late 1988 when Los Angeles mayor Tom Bradley, in the midst of his fifth election campaign, decided to take on the eighteen-wheelers. Large trucks produce 17 percent of the air pollution in the Los Angeles basin, the nation's most degraded urban area.[3] The City and County of Los Angeles had been living for almost a decade under the threat of drastic state and federal action if Los Angeles did not demonstrate a determination to clean its air. In response to growing political pressure, the mayor proposed a draconian plan to control truck access to Los Angeles that invited the opposition of powerful political and economic interests, including the California Trucking Association, the California Manufacturers Association, and many major state and national trucking firms. The mayor's proposal would have prohibited 70 percent of local heavy-duty trucks from operating within the city during the morning and evening rush hours. It would have required shippers and receivers with five or more deliveries or pickups weekly to remain open at least four hours between 8:00 P.M. and 6:00 A.M., and all city agencies were ordered to accept deliveries only between 8:00 P.M. and midnight.

Mayor Bradley's foray against the eighteen-wheelers ended in impasse when the contending sides agreed to postpone further debate about the matter until regional air-quality authorities had made a more comprehensive air pollution control proposal, which was expected within a year. This came in the form of the most radical urban air-quality management plan in U.S. history. At a time when acts of regulatory desperation are becoming political style in Southern California, Tom Bradley no longer seems an environmental radical, so acute have air and water problems become in his city. Los Angeles is far from alone in the urgency of its air-quality problems, however. More than 350 counties, mostly embracing the largest urban areas, currently fail to meet federal and state air-quality standards—more than one hundred of these sites were added to the list in 1988.[4] The air quality in many of these urban areas approaches a level of degradation posing severe health risks to vulnerable populations. Water-quality problems, while less dramatized, are equally serious and pervasive in many rural and urban counties. Air and water quality remain at the forefront of the nation's urgent environmental problems.

This chapter examines the implementation of the Clean Air Act and the Federal Water Pollution Control Act Amendments during the last two decades, with emphasis upon their major substantive goals, long-term impact, and significant implications for the 1990s. It will be helpful to begin by first describing briefly the "standards-and-enforcement" regulatory framework used in both laws, giving particular attention to the administrative and political consequences.

Standards and Enforcement

Like all other regulatory programs affecting the U.S. environment, the CAA and FWPCAA are based on the standards-and-enforcement approach to regulation, sometimes called "command and control." The structure and philosophy of this approach create many of the characteristic processes and problems associated with governmental management of the environment. In recent years this regulatory philosophy has been increasingly criticized as economically inefficient, excessively complicated, and counterproductive. Regulatory horror stories abound, many doubtless true, convincing believers that a better approach lies in less direct governmental involvement and more economic incentives to encourage pollution abatement. In fact, both approaches have virtues and liabilities.

Understanding current issues in pollution regulation requires an appreciation in broad outline of the standards-and-enforcement method and its purposes. Essentially, this method consists of five phases through which pollution policy evolves.

Goals

In theory the first step in pollution abatement begins with a determination by Congress of the ultimate objectives to be accomplished through pollution regulation. In practice these goals are often broadly and vaguely worded. Sometimes, as when Congress decides to "press technology," goals deliberately are made extremely ambitious as an incentive to vigorous regulatory action. The principal goals of the Clean Air Act are, for example, to protect public health and safety. Vague goals are not as important in defining the operational character of a regulatory program as the more detailed specifications for the setting of pollution standards, emission controls, and enforcement—the real cutting edges of regulation. Statements of goals, however, may be very politically significant as signals to the interests involved in regulation concerning which pollutants and sources will be given priority and how vigorously Congress intends to implement programs. The Clean Air Act's goal of establishing national air-quality standards for major pollutants, for instance, was an unmistakable signal that Congress would tolerate no longer the continual delays in controlling air pollution caused by past legislative willingness to let the states create their own air-quality standards. It was also evidence that regulated interests had lost their once-dominant position in the formation of air pollution policy.

Criteria

Criteria are the technical data, commonly provided by research scientists, indicating what pollutants are associated with environmental damage and how such pollutants, in varying combination, affect the environment. Criteria are essential to give public officials some idea of what pollutant levels they must achieve to ensure various standards of air or water quality. If regulators intend to protect public health from the effects of air pollution, for example, they must know what levels of pollution—sulfur oxides, for instance—create public health risks. In a similar vein, restoring game fish to a dying lake requires information about the levels of organic waste such fish can tolerate. Criteria must be established for each regulated pollutant, and sometimes for combinations of pollutants.

As noted earlier, obtaining criteria frequently is difficult because data on the environmental effects of many pollutants still may be fragmentary or absent. Even when data are available, there is often as much art as science in specifying relationships between specific levels of a pollutant and its environmental effects because precise correlations may not be obtainable from the information. The reliability of criteria data also may vary depending upon whether they are obtained from animal studies, epidemiological statistics, or human studies. Criteria are often likely to be controversial, especially to those convinced that a set of data works to their disadvantage. Given the limitations in criteria data, regulatory agencies often have had to set pollution standards with information that was open to scientific criticism but still the best available.

Quality Standards

Goals and criteria are a prelude to the critical business of establishing air- and water-quality standards—the maximum levels of various pollutants to be permitted in air, soil, workplaces, or other locations. As a practical matter, defining standards amounts to declaring what the public, acting through governmental regulators, will consider to be "pollution." An adequate set of quality standards should specify what contaminants will be regulated and what variation in levels and combinations will be accepted in different pollutant categories.

Creating quality standards—in effect, another means of defining acceptable risk—is ultimately a political decision. Criteria documents rarely provide public officials with a single number that defines unambiguously what specific concentration of a pollutant produces precisely what effects. A rather broad range of possible figures associated more or less closely with predictable effects is available; which one is accepted may be the result of prolonged struggle and negotiation among interests involved in regulation. This battle over numbers is a matter of economics as much as science or philosophy. The difference between two possible pollution standards, only a few units apart, may seem trivial to a layman.

Table 6-1 *National Air-Quality Standards*

Pollu-tant	Primary (health related)		Secondary (welfare related)	
	Averaging time	Concen-tration	Averaging time	Concen-tration
TSP	Annual geometric mean	75 μg/m^3	Annual geometric mean	60 μg/m^{3a}
	24-hour	260 μg/m^3	24-hour	150 μg/m^3
SO$_2$	Annual arithmetic mean	(0.03 ppm) 80 μg/m^3	3-hour	(0.50 ppm) 1300 μg/m^3
	24-hour	(0.14 ppm) 365 μg/m^3		
CO	8-hour	(9 ppm) 10 mg/m^3	Same as Primary	
	1-hour	(35 ppm) 40 mg/m^3	Same as Primary	
NO$_2$	Annual arithmetic mean	(0.053 ppm) 100 μg/m^3	Same as Primary	
O$_3$	Maximum daily 1-hour average	0.12 ppm (235 μg/m^3)	Same as Primary	
Pb	Maximum quarterly average	1.5 μg/m^3	Same as Primary	

SOURCE: Council on Environmental Quality, *Environmental Quality, 1984* (Washington, D.C.: Government Printing Office, 1985), 12.

Note: The standards are categorized for long- and short-term exposure. Long-term standards specify an annual or quarterly mean that may not be exceeded; short-term standards specify upper limit values for 1-, 3-, 8-, or 24-hour averages. The short-term standards are not to be exceeded more than once per year. For example, the ozone standard requires that the expected number of days per calendar year with daily maximum hourly concentrations exceeding 0.12 parts per million (ppm) be less than or equal to one.

[a]This annual geometric mean is a guide used in assessing implementation plans to achieve the 24-hour standards of 150 μg/m^3.

But the higher standard may involve millions or billions of additional dollars in pollution control technologies for the regulated interests and possibly many additional years before standards are achieved. Sometimes Congress establishes a standard based on a number's political "sex appeal." The original requirements in the Clean Air Act that automobile emissions of hydrocarbons and carbon monoxide be reduced by 90 percent of the 1970 levels no later than 1975 were largely accepted because the 90 percent figure sounded strict and spurred the auto industry into action. In practical terms the figure might have been set at 88 percent or 85 percent, or some other number in this range, with about the same results. Air-quality standards created by the Environmental Protection Agency (EPA) for the major criteria pollutants are identified, and their method of calculation explained, in Table 6-1.

Emission Standards

Standards for clean air or water are only aspirations unless emission standards exist to prescribe the acceptable pollutant discharges from important sources of air or water contamination. If emission standards are to be effective, they must clearly indicate the acceptable emission levels from all important pollution sources and should be related to the pollution control standards established by policy makers.

Congress has used two different methods of determining how emission standards should be set. In regulating existing air pollution sources under the Clean Air Act, Congress requires that emissions be limited to the extent necessary to meet the relevant air-quality standards; determining what emission controls are necessary depends upon where the quality standards are set. In controlling new air pollution sources, and most water polluters, the emission controls are based upon the available technologies. This "technology-based" approach sets the emission levels largely according to the performance of available technologies.[5]

There is a very direct and critical relationship between air-quality standards and emission controls. For example, once EPA declares national ambient air-quality standards, each state is required in its State Implementation Plan (SIP) to calculate the total emissions of that pollutant within an airshed and then to assign emission controls to each source of that pollutant sufficient to ensure that total emissions will meet air-quality standards. In effect this calls for the states to decide how much of the total pollution "load" within an airshed is the responsibility of each polluter and how much emission control the polluter must achieve. This has become a bitterly controversial process. Experts often have difficulty in determining precisely how much of a pollution "load" within a given body of water or air can be attributed to a specific source; this compounds the problem of assigning responsibility for pollution abatement equitably among a large number of polluters.[6] Regulated interests, aware of the relationship between air-quality standards and emission controls, will attack both in an effort to avoid or relax their assigned emission controls. Regulated industries also chronically complain that insufficient attention is given to the cost of emission controls when government regulators prescribe the acceptable technology. Polluters often balk at installing specific control technologies prescribed by governmental regulators. The scrubber wars between electric utilities and regulatory authorities, for instance, have been continuing for more than a decade. Alleging that the scrubbers prescribed by government to control their sulfur oxide emissions are inefficient and unreliable, coal-fired utilities have fiercely resisted installing the scrubbers until compelled to do so.

The full force of the backlash against emission controls often falls upon state government officials who, under existing federal law, usually are responsible for setting specific emission levels, prescribing the proper technologies, and enforcing emission restraints upon specific sources. This is accomplished largely through the issuance of a permit to individual dischargers specifying the permissible emission levels and technological controls for their facility. Despite several decades of experience and substantial financial assistance from Washington, many state regulatory authorities still are understaffed and undertrained, chronically enmeshed in litigation over regulation, and otherwise inhibited from implementing emission controls with dispatch. Moreover, the political and economic influence of regulated interests often are far more formidable in state capitals than in Washington.

Enforcement

A great diversity of enforcement procedures might be used to ensure that pollution standards are achieved; adequate enforcement must carry enough force to command the respect of those subject to regulation. Satisfactory enforcement schemes have several characteristics: they enable public officials to act with reasonable speed—very rapidly in the case of emergencies—to curb pollution; they carry sufficient penalties to encourage compliance; and they do not enable officials to evade a responsibility to act against violations when action is essential. It is desirable that officials have a range of enforcement options that might extend from gentle prodding to secure compliance, at one end, all the way to litigation and criminal penalties for severe, chronic, or reckless violations. In reality, when it comes to enforcement, administrative authority is often the power to "make a deal." Armed with a flexible variety of enforcement options, administrators are in a position to bargain with polluters in noncompliance with the law, selecting those enforcement options they believe will best achieve their purposes. This bargaining, a common occurrence in environmental regulation, illustrates how political pressure and administrative discretion concurrently shape environmental policy; enforcement will be examined in greater detail shortly.

In the end an effective pollution abatement program largely depends upon voluntary compliance by regulated interests. No regulatory agency has enough personnel, money, and time to engage in continual litigation or other actions to force compliance with pollution standards. Furthermore, litigation usually remains among the slowest, most inflexible, and inefficient means of achieving environmental protection. Administrative agencies prefer to negotiate and maneuver to avoid litigation as the primary means of regulation whenever possible.

The Political Anatomy of Regulation

The standards-and-enforcement approach to regulation creates a number of characteristic political processes and issues regardless of which specific pollution program is involved. The technicality of pollution regulation frequently creates a language and style of action that conceals (sometimes deliberately) the extent to which political forces are operating behind the facade of regulatory procedures. Nonetheless regulation is fundamentally a political enterprise.

Opportunities for Political Influence

Political influence and conflict occur wherever administrative discretion exists in the regulatory process, just as they develop in any other aspect of bureaucracy. There are several characteristic points where such administrative discretion ordinarily is found in pollution regulation.

1. *When words, phrases, or policy objectives are unclear.* Congress may deliberately shift responsibility to administrators for settling disputes between interests in conflict over how a law should be phrased. Tossing this political "hot potato" to administrators ensures that partisans for all sides of an issue with something to gain or lose by the law's interpretation will scramble to influence whatever officials or bureaucracies resolve such obscurities. Sometimes this lack of legislative clarity results less from deliberation than from congressional confusion or ignorance. In any case, regulators usually find themselves caught between competing group pressures to interpret statutes or regulations in different ways. Such pressures, in fact, should be considered routine in the regulatory process.

2. *When technical standards must be created or revised.* Existing legislation regulating air pollution, water pollution, and hazardous substances ordinarily requires the EPA to define the standards and prescribe the appropriate control technologies necessary to meet mandated standards; often regulatory agencies also are required by such legislation to review periodically and, if appropriate, revise such standards or technology requirements. Legitimate disagreement often exists, as noted in the previous chapter, over the technical and economic justification for most regulatory standards. In the presence of expert dissension about such issues, a large measure of discretion rests with regulatory agencies for resolving such disputes. This discretion, and the conflict it invites, will reappear when regulatory standards are reviewed. In fact virtually all major technical determinations by regulatory agencies are politicized by the activity of pressure groups, Congress, competing governmental agencies, and other interests seeking to shape discretionary decisions to their respective advantage.

3. *When compliance deadlines are flexible.* Pollution legislation may bristle with explicit compliance deadlines, but administrators almost always have authority to extend them. Legislation is particularly generous in granting administrators authority to extend compliance deadlines when, in their opinion, economic hardship or other inequities may result from strict enforcement. Thus the Clean Air Act instructs the EPA to set emission standards for new air pollution sources by considering, among other things, "the degree of emission limitation achievable through the application of the best system of emission reduction which (taking into account the cost of achieving such reduction) the administrator determines has been adequately demonstrated." Such a fistful of discretionary authority in effect permits the EPA to extend compliance deadlines for specific air pollution sources by increasing the time allowed to search for pollution controls meeting these multiple criteria. In many cases a compliance deadline also may be relaxed if an agency determines that it is beyond the technical ability of a polluter to install the proper controls in the required time. Agencies sometimes can achieve "backdoor" extension of compliance deadlines by deliberately delaying the establishment of a standard long enough to permit the regulated interests to make adjustments to the anticipated standard. The EPA, for instance, waited until 1976—more than two and a half years after vinyl chloride was identified as a human carcinogen—before setting an exposure standard for that substance. The reason, the agency explained, was to avoid creating "unacceptably severe economic consequences" for the vinyl chloride manufacturers and users through an earlier standard establishing a more rapid deadline for controlling the chemical's emissions.[7]

4. *When enforcement is discretionary.* Few provisions in current pollution legislation compel federal officials to stop a polluting activity. Most often enforcement actions are discretionary, as in section 111 of the Clean Air Act, which instructs the EPA administrator to regulate any pollutant from a stationary source when "in his judgment" it may cause or contribute to "air pollution which may reasonably be anticipated to endanger public health or welfare." Even when enforcement action is initiated, officials are usually given optional methods for securing compliance.

Beyond Public View

It is worth noting that the implementation of most environmental regulatory programs does not routinely involve the public, or public opinion, in the process. Unlike the White House and Congress, the federal bureaucracy is neither highly visible nor readily understood by the public; regulation operates, in the words of Francis Rourke, behind an "opaque exterior" that the public seldom cares to penetrate. A 1981 public opinion poll that indicated 31 percent of the public knew "nothing at all about the Clean Air Act" and another 39 percent "knew a little" at a time when the act was a topic of major congressional debate typifies public attention to most regulatory matters.[8] This dearth of dependable public interest means that the constellation of political forces and actors involved in regulatory politics ordinarily is confined to organized interests, governmental officials, scientists, technicians, and other "insiders." Given the complexity and technicality of environmental issues, this situation is not surprising. But it emphasizes the extent to which regulatory politics tends to involve a process highly specialized and commonly closed to public involvement.

The Enforcement Problem

The intermingling of administrative discretion and political pressure in regulatory policy making is evident in the enforcement of environmental law. Typically, air and water pollution laws are enforced through state or local agencies with considerable discretion to decide what level of emission control will be required of an air or water polluter and when emission controls must be achieved. These become conditions for the permit that all air and water polluting firms must obtain to operate. In air pollution regulation, for instance, this discretion can arise from the regulator's authority under the Clean Air Act to decide which emission controls are technically and economically feasible and to issue "variances" that temporarily waive emission control deadlines or technology specifications.[9] Regulators seek voluntary compliance. They want to avoid penalties as a means of ensuring compliance if possible because they know that resort to administrative or judicial tribunals likely will involve a protracted, inflexible process with no assurances that the polluter will be compelled to control emissions speedily and efficiently at the conclusion. In fact polluters often provoke such action, hoping to avoid emission controls indefinitely by exploiting the complexities of the administrative or judicial procedures involved.

Regulated firms commonly balk at a regulatory agency's initial specification of acceptable control technologies and deadline dates for compliance with emission standards. The usual solution is bargaining between regulator and regulated, particularly when regulatory agencies confront an economically and politically influential firm, or group of firms, capable of creating political pressures upon the regulatory agency to reach some accommodation over required control technologies or compliance deadlines. Regulatory agencies typically will make some concession to firms concerning required control technologies or compliance deadlines. One form of these concessions is the frequently used variance that allows a firm some delay in achieving emission controls otherwise required under the law. A firm commonly is able to negotiate a variance permitting it to discharge on an interim basis at its existing emission levels and to obtain several additional variances that can significantly delay achievement of required emission controls.

Agencies also heavily depend upon firms monitoring and reporting their own pollution emissions. Most regulatory agencies lack the personnel and other resources to inspect routinely and monitor all emission controls within their jurisdictions. Thus voluntary compliance is almost a necessity in regulation. Quite often, as Paul B. Downing and James N. Kimball note in their careful review of enforcement studies, regulatory agencies accept the firm's own reports of its behavior under all but exceptional circumstances. "We find that the typical agency does not inspect frequently," they comment. "Furthermore, those inspections which do occur are usually pre-announced. Thus we find that the probability of being found in violation is virtually zero. There are two exceptions to this conclusion. One would be cases where a third party reports a violation. . . . The other occurs when a source self-reports a violation. Our case study did indicate that many violations were reported by the regulated companies."[10]

While administrative discretion and political pressure clearly do limit the vigor and strictness in enforcement of environmental regulations, these constraints are sometimes inevitable and may even be prudent. Often the use of administrative discretion to "make a deal" over pollution permits a regulatory agency to achieve more pollution abatement than would be the case if it insisted upon extremely stringent emission standards in full and immediate compliance with the law. This is true particularly when the regulated firm is either unable to comply fully and immediately with a strict interpretation of the law or willing to fight indefinitely in the courts or administrative hearing rooms to prevent any regulation. Many regulatory agencies, limited by staff and funding inadequate for their mandated responsibilities, have no practical alternative to reliance upon voluntary compliance and accommodation. Finally, regulatory agencies often confront regulated interests—including other governmental agencies subject to pollution control—too politically or economically powerful to be compelled to comply fully and immediately with the law. While this should be no excuse for exemption from full compliance with environmental regulation, it is often an immutable political reality with which regulatory agencies must make peace. In such circumstances agencies may logically conclude that it is better to bargain with the regulated interests in the hope of achieving some limited goals than to adopt what may well become an ultimately futile strategy of insisting upon stringent compliance with the law in spite of massive resistance from the polluter.

The existence of discretion in the enforcement of pollution regulation, however necessary or inevitable, also means that such discretion at times will be abused. It sometimes leads agencies to yield needlessly and negligently to political pressures preventing enforcement of essential pollution controls. Unfortunately these are among the unavoidable risks inherent in the exercise of discretionary authority without which environmental administration would be impossible.

Regulating Air Pollution: The Clean Air Act

The Clean Air Act of 1970, together with its important 1977 amendments, constitutes one of the longest, most complex, and most technically detailed regulatory programs ever enacted in Washington. Generally it creates a standards-and-enforcement program in which the federal government establishes national air-quality standards for major pollutants, the states assume primary responsibility for implementing the program within federal guidelines, and the two governments share enforcement responsibilities. In broad outline, the act mandates the following programs.

1. National Air-Quality Standards. The act directed EPA to determine the maximum permissible ambient air concentrations for pollutants it found to be harmful to human health or the environment. EPA was instructed to establish such standards for at least seven pollutants: particulates, sulfur oxides, carbon monoxide, nitrogen oxide, ozone, hydrocarbons, and lead. The agency was to set two types of National Ambient Air Quality Standards (NAAQSs) without considering the cost of compliance:

A. Primary Standards. These were supposed to protect human health with an adequate margin of safety to particularly vulnerable segments of the population, such as the elderly and infants. Originally all air quality control regions in the United States were required to meet primary standards by 1982; this deadline was extended.

B. Secondary Standards. These were intended to maintain visibility and to protect buildings, crops, and water. No deadline was mandated for compliance with secondary standards. The EPA is required by the 1977 Clean Air Amendments to review all criteria for ambient air quality every five years after 1981.

2. Stationary Source Regulations. The EPA was to set maximum emission standards for new sources (plants and factories) called New Source Performance Standards (NSPSs). In doing this, the following procedures were to be followed:

A. Standards were to be set on an industry-by-industry basis; the states then were to enforce the standards.

B. In setting NSPSs, EPA was to take into account the costs, energy requirements, and environmental effects of its guidelines.

C. For existing sources (those dischargers active at the time the act was passed), the EPA was to issue control technique guidelines for the states' use.

3. State Implementation Plans. Each state was required to create a State Implementation Plan indicating how it would achieve federal standards and guidelines to implement the act fully by 1982. The SIPs, which EPA was to approve no later than 1979, were to contain information relating to several important elements:

A. The nation was divided into 247 Air Quality Control Regions (AQCRs) for which states were made responsible. The regions were classified as "attainment" or "nonattainment" regions for each of the regulated pollutants.

B. States were also made responsible for enforcing special air-quality standards in areas with especially clean air called Prevention of Significant Deterioration (PSD) regions.

C. States were required to order existing factories in nonattainment areas to retrofit their plants with control technologies representing "reasonably available control technology." Companies wanting to expand or build new plants in nonattainment areas had to install control equipment that limited pollutants to the least amount emitted by any similar factory anywhere in the United States. This technology was to be specified by the states without regard to the cost.

D. New factories in nonattainment areas also were required to purchase "offsets" from existing air polluters. This involved purchasing new pollution equipment for an existing polluter or paying an existing polluter to eliminate some of its pollution to the extent that the offset equalled the pollution the new source was expected to emit after it installed its own control technology.

E. States in nonattainment areas were given until 1987 to meet carbon monoxide and ozone standards if the state required an annual automobile inspection and maintenance on catalytic converters on newer automobiles. In 1987 Congress extended the deadline for compliance in nonattainment areas to 1988.

F. In PSD areas, all new stationary emission sources were required to install the best available control technology.

4. Mobile Source Emission Standards (for automobiles and trucks). Title II of the act created a detailed but flexible timetable for achievement of auto and truck emission controls.

A. For autos there was to be a 90 percent reduction in hydrocarbon and carbon monoxide emissions by 1975 and a 90 percent reduction in nitrogen oxide emissions by 1976, when measured against 1970 emission levels.

B. The administrator of EPA was authorized to grant extensions of these deadlines for approximately one year. Considerable extensions were granted by EPA and others authorized by Congress:

(i) In 1973 the EPA granted a one-year extension of the 1975 deadline for hydrocarbons and carbon monoxide emissions and a one-year extension of the nitrogen oxide deadline.

(ii) In 1974 Congress granted an additional one-year extension for all emission deadlines.

(iii) In 1975 the EPA granted another one-year deadline extension for enforcement of hydrocarbon and carbon monoxide standards.

(iv) In 1977 compliance deadlines for all emissions were extended for two more years, to be followed by stricter standards for hydrocarbons and carbon monoxide in 1980 and further tightening of the hydrocarbon standard in 1981, together with higher nitrogen oxide standards.

(v) Since 1982, Congress has repeatedly waived compliance deadlines for auto emission controls; the new deadlines extend to the early 1990s.

After a decade of repeated failures, the 1990s began with the Congress and president locked in debate over legislation that would comprehensively amend the Clean Air Act. The major new provisions of the amendments are cited in "New Clean Air Amendments," page 183.

The Continuing Political Struggle

Any regulatory program intended to force polluters to develop the technologies needed to control their pollution in virtually every major economic sector will be controversial and difficult. The third decade of the Clean Air Act has arrived with many of its original objectives still unaccomplished, while new air-quality problems arise to further crowd the governmental agenda. There has been limited success, however. Surveys of national air quality in the late 1980s indicate that many regulated pollutants in ambient air have been reduced or their growth inhibited: sulfur dioxide and carbon monoxide levels have decreased by more than 30 percent, particulate levels are down 23 percent, ozone and nitrogen oxide levels have been reduced by about 14 percent.[11] The most impressive air-quality achievement has been a dramatic reduction in airborne lead, a known toxic especially dangerous to children, since the EPA mandated in the mid-1980s a sharp cutback in the lead content of gasoline. Estimated air emissions of lead have fallen by more than 75 percent since the mid-1970s.[12]

New Clean Air Amendments

Proposed amendments to the Clean Air Act debated in Congress between 1989 and 1990 will be the most important air pollution legislation passed since 1977. When passed by Congress and approved by the president, the new amendments are expected to include these major provisions:

• Automobile emission standards will be increased for hydrocarbons, nitrogen oxides, and carbon monoxide. Emission levels for these pollutants will be lowered to 40 to 60 percent of current levels by the turn of the century and lowered again at a specified date thereafter.

• New automobile pollution controls will be required to remain effective for ten years or 100,000 miles.

• The largest coal-fired electric utilities, mostly in the Midwest, will be required to reduce sulfur dioxide emissions collectively through new technology controls and low-sulfur fuel by at least 10 million tons annually.

• All major industrial and commercial sources of airborne toxics will be required to install the "best available technology" to control these releases. New, more stringent standards for determining acceptable risk from public exposure to airborne toxics will be enforced.

• Coke ovens, a major source of air pollutants from the steel industry, must be installed with the "best available technology" to control pollutants by the late 1990s and must be eliminated entirely within a few decades.

• The use of alternative, less polluting fuels will be encouraged in the U.S. auto industry and in urban areas with the most serious air pollution.

Nonetheless, many fundamental goals of the Clean Air Act remain unachieved. Levels of regulated pollutants remain dangerously high in violation of ambient air-quality standards throughout many of the nation's urban areas. New modes of air pollution on a global scale, such as acid precipitation, have yet to be adequately addressed in the legislation. And new research indicates that a variety of airborne toxics may need swift regulation. These problems arise partially from the political controversies, administrative complexities, and delays inherent in any environmental policy making. But these particular problems also illustrate how new data, technological change, and the global scale of environmental degradation have altered and complicated the implementation of environmental programs initiated in the environmental era's first decade.

Global Scale: The Acid Precipitation Issue

Acid precipitation, like the Greenhouse Effect and atmospheric ozone depletion, is an air-quality issue never anticipated when legislators were writing the Clean Air Act. Besides the technological and political complexities inherent in its domestic control, acid precipitation's apparent global scale poses the additional challenge of requiring agreement on global regulation with other affected nations. The Reagan administration's glacial approach to the problem did little to abate the damage acid precipitation is believed to have inflicted upon the nation's environment and economy, or to resolve the difficulties in creating a regulatory solution to the problem both domestically and internationally. Although scientific uncertainty persists about many aspects of the issue, Congress has felt growing political pressure to advance beyond the Reagan administration's unyielding insistence on "further study."

The Evidence Grows.   In mid-1983, the White House's initial inertia on acid precipitation received three forceful blows. The first was a report by the Interagency Task Force on Acid Precipitation, appointed by the Congress and representing twelve federal agencies, asserting that manmade pollution from industrial stack gases was probably the major cause of the acid rain destroying the fresh water in the Northeast.[13] Shortly thereafter, a report from scientists appointed by the White House Office of Science directly contradicted the administration's contention that further research was necessary prior to any federal action on acid rain. "If we take the conservative point of view that we must wait until scientific knowledge is definitive," concluded the panel, "the accumulated deposition and damaged environment may reach the point of irreversibility."[14] Finally, the prestigious National Academy of Sciences released a report asserting that acid rain throughout the northeastern United States and southern Canada could be curbed by reducing the sulfur oxide emissions from coal-burning power plants in the eastern half of the United States.[15]

The reports were greeted with considerable appreciation not only by environmental groups and northeastern governors but also by the Canadian government, which had been urging the United States, with growing impatience, to take more aggressive action on the issue. By the time Canadian prime minister Brian Mulroney visited President Reagan in mid-1988, Canada's frustration with U.S. inaction was etched into the encounter with acid rhetoric. Mulroney reminded the president that thousands of lakes, rivers, and forests had been destroyed in Canada, and that the maple sugar industry in Quebec and salmon fishing in Nova Scotia had been devastated by acid precipitation. "The Administration knows this thing up and down," he complained.[16]

In such ways Americans were learning that more than 30 million tons of sulfur dioxide and 20 million tons of nitrogen oxide annually rise into the atmosphere from the nation's industries, public utilities, and motor vehicles.[17] High-level winds often transport these gases hundreds of miles from their origin. Forming sulfate and nitrate aerosols, they combine with water vapor into precipitation returning to the earth as acid rain or snow. Acid precipitation, now found throughout the United States, has become common in the northeastern United States and eastern Canada.

As early as 1981, an interagency task force reported that the acidity of the average northeastern rainfall had risen to ten times the normal levels—in some areas, the increase was a thousandfold. This continuing acid precipitation is suspected of rendering hundreds of mountain lakes in the United States and Canada ecologically sterile and disrupting the related forest ecosystems. By 1988, environmental experts in New York state estimated that one-fourth of all lakes in the Adirondack Mountains were too acidic to support fish.[18] That same year an EPA survey reported that streams in the eastern United States were more acidified than had previously been suspected. Based on a sample of approximately 500 streams, the report concluded that 4.4 percent of the 66,000 stream miles in the Middle Atlantic states were acidic and roughly 50 percent of the streams in the area were likely to have a low capacity for neutralizing acid rain.[19]

Continuing Scientific Disagreement.   Despite the evidence of widespread acid precipitation nationally and internationally, scientists still cannot agree upon how seriously this threatens the vitality of the forests. Opponents of national acid precipitation legislation cite this lack of scientific consensus to support their contention that more study must precede any new legislation. Proponents of new legislation argue that while the evidence is still inconclusive, it is more prudent to initiate new regulations than to assume the risks involved in waiting until a final verdict is possible.

The most comprehensive federal study, the National Acid Precipitation Assessment Program (NAPAP), illustrates the ambiguities of current research findings. The program issued its first interim report in 1989. The panel's scientists, taking a moderate position on the acid rain issue, concluded that acid rain did pose a long-term threat to the nation's forests, but not alone: ozone and other natural causes were also involved. The most serious damage, the panel suggested, might be to forest soils where chemical reactions initiated by acid precipitation removed large amounts of calcium and magnesium, essential to healthy tree growth, and left the trees unable to absorb what remained of these chemicals. In some areas, moreover, aluminum leached from the soil by acid precipitation was reaching toxic levels. The full impact of these complex chemical transformations in soil chemistry, the panel concluded, might take fifty years to become apparent.[20] In March 1990 NAPAP issued a draft final report in which it concluded that, with the exception of damage to the red spruce at high elevations in the eastern United States, the national forests were not suffering serious damage from acid rain. Many experts disagreed with the panel's conclusions. Some asserted that the report did not consider forest damage that might be inflicted by acid precipitation but was not yet visible. Other critics noted that the report gave virtually no attention to serious problems in the southern forests, nor did it address soil damage that might ultimately affect the forests.[21] While the debate continues, policy makers are left without a firm scientific consensus to guide their deliberations, yet they are faced with increasing pressure to demonstrate some active response to the problem.

Political Inertia Ends.   The United States inched forward on the acid precipitation problem through most of the 1980s. During its first four years, the Reagan administration resolutely rejected arguments that acid precipitation merited much attention on the environmental agenda. Administration spokesmen asserted that evidence of an acid rain problem was fragmentary and speculative, too meager to justify the enormous costs inherent in any new regulations necessary to control acid rain precursors. Indeed, acid precipitation was officially nonexistent as late as 1984 when the annual report of the Council on Environmental Quality (CEQ), otherwise comprehensive in surveying current national air quality, nowhere mentioned acid precipitation. By the mid-1980s, the Reagan administration grudgingly yielded to growing political pressure and scientific evidence by allocating additional funds for research on the issue and by creating NAPAP. Finally, after years of resistance to any U.S. participation in a global acid rain abatement program, the administration in its final days agreed to sign an international agreement with twenty-four other nations in November 1988 to freeze national emission levels of nitrogen oxide at the 1987 levels, beginning in 1994. But the United States refused to agree with European nations to roll back its nitrogen oxide emissions by 30 percent over the next decade.

The Bush administration, in contrast, took the initiative early in proposing a major new regulatory program to abate the precursors of acid precipitation. President Bush, eager to assume the environmentalist mantle, proposed major new cutbacks for these pollutants in his comprehensive 1989 proposals to amend the Clean Air Act. Many environmentalists argued for much greater domestic cutbacks and more U.S. commitment to global acid precipitation abatement. But they were encouraged by the new White House attitude and the president's highly visible involvement in the issue. Acid precipitation, however, will still be technically and politically difficult to abate, particularly because no scientific consensus has been reached on the magnitude of its environmental impact.

The Regulatory Problem Remains. Any federal effort to address the acid rain issue places Washington in the middle of a politically volatile confrontation between the states (particularly in the Midwest and Northeast), and some of the nation's largest and most economically powerful industries. More than 80 percent of the pollutants thought to cause acid precipitation in the United States and Canada originate in thirty-one states east of the Mississippi River or bordering it. Many of these states are in the populous, heavily industrialized Ohio River Valley. Although the precursors of acid precipitation have already been reduced or controlled significantly under existing provisions of the Clean Air Act—sulfur oxide emissions in the late 1980s, for instance, had been reduced by 21 percent since the early 1970s—existing provisions of the CAA appear insufficient to achieve adequate regulatory control to abate acid precipitation.

Under current provisions of the CAA, the states are ultimately responsible for prescribing the acceptable technologies for existing stationary sources of air pollution to bring Air Quality Control Regions within national air-quality standards. Most states have accepted "tall stacks"— stacks higher than two hundred feet emitting hot flue gases—as an acceptable arrangement for achieving permitted sulfur oxide and nitrogen oxide levels in any particular AQCR. Unfortunately, tall stacks usually disperse the pollutants, primarily sulfur oxides, into the upper atmosphere where long-range transport carries them into other AQCRs or Canada, thereby "air mailing pollutants from some AQCRs to other areas."[22] Since 1979, more than 430 tall stacks, many climbing above 800 feet, have been constructed by electric utilities, smelters, pulp and paper mills, steel factories, and petroleum refineries.

Section 126 of the CAA authorizes the EPA to disapprove any State Implementation Plan that allows a source within one state to contribute to air-quality violations in another state, but acid rain and snow are not defined as pollutants in the law. Further, it is often impossible to identify the source of pollution-tainted rain or snow transported hundreds or thousands of miles in the upper atmosphere. State regulatory agencies have been extremely reluctant to require, or even to suggest, that existing industries with tall stacks install other control technologies. The political influence and economic importance of these industries within the states often ensures that no regulatory action will be taken against the tall stacks. This situation, common in environmental politics, explains why it is often easier for environmental interests to persuade Congress to regulate specific pollutants or polluters than it is for them to persuade state legislatures to act: the political weight of the regulated interests can be more effectively counterbalanced by environmentalists on a national scale.

Industries liable to any new acid rain regulations, especially electric utilities constituting more than half the total facilities involved, have argued that the evidence linking their stack emissions to acid precipitation damage is still inconclusive. Further, as scientists readily admit, it is almost impossible to assign a specific proportion of the acid precipitation in one region to some single distant source. How, ask the affected industries, can emission controls upon specific sources be assigned equitably under such conditions? All affected interests also point to the very large costs of retrofitting control technologies on existing facilities. Total U.S. costs for acid precipitation abatement have been estimated between $20 and $40 billion. Representatives for utilities in the Ohio River Valley, moreover, have argued that these abatement costs would become a crushing burden on an already faltering regional economy dependent upon moribund smokestack industries. Some midwestern utilities have asserted that new emissions controls might raise customer bills by 20 to 50 percent (utilities are especially prompt at converting any potential regulatory expense into customer cost on the well-founded premise that public enthusiasm for new regulations will thereby be dampened).

The Bush administration's proposed amendments to the Clean Air Act required an additional 50 percent reduction of sulfur oxides and 10 percent reduction in nitrogen oxides by the year 2000. Almost all these emissions controls would be imposed on coal-burning utilities. The Bush proposals were most significant as an indication that Congress and the White House agreed on the urgency of some new regulatory action to control acid precipitation. In addition to arguments over how much total U.S. emissions should be reduced, controversy continued over how the additional emission controls would be financed.[23] Among the proposals Congress is likely to consider are:

1. A small tax on electricity consumed by all users of fossil-fuel fired electric plants in states largely east of the Mississippi River. The tax would create a trust fund to help utilities defray the cost of installing the new emission controls.

2. All U.S. utilities generating electricity by coal-fired generators would pay a fee into a national trust fund based upon the total amount of electricity each utility generates. The trust fund would be used to defray the costs of emission controls to affected plants. Utilities would recover these fees through additional consumer charges.

3. A tax would be assessed against utilities based on the amounts of sulfur oxides and nitrogen oxides they emit. Fees would be set at levels

sufficient to persuade utilities to reduce their emissions to levels necessary to achieve the national emission goals established by Congress. Utilities would be permitted to recover these fees from their customers in service changes.[24]

Another major interest sure to be drawn into the political brawl over regulatory strategies is the U.S. coal industry. Fearing that regulation may mean a massive cutback in the use of high-sulfur Appalachian coal, if not all coal, the industry will seek to blunt the impact of regulation upon the utilities as much as possible.

Present proposals before Congress do not confront directly the larger problem of worldwide abatement of acid precipitation. Environmentalists argue that the proposed emission reductions are insufficient to reduce significantly global acid precipitation. They also assert that the United States should take much greater initiative in making international agreements for acid precipitation regulation. It is symbolic, however, that one of the first major environmental issues to trouble Washington in the 1990s is acid precipitation, a problem of global scale that will initiate a decade when U.S. domestic politics will increasingly be forced to face the worldwide implications of its environmental ills.

Pressing Technology: Urban Air Pollution

As the 1990s began, the only major urban area in the United States whose air quality fully met federal and state air-quality standards was Minneapolis. Despite almost two decades of effort, more than 77 million Americans were living in urban areas where serious, sometimes dangerous, air-quality problems remained. The EPA, Congress, and numerous state regulatory officials have been threatening and cajoling the nation's cities to clean their air for more than a decade. Enforcement failure and delay are often cited as explanations why urban air pollution remains so intractable. Other major reasons are inadequate control technologies and overly restricted regulatory objectives. It seems evident now that attaining the urban goals of the CAA will require much greater reliance upon many newer, more radical strategies than "pressing technology," the principal approach now in the CAA.

Years Pass, Smog Endures. Urban smog remains extremely troublesome despite substantial reductions in many of its components. Automobile emission controls have reduced ambient carbon monoxide nationally by more than 30 percent since the late 1970s and ambient ozone has fallen by more than 13 percent during that period.[25] Moreover, the number of Air Quality Control Regions nationally violating one or more federal air-quality standards has fallen from about 600 in 1978 to about 370 currently. The only states where all AQCRs fully comply with federal standards are Iowa, North Dakota, South Dakota, Wyoming, Vermont, and Hawaii. The smog problem is pervasive. The EPA estimated in 1988 that 350 counties were not complying with federal ozone standards and 211 counties were violating federal carbon monoxide standards—most of the counties cited contained major urban areas. The Bush administration's early proposals to bring the nation's cities in compliance with the Clean Air Act—not the most expensive strategy before Congress—was estimated to add between $8 and $20 billion more to the national air pollution control bill.[26]

Regulating urban smog remains difficult because so many varied sources contribute to its creation. The large stationary sources, such as fossil-fuel fired utilities, factories, mineral smelters, and chemical manufacturers, are major contributors. But thousands of small sources, most previously unregulated and many until recently unrecognized— including paint manufacturers, dry cleaners, and gasoline stations— collectively make a major contribution. The automobile stubbornly remains a chronic polluter despite the advent of efficient emission-control technologies. One reason is that pre-1970 vehicles, the worst auto polluters because they lack emission controls, are not being replaced as quickly as predicted. And 25 percent of the new car pollution-control devices, in EPA's illusive phrase, have been "disabled"—that is, deliberately destroyed.[27]

Moreover, a great many state and local governments are failing to enforce their own State Implementation Plans, although the number is hard to estimate. One recent study, for example, reveals a distaste for enforcement at the grass roots. After observing in 1988 the implementation of ozone reduction plans in three major U.S. cities with serious compliance problems (Charlotte, Houston, and Los Angeles) the General Accounting Office concluded that the cities were failing because "control measures were not implemented, control measures implemented were not enforced. . . . In addition, deficiencies identified in the three areas' ozone control programs were not corrected, indicating that EPA's oversight was not as effective as it should have been."[28] Control strategies often failed to perform as expected: in Los Angeles, sixteen of twenty-nine planned measures to control hydrocarbon emissions from stationary sources had not been implemented because the control technology was not fully developed, was too costly to use, or failed to perform as promised. And "discussions with state and local government and industry officials indicated that there is a general reluctance to implement control measures that will have a negative impact on economic development or change life-styles."[29]

Even the best available technologies may be insufficient to control adequately all important emissions. The newest Detroit emission controls now remove 96 percent of the pollutants that were allowed to be emitted before controls began in 1972.[30] Many experts believe existing auto emission controls have reached "the knife edge of technological feasibility" and further emission reductions are unlikely as long as auto engines burn gasoline. Thus, the future of urban air pollution control may lead directly into a thicket of new, unwelcome strategies including intrusive approaches that are inconvenient at least, and probably costly to the public and to regulated firms.

Ahead: Difficult Choices, Tough Strategies. The easiest strategies for reducing urban smog have been tried. If the nation means to restore urban air quality to safe levels, it will have to adopt newer, more stringent approaches that are likely to be unpopular, moderately costly to the average American, and politically distasteful to public officials. The amendments sure to be added to the CAA in the early 1990s will be the most important test of Washington's political fortitude.

Most environmentalists and many air-quality experts believe amendments added to the CAA must include many of the approaches already enacted by California, a national leader in environmental policy innovation for the last two decades. These new approaches for auto emissions include:

• Increasing performance life of auto emission control devices well beyond the 50,000 miles now required for new cars by federal law. California will require a 100,000-mile control on carbon monoxide, hydrocarbons, and nitrogen oxides.

• Requiring periodic inspection of auto emission controls on automobiles and assessing heavy fines for tampering with such devices.

• Requiring reformulation of gasoline to increase the amount of methanol or other alternative fuel in the mix, or mandating the gradual introduction of production cars with engines capable of running entirely on methanol, ethanol, or some nonfossil energy source such as electricity.

Requiring further reduction in the emissions of major stationary sources within cities may, in some cases, bring an urban area into compliance with federal air-quality standards. But in many areas, such as Los Angeles, additional strategies will be necessary, perhaps bringing the battle against smog, quite literally, into the average resident's back yard. The air-quality control plan proposed for the Los Angeles basin in the early 1990s included these measures:

• Requiring all local manufacturers to reformulate all paints and solvents;

• Banning gasoline-powered lawn mowers;

• Banning the sale of barbecues and fuels requiring a liquid starter;

- Limiting the number of cars each family may own;
- Raising parking fees for cars that carry only one person;
- Restricting new tire purchases to radials, which throw less rubber particles into the air.[31]

Regardless of the particular strategies adopted, the Los Angeles proposals are a portent of regulations to come: the average urban resident will have to assume a much greater responsibility and bear a higher cost, in dollars and convenience, for urban smog reduction. Whether millions of Americans will be willing to do this remains one of the most critical political questions of the 1990s.

Science and Regulatory Change: Particulates and Airborne Toxins

Regulation strives for predictability, consistency in interpreting and applying the law, and stability in established norms for decision making. Science breeds discovery, embraces change, promotes experimentation, and challenges tradition. Science has become the troubler of regulatory order. The Clean Air Act currently regulates both airborne particulates and toxics. But the continuing enrichment of the scientific base for regulation over the last twenty years is forcing a change in understanding which substances should be regulated and what levels can be tolerated. New scientific evidence poses difficult new regulatory choices in both instances.

New Discoveries About Particulates. In 1971, the EPA issued air-quality standards for particulates without distinction about size. Particulates—extremely small solid particles of matter found in the air and produced by dust, smoke, fuel combustion, agriculture and forest cultivation, among other sources—have been known to pose health hazards for many decades. Initially, however, EPA's standards assumed that size was not a significant factor in the health risks posed. By 1987, accumulating scientific research had demonstrated conclusively that small particulates, those smaller than 10 microns (one micron equals 1/25,000 inch), are especially hazardous to humans because they can be inhaled into lung tissue, unlike larger particulates that are caught in the air passages to the lung.[32] These smaller particulates are commonly found in cigarette smoke, diesel engine emissions, windblown dust, and many other sources. They are also dangerous because they can carry carcinogenic chemical substances into the lung. In 1987, the EPA issued new air-quality standards for small particulates. However, existing emission controls for particulates were not designed specifically to control small particulates and many sources of small particulates were not regulated at all. In effect, small particulates have become a separate emission-control problem.

Presently, about 250 AQCRs are estimated to fail the new ambient air-quality standards for fine particulates.[33] In the West, a major problem is windblown dust, which is not easily controlled by any current technology. The EPA has established tailpipe standards for emissions from diesel trucks and buses, beginning with model year 1988, that will become increasingly stringent in the 1991 and 1994 models. But monitoring data about the origin and distribution of fine particulates are inadequate and, consequently, states are only beginning to identify the magnitude of their problem and the sources that must be regulated. Control technologies for stationary sources of small particulates have not been well tested, and the control costs are not accurately known. Thus, it may be many years before it is apparent whether newly initiated regulatory approaches will have a major impact on the small particulate problem.

Regulation at a Crawl: Airborne Toxics. Section 112 of the Clean Air Act authorizes the EPA to establish emission standards for airborne toxic or hazardous substances, defined in the law as any substances that cause or contribute to "an increase in mortality or an increase in serious irreversible or incapacitating illness." More than 320 toxic chemical substances are emitted into the air annually.[34] The EPA is currently evaluating about 30 of these, but only 8 are currently regulated: asbestos, beryllium, mercury, vinyl chloride, arsenic, radionuclides, benzene, and coke oven emissions. The federal government has identified at least 60 airborne chemicals as known carcinogens, including carbon tetrachloride, butadiene, acrylonitrile, and cadmium. Other toxics are known to cause birth defects or neurological disease.

EPA officials have complained that the CAA's provisions affecting airborne toxics are so cumbersome and expensive, and so vulnerable to legal challenge, that they have been unable to add more substances to the regulated list.[35] Regulation is indeed slow and expensive. The EPA must take the initiative in assembling the list of prospective chemicals to be examined, in gathering the appropriate scientific data and reviewing it, and in determining which among hundreds of chemicals merit more detailed study. The agency must then identify the sources of chemicals on its "short list" of substances, obtain data if possible from these sources about the character and volume of their chemical releases, and visit at least some emission sites to verify their estimated releases. If the EPA decides to regulate a substance under Section 114, the federal government bears the burden of proof in demonstrating that the risks of exposure to that substance are sufficient to merit regulation if the decision is challenged legally. This obligation encourages an extremely cautious approach to decision making, made even more deliberate by the frequent inadequacies and gaps in scientific data on the health effects of many suspected chemicals. And it is an expensive business. In the middle 1980s, the EPA's ten on-site emission tests for chromium—just one phase of its evaluation—cost between $300,000 and $400,000.[36]

The annual national survey of chemical emissions, now required by the Superfund Amendments and Reauthorization Act (SARA), will contribute considerable information to the presently meager data on the extent of these emissions nationally. But the variety and distribution of emission sources pose serious problems because many are not easily or economically controlled. Although the chemical industry is the single greatest source of these emissions, other sources include manufacturing plants, dry cleaning and paint removal processes, sewage treatment plants, hazardous waste processing and disposal facilities, smelters, and metal refining industries. Data are especially scarce on the long-term effects of low-level exposure to hazardous chemicals because most current information is obtained from industrial workers; additionally, the EPA has now excluded from SARA's reporting requirements even large releases of substances with low toxicity.

Another highly productive cause of regulatory delay is the frequent opposition of chemical manufacturers and commercial users to such regulation. Since the scientific base for estimates of risk from exposure to these substances is often meager, legal and administrative challenges even to the designation of a proven carcinogen can postpone regulation for years. The asbestos industry's ferocious resistance turned control efforts into a regulatory trench warfare that lasted many years. The asbestos manufacturers agreed to virtually nothing, rejecting among other things a proposal that the federal government inform the public about the potential harm that might afflict children spending much time in school buildings containing asbestos insulation.[37]

Acid precipitation, urban smog, airborne toxics, and small particulates are a few among many ambient air problems challenging the nation's ability to realize the ambitious goals set by the CAA more than twenty years ago. These problems test the nation's technological skill and economic resiliency. They will challenge the political determination of its officials and the public's commitment to the environmental protection the majority professes to support. These problems are also reminders of how incrementally slow has been the implementation and how modest have been the achievements of the Clean Air Act. The nation's experience with water pollution has been much the same.

Regulating Water Pollution: Different Systems, Different Laws

The nation's aquatic inheritance is not just water but different water systems, each essential to modern U.S. society and each currently threatened, or already degraded, by different combinations of pollutants. There have been conspicuous achievements in water-quality control in the last twenty years and dangerous failures. And there have been new, troubling revelations that the full magnitude of the nation's water degradation is not yet accurately understood, and that effective remedies have not been applied.

Surface Water

The nation's streams, rivers, and lakes are, together with the sea, the most visible of all water resources. Almost 99 percent of the population lives within fifty miles of a publicly owned lake. Streams, rivers, and lakes account for a very high proportion of all recreation activities, commercial fishing grounds, and industrial water resources. Because surface waters are used so intensively and are highly visible, their rapidly accelerating degradation was the most immediate cause for congressional action in the 1960s and 1970s to arrest water quality degradation. Indeed, to many Americans "water pollution" is surface water pollution. Most of the still fragmentary data on national water quality during the last three decades come from monitoring surface-water conditions.

The Federal Water Pollution Control Act Amendments.   The federal government's major water pollution regulatory program is embodied in the Federal Water Pollution Control Act Amendments of 1972 and concerns primarily surface water quality. The 1972 legislation amended the earlier Water Pollution Control Act of 1948. The 1972 amendments completely changed the substance of the earlier legislation and established the regulatory framework prevailing ever since. This 1972 legislation was greatly strengthened by new amendments passed in 1987 as the Water Quality Act. In more than 120 pages of fine print, the FWPCAA mandates the following regulatory program for the nation's surface waters:

1. Goals. The amendments established two broad goals whose achievement, if possible, assumed an unprecedented regulatory structure and unusually rapid technological innovation:

A. "the discharge of pollutants into navigable waters of the United States be eliminated by 1985."

B. "wherever attainable, an interim goal of water quality which provides for the protection and propagation of fish, shellfish and wildlife and provides for recreation in and on the water be achieved by 1 July 1983."

2. Regulatory Provisions for Existing Dischargers. The legislation required that all direct dischargers into navigable waterways satisfy two different standards, one relating to water quality, the other to effluent limits. The water-quality standards, established by the states according to EPA guidelines, were to identify the use for a body of water into which a polluter was discharging (such as recreation, fishing, boating, waste disposal, irrigation, etc.) and to establish limits on discharges in order to ensure that use. Effluent standards, established by the EPA, were to identify what technologies any discharger had to use to control its effluents. In meeting these dual requirements, the polluter was required to achieve whichever standard was the more strict. A different set of standards was established for publicly owned waste treatment facilities.

A. *Effluent Limits for Existing Nonmunicipal Sources.* Except for city waste treatment plants, all existing dischargers were required to have technological controls, prescribed by the EPA, which were to meet the following criteria:

a. The "best practicable control technology currently available" by 1 July 1979.

b. The "best available technology economically achievable" by 1 July 1983.

B. *Effluent Limits for Municipal Treatment Plants.* All treatment plants in existence on 1 July 1977 were required to have "secondary-treatment" levels. All facilities, regardless of age, were required to have "the best practicable treatment technology" by 1 July 1983.

C. *Effluent Limits for New Nonmunicipal Sources.* All new sources of discharge, except municipal treatment plants, were required to use control technologies based on "the best available demonstrated control technology, operating methods or other alternatives."

D. *Toxic Effluent Standards.* The EPA was required to establish special standards for any discharge determined to be toxic.

3. Regulatory Provisions for Indirect Dischargers. Many pollutants, including chemical toxics, are released into municipal waste water systems by industrial and commercial sources and later enter waterways through city sewage treatment plants unable to eliminate them. The law required the EPA to establish "pre-treatment" standards, which were to prevent the discharge of any pollutant through a public sewer that "interferes with, passes through or otherwise is incompatible with such works." The purpose of this provision was to compel such "indirect dischargers" to treat their effluent before it reached the city system.

4. Federal and State Enforcement. The EPA was authorized to delegate responsibility for enforcing most regulatory provisions to qualified states who would issue permits to all polluters specifying the conditions for their effluent discharges.

5. Waste Treatment Grants. The act authorized the expenditure of $18 billion between 1973 and 1975 to assist local communities in building necessary waste-water treatment facilities. The federal government assumed 75 percent of the capital cost for constructing the facilities.

6. Nonpoint Pollution Regulation. Amendments added in 1987 require each state to have an EPA-approved plan for controlling pollution from nonpoint sources. Such plans must include "best management practices" but states are permitted to decide whether to require owners and managers to use such practices or to make them voluntary.

The 1972 legislation was written by a Congress unchastened by the political, economic, and technological obstacles to pressing technology in pollution regulation. The legislation, as originally written, was the purest example of "technology forcing" in the federal regulatory code. The use of effluent standards in addition to water-quality standards for dischargers was based on the premise that "all pollution was undesirable and should be reduced to the maximum extent that technology will permit."[38] Compliance deadlines were almost imperiously ordained for the total elimination of water pollution in a decade. The administrative and technical complexities of making the legislation work seemed surmountable. It serves as an enduring monument to the American politician's belief in the possibilities of social engineering and to the political muscle of the environmental movement in the early 1970s.

Even among the legislation's most ardent advocates, however, few were confident that the rigorous compliance deadlines for effluent treatment and waste-water treatment facility construction would be attained. They were certainly convinced that pressing technology ultimately worked—eliminating all pollutants from the nation's waters hardly seemed impossible to a people who could launch satellites carrying their language a billion light years into space. The likelihood of short-term failures was at least tacitly recognized. But advocates of the legislation were convinced that only by pressing ceaselessly for rapid compliance with regulations could they sustain the sense of urgency and bring sufficient weight of federal authority to bear upon polluters to obtain their long-term objectives. Thus, from the beginning, proponents and implementers of the 1972 legislation have had to temper militancy with compromise, to accept some failure as inevitable.

The Political Setting. The political struggle over implementation of the FWPCAA has been shaped by several factors. First, the implementation of the legislation is largely federalized. The 1972 act made concessions to the states that Congress had been unwilling to make in the Clean Air Act of 1970 and that environmentalists generally opposed. The 1972 amendments permitted the states to decide upon the designated use for a body of water. Generally, state regulatory agencies are more vulnerable than Washington to pressure from local water polluters to designate uses for bodies of water that will permit moderate to heavy pollution. This propensity of local regulatory agencies to accommodate regulated interests extends, as well, to enforcement of designated water uses and the associated emission controls. Thus, regulated interests often are likely to press vigorously for a major state role in the administration and enforcement of water-quality standards, believing that this works to their advantage more than implementation through the EPA's regional and national offices.

Most states, given the opportunity, have assumed major implementation responsibilities, such as issuing and enforcing permits for effluent dischargers, initiating requests for federal grants to build new local waste treatment facilities, and supervising the administration of the grant programs in their jurisdiction. The states thus exercise considerable influence upon program implementation directly through their own participation—and the pursuit of their own interest in the program—and through their congressional delegations, which remain ever vigilant in protecting the interests of the folks back home. Moreover, conflict arising from differing state and federal viewpoints on program implementation becomes interjected immediately into the daily administrative implementation of the law.

The political character of the program also depends upon the enormous administrative discretion left to the EPA in prescribing the multitude of different technologies that must be used by effluent dischargers to meet the many different standards established in the law. At the time the Clean Water Act was amended in 1972, for instance, about 20,000 industrial dischargers were pouring pollutants into more than 2,500 municipal waste treatment facilities. The EPA was charged with identifying the pretreatment standards to be used by each major class of industrial discharger. This might eventually require standards for several hundred different classes and modified standards for subclasses. The final standards issued by the EPA in 1976 for industries producing "canned and preserved fruits and vegetables" alone contained specifications for fifty-one different subcategories. Administrators also are limited by the state of the art in treatment technologies and by dependence upon the regulated interests for information concerning the character of the discharger's production processes and technical capacities. We already have noted that administrative discretion invites political pressure and conflict. The technical determinations required in setting effluent standards also invite controversy and litigation.

Finally, the program's implementation has been continually affected by the active, if not always welcome, intervention of the White House, Congress, and the federal courts in the program development. Federal and state regulatory agencies have had to conduct the program in a highly political environment, where all major actions have been subject to continual scrutiny, debate, and assessment by elective public officials and judges. This is hardly surprising for a program involving so many billions of dollars and so many politically and economically sensitive interests. But, as we shall observe, the economic and environmental costs of such politicized administration are high.

Results: Is "Significant" Really Significant?　The nation did not eliminate all pollution discharges into its waters by 1985, nor did it make all, or even most, waterways "fishable and swimmable" by mid-1983 as the FWPCAA intended. The combined impacts of the multibillion dollar Construction Grants Program and the national permit system for pollution dischargers have prevented the further degradation of many surface waters, reduced pollution in others, and undoubtedly saved some high-quality waters from degradation. But the evidence of a major, long-term improvement in the overall quality of the nation's surface waters is elusive. Considering the nation's population growth and economic expansion of the last two decades, the stability of water quality must be considered an achievement of sorts—it could have been much worse. But the quality of the nation's surface water is apparently not greatly improved, either—"apparently" because adequate data are often unavailable. The goals of the FWPCAA still seem decades from achievement.

The EPA has tried to salvage optimism from this ambiguity. "State and federal data indicate," it reported in 1988, "that our water pollution efforts have made significant headway to restore or protect surface water quality."[39] As evidence, the agency cited the 1986 state data found in Table 6-2. According to state reports, 99 percent of the nation's streams had been designated by the states for uses equal or better than the "fishable and swimmable" goal mandated by the 1972 legislation, and Table 6-2 indicates that 74 percent of these streams had water quality "supporting" this use. Most environmentalists, however, would find this to be cheerless news. The survey includes only 21 percent of the nation's stream miles, only 32 percent of the nation's lake acres, and only 55 percent of national estuarine miles. The data also fail to indicate what portion of the assessed lakes and estuaries are "supported" at their highest quality levels. At least 10,000 major U.S. lakes, for example, are considered to have serious pollution problems.[40] Moreover, the states and EPA base their water-quality indices largely on measurement of only six indicators: fecal coliform bacteria, dissolved oxygen, total phosphorus, total mercury, total lead, and biochemical oxygen demand. These indices exclude such important sources of water degradation as heavy metals, synthetic organic compounds, and dissolved solids. Other national studies suggest that, at best, most of the nation's surface waters have maintained about the same quality they had in the mid-1970s.[41]

Table 6-2 *Degree of Designated Use Supported by the Nation's Waters,*
1986

Degree of support	Rivers (miles)	Lakes (acres)	Estuaries (sq. miles)
Total in United States	1,800,000	39,400,000	32,000
Assessed	370,544	12,531,846	17,606
(% of total)	(21%)	(32%)	(55%)
Fully supporting	274,537	9,202,752	13,154
(% of assessed)	(74%)	(73%)	(75%)
Partially supporting uses	70,916	2,181,331	3,224
(% of assessed)	(19%)	(17%)	(18%)
Not supporting uses	22,974	859,080	1,177
(% of assessed)	(6%)	(7%)	(7%)
Unknown	2,127	288,684	51
(% of assessed)	(1%)	(2%)	(0.30%)

SOURCE: Environmental Protection Agency, *Environmental Progress and Challenges: EPA's Update* (Washington, D.C.: Environmental Protection Agency, August 1988), 48.

Note: Based on 1986 Sec. 305(b) data as follows: for rivers, forty-two states and territories reported; for lakes, thirty-seven states reported; for estuaries, twenty states reported.

There is no convincing evidence that massive governmental spending on municipal waste-water treatment plants has significantly improved the nation's waters. Since 1960, the nation's governments have spent more than \$113 billion to construct or upgrade these facilities.[42] This governmental largess has certainly produced high-quality treatment plants in abundance. Since 1970, more than 8,000 projects in 5,000 municipalities have been undertaken. Today almost three-quarters of all municipal facilities achieve at least secondary treatment for their wastes and the proportion of the nation served by these high-quality plants has risen from 42 to 56 percent.[43] But more high-tech treatment plants do not necessarily mean better water quality. The amount of pollutants dumped into the nation's surface waters from municipalities has decreased, but it is unclear how much this has improved water quality.[44] Monitoring data and other information essential to assessing the impact of the construction grants on surface water quality are inadequate. Existing information is often inconsistent. And so things will remain as long as the dull but essential task of data collection remains politically unattractive and underfunded.

The Nonpoint Pollution Problem.   The most common source of surface-water pollution has remained virtually uncontrolled in every state since the 1972 passage of the FWPCAA. Nonpoint pollution—pollution arising from diffuse, multiple sources rather than from a pipe or other

Table 6-3 *Probable Sources of National Water Pollution Reported for 1982*

	River miles	
Probable source[a]	Total	Percent
Nonpoint		
Agricultural	281,241	29.5
Natural	212,389	22.2
Silviculture and logging	71,736	7.5
Feedlots	59,947	6.3
Individual sewage disposal	47,823	5.0
Urban runoff	40,376	4.2
Mining	31,847	3.3
Construction	29,110	3.1
Grazing[b]	21,970	2.3
Landfill leachate	5,504	0.6
Bedload movement[b]	5,299	0.6
Roads	3,569	0.4
Total	**367,244**	**38.4**
Point		
Municipal	63,816	6.7
Industrial	47,097	4.9
Combined sewers	29,246	3.1
Mining	28,686	3.0
Dam releases	19,314	2.0
Total	**117,684**	**12.3**
Other	19,445	2.0

SOURCE: U.S. General Accounting Office, "The Nation's Water: Key Unanswered Questions About the Quality of Rivers and Streams," Report no. GAO/PEMD-86-6 (September 1986), 80.
[a]Subcategories are not additive.
[b]Category developed from clarification by respondents under "other."

"point" source—is estimated to be the major cause of pollution in 65 percent of the stream miles not meeting state standards for their designated use.[45] Overall, more than one-third of the stream miles in the United States appear to be affected by nonpoint pollution. The great variety of nonpoint pollution sources is presented in Table 6-3, which identifies the total stream miles polluted in the United States and the apparent source of degradation. Nonpoint pollution also affects ground water quality. In a mid-1980s survey, thirty-four states reported nitrates as the most common nonpoint pollutant affecting ground water and thirty-one states identified organic chemicals as another major source.[46]

Nonpoint pollution is especially troublesome for several reasons. Pollution originating in diffuse sources is not easily controlled technically, or economically. Many different sources require many different control strategies. By far the largest source of nonpoint pollution is agriculture: crop lands, pasture, and range lands together pollute about one-third of the nation's stream miles with metabolic wastes from animals, sediment, fertilizers, pesticides, dissolved solids, and other materials. Agricultural nonpoint pollution and urban storm-water runoff are the major causes for the eutrophication of lakes, whereby dissolved organic substances create such a high level of oxygen demand in the waters that higher forms of plants and animals die from oxygen deprivation. Eutrophication eventually leaves most lakes lifeless.

Reducing agricultural pollution requires a number of difficult strategies because technological solutions are rarely available. Most often, production practices must be altered. Farmers might be encouraged, or required, to reduce the volume of fertilizer, pesticides, and other chemicals used in crop production. Animal populations might be limited or dispersed. New crop and land management techniques might reduce soil runoff. In many instances, land-use planning might be used to prevent, or reduce, agricultural activities. But powerful agricultural groups and members of Congress for whom they are a major constituency believe such strategies will have adverse economic impacts and have opposed most measures intended to reduce agricultural runoff by most of these methods. Many state governments, fearful of damaging a major component of the state economy, are reluctant to do more than encourage farmers to voluntarily seek ways to limit their pollution runoff.

Attempts to manage other major nonpoint pollution sources will set regulators on a collision course with the commercial timber industry, the commercial and residential construction industry, meat packers and shippers, coal mining firms, and a multitude of trades and professions associated with each. Because technological controls are seldom available to manage these pollution sources, the alternatives are usually costly and difficult to implement. Regulators understandably prefer to avoid as long as possible the political bloodletting likely to arise when nonpoint source controls must be implemented. That day will be forced upon them if the nation's surface waters are ever to meet state water-quality standards. In the late 1980s, thirty-three states reported that nonpoint pollution was a serious problem and an additional fourteen states considered it moderate. The states experience the effects most acutely and the states will have to undertake the arduous job of solving the problem if it is to be solved.

Ground Water

Ground water flows beneath the earth's surface, between the porous upper layer and a lower layer of impermeable rock. Surface water percolates through the upper layer and collects until eventually it saturates soil and rock. Much of this water flows slowly to the sea through permeable layers of sand or gravel called aquifers. These aquifers sustain the life and vitality of communities throughout much of the United States. Indeed, ground water is as essential as surface water to the nation's existence and far more abundant: the annual flow of ground water is fifty times the volume of surface flows, and most aquifers are within a half mile of the earth's surface. Fifty percent of all Americans and 95 percent of rural residents depend on ground water for drinking. Ground water supplies 50 percent of the nation's agricultural water and 25 percent of all industrial water. For most of its history, the nation treated ground water as if it were endlessly renewable—as both spring and sewer. Only within the last two decades has it become obvious that steeply increasing ground-water withdrawals and growing chemical contamination now threaten most of the nation's aquifers.

Many Programs, Many Governments, Many Agencies.   Ground water was unrecognized as a threatened resource until the 1970s (the CEQ finally gave it attention in its 1979 report).[47] The 1977 discovery of massive ground-water contamination caused by the abandoned hazardous waste site at New York's Love Canal became the nation's first ground-water crisis. Ground-water contamination has been a crisis-driven issue, thrust upon governmental agendas by waves of public apprehension following revelations of widespread ground-water contamination from hazardous waste dumps, agricultural chemicals, and industrial and governmental chemical accidents. Improved monitoring has also added urgency to the ground water issue by revealing widespread and previously unknown chemical contamination. But monitoring has only begun and the quality of most underground waters remains unknown.[48]

Traditionally, ground-water management has been considered a state and local governmental responsibility. Although the federal government has no comprehensive ground-water management program, approximately forty-five different federal programs affect ground water in some manner.[49] The primary federal responsibility for implementing many of the major programs affecting ground water rests with the EPA. In addition to the FWPCAA, other important legislation affecting ground-water quality includes the Marine Protection, Research and Sanctuaries Act (1972); the Safe Drinking Water Act (1974) and its 1986 amendments; the Resource Conservation and Recovery Act (1976); and the "Superfund" legislation (1980) together with its 1984 amendments. However, many other agencies and programs are also involved. The mélange of federal agencies and programs involved in ground-water management assures incoherence, inconsistency, and overlapping and competing authority in Washington's approach to ground-water problems.

The states' considerable responsibility for ground-water management has been acquired through federal legislation and their own initiative. Forty-one states currently have their own ground-water quality standards, although little consistency exists among them. The number of ground-water contaminants currently regulated varies from 14 in one state to 190 in another.[50] Additionally, approximately fifteen states have enacted laws specifically regulating drinking water quality and almost all the states have assumed responsibility for implementing federal drinking water standards established under the Safe Drinking Water Act. Thus, the states today assume the primary responsibility for ground-water management. How well they discharge this responsibility, if at all, remains an open question.

Controlling subsurface pollution is troublesome because ground water filters very slowly as it flows. An aquifer may move no more than ten to one hundred feet annually. In any case, many toxic contaminants are not captured or neutralized by filtering. Moreover, the extent of ground-water pollution may be impossible to estimate adequately because the pollution plume radiating outward through an aquifer from a pollution source can take a number of unpredictable directions. Often, plumes will contaminate millions or billions of gallons of water. Some idea about the variety of dangerous chemicals found in ground water can be gleaned from Table 6-4, which indicates the concentration of selected volatile chlorinated solvents, a major class of potentially toxic chemicals, in the raw and treated ground water used for drinking in thirty-nine U.S. cities with populations between ten thousand and 1 million.

Continuing Chemical Contamination. The many substances known or suspected to contaminate ground water defy concise enumeration. One survey indicated that the states have collectively set standards for approximately 35 inorganic compounds, 39 volatile organic compounds, 125 nonvolatile organic compounds, and 56 pesticides, among other substances.[51] These represent only a small portion of the chemicals used in the U.S. economy and found in ground water. These contaminants originate from many sources. The states are only beginning to regulate many of these sources, such as underground storage tanks, underground injection wells, and abandoned waste sites. Although most states have at least some standards for ground-water quality, it is unclear how well they are enforced. "It is very difficult to know precisely how the states' standards were used," concluded a 1988 GAO survey. "At best, we could identify only the principal areas where they were used. . . . However, how the states actually implemented these objectives in state programs and how well the objectives were met is completely unknown at the present time."[52]

Among ground water contaminants, chemicals remain especially dif-

Table 6-4 Concentrations of Selected Organic Compounds in Raw and Finished (Treated) Ground Water

| Compound | Number of cities sampled | | Percentage with chemical present | | Concentration[a] | | | | | |
| | | | | | Mean | | Median | | Range | |
	Raw	Fin.	Raw	Fin.	Raw	Fin.	Raw	Fin.	Raw	Fin.
Trichloroethylene	13	25	38.5	36.0	29.72	6.76	1.3	0.31	0.2–125.0	0.11–53.0
Carbon tetrachloride	27	39	7.4	28.2	11.5	3.8	11.5	2.0	3.0–20.0	0.2–13.0
Tetrachloroethylene	27	36	18.5	22.0	0.98	2.08	0.6	3.0	0.1–2.0	0.2–3.1
1,1,1-Trichloroethane	13	23	23.1	21.7	4.8	2.13	1.1	2.1	0.3–13.0	1.3–3.0
1,1-Dichloroethane	13	13	23.1	23.1	0.7	0.3	0.8	0.2	0.4–0.9	0.2–0.5
1,2-Dichloroethane	13	25	7.7	4.0	0.2	0.2	NA	NA	0.2–NA	0.2–NA
Trans-dichloroethylene	13	13	15.4	15.4	1.75	1.05	1.75	1.05	0.2–3.3	0.2–1.9
Cis-dichloroethylene	13	13	38.5	30.8	13.56	9.35	0.1	0.15	0.1–69.0	0.1–37.0
1,1-Dichloroethylene	13	13	15.4	7.7	0.5	0.2	0.5	NA	0.5–0.5	0.2–NA
Methylene chloride	27	38	3.7	2.6	4.0	7.0	NA	NA	4.0–NA	7.0–NA
Vinyl chloride	13	25	15.4	4.0	5.8	9.4	5.8	NA	2.2–9.4	9.4–NA

SOURCE: Council on Environmental Quality. Environmental Quality, 1981 (Washington, D.C.: Government Printing Office, 1982), 93.
Note: Micrograms per liter = parts per billion. NA = not applicable.
[a]Micrograms per liter.

ficult to regulate because of their great number and wide diffusion in the ecosystem. Most states set standards for and monitor only a fraction of the chemicals likely to be present in ground water. Almost all states identify toxics as a major source of water-quality problems. These toxics can originate in thousands of abandoned and poorly regulated hazardous waste sites, from agricultural activity, underground injection wells, municipal landfill, and sludges. Sludges—the semisolid wastes produced in many air and water pollution control activities—often contain many hazardous or toxic chemicals. Municipal waste treatment plants in the United States annually produce more than 26 million tons of hazardous sludge. The dangerous chemicals removed from water as sludge frequently infiltrate the ecosystem again when they migrate to surface and underground water. Many states as yet have no regulatory program to manage this cross-media pollution migration.

Why have the states undertaken ground-water regulation at such a glacial pace? Many states, reporting they lack the necessary staff and technical expertise to set their own ground-water standards, depend upon federal standards whenever issued. Many state legislatures and governors have shown little interest in the ground-water monitoring that is essential to sound regulation. Potent political opposition to more aggressive regulation also exists in many states, especially from agricultural, industrial, and petroleum-producing interests likely to be the major targets of increased regulation. Ground-water regulation has yet to acquire the political weight and public attention given to surface-water pollution. As monitoring improves and toxicity evaluation of new chemicals continues, a more accurate and probably more threatening assessment of the nation's ground-water quality will likely result. Unfortunately, it may take more Love Canals or other ground-water crises before the federal government and the states give the issue the political attention appropriate to its importance.

Drinking Water

One need look no further than the kitchen faucet for the next potential ground-water crisis. All ecosystems are intricately and subtly interrelated. The negligent dumping of contaminants into surface water and ground water eventually follows a circle of causality, delivering the danger back to its source. So it is in the United States. More than 80 percent of the nation's community water systems depend upon ground water for domestic use and the remainder use surface water.

Recognizing that community drinking water was threatened by the rising volume of pollutants entering surface and ground water, Congress passed in 1974 the Safe Drinking Water Act, amended in 1986, to ensure that public water supplies achieved minimum health standards. In 1977 the EPA, following the act's mandate, began to set National Primary Drinking Water Standards that established maximum contamination levels in drinking water for microbiological contaminants, turbidity, and chemical agents. Currently, standards exist for approximately thirty substances. Standard setting is badly lagging at the EPA, however. In another demonstration of congressional overcontrol, the 1986 amendments required the EPA to adopt standards for sixty-one more contaminants by mid-1989, create twenty-five more standards from a new list by 1991, and set standards for twenty-five additional chemicals every three years thereafter. Once standards are established, the states are given primary responsibility for enforcing them, and other provisions of the act, on more than 79,000 public water systems.

Fragmentary evidence suggests that many of the nation's water systems, including some of the largest, have been infiltrated by dangerous concentrations of chemical and biological contaminants, many for which no standards exist and, consequently, no regulatory controls exist. In 1988, the EPA listed among the major problems:

• In the period 1975–1985, between 1,500 and 3,000 water supplies exceeded EPA standards for inorganic substances, particularly fluoride and nitrates;
• Major problems with toxic organic substances were reported in some wells in almost every state west of the Mississippi River;
• In the early 1980s, about 20 percent of all public water systems and 29 percent of those in urban areas had detectable levels of at least one volatile organic compound.[53]

Increasingly sensitive monitoring is revealing a mounting number of chemicals in the nation's drinking water, most posing unknown risks to human health. A 1988 study by Ralph Nader identified 2,110 chemical compounds found in one-fifth of the nation's public water systems. Among these chemicals 190 were known or suspected to endanger human health.[54] In another study, Iowa environmental officials discovered that the EPA's standards do not require drinking water monitoring for thirty-six of the thirty-seven chemical pesticides widely used in that state.[55] The EPA has conceded that existing drinking-water standards are often unenforced, especially for hotels, schools, and other institutions not linked to municipal systems. With a staff of less than fifty supporting the national drinking-water program, EPA's erratic enforcement is probably inevitable.[56]

Injection wells, used to dispose of hazardous and solid wastes by flushing them into deep aquifers, appear to be a major source of drinking-water contamination. About half of the liquid hazardous waste generated in the United States is pumped into these injection wells. While liquid hazardous wastes are subject to federal regulation, no detailed national standards exist for solid waste eliminated through injection wells. Oil and gas well wastes are a frequent source of drinking-water contamination in petroleum-producing states. These wastes, or brines, consist primarily of strongly saline water that is used in oil and gas extraction and then injected underground below drinking water sources. Federal and state laws controlling these brines are often poorly enforced. Consider, for example, the Government Accounting Office's report of conditions at an abandoned Ashland Oil Co. site in Lawrence and Johnson counties, Kentucky, in the latter 1980s:

> The Ashland field contained 1,450 abandoned oil and gas wells that had not been plugged, and brines had entered drinking water supplies through cracks in the casing of these wells. EPA therefore required Ashland to properly plug the abandoned wells . . . and fined the company $125,000 for violating the Safe Drinking Water Act. Because of the extent of the contamination, EPA officials decided it would not be technically feasible to clean up the aquifer. Drinking water supplies will consequently remain contaminated for perhaps another 20 years. . . .[57]

Rural water supplies seem especially vulnerable to contamination from injection wells and abandoned hazardous waste sites. A 1984 EPA assessment of rural water quality reported unsafe levels of cadmium in about one-sixth of the nation's rural wells, mercury concentrations above safe levels in about one-quarter of the wells, and lead at dangerous levels in one-tenth of these wells.[58]

Conclusion

Air and water are the primary issues on the environmental agenda; they are the first, most essential, most politically visible and important tasks of environmental restoration and regulation. The state of the nation's air and water has been examined in considerable detail to emphasize the daunting scope and complexity of the challenge of ecological restoration and to illustrate how short a distance we have traveled toward that goal in three decades and two eras since environmentalism emerged as a major political force in the United States.

This chapter illustrates that difficulties in cleaning up the nation's air and water cannot be blamed solely upon political incompetence, policy deficiencies, administrative failures, or scientific bungling. Rather, scientific and technological development continually poses new challenges to regulation by creating new chemicals, and new technologies, with unanticipated environmental effects. Further, scientific research continually redefines and elaborates the nature of environmental degradation and its consequences—as shown in the study of acid rain, climate warming, and atmospheric ozone depletion—forcing continual rethinking and change in regulatory strategies. And even so unexciting and obscure an activity as environmental monitoring leads to new definitions of environmental degradation, as the study of ground-water contamination reveals. Thus, the United States, like all other nations now committed to environmental restoration, must live through a long learning curve during which it must acquire experience in a policy domain with which no government on earth was involved a scant few decades ago. Governments can learn, but it takes time.

This review of the nation's current air and water pollution control programs is a sobering reminder that it will take a very long time, and require an enormous amount of money, scientific resources, and administrative skill, to give us back the healthful air and water we once had and hope to have again. So formidable a goal will not be easily realized. It may not happen in the lifetime of any American living today.

Notes

1. David Brower, "Third Planet Operating Instructions," in *Progress as If Survival Mattered*, ed. Hugh Nash (San Francisco: Friends of the Earth, 1981), 26.
2. Estimate made by Richard L. Hembra, director, Environmental Protection Issues, Resources; Community and Economic Development Division; U.S. General Accounting Office, in "Observations on the Environmental Protection Agency's Budget Request for Fiscal Year 1991" (Statement before the Committee on Environment and Public Works, U.S. Senate, March 7, 1990).
3. *New York Times*, September 29, 1988.
4. *New York Times*, May 28, 1988.
5. A useful discussion of the distinction between the two approaches may be found in *Current Issues in U.S. Environmental Policy*, ed. Paul R. Portnoy (Baltimore: Johns Hopkins University Press, 1978), especially chap. 1; and Erica L. Dolgin and Thomas G. P. Guilbert, eds., *Federal Environmental Law* (St. Paul, Minn.: West Publishing, 1974), especially Robert Zener, "The Federal Law of Water Pollution Control," 682–791, and Thomas Jorling, "The Federal Law of Air Pollution Control," 1058–1148.
6. On the problem generally see Allen V. Kneese and Charles L. Schulze, *Pollution, Prices and Public Policy* (Washington, D.C.: Brookings Institution, 1975), chap. 2.
7. David D. Doniger, *The Law and Policy of Toxic Substances Control* (Baltimore: Johns Hopkins University Press, 1978), 67.
8. *Public Opinion* (February/March 1982): 36.
9. Paul B. Downing and James N. Kimball, "Enforcing Pollution Laws in the U.S.," *Policy Studies Journal* 11, no. 1 (September 1982): 55–65.
10. Ibid.
11. Environmental Protection Agency, *Environmental Progress and Challenges: EPA's Update* (Washington, D.C.: Environmental Protection Agency, August 1988), 14–15.
12. Ibid.
13. *New York Times*, June 9, 1983.
14. *New York Times*, June 28, 1983.
15. National Research Council, *Acid Deposition Atmospheric Processes in Eastern North America: A Review of Current Scientific Understanding* (Washington, D.C.: National Academy Press, 1983).

16. *New York Times*, April 23, 1988.
17. U.S. General Accounting Office, "The Debate over Acid Precipitation: Opposing Views, Status of Research," Report no. EMD-81-131 (September 1981), 28.
18. *New York Times*, July 7, 1988.
19. *New York Times*, May 22, 1988.
20. *New York Times*, December 31, 1989.
21. *New York Times*, March 20, 1990.
22. Executive Office of the President, Council on Environmental Quality (CEQ), *Environmental Quality, 1980* (Washington, D.C.: Government Printing Office, 1980), 398ff.
23. A comprehensive survey of alternative regulatory strategies can be found in James L. Regens and Robert W. Rycroft, *The Acid Rain Controversy* (Pittsburgh: University of Pittsburgh Press, 1988), chaps. 3, 4, 5.
24. Ibid., chaps. 3, 4.
25. Environmental Protection Agency, *Environmental Progress and Challenges*, 15.
26. *New York Times*, May 28, 1989.
27. *New York Times*, August 27, 1985.
28. U.S. General Accounting Office, "Air Pollution: Ozone Attainment Requires Long-Term Solutions to Solve Complex Problems," Report no. GAO/RCED-88-40 (January 1988), 3.
29. Ibid., 4.
30. *New York Times*, March 29, 1989.
31. *New York Times*, March 18, 1989.
32. Environmental Protection Agency, *Environmental Progress and Challenges*, 21–22.
33. Ibid.
34. *New York Times*, March 23, 1989. See also Sandra Postel, *Altering the Earth's Chemistry: Assessing the Risks* (Washington, D.C.: Worldwatch Institute, 1986).
35. *New York Times*, March 23, 1989. See also David M. O'Brien, *What Process Is Due?* (New York: Russell Sage Foundation, 1987), chap. 2.
36. U.S. General Accounting Office, "Chemical Data: EPA's Collection Practices and Procedures on Chemicals," Report no. GAO/RCED-86-63 (February 1986), 6.
37. Lawrence Mosher, "Time Bomb," *National Journal*, May 1, 1982, 778.
38. Zener, "The Federal Law of Water Pollution Control," 694.
39. Environmental Protection Agency, *Environmental Progress and Challenges*, 49.
40. CEQ, *Environmental Quality, 1984*, 52.
41. U.S. General Accounting Office, "The Nation's Water: Key Unanswered Questions About the Quality of Rivers and Streams," Report no. GAO/PEMD-86-6 (September 1986), 63.
42. Ibid., 87.
43. CEQ, *Environmental Quality, 1986*, C-38.
44. U.S. General Accounting Office, "The Nation's Water," 3.
45. Environmental Protection Agency, *Environmental Progress and Challenges*, 46.
46. Conservation Foundation, *State of the Environment: A View Toward the Nineties* (Washington, D.C.: Conservation Foundation, 1987), 105.
47. CEQ, *Environmental Quality, 1979*, chap. 2.
48. Conservation Foundation, *State of the Environment*, 96.
49. U.S. General Accounting Office, "Groundwater Quality: State Activities to Guard Against Contaminants," Report no. GAO/PEMD-88-5 (February 1988), 13.
50. Ibid.
51. Ibid., 38–39.
52. Ibid., 95.
53. Environmental Protection Agency, *Environmental Progress and Challenges*, 52–53.
54. *New York Times*, January 6, 1988.
55. *New York Times*, November 22, 1987.
56. *New York Times*, December 12, 1988.

57. U.S. General Accounting Office, "Drinking Water: Safeguards Are Not Preventing Contamination from Injected Oil and Gas Wastes," Report no. GAO/RCED-89-97 (July 1989), 26–27.
58. Conservation Foundation, *State of the Environment*, 98.

Suggested Readings

Commoner, Barry. *Making Peace with the Planet*. New York: Pantheon Books, 1990.
French, Hilary F. *Clearing the Air: A Global Agenda*. Washington, D.C.: Worldwatch Institute, 1990.
Regens, James L. and Robert W. Rycroft. *The Acid Rain Controversy*. Pittsburgh: University of Pittsburgh Press, 1988.
Schneider, Stephen H. *Global Warming*. San Francisco: Sierra Club Books, 1989.

Chapter 7

A Chemical Plague
Toxic and Hazardous Substances

> *Outdated birth control pills, 96,000 drums of chemicals, hospital*
> *wastes including extracted tumors and tapeworms, carcinogenic sol-*
> *vents, toxic metals, radioactive substances, dioxin, 28 million pounds*
> *of contaminated soil and ash, phosgene nerve gas, 500 pounds of TNT,*
> *nitroglycerin, and picric acid.*
>
> —Partial inventory of Chemical Control Company's Elizabeth (N.J.) site
> shortly before it exploded on April 21, 1980

Crystal City, Texas, is the Spinach Capital of America—or so the local Chamber of Commerce insists. The small community of 8,000 residents in southwest Texas, not far from the Mexican border, has another unadvertised distinction: it is home to an abandoned hazardous waste site so dangerous that it has been listed among the nation's worst toxic waste dumps. In 1988, the efforts of the Environmental Protection Agency (EPA) to clean up Crystal City's abandoned waste site, located at the long-closed municipal airport, triggered a nasty confrontation with the city government.[1] The issue was how to dispose of the wastes and who should decide. The wastes, the toxic residue of a crop-dusting business once located at the airport, included arsenic, DDT, toxaphene, and other known carcinogenic chemicals, many long banned from commercial agriculture. The EPA intended to bulldoze the contaminated soil into a pit covered with waterproof synthetic material. The EPA's experts insisted this arrangement would assure that no chemicals would leach into the soil to pollute ground water or menace children and adults at a nearby school and housing project.

The mayor, most other civic leaders, and lots of local residents were convinced the EPA was wrong. The city argued that the EPA's site cleanup plan would not protect the safety of residents and did not meet the standards of the 1986 Superfund Amendments and Reauthorization Act (SARA). The amendments, argued local officials, required the site to be cleaned up to the maximum extent possible and the EPA was not doing that. Further, the city asserted that local leaders were not given the opportunity or the resources to participate in the creation of the site management plan as federal law requires. "We know what we want," the mayor stated. "We want a safe, healthy place for our children." Crystal City's confrontation made national news, but not because its waste site was exceptional—hundreds of sites authorized by the Comprehensive Environmental Response, Compensation and Liability Act ("Superfund") are bigger, costlier, and more menacing. Rather, Crystal City's controversy was almost a routine Superfund event, a microcosm of the problems plaguing that troubled program despite an expenditure of several billion dollars to solve them.

The Crystal City dump had been on the "priority list" of the nation's worst abandoned chemical waste sites for more than six years. Congress had authorized $1.6 billion in the original Superfund legislation to clean up those priority sites. By 1986, the EPA had identified more than 27,000 abandoned hazardous waste sites across the nation, and had assigned almost 1,000 of the most dangerous to its National Priority List (NPL). It had cleaned up only six.[2] In 1986 an angry, impatient Congress passed the SARA legislation that authorized an additional $8.6 billion for the Superfund program, set specific standards for site cleanup, and established a timetable for cleaning up a specified number of sites. Two years later, the Crystal City airport site seemed to epitomize Superfund's problems: sluggish implementation, technical disputes over cleanup strategies, rising costs, and public mistrust.

Regulating the nation's hazardous wastes, and the thousands of dangerous substances that eventually become these wastes, has proven to be enormously difficult, costly, and time consuming. After almost two decades of massive public investment in a multitude of regulatory programs aimed at almost every aspect of hazardous waste utilization, accomplishments are few. Today, the EPA enforces thirteen major laws affecting hazardous substance use and disposal in the United States. Most are burdened by the daunting variety of materials to be regulated, by inadequate data on the distribution and effect of these substances on man and the environment, by political and administrative impediments to implementation, and by widespread public criticism and distrust. These chronic problems debilitate the nation's waste management laws so gravely that their continuation is likely to create a crisis of regulatory capacity before the decade's end.

An Ambiguous Inheritance

The nation's difficulties with hazardous and toxic wastes are the inheritance of a worldwide technological revolution that was initiated in this century and that expanded explosively after World War II. It began with the creation and manufacture of synthetic chemicals on a rapidly increasing scale by the world's industrialized nations after the turn of the century. By the end of World War II the United States, leader among industrialized countries in producing new chemicals, began three decades of uninterrupted discovery and marketing of thousands of new chemical substances that would eventually become chemical wastes.[3] By 1965 the American Chemical Society had registered more than 4 million chemicals, an increasing proportion of which were synthetics created by American chemists since 1945.

Most chemicals are not dangerous to humans or the environment when properly used. Many have vastly increased human longevity, improved public health, stimulated economic development, or otherwise improved the world's quality of life. But a relatively small proportion of these substances, those currently identified as hazardous or toxic, are known to pose risks, and a much greater number of substances are suspected of posing risks to humans or the ecosystem. Numerous federal laws before 1970 attacked the most obvious risks from chemicals, such as dangers from food additives and cosmetics, but only in the last two decades has science begun to suggest the full scale and subtlety of the risks associated with many of these substances.

Hazardous and Toxic Substances

Governmentally regulated substances are usually classified, not always with precise distinction, as "hazardous" or "toxic." Generally, hazardous substances are toxic, corrosive, ignitable, or chemically reactive materials posing a threat to humans; in the last several decades, the term sometimes has been expanded in federal law to include threats to the ecosystem.[4] Toxic substances, a smaller category, includes only those materials that produce "detrimental effects in living organisms." Usually, these effects are further differentiated into the following categories:

Acute Toxicity: an effect from short-term exposure to a chemical substance. The most important effects include neurological damage, injury to the lungs, liver, kidney, or immune functions, and acute effects upon the offspring during gestation.

Subchronic Toxicity: an effect resulting from prolonged but time-limited exposure. Effects studied are the same as those identified under acute toxicity.

Chronic Toxicity: effects produced by prolonged, continuing exposure. These include delayed toxic reactions, progressive degenerative tissue damage, reproductive toxicity, and cancer.

Environmental Toxicity: a toxic effect upon fish, birds, or other organisms in the ecosystem.[5]

A substance's degree of toxicity is often difficult to describe with scientific precision yet important economically and politically. Magnitudes of toxicity become important in calculating the benefits to be expected from regulating a substance and, hence, a consideration when public officials must decide what forms of regulation, and what costs, ought to be accepted. The dangers associated with a substance—or, at least, the public's beliefs about the dangers—become a major factor in governmental decisions to initiate regulation itself. And regulated interests liable to bear high costs in money and administrative work from regulation usually will attack the evidence establishing the toxicity of a substance as one strategy for eliminating or reducing the regulatory burden upon themselves.

About 98 percent of more than 70,000 chemical substances used commercially in the United States are considered harmless to humans and the ecosystem. About 1,500 new chemicals are now introduced annually. In 1980 less than 7 percent of approximately 1,000 new chemicals proposed for manufacture and reviewed by the EPA aroused any concern among the scientific review panels.[6] However, with the chemical industry's continual growth into a major economic sector, the capacity to produce and distribute still more new substances increases. About 120,000 establishments in the United States, whose production represents about 8 percent of the Gross National Product, create and distribute chemicals. As new chemicals proliferate and the long-term risks associated with older chemicals are better understood, the need to protect humans and the environment from the relatively small but enormously diverse set of hazardous or toxic substances grows more imperative.

While many chemicals have been tested to determine their hazardousness—it is often relatively easy to decide if a chemical is corrosive, or ignitable, or otherwise clearly dangerous when handled or abandoned in the environment—few have been rigorously tested to determine their toxicity. Testing is particularly difficult and expensive when the long-term effects of a chemical are being investigated. Studies may require decades.

Cancer is the gravest and most widely feared of all toxic impacts from hazardous substances. In the mid-1980s perhaps 1,500 to 2,000 of all chemical substances, a small proportion of all suspected carcinogenic chemicals produced in the United States, had been tested sufficiently to determine their carcinogenicity. Among those tested, between 600 and 800 have shown substantial evidence of carcinogenicity.[7] The substances, or industrial processes, most strongly linked to human cancer are identified in Table 7-1. The list of chemicals convincingly associated with acute or chronic human cancer is slowly growing with additional research. Currently, more than twenty-four federal laws and a dozen Washington agencies are concerned with regulating the manufacture, distribution, and disposal of carcinogenic substances; yet, as the data indicate, their work is seriously impeded by a chronic lack of accurate information on a multitude of chemicals within their jurisdiction.[8]

Hazardous and Toxic Wastes

Pesticides are a very large component of hazardous and toxic waste. More than 50,000 pesticides are currently registered for use in the United States. In the early 1990s, the United States was producing more than 1.18 billion pounds of pesticides annually, with more than 600 active ingredients.[9] Pesticides are so widely and routinely used in U.S. agriculture that many farmers believe productivity cannot be sustained without them. Common foods are treated with dozens of possible carcinogens used widely in commercial agriculture; there are, for example, twenty-five for corn, twenty-four for apples, twenty-three for tomatoes, and twenty-one for peaches.[10] Consider the chemical bath in which the dinner table onion was likely raised:

Fungicides: Bravo, 2 pints per acre, seven to ten times a year. Manex or maneb, 1 to 3 pounds per acre, seven to ten times a year. Ridomil, 1.5 to 2 pounds per acre, once a year.

Insecticides: Parathion, one-half pint per acre, or guthion, 1 to 1.5 pounds per acre, two or three times a season. Lorsban, placed in furrow at planting and sprayed twice to control onion maggots.

Herbicide: Goal, 0.25 ounces per acre, one application a season.

Sprout inhibitor: Maleic hydrazide, 2 pounds per acre before harvest to prevent onions from sprouting before they reach market.[11]

Another large component of hazardous and toxic waste is industrial and commercial chemicals. In addition to the 70,000 chemicals currently used in U.S. manufacturing, more than 1,500 new ones appear annually. At the moment, the EPA has more than 13,000 new chemicals on its list for review. Agricultural, commercial, and industrial chemicals constitute more than half the volume of hazardous waste generated in the United States. Approximately 23 percent of all hazardous waste is disposed of in landfills and another 25 percent by deep well injection.[12] Both landfills and deep well injection are major sources of ground-water and surface-water contamination.

Table 7-1 *Chemicals or Industrial Processes Associated with Cancer Induction in Humans*

Chemical or industrial process	Main type of exposure[a]	Target organs in humans	Main source of exposure[b]
Aflatoxins	Environmental, occupational[c]	Liver	Oral, inhalation[c]
4-Aminobiphenyl	Occupational	Bladder	Inhalation, skin, oral
Arsenic compounds	Occupational, medicinal, environmental	Skin, lung, liver[c]	Inhalation, skin, oral
Asbestos	Occupational	Lung, pleural cavity, G.I. tract	Inhalation, oral
Auramine manufacturing	Occupational	Bladder	Inhalation, skin, oral
Benzene	Occupational	Hemopoietic system	Inhalation, skin
Benzidine	Occupational	Bladder	Inhalation, skin, oral
Bis(chloromethyl)-ether	Occupational	Lung	Inhalation
Cadmium-using industries (possibly cadmium oxides)	Occupational	Prostate, lung	Inhalation, oral
Chloramphenicol	Medicinal	Hemopoietic system	Oral, injection
Chloromethyl ether[d]	Occupational	Lung	Inhalation
Chromate-producing industries	Occupational	Lung, nasal cavities[c]	Inhalation
Cyclophosphamide	Medicinal	Bladder	Oral, injection
Diethylstilbestrol (DES)	Medicinal	Uterus, vagina	Oral
Hematite mining	Occupational	Lung	Inhalation
Isopropyl oil	Occupational	Nasal cavity, larynx	Inhalation
Melphalan	Medicinal	Hemopoietic system	Oral, injection
Mustard gas	Occupational	Lung, Larynx	Inhalation
2-Naphthylamine	Occupational	Bladder	Inhalation, skin, oral
Nickel refining	Occupational	Nasal cavity, lung	Inhalation
N.N-bis(2-chloroethyl)-2-naphthylamine (chlornaphazine)	Medicinal	Bladder	Oral
Oxymetholone	Medicinal	Liver	Oral
Phenacetin	Medicinal	Kidney	Oral
Phenytoin	Medicinal	Lymphoreticular tissues	Oral, injection
Soot, tars, and oils	Occupational, environmental	Lung, skin, scrotum	Inhalation, skin
Vinyl chloride	Occupational	Liver, brain,[c] lung[c]	Inhalation, skin

SOURCE: Council on Environmental Quality, *Environmental Quality, 1979* (Washington, D.C.: Government Printing Office, 1980), 199–200.

[a]The main types mentioned are those by which the association has been demonstrated.
[b]The main routes given may not be the only ones by which such effects could occur.
[c]Denotes indicative evidence.
[d]Possibly associated with bis(chloromethyl)-ether.

Unregulated land disposal of dangerous chemicals and the continual proliferation of municipal waste at landfills have created thousands of hazardous chemical dumps across the United States. These chemical junkyards, the backside of technological progress, are growing in volume by 3 percent to 10 percent annually; figures are always tentative. At best, perhaps 10 percent of this waste has been properly disposed. Accidents and investigations have disclosed more than 50,000 known hazardous waste sites. No accurate count of the abandoned sites posing acute threats to public health is yet available in the United States. Currently, the EPA has identified more than 30,000 abandoned and potentially contaminated waste sites and has assigned approximately 1,200 of the most dangerous to its National Priority List as required by the Superfund law.

With the exception of Nevada, every state has at least one NPL site; five states (New Jersey, Pennsylvania, California, New York, and Michigan) have more than seventy-five sites each (see Table 7-2). If the number of currently managed waste sites considered to be hazardous is added to the Superfund list, the total exceeds 100,000. In 1987 the General Accounting Office (GAO) estimated that the number of potentially hazardous U.S. waste sites of all kinds might exceed 425,000. The federal government itself is responsible for many abandoned hazardous waste sites. Among the NPL inventory of the worst sites are forty-one located on military bases.[13] More than 1,800 potential NPL sites have been identified in the jurisdiction of eleven federal agencies.[14]

Public apprehension about hazardous waste has been heightened by repeated discoveries, often sudden and dramatic, that citizens have been exposed unknowingly to toxic substances originating in previously undiscovered or neglected waste sites or transported through the ecosystem through careless chemical use. While Love Canal has become a national synonym for chemical contamination, incidents of real or suspected community exposure to hazardous waste are now commonplace.

More subtle is the quiet, gradual accumulation of hazardous wastes in soil, air, or water through normal industrial, commercial, or agricultural use. Such waste rarely accumulates in quantities sufficient to attract public attention. Its existence is often revealed only through deliberate monitoring by public or private organizations, sometimes only after sophisticated and lengthy testing. The following incidents testify to the ease with which these wastes can disperse throughout the ecosystem:

In the early 1980s, the Mt. Sinai School of Medicine released a study indicating that 97 percent of Michigan's residents had residual levels of the toxic fire retardant polybrominated biphenyls, or PBB, after 2,000

Table 7-2 *Superfund National Priority List: State Totals, 1989*

State/Territory	Final Nonfed.	Final Fed.	Proposed Nonfed.	Proposed Fed.	Total
New Jersey	100	3	3	3	109
Pennsylvania	84	3	9	1	97
California	53	8	17	13	91
New York	73	1	6	3	83
Michigan	68	0	11	0	79
Florida	38	0	9	4	51
Washington	23	9	8	5	45
Minnesota	39	1	1	1	42
Wisconsin	36	0	4	0	40 ⌐
Illinois	22	4	12	0	38
Indiana	31	0	4	0	35
Ohio	29	1	1	2	33
Texas	24	1	2	2	29
Massachusetts	21	0	1	3	25
Missouri	16	2	5	1	24
South Carolina	16	0	6	1	23
North Carolina	19	1	2	0	22
Iowa	10	0	10	1	21
Delaware	13	1	6	0	20
Virginia	15	1	4	0	20
Kentucky	12	0	5	0	17
Colorado	12	2	1	1	16
New Hampshire	15	0	0	1	16
Connecticut	12	0	2	1	15
Tennessee	10	1	2	1	14
Georgia	8	1	3	1	13
Alabama	8	2	2	0	12
Oklahoma	7	1	4	0	12
Utah	4	2	4	2	12
Arizona	6	0	2	3	11
Arkansas	9	0	2	0	11
Kansas	9	0	1	1	11
Louisiana	9	1	1	0	11
Rhode Island	9	0	0	2	11
Maryland	7	1	1	1	10
Montana	8	0	2	0	10
New Mexico	7	1	1	1	10
Idaho	5	0	2	2	9
Maine	6	1	1	1	9
Puerto Rico	8	1	0	0	9
Oregon	5	1	2	0	8
Vermont	7	0	1	0	8
Hawaii	0	0	6	1	7
Alaska	1	0	1	4	6
Nebraska	3	1	2	0	6
West Virginia	5	0	0	0	5
Mississippi	2	0	1	0	3
South Dakota	1	0	1	1	3
Wyoming	1	0	1	1	3
North Dakota	2	0	0	0	2
Guam	1	0	0	0	1
Nevada	0	0	1	0	1
American Samoa	0	0	0	0	0
Commonwealth of Marianas	0	0	0	0	0
District of Columbia	0	0	0	0	0
Trust Territories	0	0	0	0	0
Virgin Islands	0	0	0	0	0
Total	929	52	173	65	1,219

pounds of the chemical were accidentally substituted for feed additive on a Michigan farm in 1973.[15]

Game fish in the Florida Everglades are showing mercury levels among the highest ever recorded in the United States. The discovery has alarmed experts who cannot explain it. Fish samples contained as much as 4.4 parts per million of methyl mercury—more than four times the amount considered safe.[16]

Two EPA studies found that fish downstream from twenty-one of eighty-one paper mills contained dioxin levels far exceeding the level defined as hazardous by federal standards. Most of the problem fish were associated with "bleach draft mills" that use chlorine to make white paper products. Some fish had seven times the amount considered hazardous.[17]

David Doniger has observed that there are "boundaries of analysis" that prevent government agencies from making exact, objective, and uncontroversial decisions in regulating a suspected hazardous or toxic material.[18] Of these, notes Doniger, the most important is that all decisions must be made under substantial uncertainty about the medical and ecological risks associated with varying levels of chemical exposure. Here, as we have earlier observed in other domains of environmental regulation, limited scientific data again introduces an issue that readily becomes politicized in the regulatory process.

This chronic uncertainty arises from the lack of information about the toxicity of most chemicals used in U.S. commerce and industry. It has been estimated that useful information about toxicity is absent for 64 percent of pesticides and inert ingredients in pesticide formulations, for 78 percent of the most common commercial chemicals, and for 70 percent of food additives.[19] Even when chemicals are tested for toxicity, it is difficult to establish definitive proof that a suspected chemical will cause a given number of deaths, or other harmful effects, in a given dose over a specified time period. Thus experts often rely upon estimates, usually in the form of probability statements, when predicting the magnitude of toxic effects to man or the environment from a chemical substance.

Even after known levels of exposure can be identified, tracing the consequences to humans can be enormously complex and controversial, particularly when chronic exposure has been to small doses. Considering all these limitations, Congress and environmentalists expected too much of science by requiring in the Toxic Substances Control Act (TSCA) of 1976 that all new chemicals be screened before marketing to determine their toxicity. It is difficult, perhaps impossible, to know in advance how a chemical will be used, in what quantities, and where, even though manufacturers are required to provide an estimate in their "Premanufacture Notice" to the EPA.[20]

The difficulties inherent in risk assessment are illustrated by continuing controversy over the effects of toxic chemicals upon the neighborhood adjacent to the Love Canal dump site. In late 1982, the EPA released the results of a massive inquiry it had made, along with the U.S. Public Health Service, into the health effects of the Love Canal site. Contrary to earlier studies by the state of New York, the EPA asserted that it had found the neighborhood near Love Canal no less safe for residents than any other part of Niagara Falls, N.Y. The evidence seemed formidable. More than 6,000 samples of human and environmental materials near the site were collected and subjected to 150,000 analytical measurements to determine what contaminants they contained. This evidence suggested that only a ring of houses a block or less from the waste site had been significantly affected. But the study was challenged immediately because 90 percent of the samples were free of any chemicals. This, asserted experts, could mean either an absence of chemicals or insufficient sensitivity among the measuring procedures. Although the assistant secretary for health and the deputy EPA administrator for New York testified to congressional committees that they were confident the undetected chemicals could not be present in more than minute quantities, the Environmental Defense Fund's own scientific expert asserted that so much variance existed in the competence of the many laboratories conducting the tests and so many sources of error could exist in some tests that chemicals could indeed have been present. Officials at the National Bureau of Standards also questioned the sensitivity of the test procedures. Less than a year later, the federal Centers for Disease Control released their own study of former Love Canal area residents, indicating that they were no more likely to suffer chromosome damage than residents elsewhere in Niagara Falls. Even if such damage were present, noted the study, it was impossible to know if it was linked to the later occurrence of illnesses.[21]

Accurately describing the risks from exposure to the Love Canal site may require decades, or generations; it may never happen. Uncertainties about risk must almost be assumed to be a constant in regulating hazardous substances, and consequently errors of judgment leading to excessively strict regulation or perhaps to dangerously negligent control of chemical substances are probably inevitable. Generally, Congress and the regulatory agencies implementing congressional hazardous waste programs have been risk averse, preferring to reduce severely or to eliminate the assumed risks from toxic materials. In effect, regulators have chosen to err, if err they must, in the direction of stricter control and more willingness to accept pessimistic estimates of risk from toxic substances. However, beginning with the later years of the Carter administration and continuing with greater vigor under the Reagan presidency, federal agencies have moved toward greater attention to costs and regulatory complexity in setting standards of exposure and control.

Costs and Complexity

It is doubtful that either friend or foe of the federal regulatory programs enacted in the mid-1970s realistically understood the enormous expense that would be involved in the new hazardous substance legislation. New regulatory agencies would have to be created, or existing ones expanded. An inventory of many thousands of chemicals would have to be created, existing literature on the health effects of chemicals searched, new research initiated, new regulations promulgated, litigation involving the legality of new regulatory standards conducted, and so forth. Only as regulatory agencies began the first tentative steps in assembling data on the human and environmental effects of chemical substances did the vast vacuum of relevant information become obvious. A major reason for the protracted delays in implementing the new laws has been the tedious but essential work of building a foundation of necessary technical data upon which regulatory standards could be erected. The collective costs to the 14,000 regulated chemical manufacturers will add billions of dollars to the regulatory total.

A small sample of direct and indirect costs associated with recent hazardous substance legislation can only suggest the scale upon which such regulatory programs must operate:

The average priority abandoned waste site cleaned up by the EPA under Superfund legislation has cost $6.5 million; the aggregate expense for eliminating all the nation's worst abandoned waste sites is expected to be three or four times the initial Superfund authorization of $1.6 billion.[22]

The EPA's regulations for disposal of hazardous waste on land sites exceeded 500 pages in the *Federal Register.* EPA officials say the costs of compliance for the affected industries will exceed $1 billion yearly.[23]

The state of New York requested a grant of $20 million from the federal government to remove from the Hudson River the twenty-five-year accumulation of the toxic chemical polychlorinated biphenyl (PCB) dumped into the Hudson by the General Electric Company.[24]

When massive costs are projected against the fragmentary scientific data on the effects of many chemicals and the often tenuous evidence relating to chronic impacts from extremely low levels of exposure, arguments over the acceptability of the costs in light of the benefits inevitably ensue. Critics, especially of federal regulatory programs enacted in the 1970s, have asserted that such programs impose not only unacceptable costs for the regulation of acknowledged hazards but also staggering costs for the stringent control of substances with unproven effects. Some critics, including the leadership of the Reagan administration, have argued that costs and benefits should become a routinely important—though not necessarily the most important—factor in determining whether a substance should be regulated.

Criticism of regulatory costs often feeds upon the disparity between the timing and character of the costs and the timing and character of the benefits from regulation. The costs tend to be tangible, immediate, and massive: dollars must be spent, agencies created, rules promulgated, and other expensive actions initiated. In contrast, years or decades may pass before any apparent benefits accrue. The benefits may be in intangible terms—such as deaths and illnesses prevented, public costs of future regulation avoided, and public safety enhanced—that tend to be discounted in the present by those who must pay for regulation. Examples exist that show how the future benefits of regulation can be enormous. The number of U.S. deaths from exposure as much as forty years ago to asbestos will grow to between 8,000 and 10,000 annually by the century's end. More than 100,000 claims outstanding against major asbestos manufacturers in 1990 must be settled. The current value of these future claims has been estimated conservatively at $40 billion.[25] But few regulated chemicals have demonstrated such deadliness that the benefits of regulation become indisputable. Regulators rarely have the sure knowledge that a given chemical, if left unregulated, ever would manifest its long-term effects as unambiguously as asbestos did.

Federal Law: Regulation from the Cradle to the Grave?

Among the two dozen federal laws relating to hazardous or toxic substances, three passed in the 1970s define the fundamental framework for regulating the disposal of these substances: the Toxic Substances Control Act of 1976, the Resource Conservation and Recovery Act of 1976 (RCRA), and the Comprehensive Environmental Response, Compensation and Liability Act of 1980 (more commonly known as Superfund). These laws represent a congressional effort to create a comprehensive regulatory regime for all chemical substances from initial development to final disposal—the cradle-to-grave control that seemed essential to achieving for the first time responsible public management of chemical products. Few laws, even by the standard of recent environmental legislation, mandate a more complex and technically formidable administrative process than do these programs. A brief review of the major provisions will suggest the immense regulatory tasks involved.

TSCA: Regulating Chemical Manufacture and Distribution

The major purpose of the Toxic Substances Control Act and its important 1986 amendments (the Asbestos Hazard Emergency Response Act) is to regulate the creation, manufacture, and distribution of chemical substances so that those hazardous to man or the environment can be identified early and then controlled properly before they become fugitive throughout the ecosystem. TSCA and its amendments require the EPA to achieve five broad objectives:

1. Gather Information. EPA was required to issue rules asking chemical manufacturers and processors to submit to the administrator information about their use of important chemicals. The information was to include the chemical's name, its formula, uses, estimates of production levels, description of byproducts, data on adverse health and environmental effects, and the number of workers exposed to the chemical. In achieving these goals the administrator also was to:

A. Publish a list of all existing chemicals.

B. See that all persons manufacturing, processing, or distributing chemicals in commerce keep records on adverse health reactions, submit to EPA required health and safety studies, and report to EPA information suggesting that a chemical represents a previously undetected significant risk to health or the environment.

2. Screen New Chemicals. Manufacturers of new chemicals were to notify EPA at least 90 days before producing the chemical commercially. Information similar to that required for existing chemicals was required for new chemicals also. The EPA was allowed to suspend temporarily the manufacture of any new chemical in the absence of adequate information as required under the law and to suspend permanently a new chemical if it found a "reasonable basis to conclude that the chemical presents or will present an unreasonable risk of injury to health or the environment."

3. Test Chemicals. The EPA was given the authority to require manufacturers or processors of potentially harmful chemicals to test them. An Interagency Testing Committee, composed of representatives from eight federal agencies, was created to recommend to EPA priorities for chemical testing. As many as 50 chemicals were allowed to be recommended for testing within one year.

4. Control Chemicals. EPA was required to take action against chemical substances or mixtures for which a reasonable basis existed to conclude that the manufacture, processing, distribution, use, or disposal presented an unreasonable risk of injury to health or the environment. Permitted actions ranged from a labelling requirement to a complete ban. The control requirements were not to "place an undue burden on industry," yet at the same time they were to provide an adequate margin of protection against unreasonable risk. TSCA specifically required regulation and eventual elimination of PCBs.

5. Control Asbestos. The EPA is required to develop a strategy for implementing the congressional mandate that all schools inspect for asbestos-containing material, and develop and implement plans to control the threat of any asbestos discovered.

RCRA: Regulating Solid Waste

The major purposes of the Resource Conservation and Recovery Act and its 1980 and 1984 amendments were to control solid waste management practices that could endanger public health or the environment and to promote resource conservation and recovery. Solid wastes were defined in the act to include waste solids, sludges, liquids, and contained gases—all forms in which discarded hazardous or toxic substances might be found. In addition to providing federal assistance to state and local governments in developing comprehensive solid waste management programs, RCRA also mandated:

1. *Criteria for Environmentally Safe Disposal Sites.* The EPA was required to issue regulations defining the minimum criteria for solid waste disposal sites considered environmentally safe. EPA was further required to publish an inventory of all U.S. facilities failing to meet these criteria.

2. *Regulating Hazardous Waste.* EPA was required to develop criteria for identifying hazardous waste, to publish the characteristics of hazardous wastes and lists of particular hazardous wastes, and to create a "manifest system" that tracks hazardous wastes from their point of origin to their final disposal. EPA also was to create a permit system that would require all individuals or industries generating hazardous waste to obtain a permit before managing such waste. Permits would be issued only to waste managers meeting the safe disposal criteria created by the EPA.

3. *Resource Recovery and Waste Reduction.* The act required the Commerce Department to promote commercialization of waste recovery, to encourage markets for recovered wastes, and to promote waste recovery technologies and research into waste conservation.

4. *State Implementation.* The act provided for state implementation of regulations affecting solid waste management and disposal if state programs met federal standards. EPA will enforce these provisions in states that do not, or cannot, comply with federal regulations for the program's enforcement.

5. *Mandated Deadlines and Waste-by-Waste Review.* The 1984 amendments set deadlines for the EPA to set standards for disposal of specific wastes or congressionally mandated standards would be applied. The EPA was also ordered to evaluate nineteen specific substances and deadlines were established for it to regulate new kinds of waste disposal activity.

The 1984 amendments—bristling with mandated deadlines and meticulously detailed instructions—bespeak a profound congressional distrust of the EPA's commitment to enforcing RCRA during the first Reagan administration. The amendments were conceived in an atmosphere strident with congressional censure of the EPA. Sen. George J. Mitchell (D-Maine) captured the mood of the majority in stating that "strong congressional expression of disapproval of EPA's slow and timid implementation of the existing law is necessary, as well as a clear congressional direction mandating certain bold, preventive actions by EPA which will not be taken otherwise. . . . The Agency has missed deadlines, proposed inadequate regulations, and even exacerbated the hazardous waste problem by suspending certain regulations."[26]

Congress was determined to drive the EPA hard, to end the pervasive delay and negligent implementation that seemed to suffuse the RCRA program. And so Congress instructed the EPA in exquisite detail concerning how to implement virtually every aspect of RCRA, from the allowable permeability of liners for surface impoundments to the concentrations at which many different chemical wastes must be banned from land disposal. Twenty-nine different deadlines for specific program activities were listed: a ban on land disposal of bulk liquid in landfills within six months, new regulations for small quantity waste generators within seventeen months, interim construction standards for underground storage tanks within four months, and so forth.[27]

While RCRA attempted to provide for the first time a comprehensive federal program to control future hazardous waste disposal, it gave little attention to the thousands of abandoned hazardous waste sites across the nation. These abandoned dumps, constituting a vast chemical wasteland whose ominous proportions finally emerged to public recognition in the late 1970s, required immediate comprehensive control or elimination. In the wake of Love Canal and other abandoned waste emergencies, Congress passed in 1980 the Superfund legislation to eliminate the threat of abandoned or uncontrolled hazardous waste sites.

Superfund

When Superfund was enacted, the nation's abandoned and uncontrolled hazardous waste dumps were largely an uncharted wasteland.

The nation's governments knew little about the location or composition of many waste sites, some abandoned longer than memory of their existence. The law seldom clearly placed financial responsibility for the management or removal of these wastes with their creators; liability for damage or injury to individuals or communities from such wastes often was difficult, or impossible, to assign or to enforce. Often, procedures for cleaning up waste sites were unknown, or local officials were ignorant of them. The financial burden upon state and local governments to control or remove these wastes seemed overwhelming. Because a comprehensive, collaborative program among the nation's governments seemed essential, Congress attempted to address these and other major abandoned waste problems through four major Superfund programs:[28]

1. *Information Gathering and Analysis.* Owners of hazardous waste sites were required to notify EPA by June 1981 about the character of buried wastes. Using this information, the EPA would create a list of national sites.

2. *Federal Response to Emergencies.* The act authorized the EPA to respond to hazardous substance emergencies and to clean up leaking chemical dump sites if the responsible parties failed to take appropriate action or could not be located.

3. *The Hazardous Substance Response Fund.* The act created an initial trust fund of $1.6 billion to finance the removal, cleanup, or remedy of hazardous waste sites. About 86 percent of the fund was to be financed from a tax on manufacturers of petrochemical feedstocks and organic chemicals and on crude oil importers. The remainder was to come from general federal revenues.

4. *Liability for Cleanup.* The act placed liability for cleaning up waste sites and for other restitution upon those responsible for release of the hazardous substances.

By the mid-1980s it was obvious that the number of abandoned sites needing immediate cleanup and the costs had been grossly underestimated. The 1984 chemical disaster at Bhopal, India, had drawn congressional attention to the nation's lack of community planning for chemical emergencies. And Congress was increasingly critical of the slow pace of Superfund site cleanups. In 1986, Congress passed the Superfund Amendments and Reauthorization Act, which changed the original legislation significantly:

1. *Greatly Increased Spending.* The new amendments authorized an additional $8.5 billion for NPL site cleanups and an additional $500 million specifically to clean up pollution created by abandoned underground liquid storage tanks.

228 Environmental Politics and Policy

2. *New Cleanup Standards.* The standards mandated for all sites are to be permanent remedies to the maximum extent practicable, using the best available technologies. State standards for cleanup are to be followed when they are more stringent than federal standards. The public living near sites are to be informed about all phases of the process and involved in these activities.

3. *The Emergency Planning and Community Right-to-Know Act.* Title III of SARA authorized communities to get detailed information about chemicals made by, stored in, and emitted from local businesses. It required the formation of state and local planning committees to draw up a chemical emergency response plan for every community in the nation.

Insofar as feasible, the intent of Congress was to make the creators of hazardous waste sites bear as much financial responsibility as possible for ensuring the safety of the sites. With Superfund, Congress finished its attempt to craft within less than a decade the first truly comprehensive federal regulation of virtually all hazardous or toxic materials in the United States. With TSCA, RCRA, and Superfund, Congress in effect ordered the federal government, in collaboration with state and local authorities, to become the primary manager of all dangerous chemical substances currently used or planned for production.

The Regulatory Thicket

All these regulatory programs, each a morass of administrative and technical complexity, were passed in less than four years. The EPA and other responsible governmental agencies were confronted with an avalanche of new regulatory mandates, bristling with insistent compliance deadlines, for which they were expected to be rapidly prepared. It is doubtful that the agencies could have satisfactorily discharged these responsibilities under the most benign circumstances. From their inception, all the programs were afflicted in varying degrees by technical, administrative, and political problems impeding their development. By the early 1990s, most of these programs were running years behind statutory deadlines, mandated deadlines or not. The nation is still at serious risk from the hazardous and toxic waste problems Congress intended to remedy with TSCA, RCRA, and Superfund. Serious doubt exists that the programs will ever achieve their legislative objectives without radical reformulation.

Regulatory Achievements: Significant But Few

There have been a few conspicuous successes. Federal regulations have largely eliminated the manufacture of PCBs, a chemical used pri-

marily in commercial electrical equipment such as capacitors and transformers. Of the billion pounds produced in the United States between
1929 and 1976 (when PCB production was halted), about 312 million
pounds are still in use in millions of electrical devices.[29] High levels of
PCBs in human tissue declined from 12 percent of the population in
1979 to virtually none in the late 1980s. Trace amounts, once found in
as many as 62 percent of the U.S. population, declined to approximately
9 percent by the late 1980s.[30]

In conjunction with the Federal Insecticide, Fungicide, and Rodenticide Act of 1947, the newer regulatory programs have largely eliminated
all domestic uses of the pesticides DDT, aldrin, dieldrin, toxaphene, and
ethylene dibromide and most domestic uses of chlordane and heptachlor,
all known carcinogens. Asbestos is slowly being eliminated from domestic commerce and industry. U.S. production of asbestos has dropped by
more than half since 1976 and practically all industrial and commercial
uses are being eliminated. In 1978, the EPA banned the use of chlorofluorocarbons from domestic aerosol cans, an important first step in controlling the destruction of the atmospheric ozone layer. The elimination
or reduction of these substances removes some of the most dangerous
and widespread chemicals in the United States, yet these represent only
a tiny portion of the chemicals known, or strongly suspected, of posing
grave risks to humans or the environment.

Administrative Overload

TSCA and RCRA abound in delays and complications. Many of these
problems arise from the volume and complexity of work thrust upon
the EPA within a few years. The numerous failures in program implementation also testify to the difficulty in obtaining technical data, to
protracted scientific disputes over regulatory decisions, to lack of resources and experience in program management, and to past political
interference that plunged the EPA into demoralizing and acrimonious
disputes with Congress.

One formidable problem is that each new law requires the EPA to
assume the initiative for creating and interpreting a vast volume of
integrated technical information. Obtaining the data often requires that
chemical manufacturers, processors, consumers, and waste depositors
provide timely, accurate information—information they previously
guarded jealously. With this heavy burden of initiative, the agency would
have been hard pressed to meet all its program obligations under TSCA
and RCRA with even the most benevolent funding and generous personnel levels. The Reagan administration's sharp budget reductions in the
early 1980s severely impaired the EPA's regulatory performance even
after modest improvements occurred in the late 1980s. For instance,

Sections 8 (a) and (b) of TSCA required the EPA to create an inventory of chemicals manufactured or imported into the United States from 1975 to 1977. By 1985, the inventory included more than 63,000 chemicals. But the EPA had no resources to verify the accuracy of the information provided. The inventory had not been updated by the end of the Reagan administration even though many chemicals listed were no longer produced, the production volume and location may have changed, and many new chemicals should have been added.[31]

The required testing of potentially harmful chemicals has been an exercise in frustration. Consider, for instance, the agency's attempt to create test rules for a whole category of chemicals.[32] Some chemical groups are quite small, but others are voluminous: the aryl phosphates include about 300 existing chemicals with more continually manufactured. The chemical industry complained that testing by broad categories would involve very high costs, would stigmatize many "innocent" chemicals along with dangerous ones in the same group, and would prevent introduction of new chemicals until all existing chemicals in a category are tested. Small wonder that the EPA explained its delay in establishing chemical testing guidelines by citing "gross underestimation of the number and complexity of the issues and time spent in resolving one-time issues."[33]

Another example of failed implementation relates to TSCA's requirements for PCB regulation. The EPA has issued regulations requiring all facilities having PCBs to properly mark, store, record, and dispose or destroy most items containing PCBs within a year after removal and storage. The TSCA required the removal from service of perhaps a million electrical capacitors by late 1988 and thousands of PCB transformers by late 1990. The EPA has estimated that between 700,000–750,000 PCB storage sites exist—but the agency can't find most of them. "Because [EPA's site] lists are limited and out of date," reports the GAO, "EPA still does not know which facilities have PCBs. As a result, EPA has continued to inspect non-PCB facilities, while facilities with PCBs have gone without inspection."[34]

The RCRA's plodding progress defies the multitude of mandatory program deadlines intended to speed its implementation. For example, Congress had mandated deadlines for five major studies of large volume waste producers. In late 1987, two of the studies had been issued, one on time and the other six years late. Both needed more information. The remaining studies were three to four years behind and the EPA did not expect to complete them until 1990.[35] The RCRA required the EPA to determine which wastes are hazardous and need regulation to protect human health and the environment. Over a thousand waste materials are likely to qualify for the list. After identifying 450 such materials in 1980, the EPA was able to add only five new wastes in the succeeding six years.[36] The disarray into which the waste identification program has fallen is suggested by the GAO's summary:

Ten years after the Congress mandated the identification and control of hazardous wastes, EPA cannot say what portion of the universe of hazardous wastes it has identified and brought under regulation, or even if it is regulating the worst wastes in terms of potential impact on human health and the environment. Its waste identification activity has been hampered by low or changing priorities and changing approaches and strategies.[37]

It is becoming evident, moreover, that the number of potential waste storage and treatment facilities in the United States requiring corrective actions under RCRA is likely to exceed vastly the initial estimates. The EPA has yet to identify which among the more than 4,800 treatment, storage, and disposal facilities will need corrective work but estimates suggest at least 2,500. If accurate, the size and scope of the cleanup program would be as large as the expected Superfund cleanup and may cost more than $22.7 billion. The cleanup of all sites may not be completed until the year 2025.

Few would dispute that Superfund's implementation has been too slow, too acrimonious, and too problematic in its impact. One reason is the difficulty in identifying all the sites qualified for cleanup and for the National Priority List. Although about 1,200 sites are now on the list, the number could exceed 2,500. The total number of abandoned hazardous waste sites requiring remedial cleanup under Superfund may eventually exceed 25,000. More than a decade after Superfund's enactment, less than forty priority sites had been cleaned up.

As the Crystal City dispute illustrates, priority site cleanups are routinely attended by strident contention between agency officials and contractors on one side and citizen groups and local government officials on the other over the adequacy of proposed solutions. The EPA's efforts to control the huge site cleanup costs have been severely criticized from many sides. The congressional Office of Technology Assessment's 1989 summary report on EPA's waste management programs further exacerbated this dispute by accusing the agency of permitting too many cheap and unproven cleanup techniques at the sites it studied.[38] It is, complained an EPA official, a no-win situation. "The agency is under pressure from two sides of Congress," observed EPA's assistant administrator for toxic waste programs. The environmental committees push for the most comprehensive cleanup, he noted, but the appropriations committees demand the most "cost-effective" remedies.[39]

The Reagan Legacy: Misadministration and Maladministration

The legacy of the Reagan administration endures in the federal government's foundering waste management programs. Some significant portion of responsibility for failed deadlines, understaffed and underfunded regulators, deficient technical resources, and erratic leadership can be attributed to the administrative turmoil created at the EPA during the Reagan years.

It is impossible to insulate environmental regulation from the influence of party zealots determined to bend policy to the shape of their ideological prejudice. Moreover, government in a democracy assumes that policy makers and administrators will be reasonably sensitive to changing public opinion and electoral majorities whose will may be expressed through changes in public policy. And so, environmental policy formulation and implementation normally proceed in a politically charged setting. It is ritual for the president's political opponents to stigmatize disagreeable changes in administrative policy as "politics." In short, a certain amount of real or alleged political influence in the implementation of environmental policy is normal and not necessarily subversive of the law or of good governmental management.

The line between tolerable and unacceptable political interference in environmental administration may be imprecise, but the Reagan administration's management of EPA programs clearly exceeded the permissible limits of political involvement. Program implementation was subverted; legislative intent was blandly ignored. Later reforms were too tardy, the remedies not potent enough, to undo much of the damage inflicted on the EPA's regulatory programs between 1981 and 1985.

Major damage was done to the waste management programs by the administration's sharp cutbacks in EPA's funding for research and development, for hazardous waste, and for toxic waste programs between 1981 and 1985. The EPA during Anne Burford's embattled term as administrator between 1981 and 1984 encouraged the use of political criteria, rather than technical or statutory standards, in awarding grants to clean up Superfund priority sites; granted privileged access for regulated businesses to EPA's top management; yielded to pressure from the Office of Management and Budget to rewrite regulations in a manner more congenial to regulated interests; abided obstruction and delay in regulation writing and implementation; and fostered the selective use, or suppression, of technical information on the dangers of suspected hazardous chemicals according to the political impact of the results. The EPA's relationship with Congress became increasingly embittered as suspicion of the EPA's commitment to enforcing the law grew. Partisan wrangling between congressional Democrats and EPA's management became EPA house style. By the time Burford resigned in 1984, the EPA's waste management programs, like its other major statutory activities, had been badly obstructed, their implementation further delayed, their professional staff largely demoralized. Better times followed, but the EPA has not recovered from the partisan mauling it received during the Burford era.

The NIMBY Problem

He appears most often as a white-collar professional or executive, articulate, well educated, politically sophisticated. She is likely to be a housewife, sometimes an executive or professional. They personify the members of a growing citizen resistance movement known as NIMBY-ism ("Not in My Back Yard").[40] NIMBYism is all too familiar to federal, state, and local officials attempting to implement state programs for permitting hazardous waste sites as required by the RCRA, or trying to plan for the designation or cleanup of a Superfund site. NIMBYism poses a formidable obstacle to waste site management under RCRA and Superfund. It is the environmental movement's problem, too. NIMBY-ism is a dissonance within the environmental ethic—a disturbing contradiction between the movement's commitment to participatory democracy and its insistence on rapid, effective environmental regulation.

NIMBYism thrives because of numerous, and still increasing, state and federal laws that empower citizen activism in the implementation of many different environmental laws and regulations. Currently, twenty-one states have legislation in which citizens are given some role in the writing, implementation, and enforcement of environmental laws. Sixteen states require the appropriate agencies to prepare Environmental Impact Statements for their activities and mandate public notice and involvement in the process.[41]

Federal law provides many opportunities for citizen participation in environmental regulation. Major environmental laws, such as the Clean Air Act, Federal Water Pollution Control Act Amendments (FWPCAA), RCRA, and Superfund, grant citizens "standing" to sue federal agencies to compel their enforcement of environmental regulations. The Surface Mining Control and Reclamation Act (1977), the 1984 RCRA amendments, and the FWPCAA, among many others, require the responsible federal and state agencies to involve the public in writing and implementing regulations. Several federal environmental laws also permit citizens, or citizen organizations, to sue private firms for failure to comply with the terms of their pollution discharge permits and to recover the costs involved in the suits.[42] Public notice and hearings are routinely required of environmental agencies before major regulations are promulgated or permits are issued for pollution discharges or hazardous waste sites. Behind these generous provisions for citizen activism, notes Michael Greve, is congressional distrust, a "reflexive suspicion that the executive, if left to itself, would systematically underenforce the law."[43]

These statutory provisions have set in motion political forces powerfully abetting NIMBYism. One is the rapid proliferation of national and state organizations specifically committed to educating Americans about hazardous waste and to helping local communities organize politically to deal with local hazardous waste problems. Among the earliest and most visible national organizations is the Citizen's Clearing House for Hazardous Waste, created in 1981 by Lois Gibbs, a housewife whose experiences with the Love Canal waste crisis of 1978 convinced her of a need to educate other communities about hazardous waste. There has also been an explosion of ad hoc state and local groups that have organized to deal with specific hazardous waste issues, ranging from the closing of city waste dumps to state policy for hazardous waste transportation.

Many existing state and national environmental organizations now give major attention to hazardous waste issues and provide technical assistance and education for concerned citizens. These groups believe they are ultimately contributing to better implementation of RCRA and Superfund by ensuring greater citizen understanding and acceptance of waste policy decisions made by government officials. Often, however, this activism arouses or emboldens citizen opposition to permits for local hazardous waste sites. Public officials and waste producers commonly complain that organized citizen groups too often agitate rather than educate in community waste issues.

Public resistance to hazardous waste site permits and management plans under RCRA or Superfund is a serious and unsolved political problem afflicting both programs. Coupled with litigation, the many political and administrative strategies available to citizen groups determined to prevent permits for local hazardous waste dumps can delay program implementation for years or decades. And it is happening. Richard Andrews, for instance, studied 179 attempts to site hazardous waste facilities across the United States between 1980 and 1986 and reported that 25 percent were rejected, 53 percent were still pending, and only 22 percent had been sited. Public opposition was a significant factor in almost all delays or rejections of site permits.[44] During the first year of Pennsylvania's hazardous waste site permit program, more than 75 percent of the state's proposed permits were challenged by organized groups. More than a third of these protests were led by municipal officials or other governmental officers.[45] Equally important, almost half of these protests led to permit rejection, withdrawal, or delay.

State governments are not innocent of NIMBYism. Almost any hazardous waste proposal can arouse it. When the Department of Energy in the mid-1980s evaluated several states as potential permanent repositories for high-level nuclear waste, state officials crowded public hearings to object. A public hearing was, observes Michael Kraft, "a perfect forum for elected officials and the general public to give vent to fears and concerns, and to denounce decisionmaking on the siting question. The public hearing procedure . . . facilitated the classic NIMBY response to siting unwanted facilities that impose localized costs and risks while offering diffuse national benefits."[46] In a 1989 variation, Alabama announced it would no longer accept hazardous waste from twenty-two other states and the District of Columbia. These states would have to find some other place for the 700,000 tons of hazardous materials they had been annually trucking to Alabama.[47]

Many administrative strategies have been tried but none seems to dispel NIMBYism. States that financially compensate local governments and citizens for risks and other problems entailed in accepting a hazardous waste site are no more successful in gaining public approval for the siting than states using only scientific criteria for site selection. Evidence suggests that most citizens who oppose a hazardous waste site will not change their minds under any circumstances.[48] Opponents may occasionally be converted if they are convinced that the local community will have continuing, accurate information about the site status and continuing control over the site's management. But converts are few. Opponents to hazardous waste sites are numerous, vocal, and unyielding. Moreover, they are apt to win their fights.

NIMBYism will continue tough, stubborn, and durable, its ranks crowded with well-educated, socially active, organizationally experienced people. NIMBYism is rarely routed by better information, more qualified experts, improved risk communication techniques, and other palliative actions premised on the assumption that the public will be more reasonable about hazardous facility siting if it is better educated about the issues. All this belies the widespread belief among scientific experts and risk professionals that NIMBYism is rooted in the public's scientific illiteracy.[49]

Why is "better" risk communication not enough? Because NIMBYs usually distrust the *source* of governmental risk information: public officials and their scientific spokesmen. Additionally, critics of governmental hazardous waste management often have their *own* experts and information sources. The conflicting sides, notes Harvey Brooks, tend to become "noncommunicating publics that each rely on different sources and talk to different experts. Thus, many public policy discussions become dialogues of the deaf. . . ."[50] Often, the true wellsprings of public anxiety about waste siting are uncomprehended by technical experts: people worry about "potentially catastrophic effects, lack of familiarity and understanding, involuntariness, scientific uncertainty, lack of personal control by the individuals exposed, risks to future generations," and more.[51]

Critics frequently hold environmentalists responsible for NIMBYism. They assert that the environmentalist rhetoric favored by NIMBYs is little more than deceptive but respectable packaging for middle-class selfishness. In reality, argue the critics, most NIMBYs want somebody else to bear whatever risks are associated with hazardous waste sites while they continue to benefit from the products and economic activities that produce the waste. Even if NIMBYism is well intentioned, critics also note, it fails to solve waste problems. Eventually, waste has to go someplace. Unfortunately, critics conclude, the waste often ends at whatever sites are the least well defended politically, not at the most appropriate places.

Whatever its merits, NIMBYism's certain continuation poses difficult problems for environmental regulation. Is it possible to secure informed public consent to the siting and management of hazardous waste facilities? If no public involvement techniques or risk communication procedures can produce public consensus or acquiescence to hazardous waste site planning under RCRA and Superfund, must solutions be imposed by judicial, administrative, or political means? Is there danger that continuing promotion of public involvement in making these decisions will enshrine procedural democracy at the expense of social equity—in effect, will citizen participation gradually result in selectively exposing the least economically and politically advantaged publics to the most risks from hazardous waste? How much responsibility for NIMBYism's worst impacts rests with the environmental movement? These questions can only grow in importance as the hazardous waste problem magnifies during the 1990s.

Conclusion

In no other major area of environmental policy is progress measured in such small increments as the regulation of toxic and hazardous wastes. The slow pace at which TSCA, RCRA, and Superfund have so far been implemented has produced a quality of regulation so tenuous and variable that a serious question exists whether regulation in any significant sense has yet been achieved. The nation remains seriously at risk from hazardous waste in abandoned or deliberately uncontrolled landfills numbering in the tens of thousands. Federal and state governments have yet to approve and implement on the appropriate scale the required strategies for ameliorating hazardous waste problems. The risks already associated with hazardous substances, and the many others to become apparent with continuing research throughout the 1990s, are unlikely to diminish within the decade without a massive and continuing federal commitment of resources to implement the programs as intended by Congress—a commitment of resources and will on a scale lacking so far.

Even with sufficient resources, the implementation of TSCA, RCRA, and Superfund is likely to be slow because these laws raise technical, legal, and political problems on an order seldom matched in other environmental policy domains. First, no other environmental programs attempt to regulate so many discrete, pervasive substances; we have observed that the hazardous substances that may lie within the ambit of these laws number in the tens of thousands. Second, regulation is delayed by the need to acquire technical information never previously obtained by government, to conduct research on the hazardousness of new chemicals, or to secure from corporations highly guarded trade secrets. Third, almost every major regulatory action intended to limit the production, distribution, or disposal of chemical substances deemed toxic or hazardous by government is open to technical controversy, litigation, and other challenges concerning the degree of risk associated with such substances and their suitability for regulation under the laws. Fourth, opponents of regulatory actions under TSCA, RCRA, and Superfund have been able to utilize to good advantage all the opportunities provided by requirements for administrative due process and the federalized structure of regulation to challenge administrative acts politically and judicially. Finally, in many instances the states responsible for implementing the programs have been unable, or unwilling, to provide from their own resources the means necessary to ensure proper implementation. None of these problems are unique to hazardous substance regulation, but few other environmental policies raise all these problems so persistently and acutely.

In a broader perspective, the enormous difficulties in controlling hazardous substances once they are released into the ecosystem, together with the problems of controlling their disposal, emphasize the crucial role that production controls must play in hazardous substance management. Indeed, it may be that the human and environmental risks from hazardous chemicals may never be satisfactorily constrained once these substances are let loose in the environment. American technology development has proceeded largely with an implicit confidence that whatever human or environmental risks may be engendered in the process can be adequately contained by the same genius that inspired technology's development—a faith, in effect, that science always will cure what ills it creates. The risk to man and his environment from now pervasive chemical substances created within the last half century ought to prompt some thoughtful reservation about the efficacy of technological solutions to technological problems. Toxic and hazardous substances pose for the nation a formidable technological challenge: how to reckon the human and environmental costs of technology development while technologies are yet evolving and, then, how to prudently control dangerous technologies without depriving the nation of their benefits.

Notes

1. *New York Times*, January 10, 1988.
2. Ibid.
3. On the proliferation of these chemicals and the ecological effects generally see Erick P. Eckholm, *The Picture of Health: Environmental Sources of Disease* (New York: W. W. Norton, 1977).
4. Executive Office of the President, Council on Environmental Quality (CEQ), *Environmental Quality, 1979* (Washington, D.C.: Government Printing Office, 1980), 181.
5. Ibid.
6. The Conservation Foundation, *State of the Environment: A View Toward the Nineties* (Washington, D.C.: Conservation Foundation, 1987), 136; and CEQ, *Environmental Quality, 1981*, 11.
7. CEQ, *Environmental Quality, 1981*, 115.
8. *New York Times*, April 23, 1980.
9. Department of Commerce, Bureau of the Census, *Statistical Abstract of the United States, 1989* (Washington, D.C.: Government Printing Office, 1989), 203.
10. *New York Times*, April 16, 1989.
11. Ibid.
12. Conservation Foundation, *State of the Environment*, 448.
13. *New York Times*, June 14, 1988. See also U.S. General Accounting Office, "Efforts to Clean Up DOD-Owned Inactive Hazardous Waste Disposal Sites," Report no. GAO/NSIAD-85-41 (April 12, 1985), i–ii.
14. U.S. General Accounting Office, "Superfund: Civilian Federal Agencies Slow to Clean Up Hazardous Waste," Report no. GAO/RCED-87-153 (July 1987), 3.
15. *New York Times*, June 13, 1982.
16. *New York Times*, March 14, 1989.
17. *New York Times*, March 14, 1989.
18. David D. Doniger, *The Law and Policy of Toxic Substances Control* (Baltimore: Johns Hopkins University Press, 1978), 9.
19. World Resources Institute, *World Resources, 1987* (New York: Basic Books, 1987), 204.
20. Joseph G. Morone and Edward J. Woodhouse, *Averting Catastrophe* (Berkeley: University of California Press, 1986), 34–35.
21. *New York Times*, August 10, 1982.
22. *New York Times*, July 8, 1983.
23. *New York Times*, July 14, 1982.
24. *New York Times*, January 3, 1983. Other useful cost estimates may be found in Environmental Protection Agency, *Administration of the Toxic Substances Control Act of 1980* (Washington, D.C.: Government Printing Office, 1981).
25. Estimates by Paul MacAvoy, *New York Times*, February 14, 1982. See also U.S. Library of Congress, Congressional Reference Service, *Six Case Studies of Compensation for Toxic Substances Pollution* (Report to the Committee on Environment and Public Works, U.S. Senate, No. 96–13, Washington, D.C., 1980).

26. Christopher Harris, William L. Want, and Morris A. Ward, *Hazardous Waste: Confronting the Challenge* (New York: Quorum Books, 1987), 87.

27. Ibid., 90–91.

28. See 42 U.S.C. 9601-9657 (1980).

29. U.S. General Accounting Office, "Toxic Substances: EPA Has Made Limited Progress in Identifying PCB Users," Report no. GAO/RCED 88-127 (April 1988), 3; and CEQ, *Environmental Quality, 1986*, Table 9-9.

30. CEQ, *Environmental Quality, 1986*, Table 9-6.

31. U.S. General Accounting Office, "Chemical Data: EPA's Data Collection Practices and Procedures on Chemicals," Report no. GAO/RCED-86-63 (February 1986), 24.

32. CEQ, *Environmental Quality, 1980*, 217.

33. Ibid., 219.

34. U.S. General Accounting Office, "Toxic Substances: EPA Has Made Limited Progress," 7–8.

35. Ibid.

36. Ibid.

37. Ibid., 23.

38. *New York Times,*, June 8, 1989.

39. Ibid.

40. On the sources and impact of NIMBYism generally, see Luther J. Carter, *Nuclear Imperatives and Public Trust: Dealing with Radioactive Waste* (Washington, D.C.: Resources for the Future, 1987); Clarence Davies, Vincent T. Covello, and Frederick W. Allen, eds., *Risk Communication* (Washington, D.C.: Conservation Foundation, 1987); and Roger E. Kasperson, "Six Propositions on Public Participation and Their Relevance for Risk Communication," *Risk Analysis* 6, no. 3 (September 1986): 275–281.

41. Patrick G. Marshall, "Not in My Backyard," *CQ Editorial Reports* (Washington, D.C.: Congressional Quarterly, June 1989), 311.

42. Michael S. Greve, "Environmentalism and Bounty Hunting," *Public Interest* 97 (Fall 1989): 15–29.

43. Ibid., 24.

44. Ibid.

45. Walter A. Rosenbaum, "The Politics of Public Participation in Hazardous Waste Management," in *The Politics of Hazardous Waste Management*, ed. James P. Lester and Ann O'M. Bowman (Durham, N.C.: Duke University Press, 1983), 191–192.

46. Michael E. Kraft, "Managing Technological Risks in a Democratic Polity: Citizen Participation and Nuclear Waste Disposal" (Paper presented at the national conference of the American Society for Public Administration, Boston, 1987), 23.

47. *New York Times*, August 31, 1989.

48. William Lyons, Michael R. Fitzgerald, and Amy McCabe, "Public Opinion and Hazardous Waste," *Forum for Applied Research and Public Policy* 2, no. 3 (Fall 1987): 89–97. See also Michael E. Kraft, "Risk Perception and the Politics of Citizen Participation: The Case of Radioactive Waste Management" in *Advances in Risk Analysis*, Vol. 9, ed. Lorraine Abbott (New York: Plenum, 1990).

49. Thomas M. Dietz and Robert W. Rycroft, *The Risk Professionals* (New York: Russell Sage Foundation, 1987), 60.

50. Harvey Brooks, "The Resolution of Technically Intensive Public Policy Disputes," *Science, Technology and Human Values* 9, no. 1 (Winter 1984): 48.

51. Kraft, "Risk Perception."

Suggested Readings

Committee on Institutional Means for Assessment of Risks to Public Health, Commission on Life Sciences, National Research Council. *Risk Assessment in the*

Federal Government: Managing the Process. Washington, D.C.: National Academy Press, 1989.

Morone, Joseph G., and Edward J. Woodhouse. *Averting Catastrophe: Strategies for Regulating Risky Technologies.* Berkeley: University of California Press, 1986.

Postel, Sandra. *Defusing the Toxics Threat: Controlling Pesticides and Industrial Waste.* Washington, D.C.: Worldwatch Institute, 1987.

Sapolsky, Harvey M., ed. *Consuming Fears: The Politics of Product Risks.* New York: Basic Books, 1986.

Wildavsky, Aaron. *Searching for Safety.* New Brunswick, N.J.: Transaction Books, 1988.

Chapter 8

Black Gold and Nuclear Dreams
The Politics of Energy

I have seen moonscapes on minesites.
—Official, U.S. Office of Surface Mining Reclamation and Enforcement,
after visiting a Tennessee mine site.

These are magnificent mountains. . . . But how is a mining company
operating a pit on the other side of this ridge going to hurt all this? . . .
We just have to have copper.
—A mining engineer discussing copper reserves in Glacier Peak Wilderness

No nation was endowed with a greater bounty of natural resources than the United States. The sinews of the American economy have been forged from a seemingly inexhaustible inheritance of all the natural resources essential for national prosperity: abundant water, fertile soil, forests reaching beyond the horizon, a benign climate, and below the soil metal ores, gold, silver, coal, petroleum, and natural gas. More than abundance, it was an extravagance of resources. Only in this century have Americans come belatedly to recognize that much of this inheritance could soon approach exhaustion or irreversible degradation. The politics of natural resources is the struggle to determine how the remaining resources will be used and who will make the decisions. That these resources are finite, fragile, or unique adds passion and urgency to the struggle. The American environment will be profoundly affected by the outcome.

This chapter concerns energy, one of the nation's greatest natural endowments. Energy policy is environmental policy. Most forms of energy production upon which the United States depends create significant, often adverse environmental impacts. Any change in the amount, variety, or duration of U.S. energy production or consumption will produce corresponding alterations in environmental quality.

Energy Consumption

The United States has a ravenous energy appetite. Americans, who collectively consume about one-fourth of the world's energy production, individually use more energy in a year than the average residents of Europe, South America, and Asia combined.[1] Many of the nation's major pollution problems are directly caused by current methods of producing and consuming this energy. Consider the environmental impact of fossil fuels. About 93 percent of all energy currently consumed in the United States comes from petroleum, natural gas, and coal.[2] The ecological consequences of this combustion include:

• Transportation and fossil fuel-fired electric generating plants annually produce 36 percent of the particulates, 37 percent of the hydrocarbons, 83 percent of the carbon monoxide, 84 percent of the sulfur oxides, and 95 percent of the nitrogen oxides emitted into the air.
• The land area disturbed by coal surface mining in the United States by the mid-1980s had reached more than 5.7 million acres, an area equal in size to the state of New Hampshire. Of this total, more than 3 million acres remained "unclaimed," creating an abandoned, sterile wasteland.
• During the 1980s, an average of more than 10,000 large spills of hazardous substances, mostly petroleum, were reported in U.S. waters yearly. More than 20 million gallons of petroleum and chemicals were spilled annually during the decade.[3]

So intimate is the association between energy and environmental quality—a linkage revealed again by the emerging problems of global climate warming and acid rain—that the nation's environmental agenda for the 1990s will become energy policy by another name. The environmental movement has always recognized the interdependence of energy and environmental policy. When leaders of the nation's major environmental organizations presented President Bush with their agenda for environmental policies in the 1990s, energy conservation ranked in priority only behind global warming and ozone destruction.[4]

Until 1990, the average American's own interest in energy matters had been fading as fast as memories of the 1970's "energy crisis." Then came Iraq's August invasion of Kuwait. Domestic gasoline prices sharply climbed, stock values vacillated unpredictably, and rising apprehension about economic turbulence in the wake of the invasion was compounded with anxiety about U.S. security. Again, Americans were compelled to recognize how dependent they had become upon Middle Eastern petroleum and, thus, how gravely their military and economic future could be affected by the volatile politics of the Persian Gulf. The dispatch of U.S. troops to the Middle East to counter the Iraqi invasion was a grim reminder that the nation's tenuous Middle Eastern oil lifeline could even lead to a war for control of the world's remaining petroleum reserves.

During the 1980s, environmentalists had joined many national security experts in warning that the United States was poised between the energy crisis it had momentarily averted in the 1970s and its certain return, hastened by the nation's failure to learn from its earlier energy troubles. That first energy crisis, lasting from 1973 to 1978, was triggered by a sudden, brief Arab embargo upon petroleum exported to the United States. Then, Americans were forced for the first time to recognize their dangerous dependence upon imported petroleum. Briefly, it appeared as if the United States might face a worldwide petroleum shortage so severe that it might be compelled to accelerate rapidly, at severe ecological risk, the mining of its huge coal reserves and the construction of more nuclear utilities. But new domestic energy regulations and the Arab cartel's failure to maintain its export controls solved the first energy crisis. By 1990, the United States had lapsed back into the patterns of energy consumption and energy policies that had invited the first energy crisis. The 1990 Iraqi invasion reawakened the specters of economic dislocation, national insecurity, energy shortages, and a new raid on nonpetroleum energy resources familiar little more than a decade ago. Whether the nation has yet learned that its continuing reliance on imported oil and other fossil fuels for almost all its energy is intolerably dangerous remains to be seen.

Imported Oil and Fossil Fuels: A Perilous Combination

The American energy economy today can be sustained only by huge infusions of fossil fuel, especially imported oil. One major cause of environmental stress is continued dependence upon nonrenewable fossil fuels. As Table 8-1 indicates, the United States in the late 1980s was as dependent upon fossil fuels for energy as it had been when the first energy crisis shocked Americans in 1973 and 1974.

U.S. dependence upon imported oil declined sharply in the years immediately following the second oil shock created by Iran's sudden 1978 cutback in U.S. petroleum exports and it seemed for a few years that the United States had learned the lesson of the oil embargoes. But imports rose again and by 1989 the nation was importing 46 percent of its daily petroleum consumption—more than the 38.8 percent imported when the first Arab embargo hit, even more than the 45.3 percent when Iran curtailed its petroleum production.[5] Moreover, an increasing proportion of this imported oil—currently about one barrel in five—originates in an Arab nation. At the same time, domestic U.S. oil production is

Table 8-1 *U.S. Energy Consumption, 1974, 1980, and 1987*
(quadrillion BTUs of energy)

Year	Coal	Natural gas	Petroleum	Other[a]	Total
1974	12.88	21.73	33.45	4.63	72.69
	(17.7%)	(29.9%)	(46.0%)	(6.4%)	(100%)
1980	15.67	20.44	34.25	5.94	76.30
	(20.5%)	(26.8%)	(44.9%)	(7.8%)	(100%)
1987	18.01	17.18	32.60	8.21	76.00
	(23.7%)	(22.6%)	(42.9%)	(10.8%)	(100%)

SOURCE: Council on Environmental Quality, *Environmental Quality, 1981* (Washington, D.C.: Government Printing Office, 1982), 235; Department of Commerce, Bureau of the Census, *Statistical Abstract of the United States, 1989* (Washington, D.C.: Government Printing Office, 1989), 554.
    [a]Includes nuclear, hydroelectric, geothermal, and wood.

slowly dwindling. In 1989, U.S. production was at its lowest level since 1963 and was not expected to increase.[6]

This resurgent U.S. addiction to imported oil occurs amid considerable uncertainty about the duration of global petroleum reserves. Many experts believe world petroleum consumption may be outpacing world production, largely due to the continuing decline in U.S. and Soviet oil production and the anticipated growth of oil consumption in Eastern Europe and Southeast Asia. However, other experts believe world petroleum reserves will continue to increase at least through the 1990s, thereby keeping the cost of petroleum relatively low for a few more years and discouraging energy conservation among the world's major consumers. The economic and political assumptions undergirding all predictions of future world energy supply are at best informed guesses, often easily confounded by unanticipated events. Given these uncertainties, and the enormous ecological, economic, and security risks entailed in continuing heavy dependence upon imported oil, the United States has reason to consider imported oil a major problem in itself.

A Fading Public Concern

Public consumption of imported oil is growing, while public concern about the consequences is not. By 1985, energy had vanished from the list produced by the major polls of important national concerns. Public apprehension about energy supply and consumption that was awakened by the energy shocks of the 1970s was hurried to extinction by the Reagan administration's rapid dismantling of the energy conservation and regulatory programs enacted in the latter 1970s, and by the return of ample world petroleum supplies and lower petroleum prices. The

Reagan administration pressed for more energy production, not energy conservation, and preached the need for more confidence in the marketplace and less in governmental regulation. In 1988, the federal government cut by 70 percent the press runs of a booklet listing gas mileage for all new automobiles. It was an epitaph for the energy crisis.

In the early 1990s, attention to energy conservation and efficiency was everywhere retreating. National energy efficiency, measured by the ratio of energy used for each dollar of Gross National Product (GNP), had increased by 24 percent from 1976 to 1986, but it remained unchanged in 1987 and declined in 1988.[7] There was another portent of changing times: "muscle cars" were back. By 1989, Ford Motor Company was installing the once-banished V-8 engine in almost half its new Mustangs. The Japanese auto manufacturers were adding to their U.S. lines high-performance, big-horsepower models such as Nissan Motors's 300-horsepower sports car to challenge the American Corvette.

Many Americans at the outset of the 1990s were not driving an energy-guzzler but were living in one. Developers were no longer promoting energy-efficient homes. Many no longer built them. "I think people would rather pay for the glitzy part of a home than they would for more energy conservation," explained one of the East Coast's largest builders. "It's unfortunate, but we live in a different age."[8] As a result of growing residential energy consumption, electricity demand in the Northeast increased by twice the anticipated average in 1987. In 1986, national residential electricity demand exceeded industrial demand for the first time in U.S. history.

The Reagan Record

The Reagan administration largely ended the federal government's promotion of energy efficiency and conservation with congressional and public approval. Auto efficiency standards mandated by Congress in 1975 had raised new U.S. cars from an average 14.2 miles per gallon in 1974 to 28.5 in 1988 before the Reagan administration's decision to end the mandatory standards at the 1986 level halted efficiency gains. Raising the national speed limit from 55 to 65 miles per hour on interstate highways added an estimated half million barrels of oil to daily U.S. consumption.[9] Federal funding for research and development promoting renewable energy technologies collapsed to 18 percent of 1980 levels and federal tax credits for residential or commercial use of wind and solar technologies were permitted to expire.[10] Not surprisingly, construction of power plants running on renewable energy such as wind or solar energy began to drop steeply in the late 1980s, leaving the United States capable of generating only about 1 percent of its electric power demand from all renewable sources, including hydropower.

The Reagan administration also accelerated the deregulation of price controls on petroleum and natural gas, hastened the demise of an ill-conceived attempt to create a national synthetic fuels industry, attempted to secure a huge increase in the amount of public lands leased for energy exploration, and ceaselessly campaigned for a revival of the moribund commercial nuclear power industry. The times were auspicious for this kind of retrenchment to traditional American energy habits: world petroleum supplies were abundant, prices low. The Arab oil cartel seemed impotent and irresolute. All this inhibited domestic price inflation and encouraged a steady, healthy growth in GNP throughout the 1980s. Neither Congress nor the public, perhaps recalling the unpleasant 1970s, was disposed to challenge the return of national oblivion about energy conservation.

By an environmental accounting, however, the national energy condition was alarming. The United States had no national energy planning and no coherent energy plan to deal with the continuing, and perhaps accelerating depletion of global petroleum reserves, including its own. It possessed only a small and faltering renewable energy sector that lacked the technology, trained professionals, and supporting infrastructure to respond quickly and effectively to any sudden need for renewable energy in the event of another severe shortfall in petroleum supply. It continued to rely upon fossil fuels, particularly petroleum and coal, which were freighted with severe ecological consequences that the United States was nonetheless committed to mitigating. And the commercial nuclear power industry, the nation's most technologically and economically advanced alternative to fossil fuels, remained economically stagnant and environmentally menacing, its ecological threat magnified by repeated failures to solve its technological problems.

The intricate interdependence of these energy problems and their ecological implications can be better appreciated by examining two major national energy issues of the 1990s in greater depth. Nuclear power and coal, both important energy sectors, pose major ecological risks that are certain to continue as long as the United States builds its energy future on a foundation of fossil fuel.

Nuclear Twilight or Second Dawn?

In the early 1990s, statistics about commercial nuclear power read like the industry's obituary. For almost two decades, the Nuclear Dream—the vision of almost unlimited, cheap electricity generated from nuclear reactors by the hundreds—has been dying. The commercial nuclear power industry has been failing under a burden of economic and technological misfortunes, an increasingly hostile political climate, inept public relations, persistent environmental risks, and regulatory pressures that have been mounting since the early 1970s. Predictions of the industry's imminent demise have been common.

The nuclear industry still hopes to revive through what might be called the "other Greenhouse Effect." Buoyed by a tenuous hope that global warming and acid rain would dispel its gathering misfortunes, the industry began in the early 1990s to promote itself as the most desirable economic and environmental alternative to fossil fuel for electric power generation. Environmentalists largely reject this assertion, citing the industry's continuing ecological risks and unresolved technological difficulties. Nonetheless, governmental and private consideration of the nuclear option has been revived. But proponents of nuclear power have massive difficulties to overcome before the technology can again be considered a plausible national energy option.

The Peaceful Atom and Its Problems

Peaceful atomic power began with the Eisenhower administration's determination to demonstrate to the world that the United States was concerned with more than the military uses of nuclear power and to prevent the global spread of nuclear materials. The nation's electric power industry was initially uninterested in commercial nuclear power until Washington promised to subsidize the initial research and development, to assume the costs and responsibilities for mining and refining the required nuclear fuels, and to share the patents it had monopolized. Washington also threatened to compete directly with the utilities by developing the technology itself if the industry refused. Once the industry agreed to the bargain, the regulation and management of the new technology were invested in the Atomic Energy Commission (AEC), which had already been created to regulate existing civilian uses of atomic energy, and in the Joint Committee on Atomic Energy, a new congressional watchdog for the commission.[11]

Soon the two Washington agencies joined the emerging nuclear power industry and the scientific community involved in the nuclear enterprise to form a powerful, politically autonomous subgovernment whose control of nuclear policy was largely uncontested for almost two decades. The industry prospered from benevolent regulation, huge infusions of federal subsidies reaching between $12 and $15 billion by the mid-1980s, public and political favor, and unique governmental concessions never given its competitors, such as the Price-Anderson Act (1957) limiting a nuclear utility's insurance liability to $540 million for any single reactor accident, thus ensuring that the industry would obtain the necessary insurance coverage. Until the 1970s, all but a handful of scientists, economists, and public officials associated with the new technology

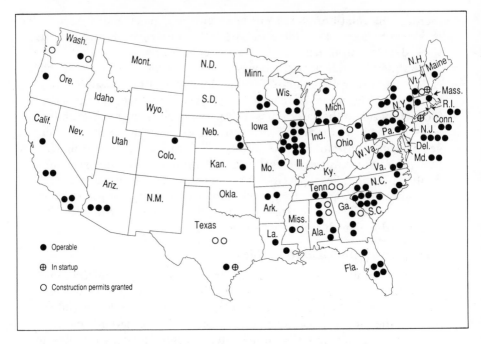

Figure 8-1 *Status of Nuclear Generating Units, December 1988*

seemed, in the words of economist Irvin Bupp, so "intoxicated" by the enterprise that they largely ignored grave technical and economic problems already apparent to a few critical observers.[12] When problems could not be ignored they were usually hidden from public view; when critics arose they were discredited by Washington's aggressive defense of the industry.

The Nuclear Dream seemed most resplendent in 1975: 56 commercial reactors had been built, another 69 were under construction, and 111 more were planned. Never again would the industry be so robust. The near catastrophic reactor meltdown at Three Mile Island (TMI), near Harrisburg, Pennsylvania, in March 1979 became the most politically damaging episode in the program's brief history, forcing national attention upon an industry already in serious trouble. Grave technical and economic problems had been evident even in the early 1970s. TMI, however, was a catalytic political event, powerfully altering public consciousness about nuclear power and strengthening the credibility of the industry's critics. Moreover, the industry's grave economic, technical, and environmental problems continued to worsen as the 1980s progressed. The May 1986 core meltdown at the Chernobyl nuclear power plant in the Soviet Ukraine was one more catastrophe in a series of baleful events hastening the extinction of the Nuclear Dream. As the 1990s began, the industry was almost moribund.

The Nuclear Industry Today.   In 1990 there were 112 operational nuclear reactors licensed to U.S. electric utilities. Most reactors are located along the East Coast, in the Southeast, and in the Midwest (see Figure 8-1). These reactors currently generate about 20 percent of peak summer electric power production. Under current schedules, half the present reactors will end their legal operating lives between the years 2005 and 2015, the remainder before the year 2075. In short, commercial nuclear power will disappear within another generation unless its fortunes are reversed. The major reason is that U.S. utilities have not ordered a new reactor since 1979, while simultaneously cutting back sharply on planned construction. This demise is evident from the data in Table 8-2, which describes the industry's reactor status at the end of 1988.

Despite notable improvements in the industry's safety procedures and technology development since TMI, its troubles remain substantially unrelieved. The malaise is compounded by economic and technical difficulties, unsolved waste management problems, and a volatile regulatory climate.

Economic Ills.   The cost of constructing and maintaining commercial nuclear power plants has climbed so steeply within the last decade that investment capital is scarce and costly. Many operating facilities

Table 8-2 *U.S. Nuclear Reactor Units, 1976 to 1988*

Year	Operable	In startup	Construction permits		On order	Announced	Total
			Granted	Pending			
1976	61	0	72	66	16	19	234
1977	65	1	80	52	13	9	220
1978	70	0	90	32	9	4	205
1979	68	0	91	21	3	0	183
1980	70	2	82	12	3	0	169
1981	74	0	75	11	3	0	163
1982	77	2	60	3	2	0	144
1983	80	3	53	0	2	0	138
1984	86	6	38	0	2	0	132
1985	95	3	30	0	2	0	130
1986	100	7	19	0	2	0	128
1987	107	4	14	0	2	0	127
1988	108	3	13	0	0	0	124

SOURCE: U.S. Department of Energy, Energy Information Administration. *Energy Facts 1988* (Washington, D.C.: Government Printing Office, 1988), 41.

are producing power at a unit cost far exceeding original projections. Facilities completed in the late 1980s and early 1990s will generally be 500 to 1,000 percent over budget.[13] New Hampshire's bitterly contested Seabrook No. 1 facility, finally granted an operating license in 1990 after a fifteen-year battle with opponents, was originally expected to cost $900 million. At startup in 1990, the costs had exceeded $5.8 billion. When Detroit Edison's Enrico Fermi II plant began generation in 1988, it was $4 billion over its original budget.[14] Discounting inflation, the real cost for constructing the nuclear facility had risen from $1,135 per kilowatt of power in 1980 to $4,590 in 1989.[15]

Among the major reasons for this cost escalation are several involving public safety and environmental protection. The time required to secure the many governmental licenses that ensure the facility will meet safety and environmental standards has been continually lengthening. Currently, surmounting these regulatory hurdles requires four to eight years and may involve almost a hundred different federal, state, and local governmental permits. Industry officials also complain of the costs imposed during plant construction through regulatory "ratcheting" by the Nuclear Regulatory Commission (NRC)—its habit of requiring facilities to make new safety modifications or other expensive design changes retroactively. Additional costs have been imposed upon many utilities by protracted litigation involving environmental groups and others challenging various aspects of plant design and safety. These costs have reduced the market competitiveness of nuclear-generated electricity in comparison to fossil fuel-fired plants.

The industry's economic ills cannot be blamed wholly on regulators and environmental critics. Operating plants seldom perform at design levels. The average facility has been "down" about one-third of its total operating time due to routine maintenance. Many plants suffer from overcapacity due to unanticipated levels of new electric power demand. And serious, expensive technical problems continue to beset the industry.

Technical Problems. Proponents of nuclear power correctly argue that its historic safety record, notwithstanding TMI, is excellent and that critics have exaggerated its technical problems. However, continuing revelations of technical difficulties suggest serious deficiencies in the basic design and operation of the plants, and frequent carelessness or incompetence in plant management. Whatever their "real" significance, these problems have worked against the industry politically. Continuing admissions of safety risks and technical difficulties at a time of growing public apprehension about nuclear power inspire the opposition.

Several technical problems have been especially damaging to the industry. First, materials and design standards for many plants currently

operating or under construction have failed essential safety requirements. Reactor parts, for instance, have aged much faster than anticipated. Steam generators meant to last a plant's lifetime—approximately
fifty years—are wearing out much sooner; this is a particularly serious
problem in New York, Florida, Virginia, Wisconsin, and South Carolina.[16] Mistakes have been made in plant specifications or construction.
Pipes have cracked and "wasted" (the walls becoming thinner) from
extended exposure to radiation. In 1988, the General Accounting Office
(GAO) recommended a mandatory inspection of all plants for pipe deterioration after finding that nearly a third of the plants it surveyed had the
problem. The NRC betrayed its own misgivings about plant safety in
1979 when it repudiated its 1974 estimate, contained in the so-called
"Rassmussen Report," that a potential catastrophic reactor accident
would occur only once in 10 million years of reactor operation—as
probable as a single meteorite striking someone on earth. The NRC
failed at the time to provide an alternative safety estimate.

Finally, continuing relevations of plant mismanagement, administrative bungling, and secrecy raise serious questions about the competence
of plant managers and technicians. The industry must contend with
such disclosures as:

• In 1987, the NRC shut down Philadelphia Electric's Peach Bottom
plant, the first time a nuclear power plant had been closed for a nonme-
chanical reason. Operations were suspended when it was discovered that
plant technicians, who came to work in jeans and T-shirts, passed much
of their time with magazines, video games, and rubber band fights, and
took turns sleeping at night, although sometimes everyone on the shift
was asleep.[17]

• In 1989, NRC records showed that four of five U.S. nuclear utilities
had failed to complete sweeping safety changes required after TMI in
1979. Only 24 of 112 licensed reactors have installed all 149 changes.[18]

• In 1986, the Mississippi Power and Light Company gave the NRC
false information about the amount of training given to engineers
applying for licenses to operate its reactor. If the correct information had
been given, the applicants would have been ineligible to take the exam.
Company officials who discovered the deception failed to correct it.[19]

Industry officials insist that critics have distorted and misrepresented
the safety record of commercial nuclear utilities by seizing upon these
disclosures as if they characterized the entire industry. Indeed, many
utilities have a virtually uninterrupted record of safe operations and
skilled management. Still, after more than twenty years of operation,
the industry continues to experience serious design, management, and
engineering failures. The risk of a major plant accident is not insignifi-

cant and several near disasters have occurred. Moreover, the industry has not solved its grave waste disposal and emergency management problems.

The Waste Nobody Wants.   No problem has proven more politically troublesome to the nuclear power industry and its federal regulators than where, and how, to dispose of the enormous, highly toxic, and mounting volume of nuclear wastes in the United States. The problem, never anticipated when commercial nuclear power was first promoted, has been especially difficult because reactor wastes incite great public fear and chronic conflict between federal, state, and local officials concerning where to put them.

This nuclear waste originates from uranium mining, civilian nuclear power plants, military nuclear weapons programs, hospitals, educational institutions, and research centers. Current controversy involves four categories of waste:

1. *High-Level Wastes.* Highly radioactive liquids created through the reprocessing of reactor fuels. These wastes are generated by both civilian and military reactor programs. Currently, more than 100 million gallons of high-level wastes are stored in temporary containment facilities in the states of Washington, Idaho, South Carolina, and New York.

2. *Transuranic Wastes.* Some of the elements in these radioactive byproducts of reactor fuel and military waste processing remain dangerous for extraordinarily long periods. Plutonium 239, with a half-life of 24,000 years, and americum-243, with a 7,300-year half-life, are among the transuranics. Other more exotic transuranic elements have a half-life exceeding 200,000 years.

3. *Spent Nuclear Fuel.* About 6,000 metric tons of spent fuel, mostly from civilian reactors, are stored temporarily in "cooling ponds" at reactor sites. By 1995, as more nuclear plants become operational, this spent fuel is expected to increase to 63,000 metric tons.

4. *Low-Level Wastes.* Any material contaminated by radiation and emitting low levels of radioactivity itself belongs in this category. This includes workers' clothing, tools, equipment, and other items associated with nuclear reactors or nuclear materials. Low-level wastes currently are stored at repositories in South Carolina, New York, and Nevada.

In the early years of nuclear power promotion, it was assumed that spent fuel from civilian and military plants would be reprocessed: the fissionable materials, primarily plutonium, would be recovered for use again as reactor fuel and the remaining high-level waste eventually would be contained and isolated at appropriate disposal sites. In the planners' early view, the high-level and transuranic wastes remaining after reprocessing posed a largely technical and readily solvable problem of finding the appropriate containment materials and geographic location for permanent storage. They did not anticipate the failure of civilian reprocessing and the resulting volume of nuclear waste. They did not foresee the necessity to store military wastes for decades longer than the containment structures were designed to last. They did not anticipate the political repercussions in trying to find a place to put the waste.

Existing and planned commercial facilities were designed to store temporarily no more than three years' accumulated spent fuel in cooling ponds until the fuel assemblies were reprocessed. Since the early 1970s, however, virtually all spent fuel has been stored in these cooling ponds. Space and time are now running out. The United States continues to reprocess its spent military fuel, thereby generating most of the high-level liquid wastes accumulating at military nuclear reservations. Until 1982, the federal government had no comprehensive plan for the permanent storage of these nuclear wastes. Washington and the states quarreled for more than a decade over how a permanent waste depository would be designed and which states would be depository sites—nobody wanted it.[20] Idaho and South Carolina, already accommodating large volumes of high- and low-level wastes from other states, were increasingly reluctant to accept more. In 1976, California ordered a moratorium on the construction of commercial nuclear facilities until Washington could certify that a permanent repository for their spent fuel existed. The nuclear waste issue was approaching crisis.

The States Play Nuclear "Keep Away." Congress finally passed in 1982 the Nuclear Waste Policy Act (NWPA), which was intended to create a process for designating and constructing the first permanent repositories for nuclear waste. The act appeared to end a decade of nasty legislative infighting during which each state scrambled to write language into the law assuring it would not be a candidate for the repository. The legislation assigned the site selection task to the Department of Energy (DOE) and created what appeared to be a meticulously detailed, impartial, and open process by which all possible sites would be thoroughly studied and reduced to a few from which the president would eventually select two, one east and one west of the Mississippi River. The president was to designate the first site by March 31, 1987, and the second by July 1, 1989. To demonstrate its confidence in the process, the DOE agreed to begin accepting high-level commercial wastes sometime in 1998.

Following procedures required by the NWPA, the DOE in 1985 nominated three permanent sites to the president from which he was to select one: Texas (Deaf Smith County), Washington (the Hanford nuclear military reservation), and Yucca Mountain, Nevada (near the Nevada atomic test site). Every stage of the designation process, however, had been accompanied by political controversy. Republican senators and representatives from each designated state complained to the White House that the designation of their state would penalize the party at the polls in 1986 and 1988. The political leadership of both parties in all three states complained bitterly that their states had been improperly designated and attempted to overturn the designation in the courts. Environmental groups in each state went to court, challenging the designations on technical and procedural grounds. And Congress could anticipate another rancorous round of the same when the president was scheduled to select the second repository site from another set of states in 1989.

Rather than abide the continuing controversy, with all its inherent political risks, Congress found a simpler solution to the designation problem. In December 1987, the Congress suddenly renounced the procedures it had ordered in the NWPA and summarily designated Nevada to be the first permanent waste site. As a consolation, Nevada was assured up to $20 million annually to manage the job. Nevada legislators were outraged. It "will turn our state into a federal colony," accused Republican representative Barbara F. Vucanovich.[21] "Instead of leadership and principle, it's a gang-rape mentality," added a spokesman for Richard Bryan, Nevada's governor. The man who arranged it all thought otherwise. "If I were a Nevadan living in the real world, I would be happy with this bill," asserted Sen. J. Bennett Johnston (D-La.). "I would bet that in a very few years, Nevada will deem this one of their most treasured industries."[22] The other states, assured they would not inherit this potential treasure, were content. In the keep-away politics of nuclear waste, the most weakly defended constituency had become "It."

Repository Problems.   "It's fair to say we've solved the nuclear waste problem with this legislation," Senator Johnston assured his colleagues with premature optimism after they voted the waste to Nevada. But after more than two years of preliminary work and an expenditure of $500 million at the Nevada site, the DOE announced in 1989 that it was abandoning its initial repository plan because it lacked confidence in the technical quality of the proposal.[23] The DOE predicted that the repository would be delayed until at least the year 2010, even though it was committed to accepting high-level wastes from commercial reactors by 1998 and the commercial utilities had already paid $3 billion in taxes to use the repository.

Reports on the DOE's nuclear waste management projects became unrelieved bad news in the latter 1980s. In mid-1989, the DOE announced that it was delaying the opening of its Waste Isolation Pilot Plant (WIPP) near Carlsbad, New Mexico. The WIPP, begun in the late 1970s, was intended to store the plutonium wastes generated at the

Rocky Flats nuclear military facility near Denver where space for the liquid wastes was fast disappearing. The underground repository had been scheduled to receive its first shipments in 1992 but DOE's scientific advisers urged a delay of two or three years because the DOE needed to complete technical diagrams of the exact structures of twenty-one systems already built into the structure, including the electrical, radiation control, and fire protection systems.[24]

The WIPP's delay adds another chapter to the already protracted, acrimonious debate about the safety of that facility, and raises doubts that the WIPP will ever be used. Thus, the nation still lacks a permanent repository for either its civilian or military nuclear wastes. Waste storage capacity at civilian utility sites continues to dwindle. At the same time, military waste-containment structures are dangerously deteriorating at places like the Hanford, Washington, military reservation where 440,000 cubic yards of high-, low-, and extremely long-lived nuclear waste are stored, some since 1943, awaiting permanent deposition.[25] This is not, however, the whole of the national nuclear waste problem. The controversy attending reactor waste deflects public attention from the emerging problem of disposing of nuclear facilities themselves after they have ended their useful life.

Decommissioning Problems.   Once civilian or military nuclear facilities have finished their useful lives, the NRC and DOE require that the owners "decommission" their facility by removing from the site the radioactive materials, including land, ground water, buildings, contents, and equipment, and by reducing residual radioactivity to a level permitting the property to be used for any other purpose.[26] Since a commercial reactor's life span is expected to be fifty years, an increasing number of the nation's reactors will have to be decommissioned beginning in the 1990s. However, no utility has yet decommissioned a large plant and none expect to do so until a permanent high-level waste depository is available. Instead, the utilities plan to partially decommission their facilities and to put them in "safe storage" while awaiting the completion of a permanent repository.

In fact, little is known about how large facilities can be taken apart and rendered safe. Few of the nation's utilities have done much practical planning for decommissioning their own plants. No reliable estimates are available for decommissioning costs, which have been calculated to range from tens of millions to $3 billion for each facility.[27] The NRC currently requires utilities to set aside $105 million to $135 million for decommissioning, but many experts believe these estimates are too low. Utilities are also required to have decommissioning plans, cost estimates, or written certification that they will meet NRC's cost estimates. Still, no utility has yet created a decommissioning fund, assessed its rate payers for the costs, or filed a decommissioning plan with the NRC in the absence of a permanent high-level waste repository.

The DOE's responsibility for decommissioning the nation's military reactors presents even more formidable problems. Investigations of the nation's military nuclear facility management in the late 1980s revealed appalling negligence in waste storage and management, leaks of dangerous radioactive materials for decades into the surrounding environment and civilian settlements, and deceit and secrecy in managing information about the lethal dangers created both on- and off-site from waste mismanagement. This legacy of a half-century's negligence leaves the DOE with an estimated cost of $200 billion to decontaminate and decommission its nuclear facilities. Some experts believe the costs will climb much higher, so intolerably high that the sites will be, as some plant engineers privately predict, "national sacrifice zones" never adequately decontaminated.[28]

Waste management and nuclear plant decommissioning problems will trouble Americans for centuries and remain a reminder of the technological optimism and mission fixation that inspired Washington's approach to nuclear technology development. Indeed, the politics of civilian nuclear power development has been as important in shaping the economic, ecological, and technological character of the industry as its science. So it will continue to be. The future of commercial nuclear power will be determined, in good part, by how the Congress, the White House, and the NRC respond to its present ills and challenges. The battle for the nuclear future is still being fought in these political arenas.

The NRC in the Middle

The NRC works in the vortex of controversy over commercial nuclear power regulation. Critics of the nuclear power industry almost ritually indict the NRC for its regulatory failures. But even its friends recognize a problem. It was an NRC commissioner newly appointed by President Reagan, a pronuclear spokesman for a pronuclear administration, who publicly complained shortly after assuming office about the "surprising lack of professionalism in the construction and preparation . . . of nuclear facilities" and "lapses of many kinds—in design analysis resulting in built-in design errors, in poor construction practices, in falsified documents. . . ."[29]

The NRC's regulatory deficiencies arise, in large part, from the political circumstances of its origin and the outlook of its professional staff. The NRC was created in 1974 when Congress abolished the AEC and vested that agency's regulatory authority in the new NRC. The new agency could not readily dissolve the strong, congenial professional and institutional relationships linking former AEC staff to the nuclear power industry, nor could it eliminate the impulse to promote and protect the industry that was so deeply rooted in the AEC's history. The NRC remains unapologetic about its commitment to nuclear power. "People who serve on this commission and on its staff do believe in the nuclear industry," retorted one to a critic.[30] Successive NRC commissioners and their staffs often tried to regulate without prejudice and sometimes succeeded, but institutional history and professional experience often— the critics say *usually*—prevailed against regulatory rigor.

In the aftermath of Three Mile Island, the NRC has made an effort to be a more aggressive and foresighted regulator and its relationship to the industry has become more complex. The NRC required a multitude of changes in plant management that cost utilities an average of $50 million. It has been quicker and harsher in assessing regulatory penalties, but the commission is still cited for serious regulatory lapses, such as the following:

• A GAO study between 1986 and 1987 of five nuclear facilities disclosed "that despite records of chronic safety violations, NRC did not close them. With only one exception, a safety incident occurred that made continued operation impossible or the utilities shut them down when the problems grew severe." Regarding plant safety standards it noted that the "NRC may take from several months to 10 or more years to resolve . . . generic issues, including those NRC believes pose the highest safety risk."[31]

• Another GAO investigation of NRC's supervision for the decommissioning of eight small reactors in 1987 found that the "NRC fully or partially released two sites for unrestricted use where contamination at one was up to 4 times, and at the other up to 320 times higher than NRC's guidelines allowed. . . . Also, for five licenses that buried waste, NRC does not know the types and amounts of radioactive waste that have been buried at four of the sites."[32]

Defenders of the NRC assert that many of its regulatory lapses result from understaffing and underfunding: the commission reportedly had only twenty-five full-time license reviewers and thirty-six inspectors to oversee 7,700 licenses for industrial and other uses of radioactive material in 1988.[33] Moreover, argue NRC's proponents, the regulatory changes required by the NRC often take years for utilities to accomplish. Some observers argue that the NRC must be doing its job reasonably well because it is also a frequent target of criticism from the nuclear power industry itself. One certainty is that the NRC operates in a radically different political environment after TMI. Relentless public exposure, politically potent and organized critics from the scientific and environmental community, fading congressional enthusiasm for nuclear power, and technical controversy over nuclear power's safety and economic prospects all produce a politically volatile regulatory climate in which the NRC must expect to operate in the 1990s. The transcendent political question for the NRC in the decade, however, is whether it will be presiding over the death of the Nuclear Dream.

Stubborn Hope: Breakthrough Technology, the White House, and the Greenhouse

If the nuclear power industry has cause for optimism about the future, it lies in the development of a new generation of safer reactors, in renewed White House promotion of nuclear power, and in nuclear power's revival as an alternative to fossil fuels, which are thought responsible for climate warming.

Spokesmen for the industry assert that the lessons learned from almost four decades' experience with commercial nuclear power are being applied in the design of a new generation of smaller, safer reactors free from the technical and economic ills of the present ones.[34] The Advanced Light Water Reactor presently at design stage is alleged to be ten times safer than present reactors in severe accident prevention. Two other promising technologies, the Modular Gas Temperature Gas Cooled Reactor, sometimes called the pebble-bed reactor, and the Liquid Metal Reactor, are also at design stage. The nuclear industry asserts that this new generation of reactors, while smaller than present ones, could be used in combination (as "modules") to produce as much power as needed much more safely and economically in future power plants. Morever, the industry now supports the adoption of a standard design for all future commercial reactors instead of the multiple designs now in use. This strategy would facilitate the rapid development and application of safety standards for the whole industry much more effectively than is possible with the present multiplicity of reactors.

The commercialization of this new generation of reactors will require a huge investment in research and development. The nuclear power industry, unable to raise capital on this scale in light of its presently bleak prospects, looks to the federal government for help. The Reagan administration strongly supported the industry but left its future largely to market forces. The Bush administration has declared its belief in the "nuclear option" and committed to support research and development for the industry.[35] In late 1989, for instance, the DOE awarded the General Electric Company and Westinghouse Electric Corporation each about $50 million to plan more efficient and reliable commercial reactors at a time the DOE was not aggressively promoting other energy technologies.[36] Congress, equally reluctant to preclude the "nuclear option," helped to keep the industry alive by renewing the Price-Anderson Act, which limits the insurance liability of utility operators, now to a maximum of $7 billion for any single commercial reactor accident. This new liability limit is still much smaller than a nuclear utility would ordinarily expect to pay in liability for an accident without the Price-Anderson Act.

Proponents of nuclear power also argue that the United States must continue commercial reactor development lest it become too dependent for electric power production upon uncertain supplies of increasingly scarce and costly petroleum or upon coal with all its environmental risks. With the resurgent growth in demand for new electric power in the early 1990s, assert nuclear power's proponents, the United States can no longer count upon the large unused power-generating capacity the nation enjoyed in the 1980s.

Advocates for continued reactor development also argue that should an alternative for fossil fuels be needed in the future, the nation cannot afford to have only the present flawed reactor technologies available. After reviewing the considerable uncertainties over future availability of fossil fuels and other energy alternatives, science policy specialists Joseph G. Morone and Edward J. Woodhouse conclude that the nuclear option still makes sense.

We cannot predict what energy the nation and world will want or need, nor what options will be available to meet the demands. . . . It is conceivable that there will be enough options to render nuclear power unnecessary in many nations, but equally conceivable that there will not be. And if such difficulties as the greenhouse effect do force a shift away from coal, and financially feasible energy alternatives are not available, much of the world may be backed into a corner: either rapidly construct a new generation of giant light water reactors, feared by a substantial portion of the population, or face the economic and other consequences of extremely tight energy supplies.[37]

The nuclear industry has been quick to seize upon national apprehension over climate warming to boost its failing fortunes. Trade associations have paid handsomely for media advertising portraying nuclear power as an attractive alternative to increased fossil fuel combustion with its climate warming threat. While most environmentalists argue that energy conservation and rapid development of renewable energy sources are better solutions to the Greenhouse problem, many politicians, scientists, and economists are giving nuclear power a hard second look. Eight pounds of enriched uranium can produce the energy equivalent of 6,000 tons of oil or 8,000 tons of coal. A large reactor can generate enough power for 1.5 million households. Nuclear technology can be beguiling in an era of climate warming consciousness if its technological risks can be reduced and a more congenial political climate created for the nuclear option. The Nuclear Dream is not yet dead.

Black Gold

Every American president from Richard Nixon to Ronald Reagan has tried to dam the flow of imported oil into the United States with a wall of coal. Coal is the nation's most plentiful fossil fuel. With reserves sufficient for 250 years at current consumption rates, it is inevitable that Washington energy planners should repeatedly attempt to substitute abundant domestic coal for expensive, insecure imported oil. Economic and environmental problems, however, continue to inhibit a massive national conversion to coal combustion. The Reagan administration, convinced that excessive environmental regulation impeded coal consumption, was determined to have more coal and less environmental regulation. Reagan's successor, however, could not afford tò regard coal so cordially. Most of the highly publicized environmental problems confronting the Bush administration have "coal" written all over them: acid precipitation, climate warming, and more than one hundred major American cities with severe smog problems. Nonetheless, coal will remain for many decades a major fossil fuel and a continuing environmental problem.

The Saudi Arabia of Coal

Coal represents about 90 percent of the remaining U.S. hydrocarbon reserves. The coal industry liked to remind Americans during the energy crisis of the 1970s that the nation had the equivalent of Saudi petroleum reserves in coal. This coal rests in three geologic reserves: Appalachia's wooded hills and hollows sprawling across parts of seven southeastern states, the midwestern plains, and the western plains and grasslands.

In the early 1990s, coal provided about 24 percent of U.S. energy consumption. Electric utilities, the prime coal consumers, generate more than half their power from coal-fired boilers and have been increasing their coal consumption.[38] Although U.S. coal production in 1988 reached a record 959 million tons, the industry has been afflicted since the 1950s with declining employment, chronic labor violence, and boom-or-bust economic cycles. The industry's economic fortunes are closely tied to the electric power and metallurgical industries that consume, respectively, 85 and 13 percent of annual coal production. Because more than eight of every ten tons of mined coal are transported by rail, many railroads have become heavily dependent upon coal production for revenue.

Every administration from Richard Nixon to Ronald Reagan proposed massive new coal consumption to diminish U.S. dependence on imported petroleum. The Nixon and Ford administrations' largely fanciful "Project Independence" promised that the United States could become almost independent of imported petroleum by 1980 through reliance on coal and conservation. President Carter, ignoring the chimera of "energy independence," still proposed in his 1977 energy plan to diminish U.S. dependence on petroleum through a 66-percent increase in domestic coal combustion within a decade and the creation of a massive new synthetic fuels industry based on coal feedstocks. The Reagan administration announced its intention to sell new coal mining leases in western public lands containing 5 billion tons of coal as a means of encouraging more production. The coal industry, sensing a possible reversal of its fortunes, was quick to proclaim coal the "great black hope of America" and to shift its political weight behind new White House coal initiatives.

There were several plausible reasons for coal's continuing attraction to energy planners despite related economic and environmental problems. According to some estimates, accelerated coal combustion might displace as much as 2.5 million barrels of imported petroleum consumed by the United States daily. A coal boom might bring 100,000 new workers to Appalachia, reviving its stagnant economy, and perhaps 50,000 more workers to the West; coal-related income in the West and Great Plains might rise by $850 million to $1 billion. Large "mine-mouth" electric generating plants, located adjacent to coal seams to reduce transportation costs, could provide dependable, secure electric power for the growing West and Midwest. The Carter energy plan might have increased railroad coal loadings by 350 percent between 1978 and 1985. Coal was secure energy, unmenaced by Middle Eastern politics and unpredictable world petroleum markets. Coal could glitter as gold if only the new coal boom could be made environmentally and economically tolerable.

Can Surface Mining Be Regulated?

The most significant adverse environmental impacts associated with coal utilization are created by surface mining and combustion. Many of the problems associated with coal combustion have been examined in Chapter 6 on air pollution. The regulation of surface mining has been no less contentious.

Surface Mining. Virtually all coal mined west of the Mississippi River and half produced in Appalachia is surface mined. Surface mining has rapidly replaced underground mining because it is cheaper, more efficient, more profitable, and less labor intensive. Unless rigorously regulated, however, surface mining is environmentally catastrophic. More than 1.5 million acres of American land have been disturbed by coal surface mining; more than a million of these acres remain a wrecked and ravaged waste, long abandoned by its creators. More than 1,000 additional acres are disturbed each week by surface mining, and more than thirty states have been scarred by unreclaimed surface mines.

In Appalachia surface miners roamed the hills virtually uncontrolled for decades; the evidence is written in thousands of sterile acres, acidified streams and rivers, decapitated hills, and slopes scarred by abandoned mine highwalls. In western prairies and grasslands, unregulated surface mining left thousands of barren, furrowed acres buried under spoil banks so hostile to revegetation they seemed like moonscapes to observers. After decades of resistance, the mining industry has come to recognize the necessity for the environmental regulation of surface mining, but vigorous controversy continues over the manner of this regulation and its effectiveness.

The Surface Mining Control and Reclamation Act.   President Carter, fulfilling a promise made during his election campaign, signed the Surface Mining Control and Reclamation Act of 1977 (SMCRA) and thereby created the first federal surface mining regulatory program. The act, strongly promoted by environmentalists against fierce resistance from the mining industry and two vetoes by President Gerald R. Ford, was intended to control the environmental ravages of surface mining by restoring surface-mined land to productivity whenever possible. The major features include:

1. Environmental performance standards with which all surface miners were to comply in order to operate. Standards were to be established to regulate the removal, storage, and redistribution of topsoil; siting and erosion control; drainage and protection of water quality; and many other matters affecting environmental quality.

2. Requirements that mined land be returned, insofar as possible, to its original contours and to a use equal or superior to that before mining commenced.

3. Special performance and reclamation standards for mining on alluvial valley floors in arid and semiarid areas, on prime farmland, and on steep slopes.

4. Enforcement of the act through a mining permit program administered jointly by the federal government and the states, according to federal regulations.

5. Protection of land unsuitable for mining from any mine activity.

6. Creation of a special fund, financed from a tax on existing surface mining, to reclaim "orphan" mine sites.

7. Creation of an agency, currently the Office of Surface Mining Reclamation and Enforcement within the Interior Department, to enforce the act.

The Reagan Onslaught.   Few federal regulations were more directly and consistently attacked by the Reagan administration than those arising from SMCRA. To the Reagan reformers, the act epitomized the excesses of federal authority, the red tape, confusion, and inflated costs inflicted upon industry and the states by federal environmental laws. Under Secretary of the Interior James G. Watt pervasive alterations in the name of "regulatory relief" were made in the administrative structure set up to enforce SMCRA. The attack fell squarely on the Office of Surface Mining Reclamation and Enforcement (OSMRE), and upon the regulations it wrote. OSMRE's field offices were drastically reduced, its full-time staff inspectors diminished by half. Estimates suggest that Watt's office may have rewritten more than 90 percent of the regulations originally formulated by the Department of the Interior (DOI) under President Carter.[39]

The Reagan administration charged into an already heated controversy when it promised to grant the states increased discretion in enforcing SMCRA. While conflict between Washington and the states over their respective authority is inevitable in regulatory federalism, surface mine regulation has been especially contentious. SMCRA encouraged the states to accept responsibility for its implementation—called "primacy"—and appeared to grant them discretion in applying its provisions to their mining industries. By the early 1980s, twenty-four of the twenty-seven states affected by SMCRA had accepted primacy. But many states soon complained that OSMRE's regulations were too strict and its willingness to give the states discretion in applying the regulations too limited. Congress was, in fact, responsible for much of the problem. SMCRA had been written to give the states maximum opportunity to take responsibility in procedural matters like processing permits. But Congress was also alarmed at surface mining's ecological devastation and determined to strike hard at eastern mining companies especially. It wrote SMCRA's stringent regulatory standards in great length and fine detail to ensure that the OSMRE would start with a strong program. The Carter administration assured that the OSMRE would be a tough, aggressive regulator by deliberately recruiting an environmentalist staff.

The states initially greeted the promise of more discretion with enthusiasm because it implied that they would have greater opportunity to ease the regulatory burden on local mining companies. But the Reagan administration also reduced federal financial and technical support at the same time that it increased the administrative burden for SMCRA's enforcement. Many states, suffering the fiscal effects of prolonged revenue shortfalls, lacked the money and personnel to compensate for this diminished federal assistance. Thus, "regulatory reform" for many states meant more responsibility and less enforcement for SMCRA. It appeared to many "primacy" states by the end of Reagan's first term that their ability to enforce SMCRA was becoming dangerously compromised and their enthusiasm for regulatory relief waned.

By the beginning of Reagan's second term, the OSMRE was approaching impotence, its personnel disorganized and demoralized. With six acting directors in its first eight years, its programs lacked continuity and credibility. The OSMRE had become a constant target of congressional criticism. Environmentalists increasingly resorted to litigation to compel the OSMRE to assume its statutory responsibilities for enforcing the law. Evidence of deliberate program subversion became abundant. With James Watt's abrupt departure from the DOI, the administration attempted to restore some credibility to the OSMRE. Donald Hodel, Watt's successor, responded to judicial orders and congressional criticism by eliminating some of the most blatant examples of program subversion. Personnel policies were modified to restore some continuity and confidence among program administrators. A modest increase in personnel and funding was achieved in the latter Reagan years and the OSMRE appeared less frequently in headlines and federal court dockets. The OSMRE promised more constructive assistance to the primacy states in enforcing their programs.

A Slow and Uncertain Recovery.   Despite improvements after 1985, SMCRA remains a troubled and debilitated program. A succession of directors continue through the OSMRE's revolving door. The amount of improvement in program administration remains questionable. It seems apparent, at least, that the OSMRE cannot or will not exercise dependable, vigorous administrative oversight over state enforcement programs. In 1986, for instance, the GAO concluded after studying program enforcement in four of the most important primacy states that they "generally do not accept evidence of violations observed by federal inspectors during oversight inspections which could be used to cite [violations] by [mine] operators."[40] A year later, the GAO studied three additional states and discovered that one collected fines on one-tenth of the violations it discovered and another collected on less than one-third of the violations.[41] Still, some observers believe that the controversies surrounding SMCRA have also had constructive results, including greater sensitivity in Washington to the needs of the states and greater economic efficiency through more flexibility in program regulations.

One important test of surface mine regulations is whether they result in an environmentally safer mining industry and a significant restoration of the many thousand "orphan" mine sites across the United States. An answer is elusive, partially because the restoration of surface mine sites is difficult under the best of circumstances.

The Restoration Gamble

Obscured in the controversy over SMCRA's enforcement has been an issue even more important to the future of surface mining: Is restoration of mined lands in the manner contemplated by the act achievable? Technical studies suggest that the capacity of mining companies to restore mined land to conditions equal or superior to their original condition is likely to be site specific—that is, dependent upon the particular biological and geological character of each mining site. Western mining sites are often ecologically fragile; relatively limited varieties of sustainable vegetation and scarce rainfall make ecological regeneration of the land difficult. With only limited experience in the restoration of western mine sites, most experts are reluctant to predict that mine sites can be restored to ecological vitality even with good intentions, generous funding, and high-quality technical resources.

The prospects for restoration are less forbidding in Appalachia where an abundance of precipitation, richer soil, and a greater diversity of native flora and fauna are available. Nonetheless, many experts believe that disruption of subsurface hydrology and the drainage of acids and salts from the mines' spoil heaps may not be controlled easily even when surface revegetation is achieved. Thus, restoration remains a gamble with nature. If restoration proves difficult, confronting public officials with the prospect that a major portion of all surface-mined land may remain virtually sterile for centuries, a further national controversy may erupt over the continuance of surface mining.

More than a decade's experience with SMCRA leaves only fragmentary evidence of its success. After studying SMCRA's enforcement among many primacy states, for instance, political scientist Uday Desai concluded that the consequences have been, at best, mixed. Environmentally safe conditions were apparently being maintained at active mine sites in Montana, Pennsylvania, and Wyoming. But in Kentucky, a major mining state, the law appeared to have had only a "marginal" impact and in West Virginia, another important coal state, it "had not been thoroughly and rigorously enforced in many areas."[42] The conclusion suggests how far SMCRA's enforcement has yet to go in achieving its purpose:

It is not possible to make an unqualified overall national assessment, but the evidence . . . indicates that, in most (but by no means all) cases, surface coal mining is being carried out in environmentally less destructive ways than before the Act. However, accomplishment of its ultimate objective has fallen far short of the expectations of many. In addition, there has been a serious deterioration of the situation on the ground in some states such as Kentucky.[43]

The nation's coal production was never higher, nor its future more uncertain, than in the 1990s. New amendments to the Clean Air Act are expected to require that national sulfur oxide and nitrogen oxide emissions be reduced, respectively, by about 50 percent and 20 percent—a policy likely to bring economic recession to Appalachia's troubled coal fields. Increasing emission control costs will create strong incentives for utilities to seek alternative fuel sources where possible. Policies to mitigate global climate warming all contemplate major reductions in U.S. fossil fuel combustion—another assault on Old King Coal. One tenuous hope for the coal industry lies in the commercialization of experimental "clean coal" technologies, such as fluidized bed combustion, which could reduce coal's sulfur content before combustion. The commercial prospects for these technologies remain unproven, and the industry's future precarious. Only coal mining's ecological devastation is assured. It will be the inheritance of unborn generations, a legacy written in Appalachia's scarred hills and acidified streams, in sterile mine waste plowed into moonscapes across the western plains and deserts.

Conclusion

Coal combustion and civilian nuclear power are two examples of the implicit and inevitable association between environmental quality and patterns of energy development. The United States is currently following a path of energy development that can make vast, and possibly irreversible, changes in the nation's environment. Continuing coal utilization perpetuates surface mining, along with all its environmental risks, across Appalachia and the American West. Industrial and utility coal combustion can intensify problems of air pollution, acid rain, and possible the Greenhouse Effect through the decade. Even if civilian nuclear power should fail to develop beyond facilities currently operating or under construction, the risks of accidents and the institutional difficulties in managing nuclear waste and plant decommissioning will remain significant well into the next decade at least. It should be evident that serious technical, administrative, and political difficulties exist in the enforcement of legislation intended to protect the nation from the most environmentally malignant impacts of these technologies.

Equally important are the environmental implications of current energy policy for the future. First, the United States today has no explicit, comprehensive program of energy conservation, nor does it have any governmental commitment to promoting the development and proliferation of energy-conserving technologies beyond what may be accomplished through the deregulation of energy prices. This implies that energy development throughout the remainder of the decade is likely to place growing stress upon environmental quality and nonrenewable resources such as fossil fuels. Second, the continuing U.S. dependence upon nonrenewable energy resources, along with the adverse environmental impacts often associated with these resources, is slowly but resolutely moving the United States into a position where it may have to contemplate a severe energy-environment trade-off should a new energy crisis emerge. Public opinion polls have long suggested that environmental quality is most politically vulnerable to an energy crisis. Should the public and its officials feel they must choose between more energy or continuing environmental protection, there seems to exist a strong disposition to opt for energy development. Continued reliance upon environmentally threatening energy sources leaves U.S. policy makers with few options but environmentally dangerous ones in the face of another energy crisis.

Finally, it should be apparent from discussions of coal and nuclear power development than many of the environmental risks associated with these energy sources are created or exacerbated by failure of institutional management or design. Stated somewhat differently, the problems of decommissioning reactors or finding a safe and publicly acceptable repository for nuclear waste illustrate the failure of policy makers to anticipate the institutional arrangements essential to ensuring the safety of energy technologies. An essential aspect in planning the future development of energy technologies through government, whether it be synfuels technologies, nuclear fusion, or something else, should be careful and prolonged consideration of the institutional arrangements essential to ensure the technologies' safety—a sort of institutional risk assessment that raises tough and realistic questions about the impact of technologies on governmental institutions and their capacities to manage such technologies environmentally.

Notes

1. U.S. Department of Commerce, Bureau of the Census, *Statistical Abstract of the United States, 1989* (Washington, D.C.: Government Printing Office, 1989), 563.
2. Executive Office of the President, Council on Environmental Quality, *Environmental Quality, 1980* (Washington, D.C.: Government Printing Office, 1981), chap. 6.
3. U.S. Department of Commerce, *Statistical Abstract, 1989*, 199.
4. Kennedy P. Maize, ed., *Blueprint for the Environment: Advice to the President-Elect from America's Environmental Community* (Salt Lake City, Utah: Howe Brothers, 1989).
5. *New York Times*, January 18, 1990.
6. Ibid.
7. *New York Times*, February 27, 1989. See also U.S. Department of Energy, Energy Information Administration, *Annual Energy Review, 1988* (Washington, D.C.: Government Printing Office, 1989), 119.
8. *New York Times*, May 8, 1988.
9. *New York Times*, February 27, 1989.
10. *New York Times*, August 6, 1989. On energy policy during the Reagan years generally see Franklin Tugwell, *The Energy Crisis and the American Political Economy* (Palo Alto, Calif.: Stanford University Press, 1988), chaps. 7, 8, 9; and

268   *Environmental Politics and Policy*

Richard H. K. Vietor, *Energy Policy in America Since 1945: A Study of Business-Government Relations* (New York: Cambridge University Press, 1984).
11. On the history of U.S. commercial nuclear power see Irvin C. Bupp and Jean-Claude Derian, *The Failed Promise of Nuclear Power* (New York: Basic Books, 1978); and Steven L. Del Sesto, *Science, Politics and Controversy: Civilian Nuclear Power in the United States, 1946–1974* (Boulder, Colo.: Westview Press, 1979).
12. Bupp and Derian, *The Failed Promise*, chap. 5.
13. Christopher Flavin, *Nuclear Power: The Market Test* (Washington, D.C.: Worldwatch Institute, 1983), 27.
14. *New York Times*, January 14, 1988.
15. *New York Times*, January 1, 1990.
16. *New York Times*, June 22, 1989.
17. *New York Times*, March 27, 1988.
18. *New York Times*, March 27, 1989.
19. *New York Times*, April 26, 1986. On technical problems generally see Joseph G. Morone and Edward J. Woodhouse, *The Demise of Nuclear Energy?* (New Haven, Conn.: Yale University Press, 1989), chaps. 3, 4, 5.
20. Walter A. Rosenbaum, "Nuclear Wastes and Federalism: The Institutional Impacts of Technology Development," in *Western Public Lands: The Management of Natural Resources in a Time of Declining Federalism*, ed. John G. Frances and Richard Ganzel (Totowa, N.J.: Rowman and Allanheld Publishers, 1984). See also Luther J. Carter, *Nuclear Imperatives and Public Trust* (Washington, D.C.: Resources for the Future, 1987), chaps. 4, 5, and Edward J. Woodhouse, "The Politics of Nuclear Waste Management," in *Too Hot to Handle? Social and Policy Issues in the Management of Radioactive Waste*, ed. Charles A. Walker, Leroy C. Gould, and Edward J. Woodhouse (New Haven, Conn.: Yale University Press, 1983), 151–183.
21. "Nevada to Get Nuclear Waste, Everyone Else 'Off the Hook,' " *Congressional Quarterly Weekly Report*, December 19, 1987, 3136–3137.
22. Ibid.
23. *New York Times*, November 29, 1989.
24. *New York Times*, June 13, 1989. See also U.S. General Accounting Office, "Nuclear Waste: Storage Issues at DOE's Waste Isolation Pilot Plant in New Mexico," Report no. GAO/RCED-90-1 (December 1989).
25. *New York Times*, December 15, 1989. See also U.S. General Accounting Office, "Nuclear Energy: Environmental Issues at DOE's Nuclear Defense Facilities," Report no. GAO/RCED-86-192 (September 1986), 2–4.
26. U.S. General Accounting Office, "Nuclear Regulation: NRC's Decommissioning Procedures and Criteria Need to Be Strengthened," Report no. GAO/RCED-89-119 (May 1989), 2–3. On decommissioning problems generally see Cynthia Pollock, *Decommissioning: Nuclear Power's Missing Link* (Washington, D.C.: Worldwatch Institute, 1986).
27. Pollock, *Decommissioning*, 25–33.
28. *New York Times*, October 31, 1988.
29. *New York Times*, December 12, 1981.
30. *New York Times*, January 21, 1985.
31. U.S. General Accounting Office, "Nuclear Regulation: Efforts to Ensure Nuclear Power Plant Safety Can Be Strengthened," Report no. GAO/RCED-87-141 (August 1987), 2–3.
32. U.S. General Accounting Office, "Nuclear Regulation: NRC's Decommissioning Procedures," 2–3.
33. *New York Times*, November 10, 1988.
34. Richard E. Balzhiser, "Future Consequences of Nuclear Nonpolicy," in *Energy: Production, Consumption and Consequences*, ed. John L. Helm (Washington, D.C.: National Academy Press, 1990), 184–204. See also Christopher Flavin, *Reassessing Nuclear Power: The Fallout from Chernobyl* (Washington, D.C.: Worldwatch Institute, 1987), 62–74.

35. Kirk Victor, "The Nuclear Turn-on," *National Journal,* September 9, 1989, 2196–2200.

36. *New York Times,* November 26, 1989.

37. Morone and Woodhouse, *The Demise of Nuclear Energy?* 147.

38. U.S. Department of Energy, Energy Information Administration, *Electric Power Annual, 1988* (Washington, D.C.: Government Printing Office. 1989).

39. Changes in OSMRE regulations during this period are discussed in Conservation Foundation, *State of the Environment, 1982* (Washington, D.C.: Conservation Foundation, 1984), 303–410. Estimates of the number of regulations rewritten are found in *New York Times,* November 5, 1983.

40. U.S. General Accounting Office, "Surface Mining: Interior Department and States Could Improve Inspection Programs," Report no. GAO/RCED-87-40 (December 1986), 3. See also Richard Miller, "Implementing a Program of Cooperative Federalism in Surface Mining Policy," *Policy Studies Review* 9, no. 1 (Autumn 1989): 79–87; and Richard Harris, "Federal-State Relations in the Implementation of Surface Mining Policy," *Policy Studies Review* 9, no. 1 (Autumn 1989): 69–78.

41. U.S. General Accounting Office, "Surface Mining: States Not Assessing and Collecting Monetary Penalties," Report no. GAO/RCED-87-129 (June 1987), 3.

42. Uday Desai, "Assessing the Impacts of the Surface Mining Control and Reclamation Act," *Policy Studies Review* 9, no. 1 (Autumn 1989): 104–105.

43. Ibid., 105.

Suggested Readings

Flavin, Christopher, and Alan B. Durning. *Building on Success: The Age of Energy Efficiency.* Washington, D.C.: Worldwatch Institute, 1988.

Lee, Thomas H.; Ben C. Ball, Jr.; and Richard D. Tabors. *Energy Aftermath.* Boston: Harvard Business School Press, 1990.

Morone, Joseph G., and Edward J. Woodhouse. *The Demise of Nuclear Energy? Lessons for Democratic Control of Technology.* New Haven, Conn.: Yale University Press, 1989.

Rosenbaum, Walter A. *Energy, Politics, and Public Power,* 2d ed. Washington, D.C.: Congressional Quarterly, 1987.

Tugwell, Franklin. *The Energy Crisis and the American Political Economy.* Palo Alto, Calif.: Stanford University Press, 1988.

Chapter 9

Our 700 Million Acres
The Battle for the Public Lands

> *What I want to speak for is . . . the wilderness idea. . . . Being an intangible and spiritual resource, it will seem mystical to the practical-minded—but then anything that cannot be moved by a bulldozer is likely to seem mystical to them.*
>
> —Wallace Stegner

In 1976, the bicentennial year of the Republic, the government of the United States officially ended after almost two centuries its policy of conveying the public lands to private control. During that time more than 1.1 billion acres of land, an expanse larger than western Europe, had been surrendered to the states, to farmers and trappers, railroads, veterans, loggers and miners, canal builders—to any interest with the political strength to make a persuasive claim on the public lands to Congress. American land shaped American character more decisively than any other aspect of the nation's environment. Though vastly reduced, the public domain remains an enormous physical expanse embracing within its continental sprawl, often accidentally, some of the nation's most economically and ecologically significant resources, a biological and physical reserve still largely unexploited. The struggle to determine how this last great legacy shall be used constitutes, in large part, the substance of the political struggle over the public lands.

Once most of the land was public domain. Over the last two centuries the federal government has owned almost four of every five acres on the continental United States. This land, held in trust for the people of the nation, is governed by Congress, in whom the Constitution vests the power to "dispose and make all needful Rules and Regulations respecting the Territory or other Property belonging to the United States."[1] Until the turn of this century, Congress had been concerned primarily to divest itself rapidly of the lands, turning them over to the states or to private interests in huge grants at bargain-basement prices. Only belatedly did Congress, powerfully pressured by the new American conservation movement, awaken to the necessity of preserving the remaining natural resources on the public domain before they were wholly lost. By this time most of the remaining public lands lay west of the Mississippi River; much was wilderness too remote and inaccessible to be easily exploited or grasslands and rangelands seemingly devoid of economic attraction.

The Public Domain

Today the federal government owns approximately 732 million acres of land, about a third of the total U.S. land area. Many western states are largely public domain: more than half of Alaska, Nevada, Idaho, Oregon, Utah, and Wyoming are federally owned; the public lands constitute more than a third of Arizona, California, Colorado, and New Mexico. Much of this land, originally ceded to the western states when they joined the Union, was rejected as useless for timbering, grazing, or farming; some was held in trust for Indian tribes by the federal government. Only later, well into this century, did exploration reveal that vast energy and mineral resources might reside under the tribal reservations, wilderness, timber, and grasslands remaining in the public domain. The economic value of the public lands was increased greatly by a 1953 Supreme Court ruling vesting control of 1.1 billion acres of submerged outer continental shelf (OCS) land, an area generally beginning three miles off the U.S. coast, in the federal government. Thus by accident and design that third of the nation, together with its spacious offshore lands, now controlled by Washington has become a public trust of potentially huge economic value.

An Unanticipated Bounty

The actual magnitude of mineral, timber, and energy reserves on the public domain remains uncertain, for many areas, including much of the gigantic Alaskan wilderness, have yet to be explored. Estimates of resources on more accessible lands also can be controversial. However, commonly cited figures suggest the reasons why the public lands have assumed such importance to major economic interests in the United States:

• About 30 percent of the nation's remaining oil and gas reserves, 40 percent of its coal reserves, and 80 percent of its shale oil may be on public domain.
• About 60 percent of low-sulfur U.S. coal resides on federal lands west of the Mississippi River.

• About 56 percent of undiscovered U.S. petroleum reserves and 47 percent of natural gas reserves are estimated to reside on federal OCS lands.

• About 30 percent of the nation's forests remain untimbered on federal wilderness land or national forest areas.[2]

Beyond those resources upon which a price can be placed, the public domain contains both incalculable natural treasures whose worth has become evident to generations—Yosemite, Yellowstone, Grand Canyon, and the other national parks—and nameless wild and free places, the wilderness that the naturalist Aldo Leopold has called "the raw material out of which man has hammered the artifact called civilization" and to which, he reminds us, we need often return, in fact and imagination, as to a sanctuary.[3] Indeed, much of what remains undisturbed on the American earth, still available to this generation in something like its original condition, can be found on this continent only in federal wilderness areas. Whether wilderness is or should be a thing beyond price and beyond exploitation remains among the most bitterly controversial of all environmental issues.

Diversity Within the Public Domain

The public domain has been divided by Congress into different units committed to different uses and administered by different executive agencies. The most important of these uses are the following:

U.S. National Wilderness Preservation System. Created by Congress in 1964, the National Wilderness Preservation System currently includes 79.8 million acres of land, including more than 50 million acres of Alaskan wilderness added in 1979. By legislative mandate wilderness lands are to be set aside forever as undeveloped areas.

National Park System. Begun more than a century ago with the creation of Yellowstone National Park, the system currently constitutes 37 parks and 257 national monuments, historic sites, recreational areas, near-wilderness, seashores, and lakeshores, altogether embracing more than 77 million acres. Closed to mining, timbering, grazing, and most other economic uses, the system is to be available to the public for recreational purposes.

National Wildlife Refuge System. The system currently includes almost 89 million acres, two-thirds in Alaska but distributed among all fifty states. The 413 refuges are to provide habitat to migratory waterfowl and mammals, fish and waterfowl hatcheries, research stations, and related facilities.

National Forests. Since 1897 Congress has reserved large forested areas of the public domain and has authorized the purchase of additional timberlands to create a forest reserve, to furnish continuous timber supplies for the nation, and to protect mountain watersheds. Forestlands are to be managed by a "multiple-use" formula that requires a balance of recreation, timber, grazing, and conservation activities. Currently exceeding 190 million acres, national forests are found principally in the Far West, the Southeast, and Alaska.

National Rangelands. The largest portion of the public domain, located primarily in the West and Alaska, is made up of grassland and prairieland, desert, scrub forest, and other open space collectively known as "rangelands." Although often barren, a substantial portion of the 328 million acres of rangeland is suitable for grazing; permits are issued to ranchers for this purpose by federal agencies.[4]

Such a classification implies an orderly definition of the uses for the public domain and a supporting political consensus, which do not exist. Behind the facade of congressionally assigned uses stretches a political terrain strewn with conflicts of historic proportions over which lands shall be placed in different categories, which uses shall prevail among competing demands on the land, how much economic exploitation should be permitted in the public domain, and how large the public domain should be. A major source of these conflicts is the congressionally mandated doctrine of multiple use, or balanced use, for much of the public domain. In this chapter we shall examine the ecological and political context in which multiple-use conflicts arise and the participants drawn into the struggles. These conflicts characteristically pit federal resource management agencies, state and local governments, commodity producers and users, and environmentalists against each other over issues that long predate the modern environmental era.

Multiple-Use Conflicts

Disputes over multiple use of the public domain customarily evolve in roughly similar political settings. Conflict focuses upon land administered by one of the federal resource agencies, usually the Interior Department's Bureau of Land Management (BLM) or the Agriculture Department's Forest Service, charged with the stewardship of millions of acres of the public domain under a multiple-use mandate. Struggling to interpret an ambiguous congressional mandate for land management, the agency will commonly find among the parties in conflict over its interpretation of multiple use the states within whose jurisdictions the land resides, the various private economic interests with a stake in the decision, congressional committees with jurisdiction over the agency's programs, and perhaps the White House. Especially within the last two

Table 9-1 *Public Land Owned by Federal Agencies*

Agency	Millions of acres owned	Percent of U.S. land area
Bureau of Land Management	334.0	14.7
Forest Service	192.5	8.5
Fish and Wildlife Service	89.9	4.0
National Park Service	74.9	3.3
Dept. of Defense	29.1	1.3
Dept. of Interior (other)	8.2	0.3
Dept. of Energy	2.4	0.1
Tennessee Valley Authority	1.0	0.0
Total federal	732.0	32.2
State and local	154.4	6.8
All publicly owned	886.4	39.0
Total U.S.	2,271.3	100.0

SOURCE: Council on Environmental Quality, *Environmental Quality, 1986* (Washington, D.C.: Government Printing Office, 1987), 179.

decades, environmental interests have been important and predictable participants. Sometimes the issues are resolved—that is, if they are resolved—only by congressional reformulation of land-use policy.

The Land-Use Agencies

Management of the public domain is vested principally in four federal agencies whose collective jurisdiction, more than a million square miles, exceeds the size of Mexico. As Table 9-1 indicates, the Forest Service, the National Park Service, the BLM, and the Fish and Wildlife Service control more than 690 million acres—about 90 percent of all the land currently in the public domain. The Forest Service and the BLM control by far the largest portion of this collective jurisdiction. Unlike the National Park Service and the Fish and Wildlife Service, Congress requires that the BLM and the Forest Service administer their huge public trusts under the doctrine of multiple use. The two agencies come to this task with strikingly different political histories and territorial responsibilities.

The Forest Service.   Created as part of the Agriculture Department in 1905, the service is one of the proudest and most enduring monuments to America's first great conservation movement. Founded by Gifford Pinchot, one of the nation's greatest conservationists, the service has a long and distinguished history of forest management. Widely recognized and publicly respected, the service has been adept at cultivating a favorable public image—who is not familiar with Smokey the Bear and other service symbols of forest preservation?—and vigorous congressional support. The service's jurisdiction includes most of the land, including, some grasslands, within the U.S. Forest System. With more than 39,000 employees and a budget exceeding $3.1 billion, the Forest Service historically has possessed a strong sense of mission and high professional standards. "While the Forest Service has frequently been at the center of political maelstroms," writes political scientist Paul Culhane, "it has also been regarded as one of the most professional, best managed agencies in the federal government."[5] Operating through a highly decentralized system of forest administration, local forest rangers are vested with great discretion in interpreting how multiple-use principles will apply to specific forests within their jurisdiction.

The Bureau of Land Management. The BLM manages more than 300 million acres of public domain and leases another 200 million acres in national forests and private lands but remains obscure outside the West. The bureau has struggled to establish standards of professionalism and conservation that would free it from its own long history of indifference to conservation values and from unflattering comparisons with the Forest Service.

The BLM was created in 1946 when President Harry S Truman combined Interior's old Grazing Service and General Land Office to form the new bureau with the largest land jurisdiction of any federal agency. Starting with responsibility for managing federal grasslands and grazing lands, the bureau gradually added to its jurisdiction other lands with mineral resources and, more recently, 78 million acres of Alaskan lands, including many large wilderness areas. The BLM thus has inherited a great diversity of lands with different dominant uses: the Alaskan wilderness, more than 2.5 million acres of prime Douglas timber in western Oregon, 146.9 million acres of grazing lands. BLM also is responsible for arranging the leases for mineral exploration on all public domain and the OCS.

Lacking the prestige of the Forest Service and burdened with a long history of deference to the ranching and mining interests who form a major portion of its constituency, the BLM has struggled to create greater professionalism, more sensitivity to conservation, and more aggressive enforcement of land-use regulations within its jurisdiction. Throughout its history it also has suffered chronic understaffing and underfunding— its budget and staff are less than a third of the Forest Service's despite its greater jurisdiction. And the BLM has never enjoyed the relative insulation from top departmental management that the Forest Service has experienced. This, to many environmentalists, is one of its chronic problems. According to resource expert James Baker, "The multiple-use concept suffers at the BLM because management decisions are influenced by top policy personnel appointed by the administration in power, who inherently focus on one single use, such as mining, and ignore or give short shrift to such other legitimate uses as wildlife and recreation."[6]

These agencies work in a political milieu whose character is shaped by the ambiguous, and sometimes inconsistent, requirements of multiple-use land management; by pressures from the private interests seeking access to resources on land within agency jurisdictions; by conflicts with environmentalists over the appropriate balance between environmental protection and resource use—both of which the agencies are expected to promote; by frequent conflicts between the president and Congress over their respective authority over the agencies; and by state governments, particularly in the West, determined to press upon the agencies, Congress, and the White House the states' claims for preference in policy making. All these conflicts were exacerbated in the 1980s by the White House's determination to force major changes in existing understandings about such issues.

An Ambiguous Mandate

In carrying out their assigned tasks, managers in these agencies often must walk an administrative tightrope fashioned from the inconsistencies and vagaries of their legislatively defined missions. Three different federal statutes charge the BLM and Forest Service to administer the lands in their trust by multiple-use principles. The most elaborate definition of the doctrine, ripe with the ambiguities that create so many problems in its implementation, is found in section 531 of the Multiple Use-Sustained Yield Act (1960):

"Multiple use" means: the management of all the various renewable surface resources of the national forest so that they are utilized in the combination that will best meet the needs of the American people; making the most judicious use of the land for some or all of these resources or related services over areas large enough to provide sufficient latitude for periodic adjustments in use to conform to changing needs and conditions; that some land will be used for less than all of the resources; and harmonious and coordinated management of the various resources, each with the other, without impairment of the productivity of the land, with consideration being given to the relative values of the various resources, and not necessarily the combination of uses that will give the greatest dollar return or the greatest unit output.[7]

The intent of this complicated mandate is to make sure that in land management "any use should be carried out to minimize interference with other uses of the same area and, if possible, to complement those other uses."[8] But it provides to agency managers scant information concerning how these differing values are to be defined and balanced when differing claims upon land use must be resolved. Since almost 60 percent of all public lands are held by federal agencies under some form of multiple-use law, such problems are commonplace and conflict over their resolution predictable. The BLM, for instance, has wrestled for years with managing desert areas east and north of Los Angeles to the satisfaction of both conservationists and racing enthusiasts. Each year the BLM processes more than one hundred applications for motorcycle races, some annual events with as many as 3,000 competitors. Conservationists have argued that the races permanently scar the land, alter the native ecological balances, and create noise and other disruptions for other recreationists.[9] In trying to reduce the impact of such racing, the BLM must determine the proper balance between recreation and conservation values in terms of these specific desert lands; any decision becomes controversial.

The agencies frequently discover that multiple use also leads to a conflicting mandate. The Forest Service is expected to protect the national forests from excessive timbering but at the same time to assist state and private forest owners in obtaining access to federal forests. Wildlife refuges are supposed to protect and preserve the ecologically viable habitation for endangered species but also to provide grazing, hunting, and perhaps mining opportunities to private interests.

But the multiple-use doctrine also gives both agencies, and particularly the local resource managers who must often translate the doctrine into operational terms, a means of managing the conflicting interest pressures upon the land. Multiple use requires a balancing of uses, and concern for a variety of claims upon the land, without ensuring any one dominance—a formula that leaves resource managers with the opportunity to balance and negotiate among interests claiming use of public resources. It also promises constant pressure upon the agencies to create or alter interpretations of multiple use by whatever interests feel existing interpretations discriminate against their claims upon the land.

State and Regional Interests

State governments, particularly in the West, historically have been deeply concerned with federal land-use policies and for more than a century have pressed Washington for greater control over public lands within their boundaries. Since the public domain constitutes so large a portion of many western states, decisions made in Washington affecting land use can have an enormous economic, political, and social impact upon the western governments. The states have a direct economic stake in multiple-use management. Approximately 20 percent of Forest Service receipts for timber sales are returned to local governments in lieu of property taxes on federal lands. More than a third of the BLM's annual receipts for mining royalties and other uses of its land is returned to the states. There are also large political concerns. Generally, the western states have long believed that they have been denied a properly important voice in decisions affecting their lands; they often perceive themselves to be governed by a remote and unresponsive bureaucracy insensitive to their special concerns. In particular, the western states want a larger voice in determining grazing rights, in setting conditions for mineral exploration, in establishing timbering quotas, and in deciding how revenues from resource use on the public domain will be allocated. Many states, such as Utah, have insisted that the federal government ought to divest itself of much land within the state borders, turning the land and all its resources over to the states. By the 1980s the western determination to assert greater state and regional control over federal lands had assumed a political identity as the "Sagebrush Rebellion" for which the Reagan administration, with deep western political roots, professed considerable support.

Conflict between Washington and the states over land use was exacerbated by the energy crisis of the 1970s. Even before the 1973 oil embargo, the states had fought bitterly and unsuccessfully with Washington to control the energy resources immediately off their shores in the OCS. By the late 1970s many western political leaders shared Colorado governor Richard D. Lamm's "growing feeling of regional paranoia" because they suspected the western lands might be reduced to an "energy colony" through exploitation by the more populous, politically powerful, and energy-hungry states in the Northeast and Sun Belt. Animating this fear is a realization that conditions for coal, oil, and natural gas exploration in the West are largely determined in Washington. At the same time, western states want to know that they will receive a substantial royalty for any mineral resources extracted from federal lands within their jurisdiction. In the opinion of many northeastern states, the royalties have become too substantial. These states, as major consumers of western coal, have complained of excessive severance taxes. By the late 1980s the severance taxes going to western states for coal and other energy resources will exceed $4 billion annually. One spokesman for northeastern and midwestern states feared that the western energy states were becoming "a United Arab Emirates of Western states which will have all the resources."[10] So long as the federal government continues to push aggressively for greater energy exploration and production on the public lands, the states will continue to press with equal determination for greater influence, if not control, over decisions about such activities within their own borders.

State and regional interests, in short, constitute one of the organizational givens in the policy arena where federal land-use decisions are fashioned. They represent the continual problem of reconciling national land-use needs and policies with local considerations, of balancing one set of public interests against another.

Private Resource Users

Interests using resources on the public domain, or ambitious to be among the elect, are important participants in the process of making public land-use policy. Each of the major federal land-use agencies has its "clientele," that coalition of organized groups with a major economic or ideological stake in the agency's programs. Generally, resource users want to expand their access to resources on the public domain, to use the resource as cheaply as possible, to protect the continuing availability of renewable resources, and to maintain or enhance their influence within the agencies making decisions about resources strategic to them. Thus, ranchers, sheepmen, and cattlemen customarily participate actively in the political struggles over BLM rangeland regulations; individual timber companies, such as Weyerhaeuser and Crown Zellerbach, and timber trade associations, such as the National Forest Products Association, are involved in Forest Service determinations about allowable timber harvests; Peabody Coal and Climax Coal, two of the largest coal-mining companies, will be found with the spokesmen for the National Coal Association actively attempting to influence the BLM or the Fish and Wildlife Service in writing regulations for coal leasing on land within their agency jurisdictions.

This intimate and historic involvement of clientele in land agency politics often has been criticized sharply, first by the earlier conservation movement and currently by environmentalists. Critics have asserted that agencies are easily "captured" by the clientele, who then promote resource exploitation at the sacrifice of balanced use and, particularly, with little regard for environmental values. Often environmental and conservation groups constitute practically the only politically active and effective force for balanced use within the private pressure group system. Conservationists once dismissed the BLM as the "Bureau of Livestock and Mining"; environmentalists routinely sued the BLM in the 1980s for allegedly failing to enforce surface mining regulations on coal lessees in New Mexico and Wyoming. The Forest Service's exemplary reputation has been no shield from accusations that it sanctions "clear cutting" and other timber practices abhorrent to environmentalists because the service allegedly has come to define its mission largely as timber production in response to commercial timber company demands. Agency administrators, however, often have a legislative mandate to promote resource use within their jurisdictions, and consequently some community of interest with resource users is inevitable. And, as we have often observed, the right of access by affected private groups to those administrators making decisions affecting such groups is regarded as fundamental principle in American politics. Thus, both tradition and law make the continued involvement of resource users in agency decisions inevitable and their self-interested pressures upon the agency a continual threat to the concept of balanced use.

Congress and the Public Domain

Congress ultimately decides how the public domain will be used. Although it cautiously shares some of this authority with the president, Congress traditionally has been a jealous and vigilant guardian of its prerogatives to decide finally how the states, federal land management agencies, private resource users, and others shall use the lands it holds in trust for the people of the United States. This authority flows from Article IV of the Constitution and from numerous Supreme Court decisions affirming the primacy of legislative authority in determining the character of the federal lands. Recent Supreme Court decisions have compelled Congress to share with the president the power to withdraw public lands from private use, but Congress has been quick to challenge presidents and their executive agencies when it felt they were usurping a legislative prerogative in land management.

As in other policy areas, congressional control over the public domain is exercised through the committees and subcommittees in each chamber with jurisdiction over federal land management agencies. However, while Congress vigorously defends its authority to define agency programs, it has also left the agencies with enormous discretion, as we have seen, in deciding how lands within their jurisdictions will be used; the many multiple-use laws enacted in the last several decades leave to local land managers great latitude in establishing the character of specific land uses. These agencies, as a result, operate in a politically risky milieu, where discretion is always subject to congressional challenge. When the presidency and Congress are controlled by the same party, conflicts between the two branches over agency decisions are seldom prolonged or serious. But the situation becomes ripe for conflict when differing parties control the White House and one, or both, congressional chambers. Then agency managers, exercising what they believe to be their discretionary authority on behalf of the president's program, may find themselves and their agency under congressional attack. Many of the most publicized conflicts over the Reagan administration's land-use policies erupted as battles between the secretary of the interior and Democratic-controlled House committees with jurisdiction over the department's land programs. Feeding the conflict were partisan disagreement over which programs the department should implement and traditional disputes over the limits of executive discretion.

In the last several decades Congress has demonstrated an increasing concern for environmental values by enacting legislation requiring federal land management agencies to give conservation greater importance in land-use decisions. The Wilderness Act of 1964, an early manifestation of this growing ecological sensibility, designated by statute for the first time more than 9 million acres of public lands as wilderness and provided for additional future designations. Later, the National Environmental Policy Act of 1970 (NEPA) required federal land management agencies, among many other executive agencies, to create Environmental Impact Statements (EISs) in which the environmental consequences of land-use decisions had to be identified and considered in decisions affecting the public domain. Several major multiple-use laws passed in the 1970s, to be examined later, explicitly required the relevant federal agencies to incorporate ecological protection among the uses to be protected on the affected public domain. This concern for environmental value demonstrated in good part the rising political strength of environmental groups in the legislative process. Congress, particularly the House of Representatives, came to be the principal institutional bastion within the federal government from which environmentalists mounted their attack on President Ronald Reagan's land-use policies at the Department of the Interior.

The Environmental Movement and the Public Lands

Environmentalists always have given the management of public lands a high priority. Both the National Park Service and the Forest Service were created at the turn of the century in response to vigorous promotion by the great American conservation movement, the ideological and political predecessor of the existing environmental movement. Historic legal and political battles had been waged by the Sierra Club, the Audubon Society, and other environmental groups against ecologically reckless projects promoted by federal water resource agencies long before the environmental era was named. In the 1970s environmentalists achieved a number of legislative and judicial victories that vastly expanded their influence in federal land management activities and compelled even the ecologically primitive BLM to develop, at least fitfully, an environmental conscience.

Among the most important of these achievements was passage of NEPA. As defined by the Council on Environmental Quality, which is responsible for its implementation, NEPA required that EISs be prepared by federal land management agencies for major land-use decisions affecting the environment—in effect, for most major land management planning. Draft statements had to be circulated for public review and comment prior to completion; agency officials were obligated to give the statements careful consideration in all relevant decisions.

In practical terms, the EISs became an early warning system for environmental groups, alerting them to the implications of numerous agency policies whose importance might otherwise have been ignored. Environmentalists thus had opportunity to organize a political strategy for influencing land management decisions. Further, the statements often forced agencies, such as the BLM, to give greater attention to the ecological impacts of their management practices. Not least important, the EIS was a legally enforceable procedure; environmental groups skillfully exploited many opportunities to use the federal courts to delay or frustrate agency decisions they opposed by challenging the adequacy of impact statements.

Federal courts, often with the explicit approval of Congress, greatly expanded the environmentalists' "standing to sue" federal agencies for alleged failures to give environmental values sufficient attention in land-use planning. This greatly liberalized standing often enabled environmental interests to compel federal agencies to give them a voice in agency proceedings. Critics charged, sometimes justifiably, that environmentalists were seizing upon these new strategies primarily to disrupt administrative procedures and thereby to harass their opponents even when their case lacked merit. But the environmental activities inspired by enlarged standing, as well as the impact statement procedures, quite often resulted in valuable ecological improvements in federal land management and greater federal attention to the balanced use of land, to which many agency managers had previously given little more than lip service.

Finally, congressional attempts to encourage greater public involvement in the making of land management decisions by the Forest Service, Park Service, and BLM also provided environmentalists with effective strategies for influencing federal policies, particularly at the local level where so many land-use decisions were made. Indeed, environmental groups have perceived correctly that generous provision for public involvement in federal land-use planning has been among the most effective structural means of giving them access and influence in the administrative process generally. For this reason, they have been acutely concerned about the enforcement of these participation provisions in federal land law and convinced that any attempts to narrow such opportunities, by law or administrative manipulation, were covert attacks upon their political base.

The many institutional interests, organized groups, agency programs, and conflicting philosophies of land use involved in managing the public domain mean that conflict and disagreement over policy are inevitable. The 1980s were characterized by unusually open and bitter conflict over management of the public domain triggered by the Reagan administration's vigorous attempts to change land policies in a manner that angered and alarmed conservationist and environmental groups across the nation. At issue were fiercely held and strongly felt convictions on both sides.

Energy and Public Lands

The Reagan administration began the 1980s with a determination to open the public lands to energy and mineral exploration and to transfer tracts of the public lands to state and private control on a scale unmatched by any other administration in this century. The responsibility for achieving these ambitious objectives was largely vested in Secretary of the Interior James G. Watt, whose agency controlled the largest portion of the public domain. The administration's aggressive and unapologetic determination to turn much of the public land and its resources over to private use was based on a conviction that too many resources, particularly coal, gas, and petroleum, had been locked up on the public domain. "I want to open as much land as I can," Watt remarked in explaining a philosophy that would prevail long after he left the department. "The basic difference between this Administration and liberals is that we are market-oriented, people-oriented. We are trying to bring our abundant acres into the market so that the market will decide their value."

The Reagan Land Program

What opening up the public lands meant to the Reagan administration became evident between 1981 and 1983 in a series of proposals to alter profoundly the character of vast tracts within the public domain. Among the most disturbing to environmentalists were:

The Interior Department's proposed leasing of exploration rights to more than 11 billion tons of coal on federal rangeland, timberland, and wilderness areas in New Mexico, southwest Utah, Montana, and North Dakota. This plan, opening more coal to exploration than Washington had done in the previous decade, would affect several hundred thousand acres of previously undeveloped open land.

The department's proposal to open for gas and petroleum exploration by 1987 about 1 billion acres of the OCS, virtually all the offshore lands within federal jurisdiction, including forty-one lease sales—sixteen off the Alaskan coast—that would likely result in exploration before the end of 1984.

A plan to sell to state and private bidders 35 million acres of public land, an area roughly equal in size to Iowa. This property, including abandoned military bases, urban land and parks, and a great diversity of other tracts not included within any of the major federal land-use programs, would have amounted to the largest transfer of public lands to private control in the century. The Reagan administration anticipated receiving $1.3 billion from sales the first year and then $4 billion annually for an indefinite period.

A proposal to permit the Forest Service to open wilderness areas within the national forests to mineral and energy exploration before 1984, when such lands had to be placed beyond exploration in the U.S. Wilderness System.[11]

The scale of these proposals appalled environmentalists; so did the administration's untroubled conviction that resource use, especially energy production, should have a higher priority than any other value on most federal land, including many wilderness areas.

The Department in the Middle

The Interior Department was inevitably the focus of controversy over energy exploration on the public domain. More than 200 billion tons of coal, perhaps a fourth of the nation's coal reserves, lie below western lands under the department's jurisdiction. Since passage of the Mineral Leasing Act of 1920, the interior secretary has had the discretionary authority to sell leases and to establish conditions for private mineral and energy exploration on the public lands. Such leases, to be sold at "fair market value," must be "diligently developed" into mining operations within a decade; both federal and state governments charge royalties for coal production within their boundaries. Until the 1980s, however, the department promoted coal and other resource exploration on its lands rather indifferently, and during the 1970s leasing was virtually suspended while the department, Congress, and the White House struggled to fashion a comprehensive leasing program. One finally emerged in the late 1970s but soon was challenged by the Reagan administration's new coal programs.

The change in coal leasing philosophy under the Reagan administration was immediate and dramatic. In 1981 alone, Interior leased more than 400 times the acreage for coal exploration than it had the previous year. Proponents of a greatly accelerated leasing program asserted that the nation needed the energy resources lying unused on the public domain, that federal regulations could protect the lands from the ravages of surface mining, and that the economic productivity created by private use of the energy resources would generate more jobs and greater prosperity. Many of the department's political leadership would have said a hearty, if perhaps private, "amen" to the summary conclusion on the subject by the president of the American Mining Congress: "Our society is built on the stuff that comes out of the hole in the ground and if we don't unplug the red tape stuffing the hole, this country is going to be in one hell of a mess."[12]

The department's announced intentions to accelerate the sale of leases for oil and gas exploration on the OCS and its interest in leasing when legally possible even wilderness areas for exploration convinced environmental groups and congressional opponents of the Reagan programs that a massive public campaign to counteract the new policies was imperative. Congress became the institutional weapon.

The Congressional-Environmental Connection

"The probability of our developing any meaningful dialogue with this Administration is low indeed," lamented Russell Peterson, the politically seasoned president of the National Audubon Society, after talking with White House officials less than a year after President Reagan's inauguration.[13] Most environmentalists agreed and turned instead to Congress where they were able to exploit constitutional and partisan rivalries to their advantage in seeking an institutional restraint on the president's land policies. Constitutional checks and balances became one lever with which to move the executive branch, for the issue aroused the institutional rivalries at the heart of the constitutional order. The White House programs awakened among many legislators, particularly those House and Senate committees with oversight of Interior's programs, a conviction that the department, with White House blessing, was abusing its delegated authority and subverting congressional intent in handling the new energy programs. Democrats on the oversight committees, especially in the House, sought opportunities to challenge and embarrass the White House by attacking its land programs. In the battle over land policy, the House Interior Committee became the most aggressive congressional antagonist to the White House.

Congressional opposition to Reagan's land programs was most effective when the administration had to draw upon discretionary authority clouded by ambiguity and unbuttressed by tradition. Effective opposition also required that environmentalists be able to discover when administrative actions by the department or the White House amounted to major land-use decisions—administrative language manipulated by skilled practitioners can shroud the intention of an act in a fog of obscurity. Such circumstances did not always prevail. Many land-use policies were implemented in spite of the congressional-environmental coalition.

State and Regional Opposition

Despite Sagebrush Rebellion rhetoric, the states are often guilty of doublethink about resources on the public domain, as the controversy over land policy in the 1980s illustrates. Anxious to reap the economic advantages of greater resource use on lands within their domain—more royalties, more severance taxes, greater industrial development, and the like—the states were equally determined not to pay calamitous ecological and economic costs for rapid resource exploitation. Washington's new public land policies often aroused not enthusiasm but hostility among the western states. They wanted resource development *and* environmental protection.

Conflict between the federal government and the states was focused most sharply on Washington's proposal for accelerated leasing of exploration rights to oil and gas on the OCS. In 1978 Congress had passed the Outer Continental Shelf Amendments to increase greatly the environmental safeguards required for OCS exploration; to this end, extensive federal consultation with the states was required prior to any lease sales off their shores. Washington's announced intention to sell thirty-two oil lease tracts off the central California coast sent California to the federal courts seeking an injunction to prevent the leasing; citing federal failure to consult with the state under terms of the 1978 legislation, the court issued the injunction and the Interior Department subsequently withdrew most of the disputed tracts from auction.

Responding to pressure from California state officials, including the new Republican governor, most environmental groups, and most of the state's congressional delegation, Congress in 1982 and 1983 further restricted lease sales off the northern and central California coast by denying appropriations to implement the leasing. In 1984 Congress further banned leasing in several OCS basins off Florida and Massachusetts. Thus, the OCS states had succeeded in substantially reducing, at least temporarily, the scope of offshore energy exploration through a combination of legal and political strategies. Environmentalists, however, were uneasy about the future, for substantial OCS leasing was still permitted, and the administration seemed determined to press ahead on its OCS development plans whenever it was not massively challenged.

The Continuing Conflict

Watt's resignation as interior secretary in October 1983 did not end the conflict over land policies initiated by the Reagan administration, nor did it diminish the administration's determination to open up the public domain to further energy exploration.

Through the use of existing budgetary authority, established discretionary freedom, and "a thousand small changes," the secretary had managed in the face of formidable opposition to move federal policy strongly toward more resource development on public lands. Interior had accelerated the sale of leasing rights on OCS lands, including the largest leasing sale in history: seventy-eight energy companies had bid $3.5 billion to explore about 3.2 million acres of OCS territory off the Louisiana and Alabama coasts. The BLM had issued more than 38,000 leases, covering about 95 million acres, for energy exploration on its territory—about twice the total of the Carter administration. Interior's Office of Surface Mining Reclamation and Enforcement had been severely depleted of personnel and much of its regulatory responsibility entrusted to the uncertain will and capacity of the states to implement. The BLM had succeeded in opening more than 400,000 acres of recreational areas for mineral exploration, mining, and drilling, including Glen Canyon (Utah) and Lake Meade (Nevada and Arizona).

While Watt's successors, William P. Clark and then Donald P. Hodel, created less public stir than their predecessor, the department's new leadership pursued the same land policies and objectives throughout the tenure of the Reagan administration. Pressure to develop energy resources persisted. By the beginning of Reagan's second term, more than 1,000 applications for oil and gas exploration rights in wilderness areas and perhaps 50,000 other kinds of mineral claims were pending. During Reagan's second term, Secretary Hodel was especially diligent in seeking quietly to remove restrictions on oil and gas exploration on the outer continental shelf. Environmental groups were particularly critical of his proposal that Congress remove restrictions against oil exploration along 125 miles of OCS land within the Arctic Wildlife Refuge.

In the administration's waning days, the department attempted a number of actions that convinced environmentalists that the spirit of James Watt still roamed departmental corridors. In the last week of the administration's tenure, for instance, the department attempted to transfer title to an additional 24,000 acres of western shale oil lands to private owners for $2.50 an acre—228,000 acres had already been sold. This was a "fire sale" price in the opinion of environmental and congressional critics. At the same time, the department was preparing rules that would lower the royalties paid to the government for coal mined on public land.[14] Congressional opposition and a court injunction obtained by environmentalists thwarted these eleventh-hour initiatives. And so the Reagan administration's Department of the Interior left as it had entered, embattled with environmentalists.

The Bush administration began on a more conciliatory note, with the president committing himself to an active environmental agenda and implicitly distancing himself from the Reagan public land policies. But the environmental community was not pleased with the administration's new secretary of the interior. The president's choice, Manuel Lujan, a former New Mexico congressman, had been closely identified with mining, timber, and other corporate resource users during his legislative tenure. He was widely perceived within the environmental community as more antagonist than ally. Lujan's early pronouncements, including advocacy of greater energy exploration on OCS lands, did little to dissipate this image. At the same time, the department seemed curiously ambivalent and indecisive in its policy agenda, leaving environmentalists unsure about its future course or priorities.

The Fate of the Forests

More than one in every ten acres on the public domain could be used for commercial timber production. This land, about 89 million acres, lies mostly within the jurisdiction of the Agriculture Department's Forest Service. Since the end of World War II, pressure has been unremitting on the Forest Service to increase the size of the annual timber harvest from national forests to satisfy the nation's growing demand for wood products. Recently, there has been increased pressure to open many undisturbed "old-growth" timber stands and wilderness areas to commercial logging. Against this economic pressure, the Forest Service is required not only to enforce the doctrine of multiple use, which forbids the service from allowing timber cutting to preclude other forest uses, but it also must manage timber cutting to ensure a "sustained yield" from any forest reserve used for commercial timbering. Congress has left to the service the difficult and politically contentious responsibility for defining how much timber cutting is compatible with multiple use and sustained yield.

The struggle over competing timber uses is fought in the arcane language of forest economics—"nondeclining, even-flow" formulas, "allowable cuts," and "allowable-cut effects"—but the larger interests and issues at stake are apparent. The struggle represents a collision between preservationist and developmental priorities for timber, between competing definitions of the nation's economic needs, and between differing definitions of the Forest Service's mission. It is a struggle likely to intensify throughout the 1990s.

A Disputed Treasure in Timber

About half of the nation's softwood sawtimber reserves and a very substantial portion of its remaining hardwoods grow today in the national forests. The Pacific Coast region, particularly the timbered hills and lowlands of the Pacific Northwest, contains the largest of these timber stands within the public domain; the Pacific Coast area contains almost half the pine, spruce, fir, and other softwoods in the national forests. These timber reserves, more than three times the size of all the private commercial forests in the United States and currently worth more than $20 billion, will increase in value.

Although timber cutting was permitted in the national forests from their inception, the demand for commercial timber in the forests assumed major proportions only after World War II. In the early 1940s the service sold about 1.5 billion board feet of timber a year; by 1973 the cut exceeded 12.3 billion board feet. Driven by the nation's ravenous postwar desire for new housing, the demand for wood products rose steadily in the three decades following 1945. Private timber companies, approaching the limits of their own production, began to look increasingly to the national forests as an untapped timber reserve. This demand, if wholly satisfied, would likely result in a doubling of the annual timber harvest from the national forests in keeping with the industry's estimates that the U.S. demand for wood products would double before the turn of the century.

Pressure to expand the allowable timber cut has been particularly intense in the Pacific Northwest. Many of the Douglas fir forests in Oregon and Washington are old-growth stands, virgin forests never touched by a logger's saw, growing in a continuity of development many centuries old. These forests are among the most ecologically diverse and historically unique of all timber stands in North America, reminders of a continent once largely timbered with a profusion of species greater than all of Europe's. Many virgin forests, together with other less spectacular timberlands, are on Forest Service lands still classified, or eligible for classification, as "wilderness." To many environmentalists and to organized preservation groups such as the Sierra Club and the Wilderness Society, these lands are the living expression of the preservationist ethic, the values of the movement made visible. They are, in political terms, "gut issues."

Multiple Use and Sustained Yield

Since Congress has chosen not to specify how it expects the foresters to define multiple use or sustained yield in specific jurisdictions, the Forest Service has been left with enormous discretion in translating these formulas into practice. Like the multiple-use doctrine, the congressional definition of sustained yield is open to diverse interpretations, as section 531 of the Multiple Use–Sustained Yield Act suggests:

Sustained yield . . . means the achievement and maintenance in perpetuity of a high-level annual or regular periodic output of the various renewable resources of the national forests without impairment of the productivity of the land.

Conflict over interpretation of multiple-use mandates has been intensified by requirements in the Resource Planning Act of 1974, as amended by the National Forest Management Act of 1976, that the Forest Service prepare comprehensive development and management plans for each of the more than 120 management units it operates. The service began this process in the latter 1970s and still has not adopted final plans for all its management units. These management plans often become a catalyst for controversy among interests with competitive demands upon particular planning units. Final adoption of a management plan does not necessarily end the controversy, however, for arguments often continue over whether the plan is being properly implemented. Thus, the Forest Service often finds itself in the middle of a continuing, and often unresolvable, conflict over what pattern of multiple use is, or should be, implemented in a given forest tract.

Both sustained-yield and multiple-use doctrines become important to the commercial timber industry because they provide the basis for the service's determination of the allowable cut in a given timber reserve—the amount of timber that can be removed from a particular resource area in a given chronological period. The service has interpreted sustained yield to require a nondeclining, even-flow policy, which limits the timber cut in a given area to a constant, or increasing rate—but never a declining one. In effect, this has severely limited the cutting of old-growth forests, particularly in the Pacific Northwest, to the ire of the timber industry, local communities, and some forest economists who believe a larger cut of old-growth timber is more economically efficient and compatible with the multiple-use doctrine. Environmentalists, however, generally support protection of old-growth forests and advocate further reductions on the allowable cut elsewhere.[15]

In response to pressure from the timber industry and the Reagan administration's own preferences, the Forest Service began to increase the timber harvest substantially in the middle 1980s and to plan for increasing harvests through the 1990s. Between 1982 and 1989 the total timber cut in the national forests grew from 6.7 to 12.7 million board feet.[16] Forest Service professionals contend that this expansion is consistent with the statutory mandate to maintain a sustained yield. But the timber industry wants more production. With its own reserves rapidly depleting, the industry contends that only a timber harvest from the national forests significantly above the currently projected levels will provide enough wood for the U.S. economy in the next several decades. The Carter administration, responding to the rising cost of new housing, had ordered the Forest Service to depart "in a limited and temporary way" from its general sustained-yield principles and to open up some wilderness areas not specifically included in the Wilderness System for timber harvesting. The Reagan administration, more sympathetic to the viewpoint of the National Forest Products Association, advocated that the service permanently modify its sustained-yield practices to permit greater timber cuts without violating the balanced-use principle. In keeping with this production bias, the Reagan administration's budgets substantially increased spending for Forest Service activities closely associated with timber production, such as new forest road construction.

The Forest Service asserted that it could meet the higher timber production levels demanded by the Reagan administration only by cutting deeply into the Pacific Northwest old-growth timber, including many of the nation's remaining virgin forests. While towering stands of old Douglas fir and associated species within these forests provide incomparable vistas and sustain a great variety of plant and animal life, they are not particularly productive from an economic viewpoint. About a quarter of the trees will rot once they mature. Most of these forests have already matured and most timber has ceased to grow: they cover highly productive land upon which second- and third-growth timber would flourish, producing much greater income over the next century than could be realized from current use. Professional foresters associated with the commercial timber industry have asserted that protecting most of the old-growth forests from commercial cutting largely prevents decaying old forests from being converted to more productive young stands. Moreover, note the service's critics, higher timber cuts do not mean an end to all, or even most, of the old-growth stands but a selective cutting of some and the conversion of others to second-growth production.

Environmentalists have long opposed the logging of old-growth forests, citing the soil destabilization and ecosystem disruption they assert is almost inevitable. Nor do they find the economic arguments persuasive. The battles tend to be fought on a forest-by-forest basis, as the service proposes the required long-range plans for each forest and then files the necessary EISs. Environmentalists often challenge the overall adequacy of the impact statements and the specific timber production goals. The struggle over timber use spills into the related issue of wilderness designation, where the Forest Service also exercises discretionary authority. The Bush administration inherited one of these struggles, an especially emotional and public dispute provoked by Forest Service plans to permit greatly expanded timber cutting in old-growth northwestern forests. The plan might have succeeded, save for ecological serendipity in the form of the Northern Spotted Owl.

The Northern Spotted Owl versus the Timber Industry

In the mid-1980s, the Forest Service had planned to permit commercial timber companies to make substantial cuts in old-growth Oregon forests, whose 2.3 million acres represent the last 1 percent of the nation's original forest cover. In 1985, biologists in the Department of Interior's Fish and Wildlife Service reported to the departmental leadership that the Northern Spotted Owl, whose habitat was almost exclusively northwestern old-growth forests, was fast disappearing and should be designated an "endangered species." Estimates indicated that about 1,500 nesting pairs of owls remained, all in the first-growth stands. One consequence of this designation would be to protect this habitat, if geographically unique, from almost all forms of development. This recommendation was initially overruled by the department's leadership under considerable pressure from the timber industry and a variety of local Oregon and Washington interests, including timber mills, community leaders, unions, local congressmen, and timber industry workers.

Spokespersons for these interests argued that designating the Northern Spotted Owl an endangered species would virtually end logging on 1.5 million acres of old-growth timber in Oregon and Washington. The federal government estimated that between 4,500 and 9,500 jobs would be lost, but the timber industry asserted that the actual figure was ten times that amount. "You're talking about complete devastation of communities," protested Sen. Slade Gorton (R. Wash.)[17] The president of the Northwest Forestry Association, a trade group, repeated a familiar refrain among local economic interests in Washington and Oregon: "To devastate a regional economy over the spotted owl seems absurd. You're talking about affecting half our industry. . . ."[18] The timber industry's outrage was further exacerbated because much of the old-growth, softwood timber was exported, primarily to Japan, where it could command several times the domestic price.

Environmentalists had opposed commercial logging in old-growth forests long before the specific tracts in Oregon and Washington entered the dispute. Environmentalists have argued that intensive logging in old-growth forests, with the building of logging roads and disruptive soil practices sure to attend it, greatly reduce the forest's ability to conserve water and to prevent soil erosion, thus violating the principle of balanced use. Spokespersons for environmental organizations have also contended that much of the old-growth timber is found in poor soil—at high elevations and on steep slopes—and exposure to weathering will cause rapid erosion after logging begins. Moreover, they assert, these forests support a unique ecosystem with a great variety of important and irreplaceable flora and fauna. Finally, environmentalists generally challenge the presumption that a major increase in the timber harvest would significantly decrease housing costs. In any case, there are many acceptable substitutes for wood in the U.S. economy that can be had without sacrificing virgin forests, they note.

But for the Northern Spotted Owl, these arguments might have suc-
cumbed to the political weight of local, regional, and national interests
defending commercial access to first-growth timber. In the fall of 1988,
environmental organizations obtained a federal court order that instructed the secretary of the interior to list the Northern Spotted Owl
as endangered and in mid-1989 that decision was made. The designation
appeared almost to end commercial logging in northwestern first-growth
forests, but it did nothing to diminish the rancor, or the economic stakes,
involved in the continuing controversy over the appropriate use of the
national forests.

The Bush Administration and Timber Sales Reform

The Bush administration came into office committed to an active
environmental agenda, implicitly distancing itself from the Reagan-Watt
era in its goals for the public lands. While the environmental community
had been displeased with the administration's new secretary of the interior, it was considerably more receptive to the administration's proposal
in early 1990 to reduce substantially timber sales in twelve national
forests. The new proposal seemed to repudiate the previous administration's resource policies and to signal a major effort to reform traditional
Forest Service sales practices, which had long been criticized by environmentalists. The sales-below-cost controversy—"political dynamite" in
the western states—seemed to set the new administration's public lands
policy on a collision course with vast segments of the Forest Service's
constituency.

The controversy had been simmering for decades. "The Forest Service
typically constructs the roads and assumes other management and administrative responsibilities that allow private companies to harvest
[public forest timber] economically," notes the Conservation Foundation. "However, several studies have alleged that the nation actually
loses money (as well as valuable wilderness and wildlife habitat) in many
cases, particularly in the Rocky Mountain region, because the Forest
Service must spend more to allow the harvesting to occur than it receives
from the harvests. The Forest Service denies that the economics of
sales such as those in the Rocky Mountains and the Northwest are as
unfavorable as many critics claim. . . ."[19] Environmentalists, as well as
critics within the service, had long asserted that this practice amounted
to public subsidies for the commercial timber industry and a sacrifice of
all other multiple-use values, such as recreation or wildlife habitat,
to timber sales. "We think the Forest Service overestimates what is
sustainable," argued a spokesperson for the National Wildlife Federation. "They overestimate how much timber a given area can produce,
they overestimate the potential for the lands to be reforested and they

underestimate the impacts on fish and wildlife. The bottom line is they are timber-dominated."[20]

When the Forest Service initiated a new bookkeeping system in 1987, it appeared to demonstrate that the agency was losing money on about two-thirds of its timber sales. Critics cited Alaska's Tongass National Forest as an example of the losses disclosed by the new bookkeeping: the agency had spent about $50 million annually to finance the cutting of 450 million board feet of timber that brought less than $1 million to the government in revenue.[21] Nonetheless, there were many formidable opponents to the new proposal, including loggers, timber companies, state and congressional political spokespersons for the affected areas, and the Forest Service itself. Since much of the Forest Service budget was spent on preparing and auctioning acreage for commercial logging, a reduction in these sales would mean a substantial budget reduction for the service. In effect, the administration's plan represented the first major assault on a forest management practice that had endured for more than a half century, fortified by a powerful coalition of political and economic interests and defended by one of Washington's most successful and respected public agencies. The proposal's fate was uncertain at best. In broader perspective, the controversy was evidence that environmentalism had achieved enough political weight to compel a fundamental rethinking of the Forest Service's professional and institutional values.

How Much Wilderness Is Enough?

A substantial portion of the 62 million undeveloped acres under the jurisdiction of the Forest Service—the "roadless regions"—could become part of the National Wilderness System and thereby be forever excluded from timbering. A large portion of this roadless area is eligible for assignment to timber production. Timber producers, environmentalists, the Forest Service, and Congress have disagreed for more than two decades over how much of this roadless area should be designated for multiple use—in effect, opened to timbering, mineral exploring, and other nonrecreational and nonconservation uses. Perhaps as much as a third of the whole national forest system, including many old-growth stands, are in these roadless areas.

Environmentalists have been apprehensive that any multiple-use designation for large undeveloped tracts will be an invitation not only to aggressive timbering but to oil, natural gas, and coal exploring. They predict that energy industries, upon locating energy reserves, will seek exceptions to environmental regulations. Air pollution from electric power plants and energy refining operations adjacent to public lands with energy reserves will result, predict environmentalists, and the quality of the lands will be irreversibly degraded. They would prefer that most of the roadless areas under the Forest Service's jurisdiction be included in the National Wilderness System.

With some justification, environmentalists also allege that the service's strong commitment to its traditional multiple-use doctrine makes it reluctant to turn large tracts of roadless areas over to a single dominant use, such as wilderness preservation. It is this conviction that led environmentalists to criticize the manner in which the service conducted its first major inventory of roadless areas within its jurisdiction in the early 1970s.

Nonetheless, the Multiple Use-Sustained Yield Act requires the Forest Service to include wilderness protection among other multiple uses of land within its jurisdiction; the National Forest Management Act also requires it to draw up a master plan for the use of land under its jurisdiction that includes consideration of wilderness designation. Thus, the service was given both ample authority and explicit responsibility to recommend to Congress additional roadless areas for inclusion in the Wilderness System; while Congress alone possesses the authority to assign land to the system formally, the service's recommendations often influence the decisions. The White House, however, has often proposed its own plans for the roadless areas, sometimes at variance with Forest Service initiatives.

Both the Carter and Reagan administrations offered proposals to Congress for allocating the roadless areas between wilderness and multiple-use categories; both proposals departed in significant ways from the Forest Service's own proposals. The Carter administration's plan, the more conservative, would have allocated about 10 million acres to wilderness and reserved another 10 million for further study. The Reagan administration, committed to increasing the size of territory open to timbering and energy exploring, rejected the Carter proposal. Congress, as it has often done, chose to follow its own agenda for wilderness preservation. During the remainder of the Reagan administration, few new areas were designated for wilderness because Congress and the White House could reach no agreement on priorities.

RARE I and RARE II

The three-sided debate within the federal government over the use of roadless areas—dividing Congress, the Forest Service, and the White House, together with their allied interest groups, into competing coalitions—is a reminder of how pervasively the constitutional dispersion of authority affects resource planning in Washington. It also illustrates how administrative discretion can be challenged and thwarted by skilled interest groups using the Congress, and even the chief executive, against the professional administrators of an agency.

Twice in the 1970s the Forest Service invested enormous time and money in comprehensive surveys of its roadless areas in an effort to provide Congress with a plan for their future development. The first Roadless Area Review and Evaluation (RARE I) recommended in 1976 about 12 million acres from a total of 56 million for wilderness classification. This study was shelved after environmentalists challenged the plan in the federal courts on grounds that the service had not prepared adequate impact statements and had failed to include sufficient public involvement in the plan's preparation.

The Carter administration, attempting to open more public domain to timbering in response to pleas from the commercial timber industry, ordered a second study. RARE II, completed in 1978, recommended more area for wilderness designation (about 16 million acres) but also left more area open to multiple use than had RARE I. RARE II provoked opposition from environmentalists, who still believed too many multiple-use tracts had been proposed, and from the states of California, Oregon, and Washington, which opposed the exclusion of various roadless areas within their boundaries from wilderness designation. Litigation initiated by environmentalists and the state of California kept RARE II in limbo until the end of the Carter administration. President Reagan subsequently ordered the service to begin yet another study, this time under guidelines intended to maximize opportunities to designate forest areas for multiple use. Further litigation initiated by environmentalists and disagreement between the many congressional committees involved in wilderness designation largely prevented significant growth of the federal wilderness system during the Reagan administration. The Bush administration, preoccupied with other environmental issues, has given wilderness designation a low priority.

During this whole period Congress continued to designate portions of roadless areas for inclusion in the Wilderness System and to order other areas to be reserved for further study, while leaving still other tracts open to multiple use. Congress was planning roadless area development on an ad hoc basis, allocating tracts in response to changing political pressures and circumstances in the context of RARE I and RARE II. As often happens in environmental affairs, Congress had become the final arbiter among the contentious White House, environmental, administrative, and private interest factions with a stake in RARE I and RARE II and a determination to change some recommendations to their own advantage.

Areas in Oregon and California not proposed for wilderness designation under RARE II were so designated by congressional committees. Some tracts originally proposed for wilderness were opened to multiple use. Generally, environmentalists felt that Congress was a more hospitable arena in which to fight for their vision of roadless area development than either the Reagan White House or the Forest Service operating under White House directives.

The Uncertain Future

Conflict over roadless area management continues, leaving perhaps half the undeveloped areas under Forest Service jurisdiction in limbo, awaiting final assignment to either the wilderness or multiple-use category. The Reagan administration was committed to expanding the multiple-use areas managed by the Forest Service for timbering and for energy exploration but failed in the face of massive congressional and environmentalist opposition. Although studies by the U.S. Geological Survey suggest roadless areas in the eleven western states, excluding Texas and Oklahoma, are likely to contain relatively small amounts of undiscovered petroleum and natural gas, some tracts may be sufficiently rich in energy reserves to attract massive development should they be opened to multiple use. Others, not only old-growth timber, could be heavily cut for commercial wood products. The wilderness struggle, therefore, is likely to persist well into the 1990s and remain intense so long as the need for new energy resources and increased timber harvests are considered credible claims upon the public domain.

Conclusion

The struggles over energy exploration, mining, and timbering on the public lands reveal a durable structure to the political conflicts over the use of public resources in the United States. The pattern tends to be repeated because it grows from political realities inherent in the U.S. governmental system.

First, at the center of the conflict, is a federal executive agency guarding the resource as a public trust and wrestling with an ambiguous mandate for its management. Most often this agency will be part of the Interior Department, or the Forest Service. The mandates will be vague because Congress must rely upon the professional administrator to make expert resource decisions—hence the generality of the mandates—and ambiguous because Congress often shrinks from choosing between conflicting claims on resources. Thus, multiple-use prescriptions for forest or range management appear to offer something to recreationists, conservationists, and resource developers without really settling competing claims. The administrative managers for the public resource inevitably will find their professional decisions politicized as conflicting interests seek to influence technical decisions to their advantage. And technical decisions themselves can often be made and justified in different scientifically defensible ways. All this means that resource administrators sometimes can exercise their professional judgment in the service of their own group and political loyalties. In all these ways, the resource management agency finds itself at the center of political conflicts over the public domain.

Second, both the White House and Congress will become partisan advocates of resource management policy, attempting to influence administrative decisions relevant to resource management and responding to pressure from organized interests with a stake in resource management. We have observed in timber, wilderness, and energy development policies the predictable tendency of Congress to intervene in administrative management planning in order to protect interests particularly important to legislators. So, too, presidents Carter, Reagan, and Bush, as indeed every president before them for a half century, have directed the Interior Department and the Forest Service to pursue specific objectives in resource management compatible with their ideological biases and political commitments. Indeed, Congress and the White House often compete in attempting to influence administrative determinations affecting the public domain. And the president, despite the illusory title of chief executive, has no guarantee of success in the struggle.

Third, the plurality of organized interests involved in resource decisions means that Congress, the White House, and the administrative agencies all are enmeshed in a process of coalition building with organized groups during resource policy making. These organized interests, moreover, involve not only private interests but also the states within which the public domain resides and for whom the use of the resources on the domain has significant economic and political consequences.

Finally, policy struggles quite often are waged in the technical language of resource economics and scientific management. Perhaps more than most environmental issues, public resource management is an arcane business to most Americans, particularly those living where few public lands exist. In such circumstances specialized private groups, such as environmentalists and resource users, tend to operate almost invisibly to the public; the outcome of policy struggles depends particularly upon their own organizational resources, technical expertise, and political adeptness in the administrative infighting and legal wrangling that often characterize resource policy making. It is a political arena, more particularly, where organized environmental groups often constitute practically the only expression of viewpoints not associated with resource users or administrators.

Notes

1. Article IV, Section 3, Clause 2, of the U.S. Constitution.
2. Congressional Quarterly, *The Battle for Natural Resources* (Washington, D.C.: Congressional Quarterly, 1983), chap. 1.
3. Aldo Leopold, *A Sand County Almanac* (New York: Oxford University Press, 1949), 222.
4. A useful survey of the public lands may be found in U.S. Department of the Interior, Bureau of Land Management, *Managing the Nation's Public Lands* (Washington, D.C.: Government Printing Office, 1983).
5. Paul J. Culhane, *Public Lands Politics* (Baltimore: Johns Hopkins University Press, 1981), 60.
6. James Baker, "The Frustrations of FLPMA," *Wilderness* 47, no. 163 (Winter 1983): 13. See also Jeanne N. Clarke and Daniel McCool, *Staking out the Terrain: Power Differentials Among Natural Resource Management Agencies* (Albany: State University of New York Press, 1985), chaps. 4, 5.
7. On the impact of sustained use upon the Forest Service see Culhane, *Public Lands Politics*, chap. 2.
8. Ibid.
9. Council on Environmental Quality, *Environmental Quality, 1979* (Washington, D.C.: Government Printing Office, 1980), 309.
10. Quoted in *New York Times*, June 27, 1981.
11. Congressional Quarterly, *The Battle for Natural Resources*, chaps. 4, 5.
12. *New York Times*, July 2, 1982.
13. Ibid.
14. *New York Times*, January 7, 1989.
15. Culhane, *Public Lands Politics*, chap. 2.
16. U.S. Department of Commerce, Bureau of the Census, *Statistical Abstract of the United States, 1989* (Washington, D.C.: Government Printing Office, 1989), 656.
17. *New York Times*, April 27, 1989.
18. Ibid.
19. Conservation Foundation, *State of the Environment: A View Toward the Nineties* (Washington, D.C.: Conservation Foundation, 1987). 220.
20. Margaret E. Kriz, "Last Stand on Timber," *National Journal*, March 3, 1990, 509.
21. *New York Times*, February 22, 1988.

Suggested Readings

Clarke, Jeanne N., and Daniel McCool. *Staking out the Terrain: Power Differentials Among Natural Resource Management Agencies.* Albany: State University of New York Press, 1985.

Culhane, Paul J. *Public Land Politics.* Baltimore: Johns Hopkins University Press, 1981.

Hays, Samuel. *Conservation and the Gospel of Efficiency.* Cambridge, Mass.: Harvard University Press, 1959.

Nash, Roderick. *The Rights of Nature.* Madison: University of Wisconsin Press, 1989.

Stroup, Richard L., and John A. Baden. *Natural Resources: Bureaucratic Myths and Environmental Management.* San Francisco: Pacific Institute for Public Policy Research, 1983.

Wilkinson, Charles F., and H. Michael Anderson. *Land and Resource Planning in the National Forests.* Washington, D.C.: Island Press, 1987.

Chapter 10

A New Politics for a New Era
A Political Agenda for the 1990s

> *[E]fforts to patch up the current paradigm of politics with new modes of decision making and planning or even with new policies will not succeed; these can only delay, and perhaps intensify, the inevitable ultimate breakdown. . . . Only a new politics based on a set of values that are morally and practically appropriate to an age of scarcity will do.*
>
> —William Ophuls[1]

In 1990 the United States observed the nation's second Earth Day. It was twenty years since the first Earth Day in 1970—that historic moment the environmental movement regards as the ecological epiphany for the country's political leadership. "So many politicians were on the stump on Earth Day," recalls an aide to Richard Nixon, "that Congress was forced to shut down. The oratory was thick as smog at rush hour."[2] The first Earth Day was rich in the rhetoric of political protest, animated by a missionary impulse to educate Americans and to mobilize them against a gathering ecological apocalypse. The second Earth Day was very different. It seemed to cleave political time, to pronounce an end to the Reagan administration's long, bitter, barren environmental stewardship and to celebrate a resurgent environmental movement, a new environmental era. It was a time for reflection and appraisal, a moment poised at an historic juncture in American environmentalism to ponder what had been achieved and what lay ahead.

In many ways, the first decade of the new environmental era looked promising. The Environmental Protection Agency (EPA) would soon be elevated to Cabinet rank. The EPA's budget would be significantly increased, for the first time in almost a decade. The urgently needed amendments to the Clean Air Act would soon become law. These events were all testimony that an environmental sensibility had returned to the White House. Congress, respectful of environmentalism's political appeal, was again hyperactive about environmental affairs. The Montreal Protocol had been signed a few years earlier, an indication that the United States was apparently committed to global cooperation in combating man-made climate modification. The second Earth Day seemed to testify that the movement had not only survived but prevailed after its season of troubles under Ronald Reagan. Certainly, the movement had never been better organized, better funded, or bigger. The public's support for environmentalism and its regulatory regime seemed to continue broad and firm.

Yet the promise of the early 1990s may prove counterfeit unless the environmental movement is prepared to confront profound problems, deeply grounded in the movement's fundamental politics and all but ignored in the celebratory rhetoric of the second Earth Day. Some solutions may require a substantial transformation in the political style and philosophy of the environmental movement. Other responses will probably necessitate a rethinking of traditional premises about political resources and strategies. Collectively, these issues pose a challenge for the resurgent environmentalism of the 1990s to fashion a new politics appropriate for a new environmental era.

The Problem of Regulatory Capability

No problem casts a longer shadow over the second environmental era than the continuing failure of environmental institutions and policies to achieve many essential regulatory goals. Regulatory failure, as we observed in earlier chapters, is especially serious in the management of toxic and hazardous substances, in solid waste management, and in air and water pollution abatement. This problem of regulatory capability has been incrementally building with no clear, dramatic warning of its gravity.

The Perils of Rethinking Regulation

Even as environmental spokesmen on the second Earth Day were exhorting Americans and their governments to give more attention to a multitude of issues—acid rain, the Greenhouse Effect, atmospheric ozone depletion, the preservation of biological diversity, the protection of the rain forests, agricultural cropland loss, desertification, and more—and to attack ecological ills globally, many existing policies intended to remedy fundamental environmental ills were foundering. In some cases, the problem appears to be insufficient regulatory personnel and funding. But the remedies for many other failures seem beyond the capacity of better funding or more personnel. Symbolic politics will not suffice. The EPA's elevation to Cabinet rank, however symbolically important it may have been to the environmental movement, did little to mitigate its regulatory problems.

Change will not come easily. The environmental movement itself is slow to acknowledge how refractory the problem of institutional incapacity has become, in good measure because it could entail a critical reappraisal of some existing regulatory strategies to which segments of the movement are deeply committed. Congress has powerful incentives for avoiding a searching reappraisal of its own regulatory thinking. Major substantive changes in environmental law would likely force unpredictable alterations in the administrative jurisdiction of numerous legislative committees and upset entrenched patterns of influence and interaction between members of Congress and bureaucratic agencies. Reform challenges the premises of traditional professional education for pollution control specialists and threatens the traditional professional education curricula. If new regulatory ideas are not accorded the urgent attention they merit, however, the continuing disparity between regulatory intention and capacity is likely to debilitate many of the movement's most ambitious new programs with its immobilizing contradictions.

The solution to regulatory incapacity appears to rest in a multitude of reforms whose cumulative effect may take a long while to become apparent—indeed, so long as to make them politically risky for this reason alone. Nonetheless, several proposals deserve serious consideration as the foundation for a new politics of environmentalism in the new environmental era.

Beyond Standards and Enforcement

No proposed regulatory reform is more contentious within the environmental movement than that aimed at changing fundamentally the standards-and-enforcement approach to regulation.[3] Only slightly less vexatious are proposals to adopt some variety of multimedia approach to regulation instead of the current single-media approach described in Chapter 3. Yet a rethinking of the regulatory fundamentals seems imperative. After struggling for more than twenty years with traditional regulatory strategies, particularly in the management of air and water quality as well as hazardous and toxic substances, it should be clear that existing approaches are not working well and that the problem is often more than a lack of personnel or money.

Finding an alternative or, more likely, a mix of alternative regulatory strategies that combines traditional and newer methods is difficult because environmental regulation is an historically recent process. Federal and state governments have little experience upon which to draw in evaluating alternatives. Nonetheless, a beginning lies in creating a political space for it: the environmental movement needs to make a commitment to experimentation, if only on a modest scale at first. Beyond this, the package of specific proposals ought to include some experimental mixed-media regulatory strategies, incentives for source reduction of materials and processes producing pollutants, and an experimental effluent tax at state or federal levels.

A mixed-media approach to regulating one significant pollutant can be more successfully promoted if a successful federal or state prototype program exists as a model and inspiration. The states should be encouraged to experiment with this approach through federal enabling legislation, federal grants, subsidies, or other economic incentives. Solid waste management is often suggested as a possible starting place for such an innovative policy at state or federal levels.[4]

Proposals intended to change the industrial and commercial processes creating pollutants, and to reduce the sources of solid or hazardous wastes, have long been advocated by many environmental organizations. Instead of the current emphasis on controlling pollutants after they have been released into the ecosphere, source reduction would emphasize what many experts believe to be the more economical and efficient approach to pollution management. It is important that the initiative come from government, because most private firms will not readily evaluate the economic opportunities for source reduction even when the savings might be considerable. "It's simply not enough to tell companies they're going to save money," observed one expert. "If a product is profitable and salable under current law, they don't want to muck around. There's a reluctance to change anything in a plant, and that has to be overcome with some public policy initiative."[5] In fact, the management of many corporations, including some of the nation's largest industries, is often surprisingly ignorant about the components of its own manufacturing processes and the economic possibilities of achieving significant savings by process changes.

Effluent fees, or taxes, have been so exhaustively debated that they qualify as an old idea whose time has come.[6] Congress has been extremely reluctant to sanction effluent fees, even experimentally, in federal air and water pollution control programs. Some legislators lack confidence in the government's ability to obtain the information essential to setting the fees appropriately. Many more are lawyers for whom standards and enforcement is normal jurisprudence, the customary legal approach to creating regulatory regimes. Many legislators, aware of the passionate commitment of many environmental groups to existing regulatory strategies, fear the political backlash that may ensue if they vote for new regulations that appear to sanction pollution for a price. Nonetheless, given the problems with existing legislation, experimentation with effluent fees seems reasonable and relatively riskless.

It is likely that such experimentation would first be attempted at the state level, where much administrative innovation in environmental management has occurred in the last decade. Regulations would probably have to be revised to permit such experimentation under the Clean Air Act and Clean Water Act. Also, state incentives may be necessary in the form of federal subsidies, grants, or administrative assistance. A consortium of private firms, public agencies, and private foundations might be created to underwrite and evaluate such a program.

Building the Regulatory Science Base

It should be evident from prior chapters that the implementation of many essential environmental regulations has been complicated, or entirely frustrated, by the EPA's lack of a large and dependable research and development (R&D) budget through which it can generate information and schedule future research appropriately for its statutory responsibilities and institutional needs. The need for an appropriate R&D budget is especially evident when regulatory agencies are faced with statutory risk assessment, which is required in most domains of environmental management. Closely related is the need among all environmental regulatory agencies for professionally and politically credible statistical data on environmental trends and regulatory impacts. Such data should stem from an institutional source different from the often partisan and politically controversial sources, such as regulated interests, to which regulatory agencies must often currently turn for information.

Unfortunately, R&D budgets and institutional data collection are not exciting. They do not command the attention, let alone the sense of urgency, that Congress is likely to accord a major environmental problem dramatized by the media or by organized interest groups. Moreover, even when these resources are used productively, it is difficult to prove they are "working" in some direct, tangible way. The absence of these resources often deflects the regulatory impulse into protracted, politically unproductive administrative proceedings or litigation meant to resolve regulatory issues in the absence of appropriate scientific data. While better data alone often cannot resolve regulatory issues, they can often speed the regulatory process and simplify the task in numerous modest but productive ways.

A Hard Look at the "Paradigm Shift"

In the aftermath of the second Earth Day, veteran public opinion analyst William Schneider was convinced that environmentalism had become an issue beyond debate. Noting a recent Gallup Poll disclosing that 76 percent of Americans called themselves "an environmentalist,"

Schneider concluded that "everybody is an environmentalist these days."[7] Most public opinion analysts would agree that environmentalism has become part of "the American consensus," an idea deeply fixed in the firmament of values that define America's basic political beliefs.

From Consensus to Paradigm Shift?

Many scholars, citing their own detailed attitude studies as well as the popular polls, have concluded that this broad public consensus about environmentalism reveals an ongoing transformation in the American public's belief about how the world works physically, socially, economically, and politically—a "paradigm shift" from traditional ways of perceiving the world and one's place in it to a more environmentally enlightened one.[8] This paradigm shift, they assert, represents more than a change in public mood or attitude. Rather, it is a profound redefinition of social values and a metamorphosis in self concept, an enduring transformation. Most investigators believe that only a minority of Americans fully express the new paradigm in their thinking and behavior. But leading environmental scholars often attribute the environmental movement's growth and achievements to this ongoing shift in public values. The evolution of environmentalism in the United States, writes historian Samuel Hays, "rests heavily on changing values that create a widespread desire for higher environmental standards of living and become more extensive and more deeply rooted over the years."[9] Moreover, "these values . . . have driven wide ranging innovations in public policy at all levels of government." Lynton Caldwell places the U.S. experience in a global perspective:

During the last half of the twentieth century societal changes seem to have occurred spontaneously in North America and Western Europe. Manners and morals, attitudes toward freedom of speech, dress, human rights and life styles followed a parallel course, and concern for the environment was a major dimension of the change. Globalizing of American environmentalism is merely a particular case of a globalizing of environmental movements everywhere. It is a manifestation of a worldwide trend.[10]

Ronald McDonald may have experienced the paradigm shift. The huge fast-food corporation for whom Ronald is an icon now distributes a handsome ten-page brochure of recycled paper at all its outlets, assuring patrons that it is a good environmental citizen. "McDonald's has always been committed to environmentally sound business policies," it informs. "In fact, our commitment goes way back to day one—when our founder, Ray Kroc, would pick up litter in the parking lot of his first McDonald's. And he always made sure crew members went on a daily neighborhood litter patrol."

The paradigm shift is a contagion to judge from the number of U.S.

institutions eager to exploit environmentalism's appeal. General Motors bought full-page, multicolor ads in many national publications to proclaim: "Earth Day 1990: General Motors Marks 20 Years of Environmental Progress." Another ad asks, "Do you want to solve environmental problems?" and informs the reader that New York University's Wagner Graduate School of Public Service can prepare students for an environmental career. The *haute monde* has also gone ecological. Some upscale furniture stores sell only politically correct materials: tropical hardwoods are out. One famous couturier features dresses with leaves, accessories with branches, and earth tones everywhere. Another sponsors "don't bungle the jungle" parties.

American advertising's trendy environmentalism may be shallow but it testifies to the cultural reach and potency of contemporary environmentalism's symbols. For the moment, environmentalism is a transcendent value in American public life. Whether this bespeaks a profound transformation of public consciousness implied by a paradigm shift is considerably less certain. Indeed, whether Americans are environmentalists in any enduring sense remains problematic. A critical look at American culture raises profound questions about the public strength and endurance of American environmentalism and warns that public opinion polls are not yet prophecy.

An Uncertain Verdict

It is worth emphasizing that public opinion matters enormously for the political future of environmentalism. Public opinion has been the great equalizer in the political battle between environmentalists and their opposition. It is the public opinion polls as much as the organized environmentalist lobbying that commands the respect of public officials when they calculate the political importance of environmentalism in the unceasing group competition for access and influence in the political process. Environmentalists have repeatedly demonstrated an ability to rally the public for all sorts of political purposes, from Earth Day to public hearings on environmental regulations. And one incentive for business compliance with environmental regulation has been the apprehension among numerous image-conscious American firms that they would become "polluters" in the public mind. "The game today is public accountability," argues Dow Chemical's environmental affairs director. "Anyone who doesn't understand it may not be around 10 years from now. The public has tremendous power, more than they realize."[11]

In many ways, however, the depth and tenacity of public commitment to environmentalism have yet to be tested. Moreover, a glance at recent history is sufficient to raise doubts about the public's commitment to environmentalism and its implications. The political ascendance of

American environmentalism has occurred during two decades of almost uninterrupted domestic economic growth, an extraordinarily long period without a depression or prolonged recession by historical standards. The robust U.S. economy has enabled major American businesses to spend many billions of dollars on pollution control without adversely affecting the gross national product, employment, stockholder's equity, and other critical economic sectors. For more than a decade there have been no economic shocks or other social dislocations produced by a major energy crisis. In short, Americans have not faced the politically and economically difficult choices in public policy and life styles that environmentalism could present in economically troubled times. Would the public continue to insist upon environmental protection "regardless of the cost" if pollution control entailed plant closings, work force reductions, and reduced or perhaps arrested economic growth? Would Americans be willing to pay for environmental protection in the form of higher prices for public services and consumer goods in a depressed economy if the price increases were attributed to environmental control costs? Would the average citizen, facing the prospect of unemployment or greatly reduced income, still embrace environmentalism if it were perceived that a "trade-off" existed between environmental protection and more jobs, or more energy?

Domestic reaction to the economic dislocations produced by energy shortfalls in the 1970s—relatively mild economic shocks compared to a major recession or depression—is worth recalling. Contemporary public opinion polls reported that a majority of Americans still supported environmental protection and regulation. But the polls also indicated that Americans wanted accelerated new energy production as well as energy conservation, and would tolerate some compromises in current environmental protection standards but not a broad rollback of all measures. Environmental values were, in effect, vulnerable to compromise in the face of a threatened economic crisis. Riley Dunlap's meticulous study of public support for environmentalism during this period and later led him to conclude that economic issues might have an especially important effect upon both public environmental beliefs and how those beliefs were expressed politically. "The intensity or strength of public concern for environmental quality—as reflected in electoral impact—may not be as high as it is for economic well-being."[12] And, recalling Ronald Reagan's electoral success despite his dismal environmental record, he adds: "[W]hile mindful of the environmental movement's success in maintaining public support, I cannot help but question the fundamental strength of that support in view of the Reagan administration's relatively successful challenge to environmentalists' goals."[13]

It is revealing to recall as well Washington's response to the energy crisis. Jimmy Carter was unquestionably an ardent environmentalist, yet his administration's energy plan called for massively increased coal production; he ordered utilities to switch from natural gas or petroleum to coal when possible for boiler fuel, and urged "streamlining" of nuclear power plant licensing. Facing the prospect of diminished oil imports, the Congress in 1980 voted to create the environmentally reckless synthetic fuels programs and pledged $88 billion to the enterprise—an endeavor soon ended by the return of abundant imported oil. Clearly, the prospect of an energy crisis, with all its threatening economic implications, was enough to relax many environmental restraints Congress normally felt in legislating. In short, the state of the economy, as much as the state of the environment, may determine the intensity and duration of environmentalism among Americans and their public officials.

Consumer behavior suggests that environmentalism has yet to invade the life style of most Americans. Average garbage discards in the United States continue to rise, from 2.5 to more than 3.5 pounds per day between 1960 and 1987. Gas mileage in new U.S. cars declined by an average of 4 percent from model year 1988 to 1990. Americans are still energy gluttons. The United States comprises just 4.7 percent of the world's population but consumes 24 percent of the global energy production.[14] Commenting on rising U.S. automobile use, the editor of *Automobile Magazine* attributed America's autophilia to a passion for personal freedom. "There are a lot of unpleasant aspects to modern American life," he philosophized. "But you can get in that sucker, lock it up, turn on the radio and control the climate and it takes you to where you want in a enjoyable way."[15]

The Need for Environmental Education

Scholars may be correct in describing an evolving paradigm shift among Americans. The pollsters' great consensus on environmentalism may also exist. But there is evidence enough to warn that public environmentalism ought not to be regarded as part of some irresistible historic force. Paradigm shifts are not necessarily social destiny. And so, public support for environmental values ought not to be considered a "given" in the environmental movement's political strategies. Rather, there is a need for continued cultivation and reinforcement of public environmental values, and, in particular, a need to socialize Americans into environmental sensibilities that will endure the onslaught of energy crises, economic recessions and depressions, and the social cleavages to which environmentalism may prove vulnerable.

Environmental education ought to be high on the environmental movement's political agenda. This means much more than promoting public exposure to environmental information through the mass media, or encouraging citizen involvement in environmental activities, worthy as these acts may be. Rather, environmental education ought to involve the requirement that ecology be a component in the public education of every U.S. citizen: ecological literacy should be inculcated in the nation's education as an essential attribute of scientific literacy. Environmental education within the schools is especially important because it is the most direct way of bringing the environmental message to the nonwhite young people—blacks, Hispanics, Orientals, and others—and to the economically disadvantaged, who represent the fastest growing population in the United States. It is also a population that historically has been least active in environmental organizations, for whom environmentalism has seldom been a salient issue.

In broader perspective, the environmental movement needs to make a large and continuing investment in the recruitment of minority activists and in articulating environmental issues in terms relevant to the nation's minorities and its underprivileged. Environmentalism may no longer be stigmatized by a white, upper-class, elitist image, but some public policies commonly espoused by environmentalists, like growth management, threaten to alienate minorities and the underprivileged. This has been particularly apparent in urban areas, such as Los Angeles, where "slow growth" to the white upper and middle classes means less noise, traffic congestion, and strip development, while to most minorities and the economic underclass it means less economic development, fewer job opportunities, and no social mobility.[16] As the nation's nonwhite population grows in size and political significance, the environmental movement will need to seek out issues that draw this new electorate within the movement's constituency, and anticipate demographic change rather than react to it.

Establishing the Environmental Priority

The United States has been unable, or unwilling, to create a politics of goals and priorities in which ecology will be assigned an appropriately elevated place. Rather, ecology must continually compete in the pluralistic marketplace of American politics for a place and priority in the allocation of social resources by the government. The ongoing, open-ended competition among social groups and interests for a claim on public resources is traditional American politics, a way to avoid the creation of a final order of priority for political goals and thereby to avoid the vicious political bloodletting such decision making would unloose. Indeed, American political institutions and political culture are hostile to the politics of ideology that aims at imposing a final order of political values and a fixed priority of claims on public resources.

Environmental politics, however, raises issues that vastly transcend the admittedly crucial problems of social structures and social survival, social and economic equity, and the allocation of economic resources. Environmental issues are extraordinary. They concern the survival of the nation, of global civilization, of the ecosphere. Environmentalism is now striving to sustain the biological and physical basis of life against real and potentially catastrophic threats to human survival. Environmental politics deals with the penultimate issues of human existence, even when they are packaged in the commonplace language of regulation. Put somewhat differently, environmental protection, preservation, and restoration ought to be explicitly recognized in public policy making as issues of national security, as issues with embedded values having a transcendent claim on national resources in competition with other values in the political process.

Environmental Protection as National Security

It has always been understood implicitly in American politics that national security has a prior claim, if not a preemptive one, in comparison with almost all other goals for national policy and all other claims on scarce resources. A growing number of policy analysts concerned with global security are coming to recognize, in the words of Jessica Mathews, that there must be a "broadening definition of natural security to include resources, environmental and demographic issues."[17] It is time that environmental protection be given the privileged status of a national security issue in domestic politics.

Defining environmental protection as a national security matter would also place global ecological change and the environmental policies of other nations in a national security context, as it should, because the United States shares with all other nations a common ecological interdependence. "National security is a meaningless concept," concludes the Worldwatch Institute's Michael Renner, "if it does not include the preservation of livable conditions within a country—or on the plant as a whole. Increasingly, countries are finding their security undermined by environmental threats emanating from other nations. . . . Environmental threats with the potential to erode the habitability of the planet from beneath us are forcing humanity to consider national security in far broader terms than that guaranteed solely by force of arms."[18]

Translating the Environmental Priority into Law

There is, it should now be apparent, a rational and scientifically persuasive argument for a political strategy aimed at a congressional declaration of environmental priority in which Congress explicitly invests environmental protection and regulation with a preemptive claim in competition with most other priorities. This might be accomplished through a number of legislative acts, including a comprehensive statement of ecological priorities in a single statute, or through gradual amendment of existing legislation to clarify environmental priorities in the many instances where failure to do so in the past has resulted in significant environmental damage.

Alternative approaches to this task might include some, or all, of the following:

1. Amending the Constitution to declare the right of all U.S. citizens to a safe physical environment and the government's obligation to protect the environment.

2. Amending federal "multiple-use" mandates for managing the public domain to create a priority for uses that protect environmental quality and biological diversity.

3. Amending state constitutions to include a statement of environmental rights with other fundamental rights accorded all citizens of a state.

4. According the preservation and restoration of environmental quality an explicit, high priority in (a) the charters of the Department of the Interior, the Department of Agriculture, and the Department of Energy; (b) organic legislation defining the mission of the Army Corps of Engineers; and (c) the charter of the Nuclear Regulatory Commission (NRC).

5. Using indices of environmental quality as a statutory basis for allocating a significant portion of the budget for the EPA.

In effect, these and other strategies with similar intention would insulate the process of allocating resources for environmental protection and administration from the competitive influence of the political marketplace, an act which Congress has performed numerous times in respect to other programs. Indeed, more than 70 percent of the annual federal budget—the "uncontrollable" portion of the budget—is already apportioned before the president ever proposes it because Congress has given guaranteed funding to various entitlement programs, such as social security, aid to the disadvantaged, and veterans' pensions. Designating environmental protection as a preferred social value in some of the ways indicated would no doubt be a politically turbulent affair, but there is ample precedent for establishing such a priority.

Environmental Forecasting

The ongoing debate within government and the scientific community about the urgency of government action to mitigate acid rain, global climate warming, and atmospheric ozone depletion illustrates the importance, and the difficulty, of scientific forecasting in environmental management. An increasingly varied array of sophisticated technologies and conceptual models enables scientists not only to monitor environmental conditions with great precision but also to make forecasts of long-term environmental transformations on the basis of such monitoring. As forecasting capability improves, the desirability of incorporating forecasts into environmental policy planning becomes more evident.

Environmental forecasting entails scientific and political problems, however. Continuing controversy among scientific experts over the reliability of models used to predict future climate warming, and technical arguments over the relative merit of competing models, testify that forecasting is an imperfect science. Harvard's Stephen Jay Gould, a geologist, explains the forecasting problem in global climate change: "Most people are taught that science is a discipline that makes predictions by evaluating data in terms of the universal laws of nature. They believe that when data go into a computer, which churns out complex graphs, the result is rigor in canonical form." But the truth is very different:

climatic modeling on a global scale requires not only that the computer be fed scores of variables (many of which cannot be precisely measured), but also . . . that the complex and nonlinear interactions among these variables be assessed (and here we haven't the ghost of adequate knowledge or even, in many cases, of suggestive theory). Thus, honorable people all trying their darndest to model the global climate come up with the most disparate predictions.[19]

Forecasting the future impact of atmospheric ozone depletion involves similar problems in assessing the importance of different variables to be measured. Atmospheric scientists generally agree that significant depletion has occurred, is likely to continue for at least a half-century, and may entail many ecologically disruptive and dangerous consequences. But the specific kind of "disequilibrium" to be anticipated is open to argument, for there are a multitude of alternative models. "We have a system guaranteed to be out of equilibrium," commented Stephen H. Schneider, a climate expert with the National Center for Atmospheric Research. "The physical system is going to be out of equilibrium, the biological system is going to be out of equilibrium, and so is the social system. Good luck, Charlie, trying to forecast that."[20]

Despite these technical problems, some current environmental forecast models are likely to prove reliable and, with time and experience, many others will become so. Most scientists believe that forecasting can serve a useful policy-making role when its limitations are understood. Among its important contributions, forecasting can identify potential environmental problems requiring monitoring and discussion before they achieve critical proportions, can help to clarify priorities for future public and private research, can sometimes narrow the range of options to be considered when predicting the future impacts of current environmental trends, and more. It is evident that forecasting should be accorded some important place among the scientific data to be evaluated in environmental policy making. Nonetheless, using forecasting capability to make regulatory decisions is freighted with formidable political problems. The most important, as former EPA administrator William Ruckelshaus observes, is that "models may convince scientists, who understand their assumptions and limitations, [but] as a rule projections make poor politics."[21]

Projections make poor politics partially because they always are open to challenge and disputation among technical experts; this undermines their credibility. Moreover, the future is no one's constituency. The White House and Congress are continually exposed to a multitude of immediate pressures and demands from organized interest groups, electoral constituencies, and squabbling bureaucracies. Crises and political conflict make imperious claims on time and available resources. The political rewards and perils of office for most elective officials are bound within the universe of these events. In comparison, the future has no capacity to create tangible political pressures, rewards, and penalties to get a policy maker's sustained attention. For these and other reasons, forecasting shares with the EPA's R&D programs a distinct lack of political allure. This translates into low budget priority.

Moreover, projections also pose politically unattractive economic trade-offs. Making environmental regulations on the basis of anticipated events usually means imposing tangible, short-term, often heavy costs upon some important political or economic sector in return for future benefits that can be made to appear highly speculative. In the political marketplace, future benefits are highly discounted in decision making about matters far more routine than the ecological future. Especially in the absence of some dramatic and convincing evidence to fortify a forecast model's predictions, public officials are loath to risk the wrath of those who must pay today for the future's environmental preservation.

Judged by these realities, the short-term prospects for forecasting as a policy-making tool may seem lackluster. However, plans and programs ought to be initiated now to create a more important role for ecological forecasting in policy making. Efforts should be made to increase the amount of R&D funding allocated to the development of forecasting. Greater attention should be given to educating public policy makers about the strength and limitations of forecasting, with emphasis upon successful forecasting experiences. Scientists and other professionals creating or using forecast models need to become adept at explaining these models and the utility of forecasting, in terms meaningful to public policy makers.

Technology's Institutional Risks

Many of the nation's current environmental problems arise directly from the government's failure to anticipate the legal and institutional arrangements needed to control the new technologies and the products of those technologies, which it has been promoting resolutely. The private sector is often guilty of a similar disregard for the long-term management of risks from its own technological innovations. The result has been the emergence of technological crisis—in the guise of a Three Mile Island or Love Canal incident—created or exacerbated by the absence of legal or institutional controls on technology failures. Many of the essential controls on publicly or privately promoted technologies that seemed lacking in the throes of a crisis could be anticipated. Many controls were deliberately ignored or prematurely dismissed in the early enthusiasm of technology development. In short, the ecological risks often associated with technological development arise not only from the physical and biological consequences of technologies but also from failures to provide adequately for their social management. One practical consequence should be greater governmental attention to what can be called institutional risk assessment in technology development, a procedure promising substantial environmental benefits.

Technology and Institutional Risks

As a people fiercely committed to technological innovation, Americans always have been gamblers with the future. In the United States, technological innovation has been driven by an implicit assumption that the legal, economic, and governmental resources will be available to protect society from the worst impacts of attractive technologies. It was assumed that social or scientific engineering always would be equal to the challenge of technological change. One consequence of this faith in social innovation has been the tendency for public and private institutions to create technological innovation first and worry about the social management of the technology later. Another was to define the risks of technological innovation primarily in scientific or economic terms rather than to assess the ability of social institutions to manage the technologies satisfactorily. This confidence in the social manageability of new technologies often has inhibited public institutions from planning prudent strategies for eliminating or reducing the ecological dangers often inherent in technology development.

Two kinds of institutional risk, in particular, have had major ecological importance for the United States during the last half century. First, technologies have been developed in both private and public sectors without explicit and operational contingency plans for dealing with possible technological crises. Second, public and private institutions have lacked the financial, technical, and legal resources appropriate to deal with technology problems. Such failures of institutional planning can be attributed partially to the reluctance of both public and private promoters of technology to discuss candidly the full risks lest they encourage too much opposition. The neglect of institutional planning for technology development partially reflects the absence of law or tradition requiring such deliberation. And, in the case of federally funded projects, the zeal of mission-oriented agencies to produce results in their own bureaucratic interest doubtless blunts the instinct to examine the long-term consequences of failure. In any event, perhaps some of the adverse impacts of new technologies could not have been anticipated in advance of their development. Yet experience suggests that failures in institutional planning are more likely to result from a lack of will to anticipate problems.

The Lesson of the Peaceful Atom

Perhaps the clearest illustration of institutional risk in technology development is provided by the history of commercial nuclear power in the United States. Many problems in reactor safety can be traced directly to flawed institutional arrangements for managing plant accidents. Both the federal government and the private nuclear power industry share responsibility for these failures of institutional planning and also for the related nuclear waste problems. It has become evident that neither Washington nor the private promoters of nuclear power were prepared to plan realistically for the possible financial, legal, or scientific problems in the technology. In their passion to promote the peaceful atom, private and public sponsors were loath to admit even the wisdom of exploring tentatively the institutional arrangements needed for major system failures. This aversion to institutional risk analysis has resulted in managerial crises at almost every significant stage of the commercial nuclear fuel cycle:

Reactor Safety. The nation's most publicized nuclear technology failure, the crisis at Three Mile Island beginning on March 28, 1979, was described by both major commissions investigating the incident as primarily a failure in institutional management. The Rogovin Commission, appointed by the Nuclear Regulatory Commission to investigate the incident, was the most explicit: "The principal deficiencies in commercial reactor safety today are not hardware problems, they are management problems, . . . problems that cannot be solved by the addition of a few pipes or valves . . . or, for that matter, by a resident federal inspector."[22] In light of the Rogovin Commission's emphasis upon institutional management as a problem generic to the commercial nuclear power industry, it is significant that prior to 1978 the NRC's major studies of reactor safety did not consider failures of institutional management among the several hundred "human errors" whose relevance to reactor accidents it investigated.

Nuclear Fuel Reprocessing. The nation's only commercial nuclear fuel reprocessing plant, the showpiece technology at West Valley, New York, intended to demonstrate the feasibility of commercializing nuclear fuel reprocessing, failed economically in 1971 and closed permanently in 1976. Abandoned at West Valley were more than a half million gallons of high-level liquid radioactive waste, two solid radioactive waste burial grounds, a spent nuclear fuel storage facility, and a contaminated fuel reprocessing plant. The West Valley facilities could safely contain the high-level wastes for less than forty years; no permanent depository for such waste currently exists. Further, as late as 1982, Washington and New York state continued to quarrel over which should accept the financial and technical responsibility for the site's cleanup. The terms of the original contract between Washington and New York state, signed when the facility was begun in 1962, "bear no relationship to the facts as they exist today [because] . . . the parties contemplated a successful venture and did not specifically address . . . their respective liabilities for the radically different situation which exists in West Valley today."[23]

Nuclear Facility Disposal. Although the average commercial nuclear power facility has a planned operating life of only fifty years, no comprehensive federal program exists providing the money, legal authority, and technical resources needed to ensure that the plants are safely closed, or decommissioned. In fact, the United States currently lacks an integrated program for the decommissioning of any nuclear facility, including temporary waste sites. Warned the U.S. General Accounting Office, "Unless a national policy is developed to provide for unified and effective decommissioning actions and a lead agency is designated to monitor implementation of that policy, the impact will be, at worst, potential hazards to the public's health and safety."[24] The practical problems of planning the decommissioning of a single plant are suggested by the current status of funding arrangements. While the satisfactory decommissioning of even a small plant may exceed $100 million, no public or private agencies have currently established any trust funds or other revenue allocations for the retirement of a single facility.

A Continuing Need

While the U.S. experience with commercial nuclear power development provides the most persuasive example of poor institutional planning in technology development, other examples abound. Appalachia has become the nation's showcase of institutional failure in strip mine management. The region's hills and hollows, littered by more than 250,000 acres of orphan spoil banks, were devastated between 1950 and 1977 by local, state, and federal governmental reluctance to investigate the long-term ecological and economic costs of the technology's unregulated operation. The Carter administration's ambitious program to promote a commercial synthetic fuels industry in the United States initially gave virtually no attention to governmental problems involved in managing the enormous volume of highly toxic sludges likely to arise from the industry; nor did it consider the capacities of local and state governments to regulate such a complex new technology.

To be sure, the record is mixed. Appalachia became the bitter lesson leading to the Surface Mining Control and Reclamation Act passed in 1977. Love Canal produced Superfund, and regulation of the toxic sludge associated with the production of synthetic fuels may well occur. But the time lag between the development of institutional failures in technology management and the governmental efforts to remedy them is often great; the economic, ecological, and health risks involved in such long delays is often substantial. Moreover, often a solution to a technological crisis that is formulated in the midst of the crisis itself is haphazard and expedient, lacking technical finesse, economic efficiency, and comprehensiveness.

Some Solutions

U.S. District Judge David Bazelon, a jurist experienced and perceptive in technology issues, has remarked that a major task in governmental risk assessment of new technologies is "to face the hard questions created by a lack of knowledge."[25] How can federal agencies or the private institutions they support be compelled to face the hard questions about possible technology failures and to plan realistically for prospective crises or emergencies? A conservative approach would be to encourage the White House, federal departments, and regulatory agencies to interpret a number of existing requirements for risk assessment in technology development to include institutional assessment in technology-related programs. The statutory language of the Toxic Substances Control Act, the Occupational Safety and Health Act, and several other federal laws would seem to permit institutional risk analysis under broadly defined risk assessment requirements already incumbent upon implementing agencies. Even President Reagan's Executive Order 12291 urges federal agencies to use a "regulatory impact analysis" in deciding whether to adopt new regulations or to revise older ones; this analysis is to include an "evaluation of effects that cannot be quantified in monetary terms"— language sufficiently ambiguous to permit institutional impact analysis in the regulatory process for technology development.

A more incisive but difficult approach would be for the president or Congress to issue a mandate that institutional risk assessment be conducted regularly and uniformly in all federal agencies responsible for the creation, development, or regulation of new technologies. This mandate would demand uniform procedures for assessment, similar to requirements for environmental impact statements filed by federal agencies under the National Environmental Policy Act of 1969.[26] A variety of other possible strategies for encouraging institutional risk assessment have been explored as well. In the end, the most serious obstacle to the development of better institutional impact assessment for federally managed technologies remains political feasibility. Given the enormous political costs, there is unlikely to be a political push or a public clamor for such assessment in the absence of some arresting crisis pointing to the need for better institutional planning of government-funded technologies.

Ecology and Social Equity

Environmentalism at its most enlightened is egalitarian in its commitment to protecting the environmental rights of all human beings, regardless of race, nationality, or economic circumstance. At its best, it nurtures grass-roots democracy, a spiritual and ethical standard in defining the desirable quality of life, resource conservation instead of conspicuous consumption, and a proper respect for the ecological rights of posterity. It rejects the market as the social mechanism for defining social priorities and placing a value on social or physical resources. In the mirror environmentalism holds up to itself, it sees itself committed to the public interest against private interest, to a socially inclusive constituency rather than a social or economic class. Environmentalists have bitterly resented the accusation that environmentalism is a "white movement," that it is elitist in its membership or political agenda, or that it discriminates against the economic and social interests of the poor, minorities, and nonwhites. Such accusations are manifestly false when made so categorically.

But environmentalists have been reluctant to ask some tough questions about the extent to which the movement, however, inadvertently, may be promoting social bias and discrimination in its approach to specific issues and problems. These issues need an explicit, perhaps painful airing. Such introspection is long overdue and understandably difficult because it can become highly divisive within organized environmentalism. Even worse, a full, public examination of such sensitive issues may appear to validate the opposition's most pernicious criticism and, at the very least, invite renewed attack. If environmentalism takes its own professed values seriously, however, it has an ethical obligation to look into the state of its own soul in respect to its social impacts.

One specific issue environmentalists need to examine is the extent to which environmentalism in philosophy or in specific organizational settings encourages NIMBYism.[27] An agenda for a searching examination of the NIMBY issue should include such questions as:

1. Have environmentalists used public participation procedures to encourage NIMBYism?

2. Has NIMBYism become a procedural strategy for imposing the environmental risks in hazardous materials management upon the politically and economically disadvantaged?

3. Should environmentalists accept an obligation to bear some of the risks, and pay some of the costs, for the management of hazardous materials or the conduct of hazardous activities from which they derive direct or indirect benefit?

4. Should the environmental movement take the initiative in seeking to promote the most socially equitable solutions to hazardous site management, even at the risk of controversy within the movement and specific organizations?

Another large issue bearing on social equity and environmentalism is growth management, both in the larger perspective of national economies and populations and at the micro level of individual states, counties, cities, and smaller communities. Proposals for growth limitations at the local level, for instance, have frequently provoked opposition from minority groups on the grounds that such limitation discriminates against them in housing, employment opportunities, and social mobility. Environmentalists individually and organizationally vigorously support the idea of managed growth and often constitute a major constituency for growth management campaigns in specific communities. A constructive contribution toward social equity in growth management would be more explicit and prolonged discussion within the environmental movement concerning (1) whether environmentalists and their organizations should support growth management when discriminatory impacts are likely; and (2) what substantive changes can be made in management proposals to reduce significantly, or eliminate, social bias.

These are but two issues among many, some raising the equity problem to global scale, that confront the social implications of environmentalism explicitly. They are suggested for early attention because they affect almost all Americans within their own communities, and because they are often the subject of public controversy arising from disagreement over the social bias of environmentalism in most communities. Bringing forth these issues for discussion will pose risks for the environmental movement. If the movement is to reach out to a larger social constituency than its organizational base had in the past—an act essential to its continuing vitality in the United States—these tough questions will have to be faced. Thus, what may seem at first glance a dangerously divisive venture in self-examination may turn out to be an act of enlightened self-interest.

Continuity and Change in the 1990s

Looking at the magnitude of the environmental ills and the problems of policy implementation the nation faces, it should be obvious that environmental decades are no solution. Restoring the nation's magnificent heritage and preserving it for future generations will require many decades, if not centuries. It should be abundantly clear that there are no "quick fixes," either institutionally or technologically, that will substitute for decades of committed, patient, and educated governmental and private efforts at environmental restoration. The 1990s began auspiciously for environmentalism, but the nation's environmental commitments will still be fiercely tested, its capacity to sustain the environmental ethic measured, and its ability to innovate creatively in the face of new ecological challenges assessed.

This chapter suggests that the testing of commitment to environmental protection, by government and environmentalists, will take the form of challenges to the old politics brought by changing social conditions. The challenge will be to create a new, more appropriate politics in many critical domains of environmental policy. The agenda of the new politics should include: promoting sweeping institutional rethinking and reform, increasing public ecological education, enacting institutional risk assessment, redefining environmental priorities in the context of other national concerns, examining the social implications of environmentalism, and more.

This decade will also involve a testing of this nation's global environmental vision, its capacity to see its own environmental problems in the realistic context of a world ecosystem and to take responsible initiatives to control world ecological ills. The 1990s began with governmental pronouncements of a renewed, expanded commitment to global ecological preservation—a welcome and dangerously overdue repudiation of the Reagan administration's environmental parochialism. Whether the government has the will to sustain that commitment remains a critical concern.

This much is certain: There will be no other future than that we fashion for ourselves. Ultimately, environmentalism is a determination to protect this beautiful and defiled world for another generation. It is a faith, yet to be justified, that we can develop collectively an ecological conscience and an environmental ethic. It is the hope from which books such as this are written and upon which our children will depend for a decent world.

Notes

1. William Ophuls, *Ecology and the Politics of Scarcity* (San Francisco: W. H. Freeman, 1977), 197–198.
2. John C. Whitaker, "Earth Day Recollections: What It Was Like When the Movement Took Off," *EPA Journal* 13, no. 9 (November 1987): 8.
3. On the standards-and-enforcement controversy see Allen V. Kneese and Charles L. Schultze, *Pollution, Prices and Public Policy* (Washington, D.C.: Brookings Institution, 1975).
4. See Conservation Foundation, *America's Waste: Managing for Risk Reduction* (Washington, D.C.: Conservation Foundation, 1987).
5. Margaret E. Kriz, "An Ounce of Prevention," *National Journal*, August 19, 1989, 2096.
6. The arguments are usefully summarized in Thomas G. Ingersoll and Bradley R. Brockbank, "The Role of Economic Incentives in Environmental Policy," in *Controversies in Environmental Policy*, ed. Sheldon Kamieniecki, Robert O'Brien, and Michael Clarke (Albany: State University of New York Press, 1986), 201–222.
7. William Schneider, "Everybody's an Environmentalist Now," *National Journal*, April 28, 1990, 1062.
8. Lester W. Milbrath, *Envisioning a Sustainable Society* (Albany: State University of New York Press, 1989), chap. 6.
9. Samuel Hays, "An Historical Perspective on Contemporary Environmentalism" (Paper presented at the annual meeting of the American Association for the Advancement of Science, New Orleans, Louisiana, February 15–20, 1990), 31.
10. Lynton Caldwell, "Globalizing Environmentalism: Threshold of a New Phase of International Relations" (Paper presented at the annual meeting of the American Association for the Advancement of Science, New Orleans, Louisiana, February 15–20, 1990), 23–24.
11. Kriz, "An Ounce of Prevention," 2094.
12. Riley E. Dunlap, "Public Opinion and Environmental Policy," in *Environmental Politics and Policy: Theories and Evidence*, ed. James P. Lester (Durham, N.C.: Duke University Press, 1989), 130.
13. Ibid., 134.
14. *New York Times*, April 22, 1990.
15. *New York Times*, October 10, 1988.
16. Ronald Brownstein, "Testing the Limits," *National Journal*, July 29, 1989, 1916–1920.
17. Jessica Tuchman Mathews, "Redefining Security," *Foreign Affairs* 68, no. 2 (Spring 1989): 173.
18. Michael Renner, *National Security: The Economic and Environmental Dimensions* (Washington, D.C.: Worldwatch Institute, 1989), 6.
19. Stephen Jay Gould, "It's Not Too Late, If We're Not Too Crazy," *New York Times Book Review*, April 22, 1990, 15.
20. *New York Times*, March 20, 1988.
21. William Ruckelshaus, "Toward a Sustainable World," *Scientific American* 261, no. 3 (September 1989): 166.
22. Mitchell Rogovin, *Three Mile Island: A Report to the Commission and to the Public*, vol. 1 (Washington, D.C.: Government Printing Office, 1980), 89.
23. U.S. General Accounting Office, "Status of Efforts to Clean Up the Shut-Down

Western New York Nuclear Service Center," Report no. EMD 80-69 (June 6, 1980), 15.
24. U.S. General Accounting Office, "Cleaning Up Nuclear Facilities—An Aggressive and Unified Federal Program Is Needed," Report no. GAO/EMD-82-40 (May 25, 1982), ii.
25. D. L. Bazelon, "Risk and Responsibility," *Science*, July 20, 1979, 279.
26. Walter A. Rosenbaum, "Hidden Risks in Risk Assessment: The Problem of Technology's Institutional Impacts," in *The Politics of Risk Assessment,* ed. Susan Hadden (New York: Kennicat Press, 1984).
27. On NIMBYism see Daniel Mazmanian and David Morrell, "The 'NIMBY' Syndrome: Facility Siting and the Failure of Democratic Discourse," in *Environmental Policy in the 1990s,* ed. Norman J. Vig and Michael E. Kraft (Washington, D.C.: Congressional Quarterly, 1989), 125–143: Susan G. Hadden, Joan Veillette, and Thomas Brandt, "State Roles in Siting Hazardous Waste Disposal Facilities: From State Preemption to Local Veto," in *The Politics of Hazardous Waste Management,* ed. James P. Lester and Ann O'M. Bowman (Durham, N.C.: Duke University Press, 1983), 197–211; and Seymour Martin Lipset and William Schneider, *The Confidence Gap: Business, Labor, and Government in the Public Mind,* rev. ed. (Baltimore: Johns Hopkins University Press, 1987).

Suggested Readings

Dryzek, John S. *Rational Ecology.* Oxford and New York: Basil Blackwell, 1987.
Gorz, Andre. *Ecology As Politics.* Boston: South End Press, 1980.
McPhee, John. *The Control of Nature.* New York: Farrar, Straus, and Giroux, 1989.
Paehlke, Robert. *Environmentalism and the Future of Progressive Politics.* New Haven, Conn.: Yale University Press, 1989.
Piel, Jonathan, ed. *Managing Planet Earth: Readings From Scientific American Magazine.* New York: W. H. Freeman, 1990.

List of Abbreviations

AEC	Atomic Energy Commission
AQCR	Air Quality Control Region
BLM	Bureau of Land Management
BOD	biochemical oxygen demand
CAA	Clean Air Act of 1970
CERCLA	Comprehensive Environmental Response, Compensation and Liability Act of 1980 ("Superfund")
CEQ	Council on Environmental Quality
CFCs	chlorofluorocarbons
CPSC	Consumer Product Safety Commission
CWA	Clean Water Act
DOD	Department of Defense
DOE	Department of Energy
DOI	Department of the Interior
DOT	Department of Transportation
EDF	Environmental Defense Fund
EIS	Environmental Impact Statement
EO	Executive Order
EPA	Environmental Protection Agency
ERDA	Energy Research and Development Administration
FDA	Food and Drug Administration
FERC	Federal Energy Regulatory Commission
FIFRA	Federal Insecticide, Fungicide and Rodenticide Act of 1947
FTC	Federal Trade Commission
FWPCAA	Federal Water Pollution Control Act Amendments of 1972
GAO	General Accounting Office
GNP	Gross National Product
HSWA	Hazardous and Solid Waste Amendments of 1984
LUSTs	liquid underground storage tanks
NAAQS	National Ambient Air Quality Standards
NEPA	National Environmental Policy Act of 1969
NOAA	National Oceanic and Atmospheric Administration

NPDES	National Pollution Discharge Elimination System
NPL	National Priority List
NRC	Nuclear Regulatory Commission
NRDC	Natural Resources Defense Council
NWPA	Nuclear Waste Policy Act of 1982
OCS	outer continental shelf
OMB	Office of Management and Budget
OSHA	Occupational Safety and Health Administration
OSMRE	Office of Surface Mining Regulation and Enforcement
PCBs	polychlorinated biphenyls
PPM	parts per million
PSD	prevention of significant deterioration
R&D	research and development
RARE	Roadless Area Review and Evaluation
RCRA	Resource Conservation and Recovery Act of 1976
RIA	Regulatory Impact Analysis
SARA	Superfund Amendments and Reauthorization Act of 1986
SCS	Soil Conservation Service
SIP	State Implementation Plan
SMCRA	Surface Mining Control and Reclamation Act of 1977
TSCA	Toxic Substances Control Act of 1976
USGS	United States Geological Survey
WIPP	Waste Isolation Pilot Project

Index

Interactive pollutants, 121, 122
Interagency Task Force on Acid Precipitation, 184
Interagency Testing Committee, 224
Interest groups, 76
  access to government, 74–75
  governmental advisory committees, 75
Interior Department. *See also* Office of Surface Mining Reclamation and Enforcement
  energy exploration of public lands, 283–285
  public land use management, 126, 283–284
  responsibilities of, 103
  secretarial appointments, 288
  Watt as secretary, 104–105
International Apple Association, 143
"Intervenor funding," 76
"Iron triangle," 117

J
Jackson, Henry M., 74
Johns Manville Company, 150
Johnson, Paul, 130, 160
Johnston, J. Bennett, quoted, 254
Joint Committee on Atomic Energy, 247

K
Kagan, Robert A., 130
Kanawah River Valley. *See* Nitro (West Virginia) affair
Kelman, Steven, quoted, 131–132
Kimball, James N., 179
Kneese, Allen V., quoted, 135
Kraft, Michael, quoted, 235
Kroc, Ray, quoted, 305

L
Labor unions, and OSHA regulations, 101
Lamm, Richard D., 278
Lead, 36, 101
  safe blood levels for, 155–156
Leeson, Ann, quoted, 22
Leopold, Aldo, quoted, 272
Lindblom, Charles A., quoted, 73, 75
Liquid underground storage tanks (LUSTs), 43
Lobbying, 74
Los Angeles basin
  air pollution management plan, 3–4, 9, 170
  mayor's proposal for air pollution control, 169–170
Los Padres National Forest, state opposition to oil/mining exploration, 87, 88
Love Canal toxic waste affair (*1978*), 47, 80, 113, 203, 218, 221, 226, 234, 317
Lowi, Theodore, quoted, 74
Lujan, Manuel, 288

M
McCloskey, Paul, 74
McConnell, Grant, quoted, 75
Marine Protection Research and Sanctuaries Act, 18 (table), 203
Marketplace economics, 21, 135–137, 283
Materials Transportation Bureau, 90
Mathews, Jessica, quoted, 310
Mazur, Allan, quoted, 14, 162
Melnick, R. Shep, quoted, 93, 116
Mendeloff, John M., quoted, 101
Mercury. *See* Methyl mercury
Metallic sodium, 2
Methyl mercaptan, 2
Methyl mercury, in fish, 32–33, 220
Midwest Legal Foundation, 94
Milkis, Sidney, 24–25
Mine Safety and Health Administration, 90
Mineral Leasing Act (*1920*), 284
Missing data. *See* Science and technology, data deficiencies
Mitchell, George J., 117, 226
Mitchell, Robert, 23
Montreal Protocol, 3, 9, 59, 301
Moore, John A., quoted, 114
Morone, Joseph G., quoted, 259
Mothers Matter, 32
Mount Sinai School of Medicine, 218
Mountain States Legal Foundation, 94
Mulroney, Brian, 184
Multiple Use-Sustained Yield Act (*1960*), 276–277, 289–290, 295
Muskie, Edmund S., 74

N
National Academy of Science, on sulfur oxide emissions, 184
National Acid Precipitation Assessment Program (NAPAP), 185–186
National Aeronautics and Space Administration (NASA), Ozone Trends Panel, 58
National Ambient Air-Quality Standards (NAAQS), 35, 36, 174, 180, 193
National Bureau of Standards, 90, 221
National Center for Atmospheric Research, 312